Captain Cook's
FINAL VOYAGE

Henry Roberts, *HMS Resolution*, circa 1775.
Water color drawing of Cook's flagship during the Second Voyage.
Mitchell Library, State Library of New South Wales, PXD 11, f. 34.

Captain Cook's FINAL VOYAGE

THE UNTOLD STORY FROM THE JOURNALS OF JAMES BURNEY AND HENRY ROBERTS

EDITED BY
James K. Barnett

FOREWORD BY
Richard Neville

INTRODUCTION BY
Glyn Williams

WSU PRESS

Washington State University Press
Pullman, Washington

WSU PRESS
WASHINGTON STATE UNIVERSITY

Washington State University Press
PO Box 645910
Pullman, Washington 99164-5910
Phone: 800-354-7360
Fax: 509-335-8568
Email: wsupress@wsu.edu
Website: wsupress.wsu.edu

First printing 2017

Cataloging-in-Publication Data is available from the Library of Congress.

On the cover:
John Webber, "Resolution and Discovery Beating Through the Ice, 1790."
Dixson Library, State Library of New South Wales, X989/1.

To the generations of readers committed to the study of Captain Cook's extraordinary voyages, and published during the 250th anniversary of the commencement of his three remarkable voyages to the Pacific.

CONTENTS

ILLUSTRATIONS AND MAPS

PREFACE

Captain James Cook was perhaps the most accomplished explorer and circumnavigator in history. He profoundly transformed western understanding of world geography. In his three voyages to the Pacific in the late eighteenth century, he revealed countless unknown, faraway lands and their inhabitants to an appreciative European audience. In just two decades he sailed to New Zealand, Australia, and Tahiti in the South Pacific, as well as Hawai'i, Vancouver Island, and Alaska in the North Pacific, before he met his untimely death at Kealakekua Bay in 1779. The study of his uncommon exploits remains of vital interest to historians, ethnographers, and scholars to this day.

As an Alaskan committed to the study of Cook's search of the Northwest Passage, I investigated Cook's third voyage records in far off Sydney, where I discovered a trove of important but largely unknown journals and images from the voyage at the State Library of New South Wales, the oldest library in Australia. This book is the result: the day-by-day report of the voyage from the journals of James Burney and Henry Roberts, young officers who wrote with a careful prose, now being published for the first time. Along with the timeless drawings of John Webber held in Sydney, it is my hope to offer North American scholars and readers a new and remarkable resource about the triumphs and struggles of the third voyage.

I am indebted to the State Library's Senior Curator, Louise Anemaat, who introduced me to these treasures nearly ten years ago, as well as Richard Neville and the other library experts who assisted in bringing this publication to life. I also want to thank Robin Inglis of Vancouver, British Columbia, and David Nicandri of Olympia, Washington, exploration scholars and former museum curators, not only for their considerable devotion to the accomplishments of the great captain but also for their support of this project. Their efforts also helped lead to the publication by the University of Washington Press of the recent book, *Arctic Ambitions: Captain Cook and the Northwest Passage,* and the companion exhibition at the Anchorage Museum at Rasmuson Center and Washington State History Museum in Tacoma during 2015-16. Many thanks for the leadership of Jim Pepper Henry and Julie Decker in Anchorage and Jennifer Kilmer and Redmond Barnett in Tacoma.

I am also grateful for the considerable support of my wife, Marilyn Barnett, who has not only accompanied me to the far reaches of Cook's many destinations throughout the Pacific, but has also read every word of the two journals several times. Her editorial assistance was essential for the completion of this project.

Burney and Roberts probably wrote their journals for family and friends, perhaps to remember the major events of the voyage, particularly the death of Captain Cook in Hawai'i and their struggles against Arctic ice. Since they served on different vessels during most of the voyage, this publication compares their recollections at each major destination with an editorial perspective. In order to provide context and flow for the journals, introductory material is offered at the beginning of each part and chapter. In the latter case, smaller type is utilized to differentiate it from the journal text. All other editorial insertions are noted by brackets. Where possible to maintain the flow of each narrative, the spelling, capitalization, and abbreviations offered by the journal writers, no matter how idiosyncratic, have been preserved. It is their story, written in their own hand. Their handwriting is neat and legible, and their descriptions well developed for young sailors, who were both in their early twenties on the voyage. Both Burney and Roberts periodically used parentheses, but brackets are added by the editor to offer clarity to uncertain or incomplete passages.

Like many of their contemporaries, Burney and Roberts did not often punctuate their sentences and sometimes did not finish them with a period, so the text may be edited to make sense of long or run-on sentences. It is also abridged to avoid repetitive recitation of bearings to fixed points on shore, coordinates, wind direction, and some of the mundane activities aboard. They frequently refer to the nautical measure of distance, a "league," which is no longer an official unit of distance in any nation. The league originally referred to the distance a person or a horse could walk in an hour and it is now commonly computed to be three nautical miles. Further, they often referred to the measure of water depth, a fathom, still in use. While the length today is typically six feet, in the time of Captain Cook's expeditions the measure was variable, frequently five feet. A cable length in the water, based on the length of the ship's cable, was typically 100 fathoms.

In comparing the two journals, there are some discrepancies between the dates used, as Burney followed civil time and the 24-hour clock in use today, whereas Roberts (as well as Cook) used nautical or ship's time, which begins at noon, twelve hours ahead of civil time, ending the following day at noon. Finally, the geographic coordinate for longitude, still in development at the time with the use of chronometers, lunar tables, and Observatory readings on shore, was measured from the Prime Meridian that passed through the Royal Observatory in Greenwich, outside London. While it now measures from 0° at the Prime Meridian to +180° eastward and –180° westward, at the time the sailors did not recalculate the measurement at 180° East, so because they sailed around Cape of Good Hope, the journals gave measurements of longitude in the Western Hemisphere that exceeded 180°. For example, when they first sighted the Island of Maui on November 25, 1778, Burney gave their longitude as 205°52' East of Greenwich, which would read today as nearly 154° West of Greenwich.

Both journals take considerable liberties with the indigenous spelling of places and persons and, since the authors were on separate ships, their journals frequently do not agree on spelling. Instead they simply wrote names phonetically from what they heard from the local people. For example, the name of the king of Hawai'i, known today to be Kalani'ōpu'u, is designated a variation of "Terreoboo" in the journals. This requires editorial discretion, and typically clarifications are offered in brackets or as notes to offer modern spellings and maintain continuity with current references. Where there is doubt, Beaglehole's *The Voyage of the Resolution and Discovery* is considered the final authority.

FOREWORD

Captain James Cook has been part of the fabric of the history of Australia from the first days of its settlement. His survey and description of the east coast of Australia in 1770—and the eight days HMS *Endeavour* spent in Botany Bay in May of that year—were ultimately responsible for the settlement of Sydney in 1788.

Indeed his achievements, then of recent memory, were a yardstick by which early Australian colonists judged the success of their colony. While many wondered why Cook's account of Botany Bay differed so markedly from their experience of it, others, like Philip Gidley King, on Norfolk Island in 1793, complained of the absence of copies of any of Cook's voyages, and asked for a portrait print of the navigator to be sent to his settlement.

That Australia claimed its paternity from Captain Cook was elaborately and expansively celebrated throughout the nineteenth century. Queen Victoria's own son, Prince Alfred, laid a foundation stone for a statue of Captain Cook in 1869 in Sydney's Hyde Park. It took ten years for the statue itself to be unveiled in 1879, but when it was 70,000 Sydney-siders turned out to witness the occasion.

In 1887 the New South Wales Government purchased, for the substantial sum of £1050, an extensive collection of papers, relics, and some 400 items of Pacific material culture (now in the Australian Museum, Sydney) from descendants of Cook, because "it would be desirable that the Colony should possess these interesting memorials of the Great Navigator."

By the end of the nineteenth century, the Pacific and its history (largely interpreted in the colonies as the story of its European exploration) merged into that of Australia's. Indeed when the Public Library (now State Library) of New South Wales published a catalogue of its collections in 1893, it described New Zealand, Polynesia, and New Guinea as colonies of Australia, and therefore relevant collecting areas.

So integrated was Cook in the European history of Australia that any collections or artifacts relating to any of his three voyages were eagerly acquired by our institutions. Thus it was that the Mitchell Library, that great collection of Australiana which in the 1920s was perceived as the nation's national library, acquired (mostly from a Sydney book seller) in 1921 and 1922 the four manuscript volumes of James Burney's *Journal of the Proceedings of his Maj(est)ys Sloop the Discovery*. This purchase was proudly promoted in the Library's annual report for 1923 by the reproduction of the page of Burney's account describing the death of Cook.

In 1934 William Dixson, an inspired Sydney collector of substantial capacity and great public spirit, purchased the journal of Henry Roberts for £1400 from the collection of the English anthropologist and Pacific expert, James Edge Partington. Dixson's interests paralleled that of the Mitchell Library and from the earliest days of his collecting, in the first years of the twentieth century, his intentions to eventually present his collection to the state were clear. The process of the formal transfer began in 1929, but his own personal library, which included the Roberts journal and John Webber's watercolour illustrations, were only bequeathed to what became known as the Dixson Library, part of the State Library of New South Wales, in 1952.

That such rich records of Alaska and Hawai'i history are found in Australian institutions may seem unlikely, but in fact it simply reflects the diaspora of Cook material across the globe in the nineteenth and early twentieth centuries, fanned by a reputation burnished by one of the earliest instances of truly international celebrity. Cook's achievements have particular and special meaning to so many countries around the Pacific rim. Opportunities to bring this material together again are rare and should be celebrated.

We welcome the opportunity to share these special treasures with the people of the greater Pacific in this publication of the remarkable Burney and Roberts third voyage journals, illustrated by Webber's splendid voyage watercolours. This publication, as well as the recent *Arctic Ambitions* exhibition in Anchorage and Tacoma and the publication by the University of Washington Press of a fine volume by that same name, reminds us again of James Cook's place in the foundations of our shared histories.

Richard Neville
Mitchell Librarian
State Library of New South Wales
Sydney, Australia

Introduction

On his third and final Pacific voyage Captain James Cook was aware that his journal was far more than an official record of the events of the voyage written, as naval regulations demanded, for his superiors at the Admiralty. It was also being written for publication, to be read by a far wider audience, written in a sense for posterity.

Other members of the expedition shared something of the same sense that they were making history, for by the time the *Resolution* and *Discovery* sailed Cook had already transformed Europe's map of the Pacific and had become, in the words of the First Lord of the Admiralty, the Earl of Sandwich, "the first navigator in Europe." An indication of this sense is reflected in the precautions taken by Lieutenant James Burney to safeguard his journal of the *Discovery*, for on hearing on arrival at Macao that Britain was at war he copied it "on China paper in so small compass as to be easily conceivable, that if bereft of our other journals there might be one saved for the Admiralty."

The version of his journal printed here was kept, in more conventional form, in four volumes, and ends with Burney's transfer to the *Resolution* after the death of Captain Charles Clerke in August 1779. To modern eyes perhaps one of the most striking features of the other journal printed here was the youth of the writer, master's mate Henry Roberts, nineteen at the time of sailing in the *Resolution*, but already a veteran of Cook's second voyage, as was Burney.

Cook's own journal reflected his personal sense of priorities on the voyage, his explanations of decisions made, negotiations undertaken, and disputes settled. The value of the records kept by subordinates on the voyage is that they did not always share, or were even aware of, their commander's concerns. On occasion, they helped to give a collective account of the voyage; at other times they represented a different, sometimes opposing, interpretation of events to that set out by Cook in the official record.

The journals of Burney and Roberts both provide examples of an individual voice, occasionally at odds with that of their commander, more often offering a supplementary view. Their journals differ in several ways. Burney's journal of the *Discovery* is fuller, especially on events ashore. The journal of the Roberts on the *Resolution* has more detail on the everyday details of shipboard life: repairs made and punishments meted out. The number of the latter is a reminder that forty-four of the ship's crew were flogged on this voyage compared with nineteen on the *Resolution* on Cook's second voyage. A notable feature of Roberts' journal is the quality of the dozen or so charts it included, which stand in contrast to the useful but crude surveys drawn by Burney.

Whenever the ships reached land, and boat parties dispersed away from the shore, it was impossible for the journals of Cook and Clerke to make a full record of events. So at Atiu in the Cook Islands in April 1777 Burney's account of his rough handling by a crowd near the shore has no counterpart in Cook's journal. He was separated from his companions, robbed of his possessions, and detained for an hour in "by far the most uncomfortable situation during our stay ashore." More than some on board, Burney appreciated the help given by 'Mai, the Society Islander being returned to his homeland, noting on Atiu that because of his hunting and cooking skills "we fared sumptuously," while on Nomuka (Rotterdam Island) he acknowledged that he was "by far the best linguist we have." This was a matter of some importance to Burney who had compiled a Tahitian vocabulary of three hundred words but confessed that he could "never understand the Natives when talking to each other."

Another side of 'Mai was revealed when Burney described how when drunk in Tonga 'Mai he was involved in a scuffle with a sentry and threatened to leave the ships, an incident not recorded by Cook. At Tahiti Burney gave details of the punishment of miscreant islanders. When a thief was caught "we shaved half his Head, one Eyebrow, and took off half his Beard, which . . . made him an object of ridicule and contempt to his Countrymen." A final indication of Cook's concern for 'Mai (but not mentioned in his journal) came in Burney's description of the coded message 'Mai was to send after the ships once he was settled on Huahine: two white beads if all was well, two brown beads if matters were "indifferent," and two blue beads if he were in trouble.

Roberts could be more critical of Cook, notably on the occasion at Huahine when an islander who had threatened 'Mai was allowed to escape through the neglect of those in charge of the prisoner. Cook disrated a mate and midshipman, and had two marines flogged, one with thirty-six lashes. For Roberts these were harsh punishments for an affair "that's absolutely impossible to be cleared up." On the other hand, he praised both Cook and the crews for the agreement as they left the Society Islands to accept a drastic reduction in their precious grog ration until they reached more northerly latitudes. "It remained," Roberts wrote, "not a moment under Consideration but every Man gave his approbation to it."

From the islands of the South Pacific the *Resolution* and *Discovery* sailed north, through the westernmost islands of the undiscovered Hawaiian group, and on to the northwest coast of America. There Burney was more optimistic than Cook that they would find a passage north through Sandwich Sound (Prince William Sound). One, he thought, would not only be "of great advantage to us" but was "highly probable." The frustrating route along the coast of Alaska ended when the ships passed through Bering Strait, only to find their way blocked by an unbroken wall of ice. On August 20, 1778, Burney summed up their dangerous position with a minimum of words. "Having these 3 days past been pent up by a shoal Coast on one side and Ice on the other, forming a deep Gulf which by the drifting of the Ice has been continually growing narrower and kept us under some apprehension of being closed in."

As they returned through Bering Strait Burney had harsh words for the Russian chart they had on board which made "Alaschka" an island and showed a wide strait leading north along its eastern shore. It was, he wrote, "very incorrect and almost unintelligible." While at Norton Sound he stressed the significance of Bering Strait for the geography of the North Pacific in a few succinct phrases. "In the afternoon Lieut. King returned, having seen the land of Alaschka to join with the East Main ... Alaschka being part of America makes the two Continents not 14 Leagues apart."

In January 1779 the ships reached the eastern islands of the Hawaiian group in search of repair and refreshment, and the journals printed here take on a new significance, for there is no extant journal kept by Cook from the day he landed at Kealakekua Bay, Hawai'i, and entered the last dramatic weeks of his life. Burney and Roberts had different glimpses of the violence on the beach on 14 February that resulted in their commander's death. From the deck of the *Discovery* Burney saw through his telescope Cook struck down at the water's edge, and afterwards questioned "those who were on the spot" in order to obtain a detailed account of events ashore.

For his part Roberts commanded the pinnace that landed Cook on the beach, so his brief description of the attack has the authority of an eyewitness. Both Burney and Roberts describe the tense days that followed, with Roberts the more emotional as he wrote that on the sight of a piece of flesh from Cook's body "Distraction or madness was in every mind and revenge the result of all."

One of the most moving aspects of the voyage was the decision to return to the north in a renewed attempt to find a passage—this despite the death of Cook, the mortal illness of Clerke, and the battered state of the *Resolution* and *Discovery*. The journals of both Burney and Roberts have graphic detail of the difficulties the ships encountered once through Bering Strait in the summer of 1779 as they ran against a wall of ice twenty feet high, while the jagged floes which swirled around its base tore off their sheathing. On one occasion a violent swell smashed the *Discovery* broadside against the ice; on another the height of the ice that loomed out of the fog led the crews to assume that they were about to be cast ashore on the American coast.

Finally, in late July 1779 Burney wrote, "Finding our run to the Northward as well as our approaches to either Continent obstructed by the Sea being so full of Ice, it was judged fruitless to make any more attempts," and the ships headed for Kamchatka and the long voyage home. Burney's journal finished on 24 August 1779 when he joined the *Resolution* following Clerke's death; Roberts continued his until the ships reached the coast of China when all "Journals. Charts and papers, etc." were ordered to be handed in.

Not used in the official publication of Cook's third voyage, the journals of Burney and Roberts, printed here for the first time, provide significant additional information on some of the main events of the voyage.

Glyn Williams, Emeritus Professor of History
Queen Mary University of London
West Malling, Kent, England

Prologue

No man emerges larger in the exploration of the Pacific Ocean than Captain James Cook, the celebrated eighteenth century British mariner and circumnavigator, whose three voyages of exploration were perhaps the most extensive sailing voyages in the history of the world. The heroic quality of this master mariner and his achievement in discovery and exploration are well known, but most of what is written focuses on his first and second voyages in the South Pacific.[1]

In his third and most demanding voyage, which stretched between July 1776 and November 1779, he was asked to look for the imagined Northwest Passage, a place that had puzzled speculative geographers for centuries. The British Admiralty was aware that the Russians and Spanish had begun to occupy the Northwest Coast, but there were few maps of the region and those that had been published were unreliable. So they asked Cook to confirm, once and for all, the outline of the Pacific coastline of North America and whether the legendary passage to Europe existed.

Although he started his examination of the Northwest Coast off the shores of Oregon, Cook began the search in earnest much further north at 65° North Latitude. In the years before the voyage, the Englishman Samuel Hearne, exploring the Coppermine River in central Canada for the Hudson's Bay Company, reached the Arctic Ocean and speculated there was no temperate seaway across Canada from the Pacific to Hudson Bay.[2] While Hearne's exploration dispelled hope of a warm weather passage, the British Admiralty thought there might be a route for ships at the northern extreme of the continent. Russian manuscript maps then circulating in Europe suggested a series of islands existed in "Alaschka," permitting ships to sail along a temperate Arctic Ocean to Europe.

Cook left as England prepared for war with its upstart American colonies, commanding the *Resolution*, a well-seasoned collier or coal ship that had already sailed during his second voyage around Antarctica. Small by modern standards, it was the largest of the four ships he took on his three voyages—461 tons and 110 feet in length, 30 feet wide, and 13 feet to the depth of its hold. Although modest in size, she carried a crew of 112 on the third voyage, making for very cramped quarters. The consort *Discovery* was even smaller, under 300 tons, and just 91 feet in length. It was commanded by Captain Charles Clerke and had a crew of another 70 men. Of the *Resolution*'s complement, thirteen had been with Cook before, including five who had been on both voyages. The *Discovery* had ten such veterans, including Clerke. The expedition was one of the most remarkable voyages undertaken during the era of wooden sailing ships, returning in October 1780 after over four years at sea.[3]

As with Cook's first two voyages, his experienced team of officers was noteworthy, including both James Burney and Henry Roberts. Lieutenant John Gore was second in command of the *Resolution*. A Virginian, he was the most experienced, serving as Master's Mate with Byron and Wallis in voyages to the South Seas before Cook, then as a lieutenant on Cook's first voyage. Although he had not served with Cook before, James King was second lieutenant. King was so thoughtful and erudite that his personal journal was used as the official voyage account after Cook's death. William Bligh was the ship's Master. He was already intemperate at just twenty-one years of age and, while he would soon enjoy a controversial career, there is little explanation how Bligh came to the voyage or where he might have attained survey experience sufficient to put him in charge of the Master's Mate, Henry Roberts, a favorite of Cook, who served on the previous voyage and had considerable surveying and chart making skills.

Charles Clerke commanded the *Discovery*. He knew Cook well, having served as a senior officer in the previous two voyages. Clerke's lieutenant was James Burney, who made significant contributions to the hydrography of the second voyage under Captain Furneaux and was in charge of the shore party that discovered the murdered crew in Grass Cove (Wharehunga Bay) on the South Island of New Zealand. George Vancouver was also on *Discovery*, serving on his second voyage as midshipman with Cook, still not yet twenty years old. He would also gain fame for his comprehensive survey of the Northwest Coast and Alaska nearly two decades later.[4]

Among the voyage supernumeraries was Mai, as he was known in his homeland, called "Omai" in London (the O signifies "it is"). He was a young Tahitian nobleman brought to London by Captain Furneaux. After his arrival in England in 1774, he was introduced to the naturalist and president of the Royal Society, Sir Joseph Banks, who in turn presented him to the celebrities of the day, including Lord Sandwich, Dr. Samuel Johnson, and Fannie Burney. Ms. Burney wrote, "for his manners are so extremely graceful, and he is so polite, attentive, and easy, that you would have thought he came from some foreign Court." Indeed, Mai was renowned for his charm and exotic stories and was found regularly in the company of James Burney, who befriended him as Furneaux's ship returned to England and helped translate for him as he navigated London society.[5]

During his two years in London, Mai met twice with King George III and was the subject of a theatrical production. He also had his portrait painted by Sir Joshua Reynolds, a study that epitomized the Enlightenment concept of the "noble savage." After two years, weary and homesick, Mai decided to return with Cook at the beginning of the third voyage to the Tahitian island of Huahine, where the ships' carpenters built him lavish quarters. According to Captain William Bligh, who returned to the island in 1789 on the *Bounty*, many of Mai's European possessions were stolen by his fellow islanders after Cook left for America and he died a natural death three years later.[6]

England was not the only country interested in the results of the third voyage. The respect for Captain Cook and the anticipated discoveries on the voyage were vital to the entire western world, even while it was at war. In 1779 Benjamin Franklin, then American ambassador to France, issued a letter of free passage so the expedition would not be disturbed by the Americans or their allies when it returned to European waters. Cook was probably only vaguely aware of the American Revolution and certainly did not know of Franklin's letter of praise and protection. Yet the letter demonstrated the high regard Cook enjoyed in Europe and America and the anticipated success of the voyage.

In the first year the expedition sailed around the Cape of Good Hope into the South Seas, visiting Tasmania, New Zealand, Tonga, and Tahiti. After depositing Mai in Huahine, they passed Christmas Island (in today's tropical island Republic of Kiribati) before they chanced upon the Hawaiian Islands. After a short visit to the islands of Kaua'i and Ni'ihau in January 1778, they sailed to the Oregon coastline, where they chased the fogbound, tempestuous, and rocky coastline from the Northwest Coast to Arctic Alaska searching for the imagined ice-free seaway to Europe.

Because of spring storms the expedition saw little of the American coast, stopping once at Nootka Sound on the western side of Vancouver Island. Coastal features were fully revealed when they reached the Gulf of Alaska, where the latest Russian maps told them they would find islands and channels—a vast northern archipelago to navigate in the return to Hudson Bay. While Cook doubted the existence of such a passage, he found and investigated two promising waterways in Alaska, today's Prince William Sound and Cook Inlet, but they both proved to be dead ends. The Alaska landmass then forced the ships southwest before they passed through the Aleutian Islands to regain a northern course.

Frustrated by the "late pretended discoveries" of the Russians and delay in the season, it took the expedition another two months sailing near the Alaska mainland until they passed Bering Strait and stretched to the Arctic ice pack, reaching their northernmost point at 70°44' North Latitude on August 18, 1778. After turning back for the season, Cook decided to sail into the ice a second time, the next time arriving earlier in the season, as he suspected he might find a way though the ice in early July. Because of this miscalculation, the expedition returned by way of Unalaska in the Aleutian Islands to winter in Hawai'i, where Cook was killed in a skirmish over a stolen shore boat at Kealakekua Bay.[7]

In a testament to British Naval tradition, and despite his own ill-health, after Cook's death Captain Clerke steered them north again. In the summer of 1779 the expedition tested the Arctic ice pack a second time, again finding the route impassible. On July 19, 1779, they reached 70°33', a few miles short of Cook's northernmost point from the prior summer. After Clerke's death in Kamchatka the following month, the ships found their way back to England in the command of the Virginian, John Gore, and the remaining senior officers.[8]

There were no celebrations when the voyagers returned after over four years at sea. They had not found the Northwest Passage and both captains had died. But the voyage accomplished a great deal. Although the expedition's observatories were only taken ashore at Nootka Sound and Unalaska, the chronometers, sextants, and lunar observations made aboard rolling decks enabled the expedition to chart the outline of the coastline from Oregon to Bering Strait with remarkable accuracy, determining the shape of the Alaska Peninsula and proving there was no easy route to Hudson Bay. They also made the first comprehensive written and visual record of the people of the North Pacific and, thanks especially to Burney, Roberts, and other accomplished hydrographers, published the first reasonably accurate maps of the region. But with the loss of Cook, it fell to the other journal writers to publish the voyage diary, recording the circumstances of his death and the conclusion of the voyage before the sailors returned to England.

There is considerable commentary in the journals and subsequent scholarship about Cook's poor health and temperament during the third voyage. He was weary and tired from a life at sea, nearly fifty years old when he left England for his most demanding exploratory voyage. Many incidents during the voyage suggest he was not up to the task. For example, although told by the local people of the existence of nearby Fiji and Samoa, he failed to search for the islands despite the extra time available to the expedition during 1777 in the South Pacific. He was also frequently moody and erratic, even harder on his crew and less tolerant of island people than in the earlier voyages. All of this may have contributed to his death in Hawai'i. In hindsight, retirement was probably his better option, as he had spent much of the previous decades in the demanding life at sea.[9]

James Burney

James Burney (1750–1821) was the son of Dr. Charles Burney, a famous British historian of music, and brother of Fanny Burney, a popular novelist and diarist. He was an accomplished mariner and officer who accompanied Captain Cook on his second and third voyages and later wrote a series of erudite books on the history of early European exploration in the Pacific.

At the age of ten, he was sent to sea to act as a captain's servant and by fifteen he was a midshipman in the Mediterranean Sea. In 1772, John Montagu, Fourth Earl of Sandwich, arranged a post for him as an able seaman on Captain Cook's second voyage. During the voyage, he received his first commission as second lieutenant of the *Adventure*. He was best known as the officer in command of the shore boats that discovered the horrible massacre of British sailors at Grass Cove at the hands of Maori warriors. He also spent considerable time learning the Polynesian language and struck up a friendship with Mai, whom he befriended on the return to England at the end of the voyage.

Burney accompanied Captain Cook on his third voyage in 1776 as second to Clerke on the *Discovery*. He was an active member of many shore parties, contributed to the preparation of most of the charts made on the voyage, and was one of the few sailors to witness Cook's death in Kealakekua Bay from the deck of the *Discovery*. He transferred to the flagship when Clerke died six months later in Kamchatka. In 1780, at the end of the voyage, when King left the ships in Scotland, Burney was promoted to command the *Discovery* as he brought it in to the Thames.[10]

After the third voyage, Burney was temporary captain of the *Latona* in the North Sea. Later he was promoted to be captain of the *Bristol*, which in June 1782 accompanied a convoy of East India Company ships to Madras, India. A year later, Burney commanded the ship in an inconclusive battle with the French off the coast of India. But he soon became ill with a chronic liver obstruction that required his return to England, where he retired from active service in 1784.

Given his naval background and family connections, Burney began a second career as an author and historian that focused on British maritime achievements in the Pacific. His first project was to edit William Bligh's *A Voyage to the South Sea in HMS Bounty*, which was published in 1792. His major work was *A Chronological History of the Discoveries in the South Sea or Pacific Ocean*, published in five volumes from 1803 to 1817, which traced the history of Pacific exploration from Magellan to Bougainville, so it stopped just short of Cook's voyages. Two years later he wrote *A Chronological History of North-Eastern Voyages of Discovery and of the Early Eastern Navigations of the Russians*, where he devoted several chapters to his recollections of the third voyage, including the death of Cook. Burney also wrote separate works on his scientific observations, contemporary British affairs, and his favorite card game—whist.

Due to his experiences with Cook and his growing literary reputation, Burney was elected as a Fellow of the Royal Society in 1809. In July 1821, nearly thirty years after his retirement from the navy, he was promoted to rear-admiral at the age of seventy-one, a superannuated appointment that was awarded just four months before his death.

Burney's personal journal of Cook's second voyage was published in Australia in 1975 and again in 2015. While his third voyage journal has also been available in Australia, and Burney was among the few to observe Cook's death in Hawai'i, it has never been published. Burney's claim that he observed the melee might be questioned, given the distance between his ship and the shore and the clouds of musket and cannon smoke that must have enveloped the bay during the skirmish.

Left, Portrait of Admiral James Burney, drawn from a bust and later engraved, National Maritime Museum, Greenwich. Right, Portrait of Captain Henry Roberts, by Thomas Gainsborough.

But he said he was so close that he wrote in his journal "with Glasses we could see Captn Cook receive a Blow from a Club and fall off a Rock into the Water." Captain Charles Clerke, who was probably with Burney on the deck of *Discovery*, wrote that "with my Glass I clearly saw that our People were drove off to their Boats but I could not distinguish Persons in that confused Crowd."[11]

Henry Roberts

Like Burney, Henry Roberts (1757—1796) was an officer in the Royal Navy who also served with Captain Cook on his second and third voyages. Born and raised in Shoreham, south of London, he was just fifteen when he joined Cook as an able seaman on the second voyage. He was soon promoted to prepare the charts and coastal views, achieving a reputation as the best pupil of the expedition artist, William Hodges. Roberts prepared several notable drawings on the second voyage, including the often-reproduced image of the *Resolution* lying at anchor in the South Pacific, as well as bays, mountains, and vessels in Tahiti and nearby islands.[12]

When the third voyage assembled, Roberts was appointed Master's Mate on the *Resolution*. Although just nineteen years old at the beginning of the voyage, he was entrusted with many hydrographic and cartographic tasks, working directly with Cook and William Bligh. Among other things, Cook had him prepare a comprehensive map of the world depicting the routes of all three voyages, which was completed after Cook's death and the voyage's return to England.

Although Bligh once dismissed his work in a notable tirade, Gore called him "principal assistant hydrographer" to Cook. After the expedition returned to England, he took charge of the original charts and journals and, after promotion to lieutenant, he spent many years preparing the detailed charts that went into Cook's posthumous expedition Atlas.[13]

In 1789, Roberts was appointed to command the newly built HMS *Discovery* for the Admiralty's planned round-the-world voyage to fully explore and chart the Northwest Coast of America. He selected George Vancouver, an accomplished officer in the Caribbean, as his first lieutenant. When the expedition was delayed by the diplomatic controversy that followed the Spanish seizure of British vessels at Nootka Sound, Roberts was called to duty in Africa, then the West Indies, leaving command of the expedition to Vancouver. While on the voyage in 1792, Vancouver named Point Roberts after him, which is located in northern Washington State, the tiny isthmus that separates coastal Washington from British Columbia.

While captain of the *Undaunted* in the West Indies, Roberts died of yellow fever on August 25, 1796. His two-volume log of the third voyage with Captain Cook was not known to exist until 1928 when Britain was celebrating the bicentennial of Cook's birth. A summary of the second volume was published in the London "Morning Post." Later the first volume, which had been in the library of the Roberts family, was also discovered. Both were acquired in the mid-1930s by William Dixson, who in turn bequeathed them to the Dixson Library in Sydney. It has not been published in any form.

The Voyage Journals

After the English public learned of Cook's death, Britain was captivated by the details of the voyage and particularly the expedition's exploits in Hawai'i and the North Pacific, the most distant temperate shores from England. The published third voyage journal combined Cook's narrative with that of Lieutenant King, who added the segment after Cook's death, and it was very popular, rapidly selling three successive editions that are still expensive and difficult to purchase. At the same time engravings from Webber's drawings and Roberts' charts were prepared in a separate folio atlas, offering the first comprehensive visual record of the region. French, German, and Dutch editions were also published and enjoyed the same overwhelming reception from the public. According to instructions from the Admiralty, the largest part of the profits was distributed to Mrs. Cook, though smaller provisions were made to King, Bligh, and the heirs of Clerke and the surgeon, William Anderson, who also died on the voyage.

In addition to the published journal, several other records soon appeared. Although Captain Gore and Lieutenant King intended to collect all the journals in Asia before the expedition returned to England, a Royal Navy tradition, several seamen kept their personal logs, anticipating the popularity of voyage accounts. They were not disappointed. In quick succession, the four private journals of John Ledyard, George Gilbert, John Rickman, and William Ellis were published. Except for Rickman, these journals were the product of ordinary sailors, so they were filled with hyperbole and exaggeration, particularly when describing the death of Cook in Hawai'i. Motivated by financial gain, authors often took liberties with the facts to meet the demands of their publishers and benefactors. Further, because the Admiralty frowned on unofficial publications, the decision to publish usually meant the end of a naval career. This meant the officers on the voyage, like Burney and Roberts, who might be considered more truthful and articulate, usually did not publish anything.

The journals of Cook's officers and key staff are perhaps more trustworthy, particularly about the events leading up to Cook's death at Kealakekua Bay. The journals of Clerke and King were accepted as the official logs and both were published, although Clerke's account is not highly regarded for its prose. Beaglehole also reprinted the partial journals of Anderson, the surgeon who died of tuberculosis on the journey, and David Samwell, Surgeon's Mate, who was later asked to write an embellished and somewhat emotional version of the voyage, focusing on the circumstances of Cook's death and its aftermath.[14]

The Burney Journal

On the third voyage, Burney wrote one of the few accounts from the consort vessel, which only became known to the public after his descendants sold it a century ago. It is an important, thoughtful journal of first impressions of the people and places of the North Pacific, as well as a lively eyewitness account of the skirmish at Kealakekua Bay. However, perhaps because the journal has been in Australia for nearly a century, where the third voyage does not receive significant attention, it has not been reprinted in a modern form.

Burney left two copies of his third voyage journal, one now held in the British National Archives and another in the Mitchell Library, the latter acquired in 1921 and 1922. The version in the National Archives is much shorter and ends while the expedition is on the Northwest Coast, before its return to Hawai'i. Beaglehole speculates that at least a portion of the Mitchell Library version was prepared after the voyage, since the title page of one volume is signed "Jas. Burney/Latona" and Burney commanded the *Latona* soon after his return to England in 1781-82.

Burney also rewrote his journal into a miniature version in Macao, China, compressing it into a mere fifty pages to fit inside a compass. Many of the officers worried that hostilities accompanying the American Revolution might result in the seizure of the vessels and the loss of the maps and journals of the voyage. Burney's consolidated version was supposed to provide a secret voyage log for the Admiralty in the event the journals were confiscated by enemy powers. Perplexed by the minuscule version, Beaglehole terms it one of the "curiosities of the voyage."[15]

In his *Charts and Coastal Views* of the third voyage, Andrew David treats the two journals as equals. However, the Mitchell version is far more interesting, since it has a longer duration and includes over twenty coastal charts (many including the ships' tracks), some in Alaska and Hawai'i, and two modest drawings. The British National Archives version has just nine charts, none after the voyage departure from Nootka Sound, making it less attractive for people interested in voyage outcomes in Alaska and Hawai'i. The more comprehensive Mitchell manuscript, including the charts and drawings, which is presented here, is found in four separate volumes of 289 pages extending from February 1776, before the expedition left England, to August 1779, when the expedition returned from its second struggle with Arctic ice after Cook's death. Only a modest section of Burney's journal has been published before, as a few rather insignificant entries became part of the official record after the death of Charles Clerke. So a few pages of Burney's work were published by Beaglehole as part of the official voyage summary.[16]

The four-volume Mitchell manuscript is articulate, reasonably paced, and quite legible. It is divided into four segments and, fortunately for the reader, spares much of the tables of courses, winds, and headings, tedious reports that can dominate such journals. It mysteriously concludes with the return of the expedition to Siberia in the late summer of 1779, nearly a year before the expedition returned to England. Burney had been promoted and transferred from the *Discovery* to the *Resolution* after the death of Captain Clerke, which may explain the premature end to his work before they returned to England. The four volumes are summarized as follows:

Vol. 1—February 10, 1776, to October 11, 1777 (Voyage Commencement to Tahiti)—91 pages, including four charts and a drawing of a cabbage at Kerguelen Islands. The cabbage may have been drawn by John Webber and not Burney, but inserted by Burney in his journal. The volume covers the early part of the voyage, including most of the voyage contacts in the South Pacific, particularly the expedition's brief stops in Tasmania, New Zealand, and several islands now called the "Cook Islands," as well as the expedition's celebrated visit to Tonga.

Vol. II—October 12, 1777, to July 24, 1778 (Tahiti to Bering Strait)—94 pages, including ten charts and a drawing of a pastoral scene in the Society Islands, probably sketched by Burney in Huahine. The volume completes the South Pacific leg of the voyage, including the return of Mai to Huahine, then follows the expedition north past its brief encounter with Hawai'i as it hails the west coast of North America. It then follows the voyage from Oregon to Alaska, ending just before Cook's contact with the Arctic ice pack in July 1778.

Vol. III—July 25, 1778, to February 14, 1779 (Bering Strait to Cook's Death at Kealakekua Bay)—81 pages, with six charts, including a very large chart of Burney's observation of the Northwest Coast and Alaska. This volume begins with the first contact with the Arctic ice pack in August 1778, as well as the return via Unalaska to Hawai'i, with a series of charts showing the ship's track in the Arctic. At the conclusion of the volume, Burney offers a lengthy description of the death of Cook, which he viewed from the deck of *Discovery.*

Vol. IV—February 15, 1779, to August 6, 1779 (Aftermath of Cook's Death to the Death of Clerke off Kamchatka)—Burney titled this volume "Part Two of the Death of Cook," but it is actually a narrative that discusses the developments with the Hawaiians in the aftermath of Cook's death, then leads the expedition north to Kamchatka until the death of Charles Clerke nearly six months later, after testing the Arctic ice pack a second time. There is minor duplication with Beaglehole, who uses Burney's journal briefly as the official record of the proceedings on board *Discovery* after Clerke's death until the consort anchored at Avacha Bay again on August 24, 1779.[17]

Burney was quite literate and after retirement became a specialist in the exploration of the Pacific. His published volumes continue to be of considerable interest to scholars and collectors of exploration literature. The 5-volume set, *A Chronological History of the Discoveries in the South Sea or Pacific Ocean*, concludes with the beginning of Cook's first voyage, so does not contain any personal observations of the third voyage. His later *A Chronological History of North-Eastern Voyages of Discovery and of the Early Eastern Navigations of the Russians* offers a full report about Cook's third voyage in the North Pacific in three chapters near the end of the volume. These are presented as personal recollections forty years after the actual events, though they are supplemented by quotes from Cook's journal and carefully track voyage descriptions from his own voyage journal.

The third and final chapter, chapter number twenty-one in Burney's later book, describes the expedition's return to the Big Island of Hawai'i and discusses the circumstances surrounding Cook's death at Kealakekua Bay. Burney was apparently concerned about reports that Cook was irrational and hostile to both his crew and the local people, especially the morning of his death. So he assured readers that

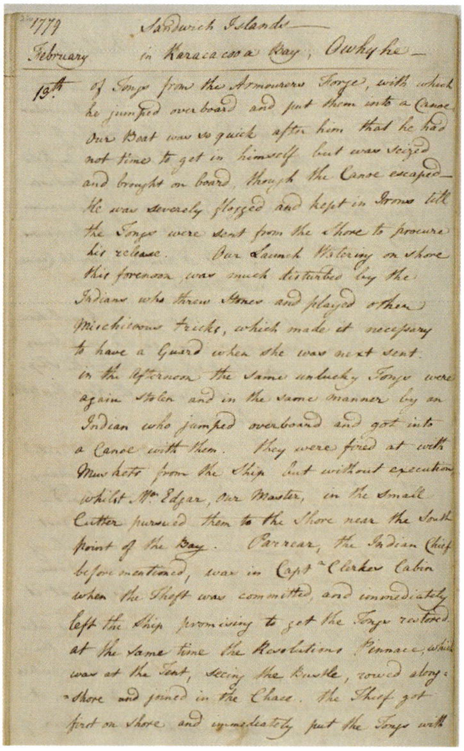
1779 Sandwich Islands
February in Karacacooa Bay; Owhyhe
13th of Tongs from the Armourers Forge, with which he jumped overboard and put them into a Canoe. Our Boat was so quick after him that he had not time to get in himself but was seized and brought on board, though the Canoe escaped. He was severely flogged and kept in Irons till the Tongs were sent from the Shore to procure his release. Our Launch Watering on shore this forenoon was much disturbed by the Indians who threw Stones and played other Mischievous tricks, which made it necessary to have a Guard when she was next sent. In the Afternoon the same unlucky Tongs were again stolen and in the same manner by an Indian who jumped overboard and got into a Canoe with them. They were fired at with Musquets from the Ship but without execution whilst Mr Edgar, our Master, in the Small Cutter pursued them to the Shore near the South point of the Bay. Parreear, the Indian Chief before mentioned, was in Captn Clerke's Cabin when the Theft was committed, and immediately left the Ship promising to get the Tongs restored at the same time the Resolution's Pinnace, which was at the Seat, seeing the Bustle, rowed along shore and joined in the Chase. The Thief got first on Shore and immediately put the Tongs with

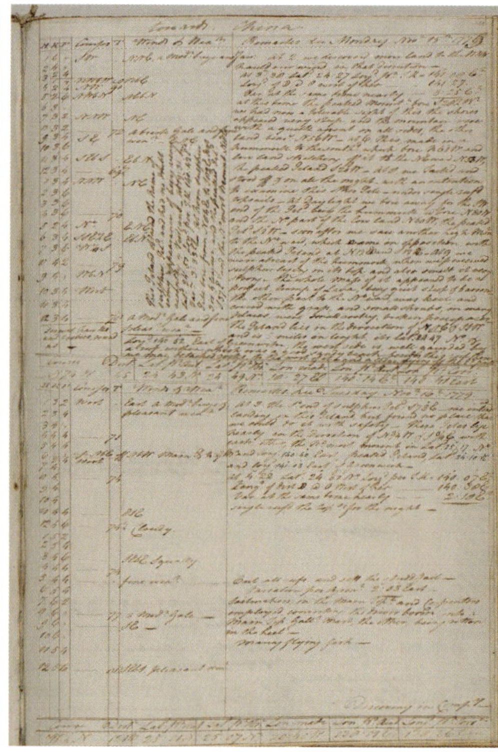

Left, Sample Page of Burney Journal (Remarks while in Kealakekua Bay, Hawai'i, February 13, 1779), Mitchell Library, State Library of New South Wales, Safe 1/64 and 1/79; Right, Sample Page of Roberts Journal (Remarks sailing toward China, November 15-16, 1779), Dixson Library, State Library of New South Wales, DLMSQ 151-52 and DLMSF 2.

the great captain was composed and objective at all times during the voyage and especially during the last hour of his life.

Burney argued that when Cook fired his musket at the Hawaiian warriors, he was not acting imprudently or irrationally, but instead he coolly assessed the situation and fired to protect the marines and other seamen who accompanied him on shore. "In the whole of Captain Cook's conduct in his voyages of discovery, so far was rashness from his character," Burney wrote, "that if the event of his death had not happened in the manner it did, he would have been not less, nor less justly, celebrated for prudence and circumspection, than he has been, and is, for enterprise and perseverance. That such was the opinion entertained of his prudence by all under his command, was evident on every occasion of difficulty or danger."[18]

The Roberts Journal

Roberts was just nineteen when he was appointed Master's Mate on Cook's vessel, the *Resolution*, and after the voyage was so well respected that he was asked by the other officers to prepare the maps of the expedition for publication, including the first published maps of the outline of the Northwest Coast of America, Alaska,

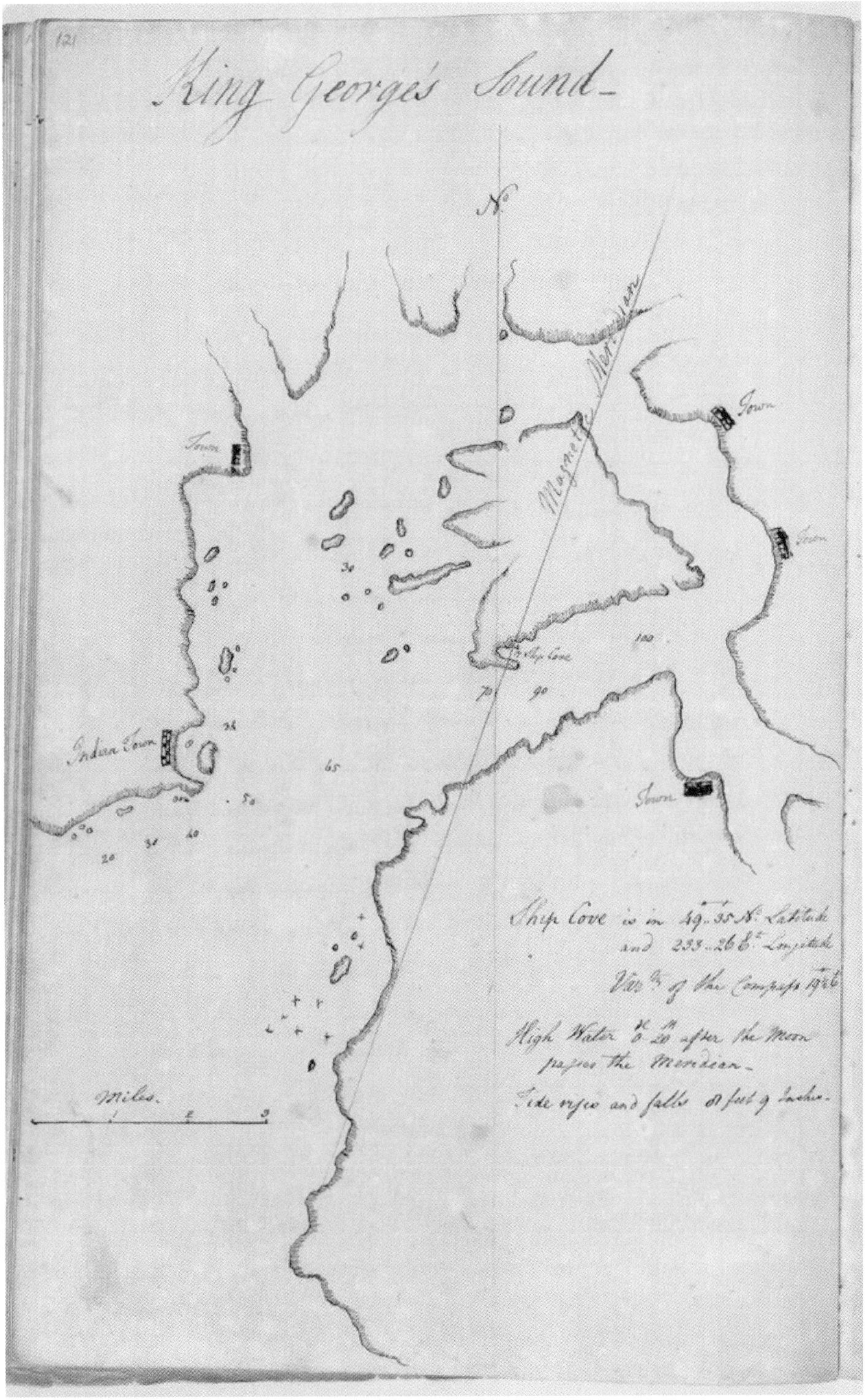

James Burney, "Sketch of King George's [Nootka] Sound," March-April 1778. Burney Journal p. 124, Mitchell Library, State Library of New South Wales, Safe 1/64 and 1/79.

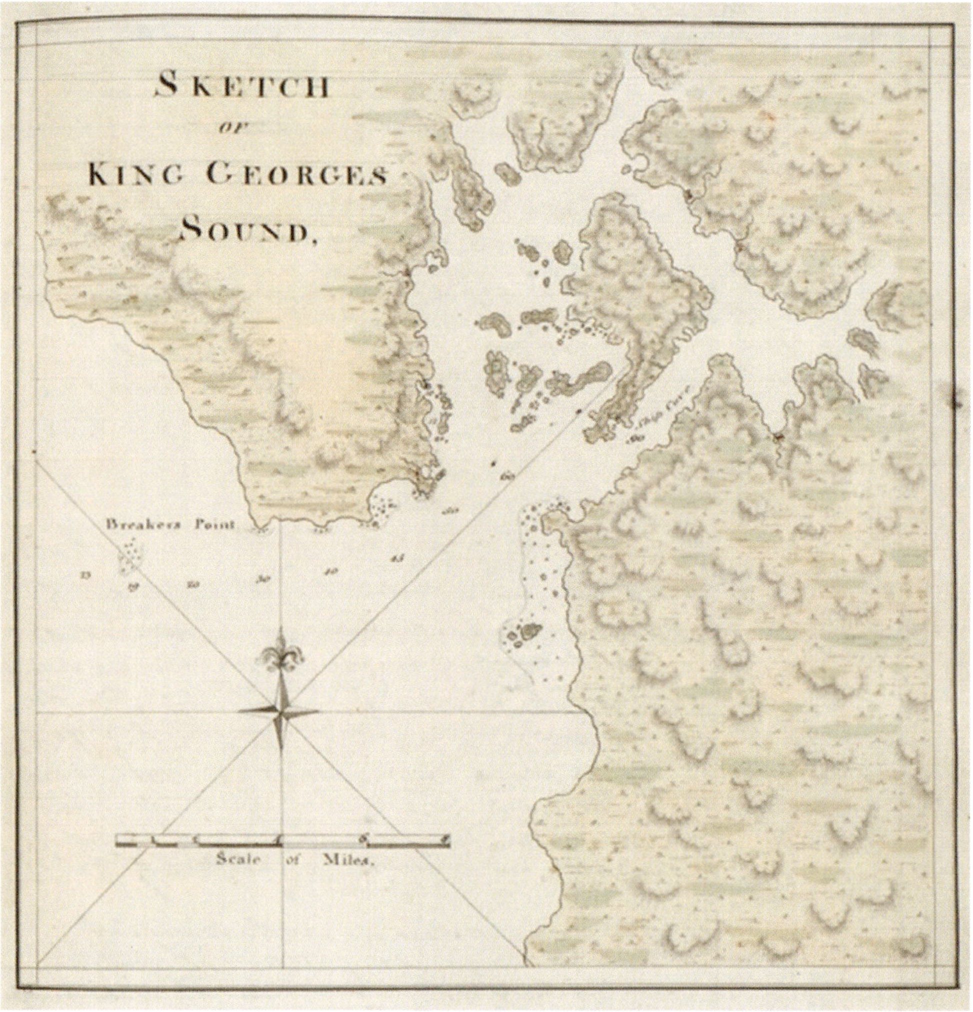

Henry Roberts, "Sketch of King George's [Nootka] Sound," March-April 1778. Roberts Journal p. 187, Dixson Library, State Library of New South Wales, DLMSQ 151-52 and DLMSF 2.

and Hawai'i. He served directly under the temperamental William Bligh, who later wrote of his frustrations that Roberts received too much glory for the published results of the third voyage. The two-volume Roberts journal, which exceeds 400 pages, was acquired by the Dixson Library from the Roberts family in 1929. It was written as a voyage logbook, so it is filled with the expected chart maker's daily report of coordinates, as well as hourly tables of courses, winds, and the changing weather. Beaglehole was apparently only aware of the second volume but both were in the library's possession when Beaglehole edited the Cook journals.[19]

The journal requires careful editing, as there are frequent references to bearings to points ashore and the change in winds and weather, important to mariners and surveyors at the time, but often tedious. It also reports on the supply of provisions on board, including the occasional feast and famine that accompanied any long journey with so many mouths to feed. Interestingly, it offers a record of the periodic lashings of the crew, the normal means of punishment in the British Navy at the time. The lash was reserved to the common sailors and marines, usually for either "drunkenness" or "neglect of duty," and often both at once. Sometimes the transgressions are more meaningful, like failing to trade fairly with local inhabitants or having sexual relations with Native women when suffering from the "venereal distemper."

Although he offers a rather tepid voyage log while under sail, Roberts alters pace to a lively narrative of the principal voyage activities when ashore. The first volume covers the period from the departure from England to near the conclusion of the Alaska season in the Aleutian Islands in early October 1778. The second volume completes the Alaska season and the return to Hawai'i, including the death of Cook. It also contains the expedition's return to Kamchatka and its second encounter with the Arctic ice pack, Captain Clerke's search for the Northwest Passage. It ends when the journals are confiscated by the captain according to tradition as the voyagers reached Macao in China.

Both volumes are well illustrated, with the best being drawings from the Cook Islands and Kaua'i in late 1777 and early 1778, as well as many illustrated charts. Burney's charts are topographically accurate, but many have the look of ill-defined sketches. Conversely, Roberts' work is more accomplished. He had already proven his chart making and artistic skills on the second voyage, so his third voyage log-journal includes remarkable drawings of coastal views, as well as colorful and detailed charts of Nootka Sound, Norton Sound, Unalaska, Kealakekua Bay, and Avacha Bay.

Roberts made good use of dark and light washes with brush strokes and, in some cases, grey, yellow, and green tones to show fertile vegetation, distant slopes, and even individual coconut palms. After they purchased the two volumes, the Dixson Library assembled four loose charts into a third volume. One of these charts is a comprehensive representation of Prince William Sound and Cook Inlet in Southcentral Alaska, probably the first map of the region and more detailed than the one found in the official third voyage publication (also prepared by Roberts).[20]

Occasionally the Burney and Roberts charts are similar, though Robert's hydrographic skills are superior. This suggests there was some collaboration among all the chart makers during the voyage, even though the two officers rarely mention one another in their logs and, until the return from Kamchatka, Burney and Roberts served on different ships.

The Webber Drawings

John Webber (1751-93) was the official expedition artist aboard the *Resolution.* Born in London, he was educated in Switzerland and Paris. He had already achieved an admirable reputation for his landscape paintings when, at the age of twenty-four, he caught the attention of the Swedish naturalist Daniel Solander and was asked to join the third voyage. Today he is best known for his images of early Hawai'i and Alaska, many of which are found at the State Library of New South Wales.

Except for the painting of the death of Cook, the Webber drawings held by the State Library of New South Wales were prepared for the engravers of the published folio atlas in the months after the voyage returned to England. They offer among the most complete and colorful visual records of the third voyage found anywhere and served as the basis for his future life's work. After the voyage, Webber spent much of his career exhibiting works from the voyage at the Royal Academy and preparing aquatint recollections of significant voyage events, which he called *Views in the South Seas.*[21]

Separated by time on the voyage, the 42 drawings and one painting in Sydney can be summarized in four parts as follows:

> First, there are twenty drawings from the South Pacific. Beginning with the Kerguelen Islands, these images depict the people and customs of New Zealand, Tonga, Tahiti, and the first encounter with Kaua'i and Ni'ihau islands in Hawai'i.
>
> Second, after leaving Hawai'i, the expedition continued to the Northwest Coast and Alaska, conducting a "running survey" of coastal Alaska before reaching the Arctic ice pack north of the Bering Strait. The Webber collection in Sydney includes fourteen unique views and sketches of the local people at Nootka Sound and along the Alaska coast to the Arctic, including Prince William Sound, Unalaska, Norton Sound, and the brief contact with the Chukchi warriors when the ships crossed to the Asia coast south of Bering Strait in Kamchatka.
>
> Third, Webber prepared six more images of Hawai'i after the expedition's return, starting with Cook's dramatic reception at Kealakekua Bay in January 1779. The collection also offers sketches of warriors and canoes and probably the most celebrated painting of Cook's death, painted in 1784 after Webber was back in England, when he portrayed the dramatic scene from the recollections of the crewmen who observed the event.
>
> Fourth, there are three drawings from Kamchatka, including the dramatic landscape surrounding the modest beginnings of Petropavlovsk, the modern-day center of the region, as well as the people and habitations of the region.

John Webber, "A Dance in Otaheite [Tahiti]," circa 1781-83. Pen, wash, and water color of a heiva or dance held in early September 1777. Two men and two women dance before a hut with spectators on either side. Three drummers play at the back under a grass-roofed awning. Dixson Library, State Library of New South Wales, PXX 2, f. 13.

The other major source of original Webber drawings is the British Library, which is the only institution with a greater number of his illustrations than the State Library of New South Wales. His other third voyage works can be found in the United States at the Bishop Museum in Honolulu and Peabody Museum at Harvard University, with fewer at the Peabody Museum in Salem, Massachusetts, and in the states of Alaska and Washington. Others are scattered throughout England and Australia, mostly at the National Maritime Museum in Greenwich, the British Museum, and the National Library of Australia. Many ethnographic and landscape drawings of the other artist on the voyage, William Ellis, are found in Australia and New Zealand. In addition, an Ellis album of "natural history" drawings is held by the British Museum.[22]

PART ONE
The South Seas

INTRODUCTION

James Cook steered the *Resolution* from Plymouth Harbor in July 1776, four years to the day after leaving on his second voyage, in full view of British warships being outfitted for the war with the American colonies. His instructions from the Admiralty gave him less than twelve months to reach the Northwest Coast of America and, even more implausible, in the meantime he was to return the Tahitian, Mai, to his homeland in Tahiti. Behind already, they left three weeks before the *Discovery* could sail, as its captain, Charles Clerke, had been bonded to his brother's creditors and was forced to serve time in the Fleet debtor's prison.

Cook soon learned the recent repairs made to the aging *Resolution* in the Royal Navy Shipyards were defective, a problem that would plague the ship for the duration of the voyage. It leaked within the first week at sea and the cabins, sail rooms, and storerooms filled each time it rained. Cook made for Tenerife in the Canary Islands as his first port, where the master navigator miscalculated the longitude and nearly crashed into rocks entering the harbor. Once in port, the *Resolution* stocked up on fresh supplies of pigs, sheep, goats, poultry, fish, and vegetables. Still missing Clerke, they continued to the Azores, then south along the African coast to the Cape of Good Hope. The passage to the Cape, which they reached by mid-October, was not nearly as eventful as the first few weeks at sea. Cook started the routine employed by the expedition at each port: erecting a camp so the astronomers could take lunar observations, sending the sailors ashore to collect wood and fill the water casks, and putting the carpenters into the shore boats to caulk and repair the leaking ship.

Clerke, Burney, and the *Discovery* arrived a month later. The consort was also frail from a flawed overhaul so, when the carpenters finished with the *Resolution*, they went to work caulking the seams between the planks of the *Discovery*. By the end of November both ships were repaired, filled with provisions, and ready to sail. They took stock animals on board from the Cape Colony to serve as presents for chiefs they would encounter in the South Seas, including cattle, horses, sheep, goats, and rabbits. The mood was positive and the course was set to the Pacific, although the duration of the mission was unknown. Cook said they would need at least two years at sea but, as it turned out, the voyage lasted over four years.

Leaving Africa, the expedition sailed to the southeast. To test his crew, Cook pushed the ships well south through stormy, foggy, and wet weather in what passed for summer in the Polar seas. This is the area dubbed today the "Roaring Forties" due to its turbulent seas and high winds. Despite adverse winds and currents, the trial was successful, as the crew used observations from the rolling decks to find two small islands discovered by the French in 1772. Three weeks later they reached another recent French discovery, the Kerguelen Archipelago, an uninhabited and desolate volcanic formation, which was also enveloped in fog, cold, and mist.

Navigation in the southern Indian Ocean was both tedious and hazardous, but Cook looked for Kerguelen's Islands not simply to chart islands of French conjecture, but also to expose his crew to what lay ahead in the Arctic. The two ships often kept in touch during foggy weather by firing their cannons. Their first landfall in the islands was a rocky cove, which they called Christmas Harbor, since they reached it on Christmas day. A bottle attached by a wire to a rock on the north side held a Latin inscription confirming the earlier French discovery of the dismal and snow covered landscape. John Webber prepared the first of his iconic drawings of the surreal anchoring place, complete with a rocky outcrop, dramatic waterfall, sparse vegetation, and a host of penguins standing sentry below the ships.[1]

After a few days in the barren islands the expedition took advantage of following winds in the "Roaring Forties" to speed across the Indian Ocean toward Australia. The journal keepers wrote little about the passage except the speed of the wind and monotonous surroundings of fog and rain. Since few of them had been this way before, the sailors kept a close watch ahead, as many feared that rocks or islands would emerge out of the thick weather. But there were no impediments to their progress. Weeks later the first land that did appear was Van Diemen's Land or New Holland, today's Tasmania. Captain Tobias Furneaux and Lieutenant Burney had visited this protected bay in 1773 during the second voyage, when they named it Adventure Bay, after their ship.

The crew was sent ashore to collect water and wood. Soon some local people appeared out of the woods, the first aboriginal Australians Cook had seen since his first voyage. While inquisitive, they seemed indifferent to the gifts of clothing, even though they were mostly naked. Yet they were pleasant and unassuming as the sailors went to work in the nearby forest, cutting spars and wood for the ships. Communication was difficult, "We addressed them in two or three South sea Languages but they did not understand any of them," the surgeon William Anderson explained, "though they immediately repeated the word "Kan'gooroo," which was mentioned on seeing a piece of skin supposed to be of that animal. Cook had already given the name "Kangaroo" to the distinctive Australian marsupial, so named by the Natives whom he met in Botany Bay on the east coast of New Holland in 1770.

To demonstrate the superiority of British weapons, Mai shot his musket at a tree, hitting his target and frightening the people, who took off suddenly. Still inquisitive, they returned the next day with their families and welcomed the sailors to their nearby village. After three days, a western breeze sprang up and Cook put to sea. Cook left before preparing a chart of the area, assuming incorrectly that Furneaux's earlier survey was accurate and that Tasmania joined the Australian mainland.[2]

In a week, Cook arrived in Ship Cove, Queen Charlotte Sound, New Zealand, also known today by the Maori name, Tōtaranui. Ship Cove is found on the inner shores of the northernmost point of the South Island and was Cook's favorite anchorage. This was the fifth time in seven years he anchored here. But it was also the site of the horrific incident on the second voyage, when the *Adventure* had a series of conflicts with the local Maori, including the murders of some of his seamen at nearby Grass Cove, which is now called Wharehunga Bay. Captain Furneaux had a difficult time staying in company with Cook and the *Resolution* during the second voyage's circumnavigation of Antarctica. Retreating to a prearranged anchorage, he guided the *Adventure* into Queen Charlotte Sound in December 1773, but it was six days after the *Resolution* left. They repaired casks, obtained wood and water, and on the day of their planned departure the captain sent a boat to nearby Grass Cove to collect greens for the men, known to prevent scurvy.

John Rowe, Furneaux's cousin, commanded the party. Rowe was an impetuous sailor who had little regard for the local people, even the warlike Maori. When Rowe's party was overdue, Second Lieutenant James Burney was sent to look for them. After searching along the coast for hours, in the late afternoon Burney and his marines came ashore at Grass Cove, attracted by several canoes surrounded by a large crowd of warriors. After they shot a few warning volleys to disperse the crowd, the sailors found an earthen oven brimming with body parts from Rowe's party, including a tattooed hand recognized to be from one of the sailors, as well as the head of their servant. Nearby baskets were also filled with roasted flesh, apparent evidence of a cannibalistic feast.[3]

Since it was getting dark, Burney and crew collected the remains and quickly withdrew. They took no action against the local warriors except to fire their weapons wildly in the air. Returning to the *Adventure*, Burney reported the details to Furneaux, but it was so horrific he did not mention the horror of possible cannibalism in his personal journal.

> We went ashore and searched [a Maori] Canoe, where we found some shoes known to belong to one of our Midshipmen who went with Mr. Rowe. One of the people at the same time brought me a piece of meat. On examining it and smelling to it I found it was fresh meat [and] supposed it was Dog's flesh, for I still doubted their being Cannibals. But we were soon convinced by most horrid and undeniable proofs—a great many baskets (about 20) laying on the beach tied up, we cut them open, some were full of roasted flesh and a hand which we immediately knew belonged to Thomas Hill, it being marked T.H. which he had got done at Otaheite with a tattow instrument. Such a shocking scene of Carnage and Barbarity as can never be mentioned or thought of but with horror.

The captain contemplated reprisals against the warriors but guessed they would be both risky and ineffectual. Instead the tragedy only redoubled his decision to abandon the voyage. The next day he sailed from Ship Cove and in six months the *Adventure* was back in England.[4]

Cook returned to Ship Cove after the massacre during the second voyage, but there was no evidence of the tragedy. But now on the third voyage, he was well-aware of the massacre, returning to the anchorage at Ship Cove anyway. When he entered the harbor on the third voyage, the local Maori assumed he came back to retaliate against the murderers. As the two ships sailed in, several Maori canoes approached, including people the British knew well, but they kept their distance until their chief waved a white flag and chanted a song of peace. Mai and Cook spoke to them at once, assuring them of their friendship. Unexpectedly, Cook carried no vengeance for the affray, which angered his crew, who nearly uniformly thought he was too moderate. As the discoverer of the crime, James Burney wrote in his journal that he was particularly appalled there was no retribution for the slaughter of his countrymen.

But Cook decided recriminations served no purpose and instead went about the business of the expedition, sending the crew with armed marines ashore to prove his peaceable intentions. The New Zealanders expected a fight, particularly when Kahura, the warrior who lead the massacre, appeared on shore four days later. Burney and even local people urged Cook to kill him, but the captain wanted to learn his side of the story. Using Mai as interpreter, Kahura offered Cook a different perspective about the quarrel, explaining the British started the fracas and that the warriors had no intention to fight, let alone kill. This confirmed Cook's decision to treat the people peaceably, despite Burney's first hand report of claimed cannibalism. Webber, like Cook, admired Kahura for his bravery and honesty and sketched his chiseled, tattooed face in Cook's cabin in late February. The drawing is an iconic voyage record of both Maori warrior and noble savage of the Age of Reason.[5]

Recognizing his crew's unhappiness, Cook did not stay long. On February 23 the tents were loaded on board and two sons of the local chief, who were enamored with Mai and wanted to accompany him to his homeland, joined the voyage. The ships then sailed north, hoping to find trade winds that would take them on a direct route to Tahiti. But they instead encountered unfavorable and indifferent breezes, which took them off track. Soon they were short of provisions for both the crew and the livestock and urgently sought an anchorage for wood, water, and greens. They approached a previously unknown island in the mid-Pacific that was surrounded by high cliffs of coral, now called Mangaia (part of today's independent Cook Islands), but found the inhabitants difficult and the landing impractical.

Days later they came upon Atiu, where the people seemed more approachable. But the island was surrounded by an impenetrable coral reef, so Mai, Burney, Gore, and Anderson were sent in shore boats, where they were transferred into local canoes on the reef. The expedition was in desperate need of provisions, but instead of trading the inhabitants became surly. The four sailors were soon separated and became both guests and prisoners for the day, with Burney writing a gripping account of the encounter. Mai's fractured discourse and timely use of a firearm prevented any harm to the foursome, but the small group rejoined their comrades without new provisions.[6]

With these disappointments, Cook changed course, sailing west, which effectively abandoned his instructions to explore America in 1777. They found and landed at the uninhabited Palmerston atoll, where they foraged a bountiful harvest of coconuts, fish, and seabirds. They then sailed to Nomuka, an island in the Tongan Kingdom encountered during the second voyage. Cook called Tonga the "Friendly Islands" in 1773, and here they found the necessary respite. As soon as they arrived canoes came alongside and began a brisk trade for hogs, fowl, breadfruit, and yams. The crisis for provisions was averted, but it was clear the voyage to America was postponed for a year.

The expedition stayed at Nomuka, which they called "Anamooka" or Rotterdam Island, for nearly two weeks. They met the Agee or Chief, Tubow, who was so generous with the available produce and pasturage that the island produce was quickly exhausted. After a week another chief named Finau arrived, who enjoyed higher status than Tubow. He accompanied the expedition in its later travels throughout Tonga. They soon learned that Finau was the supreme leader, as he was introduced to them as the king of the islands. He was a gracious host, rewarding the visitors with dramatic singing and drumming in traditional dance performances.

When it appeared they had traded for everything Nomuka could provide, Cook sailed on to the islands of Lifuka (in the Ha'apai Group), Tongatapu (today's capital of the island nation), and Eua in mid-July. Cook learned there were over 150 islands in the archipelago and the chart makers gathered the names of about 120 of them. Relations were much the same at each place. Cook and a few officers would come to shore with Mai as interpreter and meet the local chief, who would respond with a few presents. Crowds would then gather to study the ships and the pale English visitors. After these introductions the chiefs held ceremonies for the visitors, usually dances, as well as boxing and wrestling contests, frequently featuring women. The British sailors participated in the boxing and wrestling, but they always found they were no match for the local warriors.

After each ceremony, a larger quantity of provisions was presented by the local people, including hogs, fruit, turtles, sugar cane, breadfruit, roots, and other island produce. At nightfall, it was customary for the English to shoot off fireworks to the wonderment of the crowds. By Cook's estimate, 3,000 Lifuka islanders attended their fireworks display; in Tongatapu, there were more than 10,000 in the multitude. Mai was apparently so revered in the process that he could live ashore at each island, with a home and wife provided at each location. At Tongatapu a chief who held dominion even over Finau came to the ships, an elderly and corpulent man called Paulaho, who joined Finau in a large procession of canoes for the duration of their time in Tonga.[7]

The British were soon made aware of the nearby Fiji and Samoa island groups, each about two days' sail from Tonga. Although he had plenty of time to investigate, Cook did not want to look for them, a puzzling departure from his exploratory zeal. So there were few new discoveries during the early part of the voyage, except they had not previously visited Lifuka.

There were other disturbing changes in the captain's temperament. After his temperance with the Maori at Grass Cove in New Zealand, Cook became agitated with the Tongan people. He was particularly unhappy with the persistent thieving by the islanders, deciding to shave heads and take prisoners to stop it. This was a process he later perfected with even greater brutality in Tahiti. Because of this ill treatment, decades later descendants of the chiefs of Lifuka told an island missionary that Finau even plotted to kill Cook during a night dance on May 20. The plot was only abandoned at the last minute because Finau and his chiefs were uncertain whether to launch a night or day attack. More important, they decided they could not overtake the anchored ships.[8]

The advance of the seasons gave Cook considerable time to reach America, so he took his time in Tonga before sailing to Tahiti, one of his favorite stops. Cook called the archipelago the "Society Islands," a lush, compelling island nation of perhaps 200,000 people that he first visited in 1769. They first stopped in Vaitepiha Bay, located at the south side of the island, where the English learned two Spanish vessels from South America had left missionaries to Christianize the islanders. The Spaniards built a chapel and erected a cross to commemorate their visit. The cross also marked the burial site of their commander, who died when he returned to pick up the missionaries a year later. Since the cross was inscribed with the dates of the Spanish contact, Cook took it down to mark the dates of his own stops in Tahiti, apparently to prove Britain's more extensive contact with the island.[9]

After a week the ships were repositioned to Matavai Bay, one of Cook's favorite anchoring places and, because of the inclinations of the local women, a favorite of the crew as well. Cook had visited this bay many times before, when during the first voyage he commanded the bark *Endeavor* in the observation of the Transit of Venus. In the second voyage, when looking for the imagined southern continent, he drove the *Resolution* toward Antarctica each summer, then back to more temperate climates in the winter. Although he was supposed to be looking for new island nations, he was best known for his two visits to Tahiti in 1773-74, where he explored the length of the island, engaged the island people, and formed alliances with their chiefs. Returning to Matavai Bay on the third voyage, they again erected the observatories and other tents at Point Venus and effortlessly connected with the locals again. Cook tried to avoid the wanton sexual liaisons between crew and the local women, but the sailors found the Polynesian women eager in their advances and Cook relented. While at Matavai Bay the English also made presents of the stock brought from the Cape of Good Hope and Cook observed a human sacrifice.

The expedition then sailed in turn to Mo'orea, Huahine, Ra'iātea, and Bora Bora. With Mai interpreting, the initial contacts were warm and friendly. However, exasperated by continuing theft, Cook lost his temper in Mo'orea, and again in Huahine, taking hostages, cropping ears, slashing arms, and burning villages and canoes to impose British morality on the islanders. The sailors were shocked at the scale and frequency of the punishments meted out by the commander, even burning entire villages to the ground. But the sailors were still able to take advantage of friendly relations with the women and, after days ashore in the balmy paradise, several sailors decided to abandon the voyage and settle in the islands, which led to desertions and more reprisals as the captain and his marines scoured the islands to capture wayward seamen.[10]

In Huahine the British dropped off Mai and the two New Zealanders. Mai had already become well-acquainted with western ways and needed a proper place to store his accumulated possessions and enjoy European produce. The ships' carpenters built a small house for Mai overlooking Fare Harbor, near the homes of the island chiefs. His plantation included a garden and pen for the many domestic animals brought from Africa for his use.

By this time Captain Clerke was very ill with tuberculosis, which he apparently contracted in debtor's prison before the voyage began. The surgeon William Anderson was also ill, so both asked Cook if they could stay behind with Mai and not continue on to America, where they knew the weather would be ruthless. Cook was unwilling to entertain such a prospect, as it would only encourage more desertions by the crew. The lifestyle of Tahiti was a better choice than continuing northward to America, but for the enfeebled Clerke and Anderson staying aboard was a death sentence.[11]

The expedition headed north from the Society Islands to the equatorial Pacific in December 1777, crossing the equator before the end of the month. During the last week of the year, one hundred miles north of the Equator, they made landfall at an uninhabited, crescent-shaped atoll that Cook called Christmas Island. Today it is part of the Republic of Kiribati, an island nation of over thirty atolls and 100,000 people dispersed over nearly 1.5 million square miles.

Leaving Christmas Island, they again went north, hoping to intersect the west coast of North America astride coastal Oregon, the place where Francis Drake abandoned the search for the imagined Northwest Passage two centuries earlier. Cook had never been north of the equator in the Pacific and unexpectedly fell in with the Hawaiian archipelago. The Spanish, who were the only westerners in the region, may have been aware of Hawai‘i. If so, they kept their observations secret, as they did not record it or make use of its discovery.

At dawn on January 18, 1779, the expedition saw a high island on the northwest horizon, modern-day O‘ahu. Sailing with the wind they found another island in their path and by sunset they were south of Kaua‘i. Tacking against the wind, they came close enough to attract the attention of the local people and dozens of islanders launched canoes and made their way through the surf to the ships. They were friendly, though timid at first. They brought no weapons and, after Cook convinced them the English ships meant no harm, they began a brisk trade in fish and sweet potatoes. The British offered brass medals, small pieces of iron and similar trinkets, repeating the crude exchange that had been successful in their earlier anchorages.

Cook could not find a harbor so he turned his ships to coast along the southwestern side of Kaua‘i. They soon reached the village of Waimea, a cluster of about one hundred huts near the beach, and anchored offshore near the breakers. The following morning some sailors came ashore and they were quickly surrounded by inquisitive Hawaiians, many of whom climbed on board the small boats and took anything they could hold. One Hawaiian was particularly bold. He would simply not let go of a boat hook and the Marines shot him, proving the power of firearms to the unsuspecting crowd. Cook was not told of the killing until they were on their way to America.[12]

Hours later the commander came on shore and found his reception overwhelming. When he stepped from the boat the people fell to the ground and lay face down until he told them to get up. It was unclear whether they were revering him as a god or simply acknowledging the superiority of British firepower. Nonetheless, he accepted their offerings of pigs, bananas, sugar cane, bark cloth, and other produce and sent his men ashore for water and wood. While the ships took supplies on board, John Webber was guided inland, where he feverishly sketched his legendary, pastoral view of the local village. He observed the comings and goings of local residents, irrigated plantations, a sacred Morai (temple) with offerings to the Hawaiian gods, and other iconic island themes.

Although Cook was previously unaware of the Hawaiian Islands, he soon recognized that the dialect of the inhabitants was similar to the language of the Society Islands. He speculated he was at the apex of a great Polynesian triangle, based in New Zealand in the southwest and Tahiti and Easter Island in the southeast, a region he had already explored in his first and second voyages in the South Pacific. He wrote, "These people are of the same nation as the people of Otaheite and many others of the South sea islands, consequently they differ but little of them in their persons." He then wondered, "How shall we account for this Nation spreading itself so far over this Vast Ocean?" Cook named the archipelago after John Montagu, the First Lord of the Admiralty, who was the principal sponsor of the second and third voyages. He was also the Fourth Earl of Sandwich, so Cook dubbed them the "Sandwich Islands." This name was in use for the islands until the 1840s, when the local name "Hawai'i" gradually began to take precedence. By sunset the work parties had returned to the ships, stocked with wood, water, and provisions. In time they coasted further west and then across to the smaller island of Ni'ihau before embarking on the journey to America.[13]

1

THE VOYAGE BEGINS
JUNE–DECEMBER 1776

The expedition was conceived at a dinner party attended by Cook and senior members of the Admiralty in February 1776, where they planned the voyage. Cook's appointment commenced on February 10, 1776, the same date Burney began his journal. Although prior to the time of his assignment, it was the time the British government began paying wages and feeding the crew.[14]

In the first four months the two sloops were brought to Deptford, on the Thames River, where the Royal Shipyard sheathed, armed, and refitted the vessels. Cook and Burney took the ships around to Plymouth, where they separated. On July 12, the *Resolution* sailed from England; Burney and the *Discovery* waited until Clerke's discharge from debtor's prison, sailing three weeks later. After a few weeks at sea, both ships were leaking badly, a state of things to come.

The two ships came together again at the Cape of Good Hope in early December 1776, then entered the "Roaring Forties" to cross the Indian Ocean. In what passed for summer in the Southern Hemisphere, Burney described continuous fog in latitudes near Antarctica, where the ships lost sight of one another several times. Burney reports the first failures of the ships, as the starboard main trussel tree timbers, the horizontal spars that support the masts, broke in a modest storm. Burney also notes the death of a marine, who fell overboard and was drowned just two months after they left England.

The sailors tested their navigations skills passing in and out of fog and gales. While Roberts did not take up his pen until early December, both he and Burney carefully described the desolate, uninhabited, and windswept Kerguelen Islands. They were particularly fascinated when crewmen found a bottle with a parchment inside that proved the earlier discovery of the islands by a French expedition. Cook apparently placed a British coin in the bottle and returned it to its resting place. Since they arrived on Christmas day, the captain named the place Christmas Harbor. Burney drew a cabbage observed on shore; Roberts not only sketched a coastal view, but also offered charts of the inlets and islands encountered.

JOURNAL OF JAMES BURNEY

February 10th, 1776 His Majesty's Ships the Resolution and the Discovery were put in Commission at Deptford. Captains James Cook and Charles Clerke being appointed to command them.

May 12th Being rigged, stores, provisions etc. on board. The Discovery fell down to the Galleons where we took our Guns in. 8 four pounders and 8 Swivels.

John Webber, "A View of Christmas Harbour in Kerguelen's Land," circa 1781-83. Pen, wash, and water color showing the two ships at anchor in the harbor in late December 1776. The ship's boats are near shore with several seamen. There is a flock of twenty penguins to the left of a seaman on shore with a club. A sea lion is found in the left foreground, with an imposing rock cliff in the background above the ships. Dixson Library, State Library of New South Wales, PXX 2, f. 1.

June 15th Sailed out of the River in company with the Resolution whom we left at the Nore and proceeded down Channel.

June 26th Anchor'd in Plymouth Sound, and Saluted Adm'l Amherst with 13 Guns.

June 30th The Resolution, Captain Cook, came into the Sound and remained till the 12th of July, when She departed for the Cape of Good Hope.

July 22nd Our Ships Company received all their pay up to the end of June, besides 2 Months advance, an indulgence granted by the Admiralty to enable them to buy necessaries for a long Voyage.

August 1st Captain Clerke came down to the Ship. At 1 after noon Sailed out of Plymouth Sound with a SE Wind.

August 7th Passed by Cape Finistere. [Northwestern point of Spain]

Friday 9th Spoke the Diana Snow from Lisbon bound to London. Served fishing lines, hooks, etc. to the Ships Company.

Tuesday 13th Saw the Island of Porto Sancto and next day Madeira, both which we kept to the Westward of.

Sunday 18th It being intended to stop no where in our passage to the Cape of Good Hope went to a daily allowance of 2 Quarts of Water exclusive of what was used for Cooking and in moderate weather set the Still at Work which generally gave us about 10 Gallons in an Afternoon.

26th, 27th & 28th Passed within sight of the Cape de Verde Islands.

September 17th Crossed the Equator in 15 degrees West Longitude from Greenwich. From 10½ North Latitude had SW Winds till we approached the Eq. Line when it gradually veered round to the SE. At this time of the year SW Winds mostly prevail near the Coast of Africa.

Friday 20th Found the Starboard Main Trusseltree Sprung. Bolted and woulded the weak part and got the Main Toprope on the Trusseltree to Support it against the Strain of the Topmast & Rigging.

Tuesday 24th This Afternoon the Corporal of Marines, Geo. Harrison, unfortunately fell overboard and was drowned.

Tuesday 31st Saw the Land 25 Leagues to the Northward of Table Bay. A fresh Gale from the SE prevented our getting in till the 10th of November when we Anchor'd in the Bay and Joined the Resolution who had arrived 3 Weeks before. [Bearings omitted.]

Saluted the Dutch Garrison with 13 Guns which they returned.

We remained here 3 Weeks in which time we stripped the Main mast and repaired the Trusseltree Sprung at Sea. Caulk'd our Decks and Sides which had been very leaky during the latter part of the passage. Repaired the Rigging, Sails etc. & increased our Stock of Provisions, having when we left the Cape upwards of 2 Years compleat in every Species, at full allowance, Bread excepted, and of that very little Short. Entered a Seaman here, being by the loss of the Corporal of Marines, one Short of our Compliment.

Saturday, 30th Having finished our business, the people well refreshed and in good health, this Afternoon Sailed out of Table Bay in company with the Resolution who Saluted the Garrison. The Wind failing were obliged to Anchor off Penguin Island, it bearing . . . distant 2 miles. Depth of water 8 fathoms. Next morning at Daylight got under Sail again and in the evening of the 2d of December took our departure from the Cape of Good Hope. Everybody at 2/3rd allowance of Bread. We directed our Course to the SE having almost continual fair winds and foul Weather.

Thursday, December 5th The Resolution carried away her Mizzen Topmast and did not get another up till 3 days after.

Thursday, 12th [Bearings omitted.] At 1 Afternoon Saw Land which proved to be the 2 Westernmost of the Islands discovered by Marion. [Bearings omitted.] The Northernmost is about 8 and the Southernmost 12 miles in length. We ran between them keeping within 5 or 6 miles of the Southern Island which at that distance afforded a tolerable good prospect in spite of the gloominess of the weather, having many green Spots but nothing like Trees that we could discern.

Near the North End of this Island is a remarkable Shaped Rock. The south part terminates in a long low point. Saw no appearance of a Harbour or Bay.

[Bearings omitted.] At Night lost Sight of these Islands and Steered more to the Eastward for the Land discovered by Kerguelin. In this run we were in continual fear of the 2 Ships parting company, the Fogs being so thick that frequently for many hours together we have not been able to see twice the length of the Ship. Scarce a day passed without losing sight of each other. In these situations we kept company by Sound, firing Guns every hour, sometimes oftener, and guessing from the report the place of the other Ship. A Stout Jacket and pair of Trowsers was served out to every man in the Ship (being a present from Government) to enable them to stand the continual wet weather we now met with.

Tuesday 24th At 6 this morning Saw the Land SSE 2 or 3 Leagues distant, having these last 3 or 4 days sailed in a Zigzag Course as the best chance of finding it. Wind Westerly. By ½ past 7 were close in with the Land, which we found to be a Groupe of Small Islands and Rocks. At 8 being very hazy and blowing fresh Stood off to the Northward. 2 or 3 Leagues to the NNE of these Islands is a Small high Rock, the Northernmost Land we Saw. Its Latitude 48.27 South. At ½ past 11 The Weather becoming moderate, Tack'd and Stood to the Southward.

At Noon [Bearings omitted.] ran by the East Side and within a mile of the North Rock. At ½ past 2 Saw more Land to the Southward which appeared to be of considerable extent. Set all our Sails to get well in before Dark. At 4 were near the North End but Seeing no good Anchoring place, Bore away for the East Side and by 5 got under the Lee of the Land where we found a good Harbour about 2 miles from the Northernmost point. The Resolution made the Anchoring Signal, and at 8 both Ships came too in the outer part of the Harbour. We in 28 fathoms Sandy bottom near the South Shore. [Bearings omitted.] The Resolution further out in 40 fathoms. Captain Cook sent a Boat to examine the upper part of the Harbour which soon after returned with an account of good Anchorage & fresh Water. In the Night had a light breeze from the SW.

Wednesday 25th At 4 in the morning found our Anchor came home. There being no tide, very little wind, and Smooth Water. The Ship before anything of the kind was suspected drove so near the Rocks that we were obliged to make Sail with the Anchor on the Ground and 50 fathoms of Cable out. By setting all our Head Sails we luckily dragged the Anchor out into deeper Water which had it not followed easily, must have been cut away, having not more than room enough to clear the South point of the Harbour. Found one palm broke off. As we had rode with Scarce any Strain all Night this was judged owing to bad workmanship. In heaving the Anchor up we drifted out of the Harbour. In the mean time the Resolution Weighed and work'd into the upper part where we joined her in the Afternoon, and Moored the Ship. On account of the day Captain Cook named this Christmas Harbour. At the entrance on the South point is a Rock remarkable for a large Arch through it. [Bearings omitted.]

The Tide rises and falls 4 feet perpendicular, but the number of little rivulets and Falls from the Hills, particularly in wet weather, makes a continual drain or slow current setting out of the Harbour. High Water 9 ¼ Hours after the Moon passes the Meridian. The Land hereabouts is high and mountainous and has the most forlorn and desolate appearance imaginable, being a continued hump of Rock without Tree or Bush. What little Soil there is, is too rotten to bear a man's weight.

In this Latitude the Weather in Summer has been found almost always wet and foggy. The natural dreariness of the place is not a little increased by the melancholy croakings of innumerable penguins with which the Shore is lined. Nature seems to have designed this Spot solely for the use of Sea Lions, Seals, penguins and Sea Fowls. There are a few wild Duck but small and fishy. We haul'd the Sean [Seine] and tried with hooks, but caught not a Single Fish. We compleated our Water here and got a quantity of Blubber for making Lamp Oil.

Thursday 26th A bottle was found on shore in which was a paper with the French King's Titles. LUD XV in Latin, date 1772. Neither Ship or Captains Name.[15]

Sunday 29th Wind SW with fair weather. At 7 in the morning Weigh'd and came to Sail having got out and Steered alongshore to the SE. In the first 6 miles ran by 3 fine Harbours, each of which appeared better Shelter'd than the one we came from. A League and a half distant from Christmas Harbour to the SE are 4 small low Islands, Rocks & Breakers off the No. End. We sail'd within these 3 larger Islands farther out. This forenoon passed several deep Bays, the Land High and Craggy. [Bearings omitted.] Between 12 and 1 running within Some Small Islands that lay half a League from the main, got entangled amongst a great quantity of Sea Weed that grew from the Bottom and almost Stopped the Ships way. Depth of Water 19 fathoms. Seeing Breakers ahead and more Sea Weed, haul'd off Shore, more breakers without us.

At ¼ past 2 bore Round. Spoke [to] the Resolution and were ordered to make Sail in Shore and look for a Harbour, there being an appearance of one to the WSW at about 3 Leagues distant. At 4 passed a Small low island (to the North of it) which we gave a good birth on account of a large bed of Sea Weed that ran off it. Made the signal for a Harbour which Captain Cook answered by making the Signal to Anchor. At 6 Anchored in 16 fms muddy bottom in the North part of a large Bay well Sheltered without by Islands and Beds of Sea Weed. Foul ground and breakers to the South of us. [Bearings omitted.]

A Cluster of Small Islands, the nearest 1 mile distant [found] with Latitude 49.01 South, distant from Christmas Harbour 9 Leagues. Captain Cook names this Port Palliser.

Monday 30th At Daylight got under Sail. Wind NW. Ran out of the Harbour the same way we enter'd it, being frequently obliged to alter our Course on account of the Rock Weed.

All the forenoon running to the Eastward keeping a good distance off Shore having run 10 Leagues. Found the Coast, which is here low and level, turn off to the Southward on the North part of the Low Land is a remarkable Hummock. In the afternoon stood to the Southward along shore with a fresh breeze. A chain of high Snowy Mountains at the back of the Low Land. At ½ past 6 the Southernmost point of Land in sight . . . whence the coast seems to turn short round to the Westward. At 7 the weather becoming hazy, Bore away and left the Land. The winds continuing favourable got to the Eastward at a great rate. Thick foggy weather.

Journal of Henry Roberts

Roberts' journal begins on December 1, 1776, and devotes three weeks to a thorough, hour-by-hour log, with two days allotted to each page, a procedure he usually followed during the balance of the voyage while at sea. It is the expedition's record of bearings, coordinates, ship duties, and wind and weather, as well as observations of the birds, fish, and other wildlife observed from the decks of the *Resolution*. In editing his journal, such entries are usually overlooked in favor of Roberts' more lively discourse while exploring land or enjoying a port, although some entries at sea are retained. Among other things, Roberts kept a detailed record of the flogging of seamen. References made to such punishments in Robert's journal are not exhaustive, but help modern readers understand the misdeeds and punishments handed out on naval vessels of the era.

Wednesday, December 25th, 1776 Fresh Gales & hazy weather. Sailed along the north coast of this Isle about 6 miles when some craggy rocks appeared which we called the Centry Box. A Rock or Hummock between the Isles along the Shore, saw an appearance of a place for anchorage. Hauled in but the wind failing we dropped our Anchor in 45 fathoms. A Remarkable Rock with a Hole in it, resembling a decayed ruinous Castle, which forms the Southern entrance of the Bay. Hoisted out the small Cutter & sent the Master to sound the head of the Bay. At 9 the Boat returned, having found good anchorage with several streams of fresh water. In the Morning, hove up the anchor & turned into the Harbour, as did our Consort.

Thursday 26th Employed watering the Ship & other necessary Duties. Killed a great Number of Sea Lions to get Blubber, likewise many penguins, Peterals, a white Bird, nearly the size and much resembling Pidgeons (& not much inferior in taste when dressed) besides, many Ducks or rather Teal, for which are small. This Country was afterward called the Isle of Desolation.

Saturday 28th One of the People found a Bottle, with a piece of Parchment in it, with this inscription (Ludovico XV Galliarum Rege. et d. de Boynes regi a Secretis ad res maritimas Annis 1772-1773). Captain Cook put a silver three pence, coined in George the Thirds reign, into the Bottle with the parchment & replaced it; it was found on a small cliffy hill that projected into the Harbour. This place which we call Christmas Harbour, may be known by a Remarkable arched Rock, appearing like the ruins of a Decayed Castle, which forms the Southern part of the Bay. We found here prodigious numbers of Penguins, which entirely cover the sides of the Rocks & the Beach at the head of the Harbour, several Sea Lions, resembling those we find at Staten land, but not quite so much Hair of Furr on them, nor the lions those shaggy Mains, many Peterals & Albatrosses, Port Edgemont Hens & those white Birds, mentioned before & many Ducks. The Land is Mountainous & the summits of the Hills an entire Barren Rock. The lower part is covered with a kind of grass & Moss, a number of cascades, running from the Hills particularly when you have much rain.

Sunday 29th Put all Reefs, Standing along Shore the Land in General appearing high and barren, much snow lying on the Hills. At Noon five small Islands in sight.

Monday 30th Passed great quantities of long sea Weed, most of which seemed to join to the bottom. Many Beds were Drift weed. We ran over several of these patches, the sounding the same as before, never less than 40 fathoms. (Others were extremely thick and seemed to Shoal the Water.) We altered our course accordingly to Clear.

At 3 Spoke the Discovery to lead and look for a Bay, we saw an opening bearing SWBS, hauled in for it. At half past 3 we were close in with two or three small Isles when we were obliged to Tack and make about to clear them, the Bay leads in about WSW.

The Shores are bold too on each side, no way superior to any other part of the Coast in fertility, affording nothing more than a Bay, Shaggy Grass and Moss, indeed on one of the Small Isles, was a Wood of Plant, a broad leaf it is extremely good when Dressed or boiled. Saw many sea lions and most abundance of Ducks, one watering creek only, that lies about 2 miles from the Anchoring Place.

Tuesday 31st At ½ past 1 we were abreast of some low Grass land, carried Soundings from 15 to 26 fathoms. We saw some shoal Water within and appeared to extend some distance along the Shores. At 4 the Southernmost land in sight, which is very high and covered in Snow, bore 4 miles. The middle of an Island at the Entrance of a large Bay, or Sound, there seemed to be several small Isles at the back, and the Land much broken. The largest Isle was about 2 leagues.

John Webber, "The Inside of a Hippah in New Zealand," circa 1781-83. Pen, wash, and water color showing a Maori village visited in February 1777. A group of Maori people are found on a center pathway with two others seated further back. They are surrounded by homes and a stockade of stakes on Motuara Island, opposite Ship Cove. The waters of Queen Charlotte Sound, located on the north point of New Zealand's North Island, stretch out to the right. Dixson Library, State Library of New South Wales, PXX 2, f. 2.

2

TASMANIA AND NEW ZEALAND
JANUARY–FEBRUARY 1777

After leaving the Kerguelen Islands the expedition soon found following winds and in three weeks reached Adventure Bay, Tasmania, which was then called "Van Diemen's Land" after a name given to the area by Abel Tasman, the Dutch explorer who touched both Australia and New Zealand in 1642. This was Cook's first visit to Tasmania, but Burney had been there with Captain Furneaux during the second voyage. Roberts called all of Australia "New Holland" and like the others he incorrectly assumed Tasmania was connected to the mainland.

Both Roberts and Burney offered a lively portrayal of the people of Tasmania, the first encountered on the voyage, who were naked, friendly, and unarmed. They were also fascinated by the kangaroo, which Burney likened to the North American possum. Burney also found that Australia had "many snakes and such a number of troublesome vexatious insects as make it uncomfortable being on Shore." He also reported a second marine fell overboard and drowned in early February.

The expedition then sailed to Queen Charlotte Sound, New Zealand. They set up the observatory tents and sent parties ashore for wood, water, and other necessaries. They even put the horses and cattle ashore to graze. Cook then went to inspect the site of the Grass Cove massacre. Burney's party had discovered the slaughter during the second voyage and, like most of the other sailors, he now sought retribution. The Maori even expected hostilities, but Cook was not in the mood for revenge. Nonetheless, wary of the local warriors, the captain insisted that all shore parties have the protection of armed marines. Cook wrote, "for the protection of the party on shore I appointed a guard of ten marines and ordered arms for all the workmen. A boat was never sent any considerable distance from the Ships without being armed."[16]

Burney wrote of his further investigation of the fracas, finding some gratification that the warriors said they were provoked into attacking the shore party. He also wrote the Maori were surprised there was no reprisal from the British upon their arrival, explaining "many of them held us in great contempt and I believe chiefly on account of our not revenging the affair of Grass Cove." Anticipating violence, Roberts reported a sudden change in the temperament of the local people, but there was no attack and peaceful relations continued. As they sailed away, both journals revealed the captain's decision to allow two Maori boys to accompany Mai to Tahiti. Roberts said Cook soon regretted this decision, as the boys were apparently both homesick and seasick for several days after their departure.

JOURNAL OF JAMES BURNEY

Sunday, January 5th, 1777 About midnight lost sight of the Resolution and though we kept firing Guns every hour, heard no Answer till 9 next morning from which time we steered by the report of her Guns and at 2 in the Afternoon it clearing up, Saw her again. We were all this time Sailing at the rate of 4 miles an hour with a fair Wind. The 2 Ships are exceedingly well pair'd as Company Keepers being nearly equal in their Sailing. The little difference is in favour of the Discovery.

Sunday 19th At 4 in the Morning the Resolution carried away her Foretopmast and Main topgallant Mast. Till 8 at Night went under an easy sail, by which time they had got up another Topmast and Topgallant Mast and all the Sails Set.

Monday 20th Saw 2 Seals and past a quantity of Rock Weed. [Bearings omitted.]

22nd Seals & Sea Lions.

Friday 24th At 3 in the Morning Saw the SW Cape of Van demen's Land bearing N½W 4 Leagues. Ran along shore to the Eastward at the distance of 3 or 4 Leagues having a light Southerly wind till Evening when we were abreast Storm Bay. In the night had light Airs from the NE. Saw fires on shore. Little wind and Calms all the next day and Night that we Scarce got any ground.

Sunday 26th Having a breeze from the SSE both Ships in the Afternoon Anchor'd in Adventure or Frederic Henry's Bay and Moor'd. Saw the Smoke of several fires, not far distant, in the Woods on the West Side of the Bay.

Monday 27th Wooding and Watering. A party of Marines from each Ship to protect the woodcutters. In the afternoon some Brandy was sent as a refreshment for the people on Shore, but through the carelessness of those who should have seen it distributed in proper quantities, 5 of our Marines who were part of the Guard, got possession of it, and made themselves so beastly drunk, that they were put motionless in the Boat, and when brought on board, obliged to be hoisted into the Ship. For this offense they were severely punished next morning.

28th The working Cables which had hitherto been kept between decks, were Coil'd down the Main Cap Hold and 6 Tons of Cask Stowed in their Stead, which besides occupying less space are more easily moved to clean under. This afternoon some of the Natives came down on the beach and were met by Captain Cook. They were quite inoffensive and soon became very familiar. They had no arms and seemed not in the least apprehensive or suspicious. Haul'd the Sean [Seine] ashore and caught Fish enough to serve every body.

Wednesday 29th Many of the Natives came to the Wooding place and were presented with Knives, Beads, etc. with which they were much pleased. They are great talkers and their Language is neither harsh nor indistinct. Few people may more truly be Said to be in a State of Nature: both Sexes go quite naked. 2

or 3 Old Women had part of some Animals Skin tied around their Neck which just hung down to their breasts, but this probably was more for Ornament than Covering. They are of the Negroe kind, wooly headed and flat nosed, of middling Stature and not ill featured. In the most natural Actions they are without restraint, and have much less idea of decency than an English Dog, who will lift his Leg up by which you may guess what he is going about. But one of these Gentleman, whether sitting, walking or talking, will pour forth his Streams without any preparatory action or Guidance, or even appearing sensible of what he is doing, and not in the least interested whether it trickles down his own Thighs or Sprinkles the persons next him. Some had their Beards divided into separate locks, each rolled up with a Small lump of red oker and clay. The first evening of our being favoured with their company Captain Cook gave them some Fish which were found the next day left in the same place where they had been given, nor would they eat any thing we gave them. We saw no Canoes and they appeared averse to being on the water. 2 of them came into our Boat, but were very awkward and unable to steady themselves and glad to get on shore again.

A possum was Shot here, an Animal common enough in North America, and among the Natives we saw the Skin of a Beast they call Kongura [Kangaroo], which has been seen on the East Coast of New Holland in the Endeavour's Voyage. Birds here are very shy which argues the Inhabitants to have methods of catching them. They have Snares for Animals made of a Strong Grass. Here are many Snakes and such a number of troublesome vexatious insects as make it uncomfortable being on Shore.

We cut some Spars and the Resolution got a Stick for a Spare Topmast, the Trees being strong, tough and perfectly strait of all sizes, and in generally shoot up a great height before they branch out. Had plenty of Fish during our Stay and a good deal of Hay was cut for the Horses, Horned Cattle and other Stock on board the Resolution.

January 30th This morning hove up our Anchors and Sailed out of Adventure Bay. In the afternoon passed to the South of Maria's Islands and after Sunset lost Sight of the Land steering a direct Course towards Charlotte Sound, New Zealand.

Tuesday, February 4th In the night Geo. Moody, Marine, fell overboard and was drown'd.

Monday 10th In the Afternoon made the Coast of New Zealand between Rocks point and Cape Farewell. From Van demens Land have had very fine Weather.

Wednesday 12th At day light ran into Charlotte Sound and by Noon were birth'd in Ship Cove, having narrowly escaped being ashore, the Ship missing Stays under Topsails.

Bearings when Moored [Bearings omitted.] Perpendicular height of the Tide between 6 and 7 feet.

Thursday 13th The Tents of both Ships were erected at the Watering place and the Coopers, Waterers, Sailmakers etc. with a party of Marines from each Ship sent to remain on Shore under the direction of Lieut. King of the Resolution. The Astronomers Tents were likewise pitched at the Watering Place and the whole made a formidable appearance. Next day the Horses were got on shore.

A great Many Indians from different parts of the Sound have come and taken up their abode in Ship Cove. Fish plenty. Employed Wooding, Watering, Brewing Spruce Beer, Boiling down the Blubber got at Kerguelens Land, Haymaking, repairing Rigging, Sails etc. etc. The Gardens made here last Voyage were so overrun with Weeds and Under Wood that we cant scarce distinguish the remains. A few Cabbages were found and some Onion Seed that had run wild. The potatoe Garden on the Motuara was not look'd after.

Sunday 16th At Daylight the 2 Captains with a large party went up the Sound to cut Grass and at Night returned with 2 Launch Loads. In this excursion they visited Grass Cove the place where the Adventure's Cutter was attacked. Of this Accident the best account I have been able to collect is that our people were dining on the beach. During their Meal, a Zealander stole something out of the Boat and was making off with it, which being unluckily perceived by Mr. Rowe, he fired and killed the Thief on the Spot. The Zealanders immediately sallied out of the Woods and got between our people and the Boat. They say Rowe fired twice and kill'd another man, but the peoples Muskets had been left in the boat, nobody except himself having any Fire Arms, so that they were easily overpowered and fell from imagining themselves too secure.

The Adventure's Cutter was soon after taken from the New Zealanders of Charlotte Sound by those of Terrawitte (The North Side of Cooks Strait) a strong party of whom had come over on a Visit.

The Indians who are about us, are in parties or Tribes Seemingly unconnected with each other and live in different parts of Ship Cove. One of these parties are accused by the rest of being the people who cutt off the Adventures Boat. Their Chief, whose Name is Kowara, they say killed Rowe. On the Beach where this party lives were 2 Canoes that had been cut to pieces and rebuilt and it was remarked that neither of these Canoes came alongside the Ships. A little before our arrival the Inhabitants of Charlotte Sound has been surprized and 50 of them destroyed by the people of Admiralty Bay.

Thursday 20th Had a Gale of Wind from the Westward attended with hard Squalls, in one of which our Small Bower Anchor having got foul, came home and we drove alongside the Resolution but luckily got clear without hurt and Moored the Ship again. In Ship Cove and other parts of the West Side of the Sound the height and unevenness of the Land when the Wind is Westerly occasions Violent flurries from every quarter of the Compass. A Young Zealander whose Name is Tibarua, has lived on board the Resolution lately and says he will go to Otaheite. [Tahiti].

Sunday 23rd Struck the Tents and got everything on board.

Monday 24th Weighed and ran out of Ship Cove into the outer part of the Sound where we Anchord in 9 fathoms muddy bottom. [Bearings omitted.] The New Zealanders of Charlotte Sound were never So much amongst us as this time. The reason probably because they found more was to be got and on easier terms than ever before for our folks were all so eager after curiosities and withal so much better provided than in any former Voyage that Traffick was greatly altered in favor of the Indians, a Nail the last Voyage purchasing more than an Axe or Hatchet now. Before our departure, Hatchets were slung under their Cloaths instead of patows [baton or club used as a weapon].

They often appeared to have a great Friendship for us, speaking sometimes in the most tender compassionate tone of voice imaginable. But it is not a little disgusted one to find all this Show of fondness interested and that it constantly ended in begging. If gratified with their first demand they would immediately fancy something else, their expectations and importunities increasing in proportion as they had been indulged. We had instances of their quarrelling after having begged 3 things, because a fourth was denied them. It seemed evident that many of them held us in great contempt and I believe chiefly on account of our not revenging the Affair of Grass Cove, so contrary to the principles by which they would have been actuated in the like Case. Another Cause might be their getting from us so many Valuable things for which they gave the credit solely to their superior cunning. As an instance how much they trusted to our easiness one man did not Scruple to acknowledge his being present and assisting at the killing and eating the Adventures people.

No Beast can be more ravenous or greedy than a New Zealander. Nothing comes amiss; but no victuals was so highly relished by them as the rank Seal Blubber we brought from Kerguelens Land and which we boiled down here. So fond were they of this delicious food that some of our people who attended to the Boiling have for the Skimming procured very Substantial favours from the Ladies.

Tuesday 25th Wind NW. At 9 in the forenoon hove up our Anchors and left Charlotte Sound. In the Evening ran through Cook's Straits.

27th At Noon took our departure from Cape Palliser. Captain Cook has brought away another Zealander, a young Boy who was put on board by the father of Tibarua to accompany him. His name is Cogoa. Of the Hogs and Fowls left in Charlotte Sound last Voyage we have neither seen or heard any thing.

Journal of Henry Roberts

Friday, January 24th, 1777 On the Coast of Van Diemans Land, New Holland. At 8 the Mewstone on with the West point, distance 6 miles, saw seven seals & Gannets. The Land here is of a Moderate height & appeared to be very cragged

& broken, affording shelter for good Anchorage. Many small Isles & Rocks near the Coast; at Noon a Remarkable sugar loaf Hill [Tasman Head, Tasmania].

Sunday 26th The Swell setting in to Storm Bay, the Entrance of this Bay (as I mentioned before) lies between Three Hill Cape & Tasmans head, bearing from each other WSW and ESE about 6 leagues distant on the NE side of the Bay. The Southern Cape or Headland of New Holland appears to be good Shelter, two or three points forming which seemed to afford convenient cover & harbour. The land is of a moderate height & entirely covered with Trees.

Monday 27th Found riding here our Consort. At 7 sent party's on Shore to Cut wood & grass & some people watering with the launch. A party of Marines sent to protect them under the Command of the 2nd Lieut. Employed (on board) in the Hold overhauling the Rigging. At Noon, Launch returned with a Load of Water.

Tuesday 28th Employed Wooding, watering & a number of Hands cutting Grass for the Cattle on board, our Hay being expended some time before reaching this Port. In the afternoon sent the Seine with People for fishing. Returned with a Great Quantity of Elephant Fish. Carpenters on Shore cutting Spars.

Wednesday 29th This afternoon Nine of the Natives came down and visited our People on Shore. Captain Cook gave them several trifling trinkets, which seemed to please them. They stayed some considerable time & behaved very peaceable and quite. In the Evening Hauled the Seine but met with little success. More of the Inhabitants came down with few of their Women. Distributed several things among them for which they appeared very thankful, & behaved in as peaceable manner as possible & very Friendly.

Wednesday, February 12th At 3 Bore away, and Saw Point Jackson a Head. Brought to till Daylight, then bore away round Cape Jackson & stood in for Queen Charlottes Sound, frequently becalmed & sudden flaws from the High land, which [makes it] difficult to sail into Ship Cove with the Wind to the Westward. At 9 working & towing the Ship to a proper Anchoring place [and] came too in 7 fathoms, . . . Hoisted out the launch. A Number of the Natives Visited us, in their Canoes from a Hippa, to the Southward of Matavana [Motuara Island]. They immediately recollected their old Friends & particularly Captain Cook, who presented many trinkets etc to them. They appeared extremely friendly & seemed very happy in seeing us again.

Thursday 13th Sent Hands on Shore to clear a place to fix the Tent. Hauled the Seine & caught a great Quantity of Fish, chiefly the Elephant Fish with many fine Soals & Flounders. Many Canoes trading with us for Fish. Erected the Tent & Observatory & a party of Marines from both Ships under the Command of our 2nd Lieutenant sent on shore to protect the same. Hauled the Seine but had little Success. Purchased Many Fish from the Inhabitants. Got the Coppers on Shore for brewing Spruce Beer. Sent the Horses on Shore to graze during our Stay.

Friday 14th Employed sending on Shore Empty Casks & other Necessary Duties. Boiled scurvy grass & greens, with a Quantity of Portable soup and Wheat for the Peoples Breakfasts. The Natives continuing with us, residing in the adjacent Coves near the Ship & behaving in the most friendly manner possible, constantly supplying us with Fish. A party sent to Cut Grass & others to cutt wood.

Sunday 16th Employed in the Hold. This day the Natives behaviour appeared rather treacherous, the major part of them leaving us the preceding Morning & others going off seemingly much offended & paddled with great haste towards a Beach on Long Island, where our Cutter was sent with one of the Mates & party to cutt grass for the Cattle. Being alarmed at these appearances & from the intelligence we got from Omai by questioning the few Indians that still remained with us, that those people were not our Friends & advised not by any Means to send Boats unarmed towards the place they were going.

The Pinnace was therefore manned & armed & dispatched with the utmost Expedition with Mr. Williamson, our third Lieut, to order the Cutters immediately to Repair on board. The Canoes no doubt watching our Motions, instantly they saw our Boat making towards them. They paddled for a different part than possibly the first intended. Our two Boats shortly returned & the Mate remarked that the Canoes, which went off early Sunday Morning landed on the Back of Long Isle, probably waiting the arrival of their Comrades to attack our people in Front & Rear. It caused great Consternation on Board what this sudden change in their behaviour should proceed from, its most certain they have taken offense, but justly or unjustly, there's no saying. As it was Necessary to get a stock of Grass for the Cattle on Board, the Launches & large Cutters of Both Ships was ordered to be got in readiness for this purpose.

At day light the next morning we left the Ships with Captains Cook & Clerke in the Pinnace, all the Boats Armed in Case of an attack. Sailed up the Sound about 12 Miles & Landed on a Small Cove in the East side, where we filled both launches with good grass in about 4 Hours. We then came back by way of Grass Cove & these filled all the Boats with Scurvy Grass & other greens. Here a small Family of the Indians appeared on the Beach & behaved very civil & Friendly. At this spot the Adventure's Boat Crew put a sacrifice to these inhuman cursed race of Cannibals. At that time they were very numerous at this place & inhabited a large Hippa just within the Cove but their Hutts are now totally decayed. In the Evening we made the Best of our way to the Ship, the wind blowing very strong in from the Seas. The Pinnace & Cutters only getting on Board, the launches obliged to bear away and anchor under Long Island till the gale abated, which was the proceeding Morn.

Monday 17th Punished Patrick Whelon, seaman, with 6 lashes for insolence & Contempt.

Tuesday 18th Employed Wooding, Watering & other necessary duties. Served soup, boild with Greens etc for Breakfast. Few of the Natives with us & the

Family we met at Grass Cove visited us also. The Chief of this Party was constantly with Captain Cook on Board, the last Voyage from whom he received many trifling things. He never came to the Ship before. We were at his place of abode, whether he was not acquainted with our arrival here or whether it was through fear, being concerned in taking the lives of the unfortunate Adventurers, there's no determining, but I am of oppinion the former. Their Behaviour now is extremely friendly & supply us with plenty of Fish.

Wednesday 19th Began to use the Spruce Beer.

Friday 21st Many Canoes with a number of the Natives came on Board, from the upper part of the Sound, whom we had not seen before & trafficked for Hatchets, Nails, Beads etc. but Red Cloth is certainly the best trade. They are much clearer in their demands than formerly, for a small Bundle of Fish, you pay two or three large Nails, which in the Endeavours time might be purchased for a small Nail. This party were friendly & seemed to be extremely well disposed.

Sunday 23rd Got the Spruce Beer on board. Employed getting ready for Sea. Got the Observatory & Instruments on Board.

Monday 24th Got the Tent & every article on Board with the Horses. Hoisted in the launch & got ready for Sea. At ½ past 11 weighd & came to sail with our Consort. The Captain gave a pair of Goats with a Boar & Sow to one of the Chiefs. He also left two couples of Rabbits on Matuara Isle, unknown to the Natives.

Tuesday 25th Two Indian Boys intimating a Desire to accompany Omai to Otaheite. Captain Cook, after gaining the Consent & approbations of their Friends, took them on Board. After leaving the land for the first few Days, our young Adventurers abstained from Eating, chiefly from Parting with their Friends & Country, continually weeping & seemed to be greatly affected & partly owing to seasickness. But this soon wore off & they presently reconciled to their new scene of life.

3

COOK ISLANDS
MARCH–APRIL 1777

After leaving Queen Charlotte Sound and entering the tropics, the expedition battled unpredictable, baffling winds and seas that forced them too far west away from their intended route, ultimately losing a year before they could reach their planned destination in North America. Both ships were soon running low on provisions for the crew, even green plants to sustain the livestock on board, forcing them to kill some of the animals to protect the others.[17]

Burney and Roberts reported both the difficult weather and its implications, as the crew was put on reduced allowances. Roberts, who was on the *Resolution* with Cook, also told of the captain's exasperation with the delay, apparently taking out his frustrations on the crew by imposing harsh restrictions on the Ships' companies for the theft of provisions and meting out other unexpected, needless punishments.

In desperate need of provisions, the expedition attempted to anchor at different places in what is known today as the Cook Islands. But they were not successful in refreshing the ships, finding the islands difficult to reach and the Natives inhospitable. Burney called the principal islands *Modu* and *Watdu*. Since he was aboard the *Resolution* with Cook, Roberts used variations of the captain's names, *Managia-nooe-nai-naiwa* and *Wautieu*, each name suggesting a disparate interpretation of the local pronunciation.[18] The islands are *Managia* and *Atiu* today.

Burney was one of four sailors assigned to investigate the second island, Atiu, after the crews had initial success with interaction and trade. The foursome took shore boats to the reef and local canoes from the surf to shore. It was a frightening experience that was carefully documented by Burney. Once they got ashore, he explained, they were soon overwhelmed by antagonistic crowds, then separated and confined almost as prisoners. Mai's timely demonstration of the power of firearms and the intervention of local chiefs apparently prevented a melee. While the foursome was on a mission to find and replenish depleted supplies, the near hostilities prevented them from bringing much aboard.

Moving on, two uninhabited islands were passed northwest of Atiu until, in mid-April, the expedition reached Palmerston's Island. They found this island to be an atoll of about ten elevated coral banks. Although there were pieces of broken canoes and paddles scattered about, suggesting local people took refuge there during storms, they did not find any people. Here they were finally able to refresh provisions on their vessels, especially greens for the cattle and other stock on board.[19]

JOURNAL OF JAMES BURNEY

March From the coast of New Zealand we steered to the East and ENE with Variable Winds till we got in 39 degrees of South Latitude and 195° E Longitude.

March 27th, 1777 Here we had the Wind from ESE but it soon after Veered more to the East and remained so fixed that in running our Latitude down to the Tropic we could get no farther to the Eastward than 202° East at Greenwich. On board the Resolution Hay fell short on which account they were obliged to kill a great many Sheep to lessen the consumption and enable them to keep the larger Cattle alive till we should reach some place where a fresh supply might be procured. It has been remarked that in some parts of the South Seas Scarce any Birds are to be met with, which was the Case with us from New Zealand to the Tropic.

Saturday 29th At daylight passed a good deal of small Rock Weed and brushwood. Saw Land Birds and at ½ past 9 discovered Land bearing NE which proved to be a small Island. Did not set near enough before dark to distinguish any thing. Stood backwards and forwards all night.

Sunday 30th At Sunrise within a mile of the south end of the Island where seeing no anchoring place, Bore away alongshore for the West Side. A great number of Men Armed with Clubs and Spears kept walking along by the Water Side and as we did not go much more than at the rate of 3 miles an hour, held way with the Ship hallowing and Shouting, which we answered. As we rounded the SW point, they got on the Reef that surrounds the Island and walked along it, the Surf every now and then washing them up to the middle.
Under the Lee of the Island we lay too.

A Small Canoe with 2 Men came and paddled round the Ships several times. One of them gave us a Hevah something like the New Zealand War Song. Captain Cook hoisted out his pinnace and Cutter ordering our Cutter to join him, and went in Shore to see if Anchorage or a Landing could be effected. One of the Indians went with him, the other paddling the Canoe ashore himself. Several Indians swam off to the Boats. 4 of them being admitted into our Cutter were so troublesome, snatching every thing they could lay hands on, that we were glad to pull to a greater distance from the Shore out of reach of any more such Visitors. They did not know the Value of Iron. Two of them were presented with Hatchets, but Looking Glasses being afterwards given them, they threw down the Hatchet and would only take the Glasses on shore.

Finding no Safe Anchorage nor landing for our Boats, Captain Cook returned to the Ships, the Indian who first came off, going on board with him. He soon after sent the Indian ashore and at Noon we made Sail greatly disappointed. This Island is surrounded by a Reef at a Ships Length distance from the Shore. It's extent from East to West is about 6 miles and from North to South 4. All round by the Sea Shore is one continued grove, in which we could distinguish the plantain, Banana, and Cocoanut Trees and others that appeared like the Bread fruit and Shaddock. The middle of the Island rises in little Hills with, here and there, clusters of Trees along the ridges.

The people are Olive coloured, Stout, Muscular and well made. They Tattow on the inside of both Arms from the Shoulder down to the bending of the Elbow. Their Ears are bored and hang lank. Their Arms are long Spears pointed at both ends and Clubs some of which were not more than 2 feet long and Shaped like the New Zealand Patow [baton or club used as a weapon]. They tie their Hair on the Crown of the Head and in their imprudence, ferocity and martial appearance, seem not to be outdone by the New Zealanders.

We Saw no other Canoe than the little one before mentioned, which was too well finished to be their only one. It had a prow 7 or 8 feet high but for what use I could not make out. [Bearings omitted.] Stood again to the Northward. Wind ENE.

Monday 31st At Noon Saw an Island bearing NBE. The wind continuing to the Northward of East could not fetch near the Land. Kept turning to Windward all night.

Tuesday, April 1st At 7 in the morning were within 3 Leagues but directly to Leeward when we discovered another Island to the Northward much smaller and very low. Continued turning toward the large Island all day but made no progress having very little wind and a Swell against us. Saw many Fires on Shore in the Night.

Monday 2nd At Sunrise a double Canoe came off in which was a large corpulent man who seemed to be a Chief. This Canoe was soon followed by Several others. After much invitation the Chief ventured on board having first sent a bough of a plantain Tree as a Sign of peace. These Indians brought no Arms and were very quiet, peaceable, and well pleased with every thing they saw, without appearing covetous or offering to pilfer.

Lieut. Gore with 2 of the Resolutions Boats soon after came on board, and with him Omiah, who immediately entered into conversation with the Indians, they perfectly understanding each other. A Bough of a cocoanut Tree was brought and Omiah went through many ceremonies with the Chief repeating Short Sentences after him at each of which they pulled a leaf off the Bough. After these formalities the Chief invited us on shore promising plenty of Hogs, plantains, Cocoanuts etc.

This Island the Natives called Watdu. The Chief told Omiah there were 4 Otaheite men on shore. He likewise informed us the Small Island to the Northward belonged to him. It was named Modu [and] that at present nobody lived there but he frequently sent his people to catch Turtle.

This Chief was name Otenowhura. Captain Clerke presented him with a Hatchet, some Looking Glasses and red Cloth. He then went into the Resolutions Pinnace with Mr. Gore and Omiah, both Ships Cutters joining the party and some of the Indians in each. A present was made up for the Aree [chief] of the Island whose name he told us was Oterrow. On coming in Shore there was too much Surf to attempt Landing in our Boats. The Islanders in their Canoes always waited close to the Reef and took the opportunity of the first high surf to paddle over the edge of it, and as soon as the Surf began to run back jumped out on the Reef and haul'd the Canoe over. Otenowhura went on Shore in a Canoe taking with him the present for the Aree who came on the Reef to look at us.

We then Rowed alongshore from the North to the SE point of the Island without finding any opening in the Reef, or Anchoring Ground. Many of the Islanders came off to the Boats and were very peaceable and friendly. Two attempts were made to steal but on discovery, the things brought back again. A Hanger was taken out of our Cutter, and half way to Shore before it was missed. On Speaking to an Indian who came with us from the Ship he called to the Thief, who immediately sent the Hanger back. The Indian whose Authority procured this restitution was presented with a looking glass and some Knives.

After returning to the Ships, a present came from the Aree consisting of a Hog, some plantains and Cocoanuts for each Ship. At Sunset all the Canoes went on Shore. One of the Indians happening to be between decks at the time was left behind and obliged to take his lodging up with us for the Night. Our Guest was entertained in the best manner the Ship Could afford, being both fed and cloathed, but our kindness did not prevent his behaving in a very Scurvy manner.

Thursday 3rd The Swell had during the Night set the Ships considerably off Shore and it was late in the forenoon before we got near enough to send the Boats away. At 11 the Resolutions Pinnace and Cutter with our Cutter went in Shore, hoping a Market for provisions might be settled by landing in their Canoes and sending things off to the Boats.

Having brought to a Graplin within 50 Yards of the Reef, Mr. Anderson the Surgeon of the Resolution and myself got in one of their Canoes, Mr. Gore and Omiah preparing to follow us in another. On landing, a Man with a Small green bough took hold of me round the Waist to conduct me and a fellow who was Stained all over black (their Natural Colour being Olive) kept the people off with a small stick; Some Armed Men marching before to make a Lane through the crowd who during this procession Sung a Short Sentence consisting of only four words, which I could not remember though they continued repeating it all the way, keeping exact time and in one Tone. Having gone about 30 paces from the beach, an old man with a large Bough met and Saluted us by joining noses. We afterwards met a Second whom we likewise saluted, and at length came before the Aree who was seated on Mats under a Tree. The Crowd now left off singing.

We saluted the Aree and Sat down. The Aree was an elderly corpulent man with a Strong marked Sensible countenance. He received us with great Cordiality but presumed a degree of gravity rather bordering on self-consequence. His Clothing was a piece of very fine matting wrapped round his waist, and Sandals on his feet made of cocoanut Rhind slatted. He was naked above the Waist as were all the Islanders.

While sitting by the Aree we heard a hissing and Rattling Noise that resembled the Grinding of Knives and Childrens Rattles. This was followed by a party of Armed Men in three Ranks, 7 or 8 in each, with Clubs and Spears; every other Man having a Spear, which he held pointed forwards with both hands like a pike or Charged Bayonet. In this order they Marched or rather danced along without altering their pace or the direction of their Spears, the people being obliged to get out of the way as fast as they could. This procession was to clear the Road for Mr. Gore and Omiah who were soon introduced into the Aree's presence. Omiah Stopped at about 4 yards distance, and sitting down made a Speech which the Aree, answering Omiah, sent him a Small Bunch of Red Feathers and then joined us.

We were now treated by the Women with singing and dancing much in the same Stile as at the Society Islands. The Women are small and handsome, Somewhat darker coloured than the Otaheitans. Omiah to shew his Gallantry took a Cocoanut and drawing a very handsome Dirk [dagger] that had been given him in England, broke open the nut and presented it to one of the Girls. The Aree and every body admired the Dirk exceedingly and I make no doubt that people were instructed to Steal it if any opportunity offered.

The Crowd being very great and the Weather Sultry, Mr. Anderson and I rose hoping to get a little fresh Air and look about us; but we were so followed and pestered either from curiosity or for what they could pilfer (which they now began to do without minding detection so they made sure of their Booty) that we thought it safest and best to return into the Aree's company again.

On coming back, Omiah with a most rueful countenance informed us we Should not be suffered to go to the Boats. Willing to be convinced, Mr. Anderson and I again left the Company and walked towards the beach but were stopped before we reached the Water Side by a man unarmed. Not being willing to understand him we would have gone on, when two fellows with Clubs Stept before us. We went back to Mr. Gore and Omiah who were in company with another Chief, the Man who first saluted us after landing, and whom we afterwards learnt was the Chief priest, a Station in these Islands of no less consequence than that of the Aree or King. Omiah argued a good deal with this man who told him we might not go away before Sunset. However to be more fully satisfied, we all Marchd towards the beach but were again stopped.

The Crowd now robbed us without any ceremony, especially when not in company with a Chief. A Fan given me by Oterrow, the Aree, they made 3 or 4 attempts to snatch, which proving ineffectual, one of them caught hold and wrenched it away by force. In going up from the Water Side I was seperated from my companions and though I could see where they were by the Crowd that Surrounded them, was not suffered to join, but detained by a Chief I had not before seen. With him I remained an hour which was by far the most uncomfortable Situation I experienced during our Stay ashore. I made many fruitless attempts to go, giving him part of what yet remained, for I had come from the Ship well provided: at length growing impatient, I struggled with those who held me, when the Chief thinking perhaps he had had his Share, bid them let me go, and I rejoined my companions, resolved not to part again if it could be avoided.

We were now put in charge of Otenowhura, the Chief who the day before came first off to the Ships. Mr. Gore complained to him that he had lost everything out of his pockets and been robbed of a Bayonet he wore by his Side, but got no other answer than that the Thief was gone with it to the other side of the Island.

An Oblong Ring was soon after formed, Otenowhura seated at the Head and we in a Row on his left hand. Being still pestered with pick pockets, I thought it best to have the credit of giving away what was left, which I did mostly among the Women who were near us. The Sun was now near setting and Omiah again remonstrated with Otenowhura who was very reserved and scarce made any Answer. Omiah however put the best face he could on the matter and taking one of their Clubs began to talk about the Otaheite method of fighting. He then stood up in the middle of the Ring and Shewed them the Otaheite War Hevah. This a good deal engaged their attention and soon after Oterrow, the Aree, who had not been with us a considerable time, came and stood near the Ring to see Omiah perform his Exercises.

The countenances of the Chiefs gradually cleared up and they by degrees shook off that reserve and stiffness which they had hitherto observed. Oterrow seated himself by us: after laughing with Omiah about some part of the Otaheite fighting, which it seems much resembled their own, he enquired where Britannia was and how we fought. Omiah happened to have a Musket Cartridge about him, which he shewed, and taking the ball out, told them if an Englishman but saw a man at any distance, he could kill him with a Musket. The powder was put on the Ground and a live coal asked for which was thrown on it. The Islanders were much astonished at the Sudden explosion, and enquired if we had many bullets and much powder, which was answered in the Affirmative.

Whilst Omiah was thus entertaining them, I saw the Indian who was in the Boat the day before and got the Hanger restored. He was pleased at my recollecting him and afterwards presented me with a large Basket full of roasted Nuts, like Chestnuts.

Some leaves were now spread and 4 baskets brought, each containing a large portion of Roast Hog and plantains. Oterrow retired and we were told to eat, each having one of the baskets.

When we had done, the remains were tied up and put with Some bunches of Cocoanuts. We were then informed we might go. A Conductor was appointed us. The Cocoanuts and remains of our dinner were carried down to the Beach, and Canoes brought to carry us over the Reef. It was now dark and we made the best of our way on board in our own Boats. Being at liberty, I proposed finishing the remains of the dinner, but on examination found nothing but the plantains, the Black guards having Stole the Roast pork. They made shift likewise to steal the basket of Nuts. Omiah's Dirk was gone though he pretended not to miss it till after he got on board.

It is not improbable that their first intention was to have kept us wholly and that the sight of the powder and description of our Arms, which they had likewise Seen in our Boats, made them alter their plan. Certain it is, they resolved we should pay well for our Dinner, and that the Chiefs of the Island connived at most of the Thefts and robberies committed on us.

As to the business of settling a Market, they told us to return next day when we should be supplied with every thing wanted.

These islanders Tattow in different parts of the Body. It seems to be a kind of Heraldry, for those of the same family were markd exactly alike.

Our Travels ashore were so confined that we saw but One House, which was low roofed like the Amsterdam Houses. Their Arms are well carved and polished. Could we have had any intercourse with these people on an equal footing, there is little doubt but we should have found them hospitable and friendly.

Another name for this Island is Wennua not Manoo, which signifies the Land of Birds. It lays in 20.00° South Latitude and 202.00° East Longitude. It is about 6 miles in Diameter and may be Seen 7 or 8 Leagues distant from the Deck. Modu, the lesser Island, lays NW per Compass 10 or 11 miles distant from Watdu [which] is much lower and not half a League in length.[20] [Bearings omitted.]

Omiah saw the 4 Otaheite men at Watdu. They were cast away many years ago, and had families, having married Watdu Women. They never heard of the European Ships. Calm with much Lightning in the Night.

Friday 4th In the morning, stood to the Northward for Modu. Wind at ENE. At 10 Sent Boats in Shore and made Shift to Land on the Reef. Found no Inhabitants but several Old Houses and burying Grounds. Got a good number of Cocoanuts here, and some Grass etc. for the Cattle, who had been at very short allowance lately. At Sunset returned to the Ships, the Boats were got in, and we made Sail to the Northward.

Saturday 5th The light Easterly Winds having detained us so long and kept us so far to the Westward of the Society Islands as to exclude all hopes of being able to attempt any thing to the Northward this year; it was judged necessary to put the Ships Companies to 2/3ds allowance of all provisions, except Spirits, of which the full proportion still continued to be Served.

Sunday 6th At Daylight saw Herveys Islands bearing WSW 2 Leagues distant. They are 2 low Islands joined by a Reef, and extend 7 or 8 miles in length from ENE to WSW. They were first discovered in 1773 by Captain Cook. Their Latitude is 19.17 South and Longitude 201.16 East, distance 20 Leagues to the NW from Watdu. [Bearings omitted.]

At 8 Some Canoes came alongside, but the Indians could not be prevailed on to come in the Ship. They were fond of Iron for which they traffickd some Cloth, but it was not found safe to pay them beforehand. A Net which was hanging overhead with a piece of Beef intended for the Lieutenants dinner, they stole and carried on board the Resolution where it was bought and dressed for Captain

Cooks Dinner. Besides stealing every thing they could get at, they attempted to haul the Astronomers Servant out of our Cutter, and would have effected their purpose, had not one of our men jumped in the boat just time enough to prevent them. The 2 Young Zealanders are much surprized that of so many people in our power, we have neither killed or made prisoners of any.

At 1 both of the Ships Cutters were sent to the NW point to Sound. As they left the Ships, the Canoes all followed and on coming near the Shore, the Women brought their Arms down. Our Boats found 30 fathoms hard bottom at 2 Cables length from the Reef and good landing, there being very little Surf. However they did not go ashore, as the Natives Came down Armed ready to oppose them. At 4 in the Afternoon the Boats returned. The Anchorage not being very good, and the people so ill disposed, we made Sail from these Islands, to the Westward for Amsterdam, as in this Latitude there was but little Chance of getting so far to the Eastward as the Society Islands, before our Water, which now began to run short, should be wholly expended.

Monday 7th Falling little wind, steered more Northerly for Palmerstones Isles, which lay between 80 & 90 Leagues from Herveys Islands and very little out of our Rout. Having ran about 40 Leagues from Herveys Islands, the Wind which had so long continued Easterly now became Variable, mostly from the NW and Northward with unsettled Weather.

Sunday 13th Saw Palmerstones Isles at Sunset within 3 Leagues. Stood off and on all Night.

Monday 14th In the forenoon Boats were sent to look for Anchorage and landing. These Islands are 10 in Number, very low and covered with Trees. The largest is not a mile in length or more than half in breadth. They are joined by a Reef and form an Oval Lagoon, whose longest Diameter from NE to SW is 7 or 8 miles. [Bearings omitted.]

The Boats returned in the Evening, having found a landing place on the Southernmost Island, and gathered Some Scurvy Grass and other herbage for the Cattle on board the Resolution. They examined all along the SE, SW and West Sides of the Islands without finding any opening in the Reef except for Boats. Between the South and SW Island, the Reef bends in forming a Small Bay, and Soundings at 2 Cables length from the Reef [at] 20 fathoms. Sandy bottom with Rocks. The Winds being unsettled and the Sun every day increasing, this distance makes it unsafe anchoring here at present. Within the Lagoon on the North Side, seems to be deep Water. All this day and Night, the Ships standing off and on.

Tuesday 15th Boats at the Southernmost Island getting Scurvy Grass and Cocoanuts, which these Islands produce in great abundance. The Ships Standing off and on.

Wednesday 16th Employed getting Cocoanuts from the SW Island. A Small Boat from each Ship remained on shore all Night, the Cool of the Mornings and Evenings being the most proper time for the people to work.

The Lagoon affords plenty and variety of Fish. About the Skirts of the Woods near the beach, are great numbers of a species of the Crayfish that inhabit dead Shells, generally known by the name of Soldiers. Tropic, Men of War Birds and Boobies are very numerous. The Tropic Birds [are] remarkable for the long feathers in their Tails being red. Some Curlews were Shot which proved good eating. Saw Turtle Holes in the Sand, but no Turtle. These Islands, like most others in the South Seas, Swarm with Rats.

Had the good luck always to have Omiah on Shore, who proved a most useful companion for a party of this kind, being a keen Sportsman, an excellent Cook and never idle. Without him we might have made a tolerable Shift, but with him we fared sumptuously. Found in different parts of the Beaches a piece of a canoe carved, a broken paddle, some pieces of plank, in particular one very thick with Trunnel holes in it, and a piece of the Mounting of a Ships upper works painted Yellow with Nailholes iron woulderd. These things were found on the Lagoon Side of the SW Island and must have been forced over the Reef on the East Side of the Lagoon.

The Sea rises and falls here near 3 feet. It was at the highest about 5 in the Afternoon of the 17th which is 3 1/4 Hours before the Moon crosses the Meridian.

Thursday 17th All this day Employed getting Cocoanuts and Scurvy Grass. In the Evening the Boats with all the people returned to the Ships and we made sail to the Westward. Wind Northerly.

Sunday 20th Many Birds. [Bearings omitted.] Winds variable. Weather unsettled with rain.

Monday 21st Our Stock of Water being reduced to 7½ Tons went to a daily allowance of 2 Quarts, exclusive of what is used for boiling the pease, Wheat and Sweet wort. This regulation makes one Hogshead [cask] last the 24 hours. Water on board at leaving Charlotte Sound—27 Tons.

Wednesday 23rd Philip Woodfield, Carpenters Mate, broke his Leg by a fall under the Tiller which was set and he afterwards recovered. The Ships Companies, thank God, in good health. No Appearance of the Scurvy. In the Night Saw Savage Island, which we passed to the Southward of. It appears much like Watdu, somewhat larger. [Bearings omitted.]

Saturday 26th Left the Water Cask free again, having this last Week caught at different times by keeping the Awning spread, between 3 and 4 Tons of rain water.

Sunday 27th Had an Observation of the Suns Meridian Altitude, the only one we have been able to get these 6 Days. [Bearings omitted.] At Sunset thought we saw the Land, on which account Spoke the Resolution. Lay too all Night.

Journal of Henry Roberts

Sunday, March 23rd Two pieces of Pork being stolen from some of the officers & continually accidents or robberies of this kind, happening with many other before, the Captain therefore in order to put a stop to this proceeding immediately gave orders for the Ships Company to receive 2/3rds Allowance until such time the Pork should be produced or a satisfactory account given of it. They refused in a Body to receive that Allowance. The Pork was therefore brought on the Quarter Deck & every officer attending, insisted on their [not] taking it, or a punishment adequate to this Mutinous Refusal, should be instantly addicted on their First Persons. Read the Articles of War and Abstract to the Ships Company.

Sunday 30th Two points in a line on the SW Extremity offshore about ½ a mile. This Island is of a Moderate height, covered with Trees, many of which are the Cocoa Nutt. The Land gradually rising from every Point, the Shore is well defended by a reef of Coral Rocks surrounding the whole Island at a little distance from the Main. Saw many Inhabitants on Shore, in number about 400, two of them came off in a Canoe to the Ship. Gave them many trinkets etc for which they were very thankful. The Captain went to the place with the Boats but a great swell rolling in on the Reef & not the least break to shelter them, were obliged to put off & came on Board, much to His dissatisfaction.

A great number of the Natives assembled on the Reef & some swimming to the Boats, wishing them to Land. Their Complexion is nearly as light as the Otaheitians. Some few were Covered, but could not distinguish their clothing. Others were naked, only a slight covered over their privacies. Their hair tyed on the crown of the Head like the New Zealanders, those five that were on Board had sandals on the soles of their feet, many of them with a piece of white cloth like a turbain folded & wound round their Heads. Those chiefly that were armed had this. Their Arms consists of Clubs & Spears, much resembling those at the Friendly Isles. Saw only one House, directly opposite the place we proposed landing & the appearance built on the same Construction of those round thatched roofed Houses at Otaheite.

The Natives informed us that the Island produced Bread fruit & Bananas, & Cocoa Nutts we could perceive from the Ship. We saw but this Canoe that came off to us, was neatly lashed together with an outrigger & the fore part of her similar to those of the Society Isles. The stern rising very high with a kind of a swallow tail or Fork cut in the Top, their paddles, the upper Part or Handle, is round [and] the lower part flat, rounded at the Bottom, about 4 feet long.

Wednesday, April 2nd At ½ past 8 Hoisted out the Pinnace & large Cutter, the 1st Lieut sent to Explore the Island & try for Anchorage. Many Canoes coming from the Shore to the Discovery & shortly after paid us a Visit, traded for a few Cocoa Nutts & plantains.

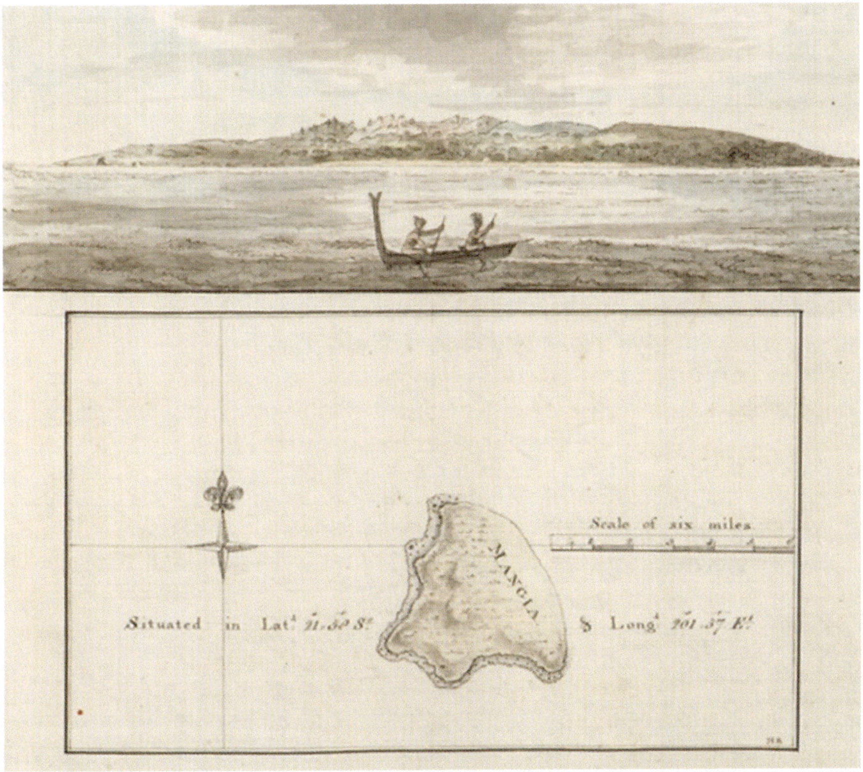

Henry Roberts, "Two Men in a Canoe off Mangaia [Cook Islands]," with accompanying chart, March 1777. Roberts Journal p. 69, Dixson Library, State Library of New South Wales, DLMSQ 151-52 and DLMSF 2.

Thursday 3rd At 4 the Pinnace and Cutter returned, finding no Anchorage, the Island being encircled by a coral Reef & steep too within ½ Cables Length of the Breakers. [There was] no break or Passage through, the Reef, & the surf rolling in with great violence prevented their Landing. The Natives however manage to land on the Reef & haul their Canoes over after them. A Number of them assembled on the Different Beaches, or Coves, looking at the Ship & some swimming off to the Boats with a few bunches of Bananas & Plantains & Cocoa Nutts. They seemed very desirous for our landing & behaved with the greatest friendliness & good nature.

In the evening a present was Brought to the Captain from the Chief of the Island, consisting of a small Hog, Cocoa Nutts & some Plantains. In the Morning sent the Boats in Shore again to endeavour to purchase some refreshments, & strive to land to get grass for the Cattle. Being much distressed for this last Article, the Cattle has suffered very much, having been near a month at a very short allowance.

Friday 4th The Inhabitants call this Island Watieu. Came on Board the Boats, the Officers with great difficulty landed, with the assistance of the Natives in their Canoes, but found it impossible to land with our Boats. The Indians behaved very friendly to them when on Shore, but would not permit them to make any excursion in the Country. The trade we got on Board was very indifferent, only a few Cocoa Nutts & plantains.

Saturday 5th In the morning stood away for the Small Island. The Boats Returned with a few Cocoa Nutts, & a quantity of grass & palm Trees for the Cattle, found it exceedingly difficult to land, being a great surf. Saw no Inhabitants but there are two or three decayed Hutts, near temporary Houses, which they use when they come from the large Island to fish. The soil is very sandy & not the least appearance of fresh water, no kind of Fruit Trees excluding the Cocoa Nutt & those a scarcity. Captain Cook sent 2 Hatchets & some Nails to be laid in a Conspicuous Place in return for the Cocoa Nutts.

Sunday 6th Saw Hervey's Isle. Several Canoes with the Natives came along side & Bartered for a few Fish. In return we gave them small Nails & slips of Red Cloth. They continued with us about 2 Hours.

Monday 7th Under the lee of the Islands, at ½ past 1 Hoisted out the Pinnace & sent her with the Discoverys Cutter, both mand & armd, to seek for Anchorage. Boats returned, found no Anchorage, being steep like the other Reef Islands & no Passage through the Reef. The Inhabitants are but few, tolerably friendly, much resembling the New Zealanders. They are great thiefs & horrid cheats, seldom returning the Article bargained for when in possession of ours. We purchased a few Cocoa Nutts, of which the Shore abounds. Their Arms are spears & Clubs, some few having these, when our Boats were near the Shore. The Canoes nearly the same as those at the other Isles. Fixed the Still for distilling Salt water into Fresh.

Monday 14th The Southernmost of Palmerston's Isles bares West Distance 2 leagues. Hoisted out the Pinnace & large Cutter & sent them with the 1st & 2nd Lieut. to examine the Shore. Bore away for the West End of the Isles.

Tuesday 15th The Small Cutter returned from the Shore with a quantity of Palm Trees & grass etc for the Cattle. At 7 the Pinnace & Cutter returned, loaded as before. Could find no Anchorage nor any Seperation in the Reef. Hoisted them in. The first Lieut. & party were left on Shore for the Night. At Daylight, Bore away round the SW Point of the Reef. Sent the Boats to the Shore where our People landed, the Boats bringing off Cocoa Nutt, Cabage, Palm Trees, Scurvy Grass etc for the Cattle.

Wednesday 16th Standing off & on while the Boats were employed bringing off provisions for the Cattle. At 8 AM Captain Cook went with the Boats & Landed on the West Isle. This Island producing many Cocoa Nutts, we found no Anchorage off the Reefs, but tolerable landing from a small break in the

Rocks, which enabled us to load the Boats with little difficulty & haul the small Boats over the Ledge at High Water, where they could not possibly receive any damage. We found several pieces of Canoes, or parts of a Canoe with a broken paddle, on the Beach. Whether Indians frequented these Isles, or whether this Vessel might have been driven from any other country, its impossible to determine, but most probable the latter, finding no other marks. We cut a great quantity of Cocoa Nutts, which were served to the People 5 per Man. Saw 2 or 3 Small Turtle near the Reefs offshore 4 miles.

Thursday 17th The Boats, bringing off Cocoa Nutts, Killed a number of Man of War Birds, Boobys, & Tropic Birds, which the Island abounds in. It did not appear that these Animals were ever, or at least often, disturbed by mankind, they suffering us to destroy them with Sticks. The Latter indeed permitted us to take them from the Ground without making the least resistance. These Differ a little from the Tropic Birds, in general, both Male & female, having the Tail Feathers Red. Saw some few Curlew, flying about the Rocks.

Punished James King, seaman, for Drunkenness & Neglect of Duty with 6 Lashes.

John Webber, "A View at Annamooka [Nomuka]," circa 1781-83. Pen, wash, and water color showing men in Cook's company visiting with Natives on shore and in nearby boats and canoes in early May 1777. A celebration is underway. Dixson Library, State Library of New South Wales, PXX 2, f. 3.

4

TONGA
APRIL–AUGUST 1777

Sailing north from the uninhabited Palmerston atoll, the expedition made for the previously known island of Nomuka, which they called "Anamooka" or Rotterdam Island, where they stayed nearly two weeks. They met the Agee or Chief, Tubow, then the younger Finau, who accompanied them throughout the islands. While accompanying the British, Finau's canoes were driven away and nearly perished from a freak storm in early June.

The journal writers could not detect the nuances of the stratified society nor chain of command between island chiefs. Burney frankly admits "their Government and degree of subordination were too difficult and intricate for us to unriddle." But the writers understood there was near constant warfare between tribes and especially between the Tongans and nearby island nations. Burney did his best to discuss local traditions and the hierarchy between chiefs. He also mentions nearby Fiji, whom the Tongans had recently battled in an inconclusive war, as well as the perplexing visit of the elderly Paulaho, an aged man with uncertain but apparently exalted status. Burney called him Powlahow and Roberts Tetta-fee-ha. He was a corpulent, inebriated man with little to commend him in comparison to the sturdy Finau.

The expedition then visited the islands of Ha'apai [Lifuka], Tongatapu, and Eua. At Ha'apai and Tongatapu, Burney was captivated with the boxing matches of both men and women, especially the first crowded celebration at Lifuka, an island he called *Happi*. Unlike Europeans he found the losers in the matches were not humiliated or, it seemed, the least affected by the defeat. Some of the crewmen participated in the boxing matches, but the local warriors were much stronger and won every match. In Tongatapu Burney recorded the lyrics of a song and carefully described the music concerts and dancing ceremonies, which were attended by large crowds. In mid-June he also reported the seizure of several chiefs as hostages to assure the return of stolen property, a practice Captain Cook followed frequently until he used it to his demise later in Hawai'i.

Burney was fascinated with the culture, customs and personality of the islanders—chiefs and commoners alike. He discusses their language, interpersonal relations, funeral ceremonies, and even the near sacred, religious-based prohibitions or "tabu." But he also wrote that the Tongans were inveterate thieves, even worse than the other islanders they observed, stealing whatever they could lay their hands on, including nails, muskets, and even Clerke's cats. The sailors were most prone to an attack while walking away from shore or alone, but thieves were even so bold as to attempt to steal from a marine sentinel, who was stationed on shore to prevent thieving.

Roberts was in his element describing shipboard life, including regular trips for wood and water on shore and the trade for locally produced provisions of coconuts, fowls, yams, sugar cane, hogs, bananas and the like. He said upwards of 2,000 hogs were "destroyed" in Tonga during their visit. He was also fascinated by the good relations between the crew and the local people, including the series of ceremonies held on shore and the amazement and appreciation of the crowd from the fireworks displays. He also mentions the flogging of several seamen.

Both journals record the complex sailing directions travelling between islands, which has been edited to avoid the repetition of bearings, tides, coordinates and wind—as the tangle of Tongan reefs and shoals were intricate and treacherous. They left Tongatapu in early July after observing an Eclipse of the Sun.

Journal of James Burney

Monday, April 28th At daylight Seeing no Land, made Sail again. At 9 Saw the Small Low Islands to the Eastward of Anamooka. At Noon were about a League distant from the Southernmost of them. [Bearings omitted.] At 4 in the Afternoon Saw Anamooka or Rotterdam and at 6 both Ships Anchord. An Island with 3 hills bearing NWBN about 4 miles and Anamooka beyond it. Many Islands all round. Bottom 10 1/2 fathoms Sand. Sent a boat to Sound round the Ships. The Ground very uneven from 7 to 25 fms [fathoms] within 2 Cables length. Have been visited this day by a great many Canoes with Cargoes of Bread fruit, Cocoanuts, Shaddocks, fowls etc. etc.

Tuesday 29th Got under Sail at Sunrise, wanting to get nearer Anamooka. Had baffling wind with much rain. At Sunset Anamooka bore NNE 5 miles. Sent a Boat to Sound intending to Anchor, but not finding less than 60 fms any where near the Ship, were obliged to keep the Sea all night.

Wednesday 30th Attempting to get nearer Anamooka. Winds and weather as yesterday. At Sunset Anchord in 47 fathoms Sand. Anamooka bearing ENE ½ E distance 5 Miles. This Day an Order of Captain Cook's, prohibiting all persons but those appointed by him, from trading with the Natives, was read to the Ships Company.

Thursday, May 1st At Daylight under Sail. At 4 in the Afternoon Anchord off the North Side of Anamooka and Moord. Best Bower to the ESE in 17 fms. Small Bower in 27 fms hard rocky bottom. [Bearings omitted.] All Ship provisions, Spirits excepted, were stopped; Fresh pork and Vegetables sufficient to serve the Ships Companies being procured.

Friday 2nd All the Cattle were sent on shore, there being good pasturage. The Agee or Chief of Anamooka, was named Tubow, a middle aged man, more modest and sedate than we found the generality of these people. Another Chief of some consequence was named Kaper. This man was remarkable for making long Orations to his countrymen. Part of a House that stood on the beach was assigned for those of our people whom it was necessary to keep on shore to attend the Cattle, Watering etc. When anything happened amiss, application was made either to Tubow or the Orator, and things went on with some degree of Order, the Natives being friendly, and well disposed.

Employed in overhauling the Rigging, Wooding and Watering. Water brackish and dirty. As to the Wood, could get no other than the Mangineal [toxic bush similar to Manzanita], which in 2 or 3 days time blinded the Wood cutters that they could not see for a fortnight after, and we were obliged to leave off cutting it.

Sunday 4th The small Bower Cable parted, being cut by the Rocks. The next day got the Anchor again. About a week after our arrival some large Sailing Canoes came from Tongitabu or Amsterdam and a Chief who we were told was Agee, not only of Tongitabu but of Anamooka and all the Islands hereabouts. The Name of this Chief was Finow, a tall handsome Man, appeared to be about 25 years of Age. Had much fire and Vivacity with a degree of Wildness in his Countenance that well tallied with our idea of an Indian Warrior. Add to this, he was one of the most active men I have ever seen.[21]

There is a ceremony among these people which an inferior Chief is obliged to perform on meeting a Superior that sufficiently indicated his dependence. He sits down before the person to whom he pays homage and bows his head so that his hair touches the others foot, which he afterwards taps gently with his hand 2 or 3 times and then rises. This is never performed but by people of distinction to their patrons. Tubow at their first meeting was obliged to acknowledge the superiority of Finow by paying him the Homage abovementioned.

Wednesday 7th The Ground about the Ship being rocky, and safer Anchorage found more to the Westward, have on the Best Bower intending to shift our Birth, but were not able to purchase the Anchor. After repeated Trials, the Cable parted, being foul of the Rocks. Set the Sails and having run nearer the Resolution, let go the Small Bower Anchor which coming home we were very near driving foul of her and obliged to carry out another Anchor. The next day got the Ship Moord in a good Birth near the NW point of the Island. Bearings when moord [Bearings omitted].

The Buoy rope of the Best Bower Anchor being stranded gave us much trouble, not being able to sweep it till the afternoon of the 13th and then chiefly by means of Some Oil thrown on the Water, which rendered the surface so smooth that the Anchor was seen at the bottom, though in 17 fathoms, and the position in which it lay discovered.

Watering had been completed some time before, and the cattle got on board, Captain Cook waiting only for our Anchor, which, as we had already broke one at Kerguelens Land, was of too much consequence to give up easily.

During our stay at Anamooka, Omiah lived ashore, as he did at every Island we visited in this neighbourhood, having a House and a Wife appointed him. Omiah does not understand these people very perfectly, nevertheless he is by far the best linguist we have. Fibarus the New Zealander contracted the Venereal Distemper here.

Wednesday 14th Wind SE with fair Weather. This morning got under Sail and Stood to the Northward. Captain Cook having been informed of some Islands to the NE called Happi or Heabbi, under the dominion of Finow who had invited him thither. Many large Sailing Canoes in company with us. Finow's among the rest.

Our passage to Happi, though not more than 14 Leagues distant from Anamooka in a direct line, took up 3 days, in an intricate Navigation amongst Small Islands and Reefs, that, had the weather not been very moderate would have been unsafe. The Sailing Canoes went on shore every night to some of the nearest Islands and as we lay too after Sunset, joined us in the morning. Their rate of Sailing was about 3 miles to our 2.

Friday 16th In the Afternoon Saw the Happi Isles very low Land and next forenoon Anchord in a good Bay. These Islands besides being called Happi or Heabbi which signifies a Cluster, have each a separate name. They are joined together by Reefs and extend considerably in length from NNE to SSW, but not much in breadth. Bearings when moord [Bearings omitted].

The Island South of the Opening is called Lofuga and is by much the longest, though from where we lay it appeared otherwise, on account of a bite to the Southward which falls in so far that we at first imagined the Land on the farther side to be a different Island. The peak of Oghas, and the Volcano on Mettafoa are in Sight both here and at Anamooka.

When the Ships were secured, Captain Cook went on Shore with Finow and Shortly after a present consisting of 7 Hogs and a great quantity of Cocoanuts,

John Webber, "The Reception of Captain Cook in Hapaee," circa 1781-83. Pen, wash, and water color showing the manner of receiving, entertaining, and making Captain Cook a present on Lifuka in mid-May 1777. The entertainment included two pairs of combatants, one pair boxing and the other pair fighting with clubs, with a large circle of spectators. Dixson Library, State Library of New South Wales, PXX 2, f. 4.

Yams, Sugar Cane, Bread fruit etc. was brought down to the Water Side and placed in two piles before a House where Captain Cook and several of the gentlemen were sitting with Finow and his Chiefs. A great Number of the Natives were assembled on this occasion, who Seated themselves in a Ring of which the House formed a part, the Space immediately before, being the center. Here some of the Young fellows Advanced and Challenges were given for wrestling, by placing their left Arm across the Breast, and Striking the bending of the Joint with the right Hand open, after the Otaheite fashion, but their wrestling was much superior.

A match being made the wrestlers grappled taking fair hold of each others Clothes which are fastened round Loins. They wrestle something like our Cornish men, and are very expert and active at it. When any one was thrown, the Victor was complimented with the following short Song in a kind of recitative.

"Too-wey. Hey. O mar to yo-e."

The first word (Too-wey) sung by a single person, dwelling on the last Syllable, and the rest in full Chorus by the men on that Side of the Ring to which he belonged. During the performance of this Song, the fallen Hero returned to his Seat and the Conqueror walked about to see if any would undertake him; if more than one, for frequently 7 or 8 would offer, he took his choice and the rest retired.

After the Wrestling a new and, to us, most extraordinary spectacle was exhibited. Women boxing. A woman advanced a little within the Ring and sat down, which was understood as a Challenge and not long unanswered.

Saturday 17th In the boxing they neither close or pull hair, and aim all their blows at the face, being very cautious not to strike lower. The Engagement is seldom decisive, not being Suffered to continue long enough; for by the time they have exchanged 5 or 6 good hearty Cuffs, Some friend parts them and they return to their seats. Two fine young Girls advancing, one of our Gentlemen got up and interposed, which produced loud Shouts of Applause and much Mirth.

This diversion having lasted some time, was succeeded by one of the most manly and hardy exercises I have ever seen. Several Young Men made their appearance with Clubs made of green branches of the Cocoanut Tree, about 3 feet long and 3 or 4 inches thick, making Motions and flourishes which were meant as general Challenges. Afterwards particular Challenges were given and all withdrew but the 2 Combatants who banged each other without Mercy. These Battles generally lasted till one of them was knockd down, or one of their Clubs broke, which put an end to the conflict, the other not taking advantage.

The Diversions and Exercises of these people were conducted with a degree of Temper truly commendable and which few Europeans are capable of. The Conqueror not Shewing any Signs of Exultation, nor the beaten party appearing in the least abashed, on the contrary he returns to his Seat with as much unaffected cheerfulness as when he entered the lists. It is not in the power of every man who feels himself disgraced at being worsted, to avoid at the same time feeling some degree of Malevolence for his Antagonist.

When any Man advances and gives a general Challenge, if another enters whom he thinks too many for him or whom he does not chuse to encounter, he returns to his place and is seldom laughd at for his defection. During the whole of these exercises, the most perfect order was preserved. When engaged they exerted their utmost Skill and Strength, but if any thing like ill blood appeared between the Combatants, the Friends of either party interposed and seperated them immediately.

The Entertainment being finished the Ring broke up; the presents were carried down to the Boats and conveyed on board the Ships. Finow next day receiving a present in return, of a very good Hanger, a Linnen Gown, and several other things.

Sunday 18th This morning an Indian was detected Stealing a Cat out of the Ship, and put in Irons. But proving to be a Son of Kaper (the Chief, remarked for his Oratory at Anamooka) it was found necessary to release him, not however, till he had promised to get 2 Cats restored that had been before Stolen. This he afterwards performed.

Tuesday 20th Was quite a Field day both on our parts and with the Indians. In the morning the marines of Both Ships (about 30) were ordered on Shore to be reviewd, and performed their Exercises, firing with ball, to the no small diversion and Astonishment of some Thousands of the Natives. This was succeeded by a War Heavah or Dance performed by Finow at the head of 200 persons who were all either Chiefs or Relations of Chiefs none of an inferior Class being suffered to miss. They had each a Small Weapon something in the Shape of the New Zealand Patows [baton or club used as a weapon] but longer and lighter as meant only for Exercising.

An Orchestra was formed the instrumental part being hollow pieces of Bamboo with which they kept time by striking one end against the Ground and Drums made of Hollowed pieces of Wood about 4 feet long and 1½ in diameter, each of which were beat upon by 3 or 4 men with Sticks. These were surrounded and accompanied by a Ring of Songsters (all Men). Their Singing being mostly Sentences pronounced in a Monotone, every now and then Shifting the Time from Common to Triple, with which the whole exactly corresponded.

The Dancing consisted of various Strange Motions, uncommonly wild. They were perfectly uniform in every different attitude and went through the whole with a graceful ease and regularity that at least equaled our performance. The War Hevah being finished, Finow went on board the Resolution and dined with the Commodore. In the afternoon some Fireworks were carried on Shore and prepared for Exhibition.

We were entertained with Matches at Wrestling and Boxing by the Men. On first approaching each other, they keep their left arm strait out as a guard and watch for an opportunity to begin with Advantage. They aim mostly at the face. If one of them is knockd down, which is frequently done the first blow, the battle is not suffered to be renewed. And if it lasts more than 5 or 6 minutes the bystanders separate them.

An hour after Sunset the Fireworks were played off with great success and the Evening concluded with a Concert of Music accompanied with Singing and Dancing by the Women of which I shall speak hereafter.

Friday 23rd Sent the Launch for Water, a place being found about 2 miles to the Southward. Water much the Same as at Anamooka. This Morning Finow with several large Sailing Canoes left us, steering to the Northward for some Islands named Vowvow which we were told lay at the distance of a days Sail in that direction. Finows business thither was to procure red feathers which were become a valuable article of Trade, our people giving any price for them on a suposition that they would turn to good Account at the Society Islands.

Monday 26th Unmoored and at Noon got under Sail. Stood to the Southward alongshore keeping a Boat a head sounding. At 2 the Ship struck on a Small patch of Coral Rocks, there being 7 fathoms depth on each Side. Threw the Sails aback and got off without hurt. At 6 anchord off the 2 Southernmost of the Happi Isles and about 2 Leagues to the South of the place we left. [Bearings omitted.]

Tuesday 27th Boats were sent in search of a passage to the SW for Anamooka, and found one, but being difficult and intricate Captain Cook did not choose to make use of it. During our Stay here some Canoes arrived from Tongitabu, and a Chief who we were told was Superior in Rank to Finow. As Finow was about on his Northern Expedition we were in doubt about the truth of this information. The new comer's name was Powlahow. [He was] elderly and seemed remarkable for nothing so much as for his great corpulency.

Thursday 29th At Sunrise Weighd and stood towards the NW to get in our old track again, being bound for Anamooka. Powlahow and 3 Sailing Canoes in company. Had a disagreeable passage with foul wind and blowing weather which obliged Powlahow to take Shelter at a Small Island.

Sunday, June 1st Wind fresh from the S. Not being able to gain Ground anchored amongst a groupe of Islands, having kept the Sea the 3 preceding Nights, in which time the Resolution twice narrowly escaped being ashore. Bearings at Anchor [Bearings omitted]. Lay here till the fourth when the weather becoming more Moderate, got under Sail.

Thursday 5th In the afternoon Anchord off the NW point of Anamooka, nearly in our old birth. [Bearings omitted.]

Friday 6th Finow returned, having been very roughly used by the Weather. He was in great anxiety about the remainder of his Fleet. Only 2 Canoes came in with him out of 9 or 10 that he put to Sea with.

Saturday 7th At daylight 3 of Finow's Canoes arrived and before the day was over only one was missing, which joined us as we left Anamooka. Powlahow likewise came in and we were convinced of his consequence by Finow performing the Same Homage, himself had received from Tubow.

John Webber, "A Night Dance by Women of Hapee [Lifuka]," circa 1781-83. Pen, wash, and water color showing Cook and other officers watching perhaps two dozen women dancers in a night time ceremony in mid-May 1777. There is a companion drawing of male dancers in the library collection. Dixson Library, State Library of New South Wales, PXX 2, f. 6.

Sunday 8th In the morning left Anamooka, and steered to the South and SSW for Tongitabu or Amsterdam. Powlahow, Finow, and a large fleet of Sailing Canoes in company.

Monday 9th At 8 in the morning were within 8 Leagues of the North Side of Tongitabu, off which lay a great many small Islands, Shoals, and Reefs. At 10 being under Topsails before the Wind, we Struck on a patch of Coral Rock but setting all the Sails, forced the Ship over it and soon after Anchord in 7 fms Rocky bottom at 5 miles distant from Tongitabu. [We anchored on the] North Side, for fear of getting too far intangled, having run over very uneven ground the last 3 miles, with soundings from 12 fms to 3, and in some places pieces of Coral Rock Sticking up within 7 or 8 feet of the Surface.

The Boats were sent to look for a Harbour and a better Channel. At 3 they made the Signal and we hove up the Anchors and stood in, having a Clear Sandy bottom and the water deepening. Falling Calm, at 5 Anchord 2 or 3 miles from the Shore in 8 fms, a great many Reefs and Islands without us, to the NE and SW.

Tuesday 10th Weighd. At 2 in the Afternoon Anchord in a very good Harbour formed by Islands and Reefs running off from the Main of Tongitabu to the Eastward and Northward of us. Bearings when moord [Bearings omitted].

Wednesday 11th The Resolutions Tents with the Astronomers Tents were erected and the Marines of both Ships ordered on Shore as a Guard. All the Cattle were got on Shore and a market for provisions opened at the Tent. The next day a party of men were sent to cut wood which was in great plenty and good. Water of the same kind as at Anamooka we got at the Island to the NNE of us.

Almost every day the first week, we were entertained with Heavahs, Concerts of Music and Dancing by the women. The Music of their Concerts is very different from the War Heavah which as before mentioned is monotonous throughout. The Instruments are the same; Drums and pieces of Bamboo surrounded by men Singers whilst the women sing and dance in a circle round all. They generally begin with a Single Voice in a Slow and Solemn Stile, the Women marching softly round. This is soon accompanied by an instrument, the other Voices and Instruments gradually joining till they arrive at the loudest pitch. They then begin by degrees to quicken their Time both in Music and dancing to the quickest possible.

Sometimes in the middle of their Career, a full Stop is made and the most profound silence Observed for about a Minute, when out they set again as if the Devil drove them. In some of their pieces they practice the diminuendo in the same degrees of graduation both with respect to Time and Noise. The whole is full, and Musical, mostly in the minor key or flat 3d, but in so uncommon a stile that I could never get hold of more than half a dozen following notes. Their organs and flutes have very little variety and are never used in their Concerts.

Some of their common Songs are in very good meter and Rhime, in particular the following which though ignorant of its meaning I thought worth noticing

O Chicheto—O Chiche matta la
O Chicheto—Vette vala vala
Keonemar, Keonemar—Koar, Koar, Koar;
Keovahey, Keovahey—Ko hey, Ko hey, Ko hey;
To Allellelay
Ki Allubey

The Sense of the latter part may in some measure be guessed at to signify Sugar Cane; Lelay, good; Ki, not; and Allubey, a pigeon, etc. At the two last words, the Singers who are all Women through aside their Cloaths, whence "To Allellelay Ki Allubey" may perhaps not improperly be construed.

Shortly after our Arrival, Omiah, in a drunken fit, took some offence at one of the Centinels on Shore and struck him, which the Corporal who was present resented by pushing him away and threatening to beat him. Omiah, who amongst these Islands had always past for a great Man, was so much incensed at this rebuff, that he immediately left the Tent and repaired to the Indian Chiefs, the 2 young Zealanders with him, declaring his resolution to return no more to the Ship. The Affair however was accomodated the next day. Some Time before this, Omiah had been invited by Finow to Stay, with an Offer of being made Agee of Oo-ha, or Middleburgh. Had he been suffered to have accepted that Station, his continuance in it, after the departure of the Ships, would have been very precarious.

Their Government and degrees of Subordination were too difficult and intricate for us to unriddle. The Chief people of the Islands were Molliwagge, Funebula, Powlahow, Fattefai and 2 of the Name of Tubow. Molliwagge, who was the Father of Finow and one of the Tubow's, was said to be King, but so old and helpless, that he scarce retained the use of his faculties. Funebula, next in rank, was of very little consequence, being a downright Idiot. Powlahow, who was a good natured, sensible old man, governed in that part of the Island where our Ships lay, and to the Eastward. Fattefai, an indolent, inactive man, was brother to Powlahow and had the SE part of the Island under his direction. One of the Tubow's had great possessions in the middle of the Island.

The Western part of Tongitabu, with Anamooka, the Happi Isles, and all the Islands to the Northward, were under the jurisdiction of Finow but what gave him more consequence was his Spirit, Activity and his post as General. Whenever the people of Tongitabu went to War they were headed by him. His followers were numerous and more attached to him than those of any other Chief. In short he was by much the most popular Man amongst the Islands. Nevertheless Finow with all his good qualities, was tainted with a degree of rapaciousness, that made him guilty of actions rather bordering on Meanness and dishonesty; and which I believe he was chiefly tempted to, from a desire of being liberal to his adherents. At Vowvow, the Islands where Finow went for red feathers, lived an Old Lady, who was stiled, Mother of all the Islands.

At present they did not seem to have any quarrel on their Hands, either foreign or domestic, but had some little time before been at War with the people of an Island called Fidgee [Fiji Islands], that they told us lay to the WNW distant 5 days Sail—which, if in a strait line, must be near 200 Leagues but their Navigation is most likely from one Island to another, which will considerably lessen the direct distance. Fidgee, by their account, is much larger than Tongitabu [and] the people not so stout, but more numerous, and in general an overmatch for our Friendly Islanders.

Superiority of Birth is held here in high estimation; they plume themselves greatly on being related to a Chief, who they sometimes stile, 'Agee taloonga tello fennua,' which signifies as near as I can make out, 'Lord in Heaven and Earth.' The greatest distinction in Dress is the Hahoo or Cloth worn by people of Rank, being very neatly plaited.

Wednesday 18th This Forenoon the Marines were exercised on Shore, and in the Evening some Fireworks were played off. Thus far every thing went on Smoothly, yet the Natives, however well disposed towards us, were not capable of withstanding Temptation when a fair opportunity offered of stealing any thing, which frequently occasioned quarrels and in the End, destroyed that mutual confidence and good fellowship we so happily set out with.

Some of the Superiour People being detected, it was hoped that making an example of them, would deter other Offenders. They were accordingly punished with a degree of severity that had never before taken place. This, unfortunately, did not answer the intention; on the contrary, desire of revenge became an additional Motive. Scarce a day afterwards passed, without some of our people being robbed and insulted. Instead of asking us into their Houses, which they had hitherto done whenever we passed by, the Doors of their Plantations were Shut and fastened against us. Most of the Sailing Canoes left the Bay and it was evident, they began to be tired of our company. An Accident happened about this time, that did not at all help to Soften matters: A Turkey Cock and some Sheep were Stole from the Tent, and as there was reason to supose this was done by the direction of the Chiefs, Captain Cook seized on Powlahow, Finow, and Fattefai, who were detained till restitution was made, which happened the same day. Notwithstanding all our Quarrels and disputes, we were upon tolerable good terms with all the Principal Chiefs again, before we Sailed; but did not recover the good will of the generality of the Natives.

Their complexion is a dark Olive. The Men are Stout, Active and perfectly well made. In wrestling with them, our people were almost constantly worsted. Their Boxing being different from the English method, which is generally looked upon as the Standard, induced some of our Men to enter the Ring against them, thinking to retrieve the Credit lost at wrestling; but in this they were so much mistaken, that, of 4 or 5 who tried, not one escaped being drubbed, and as they did not take the beating well the moderation and good temper before remarked in the Natives, were heartily laughed at.

They are very handy and have great contrivances. Some of their Thefts were executed with a degree of Genius, or rather finesse, that proved them well skilled in the Art of Confederacy. In Traffick they are fair dealers, and on the whole, I like them the best of any Indians I have been acquainted with. The Women are remarkably fine limbd and were they not rather Masculine, would be as desirable as the Otaheite Women. They are both equally kind to Strangers.

When a Relation dies, they disfigure themselves either by cutting off a little finger, burning their Arms in circular Rings, beating the Skin off their Cheek bones, or cutting the Hair Short and rubbing the Head with a mixture of Lime and Oil. Girls that were one day remarkable for their Beauty have been So altered by the lop of their Hair and the paint above mentioned as to appear quite ugly the next. This Custom is common to both Sexes.

They are very carefull of their Sick and Shew great respect and attention to the Aged. An Elderly Chief when he lays down to rest, is commonly attended by 2 or 3 women, whose business is to drum with their Hands on different parts of his Body, till he is fast asleep. This they call Tuggi tuggi.

It is customary for restrictions to be laid on individuals, which obliges them to abstain for a limited time, from some of the most common necessaries of Life. Any thing so forbidden is expressed by the word <u>Tabu</u>. Sometimes they are prohibited the use of Water or any thing cooked in water. Sometimes a Hog is under Tabu, in which case he may not be killed. If a Coconut Tree, the nuts may not be taken off, before the Term of the <u>Tabu</u> is expired. Whether this Custom is part of their Religion or what penalty is incurred by a breach, I know not; but they are very strict Observers of it. When anything is given them, they express thankfulness by laying it on their Head.

The Tongitabu Language is more distinct and intelligible than the Otaheite; being less composed of Vowels, and not affording so many instances of words nearly alike, conveying different meanings. The G and K are sounds not used by the Otaheitans and which they are not able to pronounce. In many words the Change of Language may be traced from the Society Islands to the westward as in Boa, a Hog, at Otaheite; Boakka, at Tongitabu; and Wacka at Horn Island. [Burney's list of Tongan words omitted.]

Monday 23rd The Cutters of both Ships were sent in Search of a passage to the Eastward. The next Evening they returned, having found one, but very narrow and intricate.

Wednesday 25th The Boats were sent to the Westward, but returned the same day, without finding a passage that way.

Thursday, July 3rd This morning, Hove up our Anchors and ran out of the Harbour. At 11 Anchord without the Reef that makes the Northern part of the Harbour. The Entrance of the Eastern passage being open to us. [Bearings omitted.] In the Afternoon were obliged to moor, on account of the irregularity of the Tides.

The Tents and Observatories were continued ashore, on account of the Eclipse of the Sun, July 5th and here we hoped to gain Some Credit by displaying our Skill in Prophecy, as, on a Similar Occasion, Columbus had done; but these expectations were defeated by the Cloudiness of the Weather, which rendered the Eclipse visible only at times, through a Telescope.

The following presents were made by Captain Cook to the Indian Chiefs. To Powlahow, A Bull and Cow, and a pair of Goats. To Finow, a Horse and Mare, with an English Boar and Sow. And to Molliwagge some Sheep. Whilst at Anamooka, Finow had a pair of Rabbits given him. Besides these Animals which are all new to them, they have made shift to Steal 6 Cats, since the affair of the Cats at Happi, and which can be but ill spared from Ships Swarming with Rats as ours are.

It was suposd these people had no Dogs, and the first we saw this time were thought to have been bred from a Dog and Bitch left here by the Resolution last Voyage. But from the Numbers seen afterwards, it is certain they were provided before. The Sheep given to Molliwagge being neglected, and ill used by the Natives; Captain Cook, when the Tents were struck took them on board again.

7th 8th and 9th Boats Employed sounding in the Passage to the Eastward.

Whilst we lay here a Solemn festival was observed on Shore, which they call Annachee, held on account of Powlahow's eldest Son arriving at a certain age. At this feast, which lasted 3 days, I was not present. We were told, that in a few weeks after our departure a number of men were to be sacrificed as an Offering to their Gods.

Thursday 10th Wind ESE. At 7 in the morning, got under Sail all day turning to windward between the Reefs and Islands that form the passage. Most part of the forenoon a Strong Tide in our favour. At Sunset (the Resolution having come too before) Anchord with the Best Bower in 50 fms & veered to a whole Cable; at a Short half mile distance from the Shore of Tongitabu; but being unluckily too near the Edge of a Bank, drove off, having no ground at 120 fathoms. Hove the Anchor up, and got under Sail again. At 1 in the morning Anchord near the Resolution in 47 fms. Distant from the Shore ¼ of a mile. [Bearings omitted.]

Friday 11th At 11 in the Forenoon, weighd. Wind Easterly. All the Afternoon, turning to Windward. At Sunset, got through the passage and by Midnight having Weatherd the Easternmost part of Tongitabu, stood to the SSE for Ooha, or Middleburgh.

Saturday 12th In the Forenoon, Anchord between the North and West points of Ooha and Moord. [Bearings omitted.] This is the Same Road the Resolution and Adventure Anchord in 1773. Finow was to have accompanied us hither, but was prevented by the death of an Old Lady whose funeral he was obliged to attend, and on whose account, he was to part with a very good Head of Hair. A Market was opened at the Landing place for provisions of which a good Stock was purchased and several Casks of Pork Salted for Sea Use. Captain Cook presented the Agee of Ooha with a Ram and Ewe, which he seemed to set a greater Value on than Molliwagge had.

Tuesday 15th This Afternoon, two of the Resolution's people, walking in the country, were stripped and beaten; on which account, Captain Cook sent a party of Marines ashore, whose appearance had such an effect, that not only the things were restored, but the Thief delivered up. He was next day ransomed for a large Hog. Every Article of Trade we brought was marketable before we left these Islands. Many Things not regarded at first, became Valuable as their use was discovered. The most capital Articles were blue and green glass Beads, Hatchets, Linnen, and all kinds of glass Ware.

Thursday 17th This forenoon got under Sail. Wind SE and stood to the Southward. At Sunset, took our Departure from Ooha, bearing any distant 2 or 3 Leagues, which was the last we saw of the Friendly Islands. Made the best of our Way to the South and Eastward till we crossed the 20th degree of South Latitude, after which we steered to the Northward of East having Variable Winds.

Tuesday 29th At ½ past 6 this Evening, were taken with a Heavy Squall of Wind which carried away our Main top mast, Split most of our Sails, and did us other considerable damage. By Midnight cleared the Wreck, all of which was saved, except a little of the running Rigging. Kept firing Guns in the night for the Resolution whom we lost sight of at 11. Soon after daylight saw her again.

Wednesday 30th The Weather too rough to attempt getting up another Topmast.

Thursday 31st The Sea being smoother and the weather more moderate, got the broken stump down and the Spare Main topmast up, when we found the head of the Main mast Sprung and were obliged to get the Top mast down again.

Friday, August 1st Woulded the Head of the Mainmast and Rigged a Spare Jib Boom for a Topmast on which we set a Mizen Topsail, the Mainmast being judged not strong enough to bear a larger Sail.

Sunday, 3rd Served Ship provisions to the Ships Company, our fresh Stock and Vegetables being all expended. The Anamooka & Tongitabu Water turns out much better than we could have expected.

Friday 8th In Latitude 24° South fell in with the SE Trade. The same day about Noon discovered an Island to the Northward of us. Ran towards it till Sunset when we hauld our Wind and Stood off and on during the Night.

Saturday 9th At day light Bore away for the Land. At 7 haul'd round the SW point and soon after brought too under the Lee of the Island. Had Soundings at about half a mile distant from the Reef, depth 30 fms, fine sand. The extremes of the Land bearing EBN and South.

Some Canoes came off but would not venture on board. This Island is called Otobui [Tubuai in the scattered Tubuai Archipelago in southern French Polynesia] by the Natives, and is 4 miles in length, high uneven Land. It appeared on, first making it like 2 seperate Islands being high at each end, and low in the middle. It is surrounded by a Reef at a good distance from the Shore, with openings that seem Navigable for Ships. At a little distance from the East End lay 3 small, low Islands. [Bearings omitted.]

At 9 in the forenoon, made Sail to the Northward.

Journal of Henry Roberts

Tuesday, April 29th Several Canoes [from Anamooka] visited us from the Shore & traded for Hogs, Plantains, Cocoa Nutts etc. At 8 Anamooka bore NW. Most of the morning Standing off and on waiting for the Boats. At 11 the Cutter returned, loaded with grass for the Cattle & some few fruits.

Wednesday 30th At 1 PM the Pinnace returned, having purchased 7 Hogs, plantains, bread fruit etc. Bore away for the Point of the Reef leading to Anamooka. A Number of Canoes with many of the Inhabitants along side bartering for a few small Hogs, Bread Fruit, Yams, Bananas, Haddocks, & Fowls etc. This Day Regulations & Restrictions were read concerning trading with the Indians.

Thursday, May 1st Working into Anamooka Road, soundings from 40 to 41 fathoms. Hoisted out the large Cutter. Sent her to sound to the South of Anamooka. The Natives trading as yesterday.

Punished George Barber, Carpenters Mate, with 6 lashes for Disobeying the Orders read yesterday, & James James, Boatswain Mate for Neglect of Duty. At 10 the cutter returned from soundings & reported to be a good Harbour, & free passage through the Reefs between great & little Anamooka, with a convenient landing for the Boats upon a fine sandy Beach in the Southern Part of the Island.

The Natives led them to two wells of fresh water, but these being small, & lying a considerable distance from the landing place, we made sail for the Road on the Northern side of the Isle, where we could water the Ship with less difficulty from a Pond which was much larger, yet not nearer. Stopp'd serving Ships Provisions of every specie.

Friday 2nd Sent the Cutter to the Shore to cut grass for the Cattle. Punished Richard Young, captain's cook, for Neglect of Duty. Employed in the hold. A number of Canoes with Indians trading along side. Served 1½ lbs. of fresh Pork, to each of the people & sent 3 Hogs on board the Discovery for her Crews. Served 5 fowls to every 6 Men this day.

Saturday 3rd The 2nd Lieut with a party sent on shore to trade & purchase provisions for the Ships Companys. Captain Cook, having procured a House from the Chiefs for our Peoples residence during our stay, sent the Horses & Sheep to graze & refresh on Shore. Carpenters sent to cut wood. Employed in the Fore Hold. Served one pound of Fresh Pork to each man to continue daily while we get constant supplies. Great many of the Natives on Board trading.

Sunday 4th Employed as yesterday, the party on Shore cutting grass & drying it for the Cattle. Bread fruit, plantains etc boiled in the Coppers daily for the People.

Monday 5th Punished Thomas Garraty, Marine, with 12 lashes for Neglect of Duty. Served Fowls to the Ships Company. Employed watering & stowing the Hold.

Tuesday 6th This day we were visited by the King & governor of Tongataboo or Amsterdam and this and the other neighbouring Isles, with several other chiefs & attendants. Bartering with Indians as before.

Wednesday 14th The Chief, whose name is Feenow, accompanying us with many of the Indians in their sailing & paddling Canoes. They gave us an Account of a large Island to the NE, where we intend examining.

Thursday 15th Several Canoes came off to us. The Chief Feenow came in a large sailing Canoe with Hogs, Fruit etc.

Friday 16th Bore round some Breakers, which lie off a point of the Reef, and an Island is within the point called Nanivea. These Breakers are perfectly detached from the main Reef. Many Canoes along side & Feenow, constantly visiting us every Morning & retiring to one of the Isles in the Evening with a number of his attendants. These Islands are those which the Natives made mention of to us, called Ahpie.

Monday 19th The Chief Feenow made a present to Captain Cook & Omai consisting of 4 Hogs, Fowls & 2 Boat loads of Yams, Plantains, Cocoa Nutts, Bread Fruit etc. Sent the Cutter round the Point of the Reef into a Bay to examine it. Natives continuing to supply, with many Hogs, etc.

Tuesday 20th The Marines of each Ship was sent on Shore to Exercise & seen by a vast multitude of the Inhabitants, with Feenow, who seemed highly delighted with their Manouvers. Firing afterwards, we were entertained with a War Heiva from the Natives. The proceeding Evening, Displayed a number of our Rockets & Fire works. The Indians expressing their Amazement & Admiration by their continual Shouts. In Return we were favour'd with a Dance & singing, accompanied with the Music by a number of young Cousins.

Tuesday 27th The Cutter sent with the Master to look for a Passage through the Reefs between the small Isle to the East of Callafanga. Came on board a Chief, whose name was Tetta-fee-he, with a Number of Attendants, who told us that he had greater power than Feenow. The people that were with him paid vast homage & respect.

Wednesday 28th The Cutter returned from reconnoitering the Reefs, found a Passage & no Reef to interrupt us, in Sight. The Chief Tetta-fee-he paid us another Visit & brought a present to Captain Cook [of] 2 Hogs, Yams, Cocoa Nutts etc. with an Elegant Head Dress or Bonnet of Red Feathers. A Number of the Natives round us bringing their different articles to Market.

Saturday 31st Working up to Lofanga, had irregular soundings close under the lee of the Island. Saw the Breakers close under our lee bow. Hove all aback & were round just clear of them. Fired 3 guns & made the signal to our Consort.

Tuesday, June 3rd The Boats returned with Grass, hoisted them out, the Pinnace & small Cutter sent to Ogodoo, to trade with the Natives & cut Grass & Large Cutter with the Master sounding towards Affeva & round the other Isles. Tetta-fee-he met us on those & presented Captain Cook with some Hogs, Bread Fruit & Plantains etc.

Sunday 8th Boats bringing off provisions & Refreshments from the Shore. Tetta-fee-he and Feenow came from the other Islands with seven Large Canoes & many attendants.

Wednesday 11th Punished William Butler, with 12 lashes and James King, seaman, with 6 lashes for Neglect of Duty. Sent the Master to examine a Bay. Found anchorage. In Tongatabu, promised a House from the Chiefs. Sent the people on Shore to fence it in, making a small enclosure. Put the Cattle & all the Stock there for refreshment. The Gunner on Shore Bartering with the Natives for provisions. Both ships surrounded with Canoes, at least 150, with Men, Women & Children, each bringing their different Commodities to Market.

Thursday 12th Sent the Tent with a party of Marines to the Shore under the Command of the Lieut. Sent the Topsails to the Tent with sailmakers [and] Carpenters to cut wood. Punished William Butler, seaman, with 6 lashes for Negligence. The Inhabitants continuing with us as usual.

Friday 13th In the afternoon sent the observatory & instruments to use on Shore [and later] sent Hands to clean the wells out, where we intend watering.

Natives along side as usual, the young lasses favouring us with their company & diverting us in the Evening with their enchanting Songs & Heivaa's.

Saturday 14th Natives supplying us very plentifully with large Hogs, Yams & other necessary refreshments.

Thursday 19th Punished John Griffiths, Cooper, with 6 lashes for Disobedience of Orders. Captain Cook presented the Chiefs of the Island with a Horse & Mare, a young Bull & Cow, & a Ram Sheep & two Yews, for which they appeared very thankful & Delighted.

Friday 20th In the Evening Displayed some few of our Fireworks on Shore to the astonishment & admiration of near two thousand Indians. In the Morning, the Marines of the two Ships were Manouvered with different Firings [of the cannon]. Afterwards, we was entertained with a grand Heivah from the Natives.

Saturday 21st The Natives continuing to Trade as Usual. The Chiefs brought a present to Captain Cook, consisting of 4 Hogs & a vast abundance of Yams, then accorded us with a War Hevah, performed by a Multitude of Men. The greatest Regality and Uniformity observed in each motion, concluded with a pleasing, lively Dance & singing by a beautiful assembly of Young Damsels. The Whole accompanyed with Music made up of Drums & Flutes.

Wednesday 25th The Boat returned, having found a Clear Sea to the Eastward, but a very indifferent passage leading between the Island which makes the Northern Extremity of the Harbour & a small Isle & Reefs, which lie to the Northward of it, trending in Different Directions lay about for Miles & no more than ¾ of a Cable in breadth, with a strong Eddy Tide setting to the Eastward. The Launch brought on Board a Load of Yams.

The boat out to the north trying for a clear passage. Got on board the Main Topsail & bent it. The Inhabitants, with us as usual, but thieve & pilfer every thing they can possibly clasp hands on, particularly when any of our People make an Excursion in the Country. They are guilty of Violent Acts, wrenching their Guns & other matter by force from them. The greatest threats will not retard them in [harassing our] People on Shore making Hay.

Friday, July 4th Employed occasionally. Natives with us as usual, but bring but few things to market. Found another small Channel through the Reef leading to the East, a little superior to the other, not being so long & somewhat broader. Got the tent, Observatory & Astronomical Instruments on Board.

Tuesday 8th Employed cleaning the Ship Fore & Aft. Party of Hands Sent to cut Brooms & Grass. Captains Cook & Clerke, accompanied by some of their Officers, went up the Lagoon to the East where Fetta-fee-he or Paulehow with Feenow & several other of the first Chiefs reside, at which place they gave us to understand would be a grand Ceremony of the young Son of Paulehow eating in presence of the Father, which Custom is annually performed & celebrated.

Thurday 10th The Captains & Officers returned from their Excursion having been very agreeable entertained & treated with the greatest Friendlyness & courtesy from the Indians.

Friday 11th In the Morning unmoored, Weighed & made Sail, working to Windward between the Isles & Reefs.

Saturday 12th The [expedition arrived at] Amsterdam [Eua Island]. Employed occasionally. Few of the Natives visiting us in their Canoes, with a small quantity of Cocoa Nutts, Yams, etc.

Sunday 13th Employed Drawing of Yams and making Nippers. Sent the Launch for Water and Hands to Cut Grass.

Monday 14th Employed as before, the Water we got from the Shore very breakish but servd for the Cattle's use. Punished Thomas Hereford, Marine, for refusing to Stand Centry when called on.

Wednesday 16th Punished Job Clay with 12 lashes for Neglect of Duty. Unmoored & hove into onto a whole Cable. Boats bringing on Board yams with abundance of Cocoa Nutts.

Thursday 17th During our Stay at these Isles, the Natives continued to supply us very plentifully with Hogs, Cocoa Nutts, Yams, Bananas, Shaddocks, in short, every produce of the Country. We have destroyed at a moderate computation from at least 2000 Hogs with Fowls etc, including the crew of the other Sloop. This unexpected Refreshment enabled us to Salt & Cure 4 puncheons & 1 Hogshead of pork, which proves extremely sweet & good, that's served Daily to the people 1 pound per Man. Yams we have also procured in great abundance, enough to supply the Ships Company, as a substitute for Bread [for] the passage to Otaheite, on a supposition of being 3 Months on the Seas at 10 pound per Man a Week.

The Natives, behaving with the greatest Friendliness & good Nature, but I did not perceive they were sorry or the least affected at our parting, or at any other time shew that gratitude which our Friends at Otaheite shew.[22]

Thursday 31st Fresh Gales & Squally weather with small Rain. A great SSW Swell. Made a Signal for the Discovery to make more sail. Many Pintada Birds and Petrals about.

Friday, August 1st The Discovery fired a Gun & made the Signal for speaking. Sent the small Cutter. Returned and informed us that she had sprung the Head of Her Main Mast and Shipt a heavy sea, which wash'd several of their spars overboard. Sent them a Spritsail Top Yard, with the Carpenter to inspect. The Damaged place [was] in the Main Mast [and it was] reported, that the Head was violently wrung & Doubtful whether it would bore a Main Top and sail when [repaired].

Saturday 9th The Land seen Yesterday proved to be an Island [Tubuai]. The Island encircled by a coral Reef and no Entrance for Ships, but there are small breaks which boats might pass through, and land conveniently. Saw many Inhabitants on the beach, when 2 Canoes with several of them came off near the Ship, and gaz'd with a seeming Ammuzement, but did not venture on board. Their complextion is of a Deep Copper Collour, Stout, robust made people, chiefly long Hair. Could not perceive any cloathing they had. When they returned to the Shore, they intimated we should follow them. Omai asked the name of the Isle, to which they replied imperfectly Tee-boo-ie. The Country is very hilly, but the Skirts of it is low & level, covered with trees.

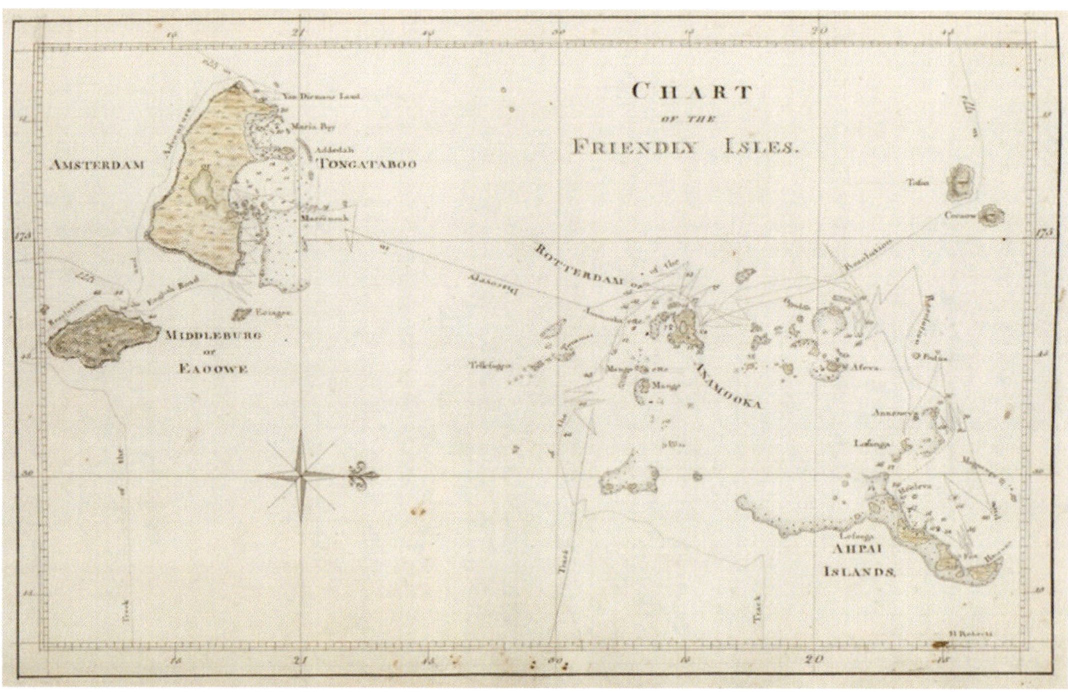

Henry Roberts, "Chart of the Friendly Isles [Tonga]," July 1777. Roberts Journal p. 103, Dixson Library, State Library of New South Wales, DLMSQ 151-52 and DLMSF 2.

5

TAHITI
AUGUST–DECEMBER 1777

The expedition entered the waters of French Polynesia at Tubuai before reaching Tahiti in mid-August. Cook decided to land at Oaitepeha Bay, on the southern flanks of the island of Tahiti, before returning to his favorite anchorage at Matavai Bay on the north. At Oaitepeha Bay they learned about the recent visit of a Spanish expedition of missionaries from Lima. While the Spaniards were gone, they had erected a modest church and left an inscribed cross, confirming the dates of their visit, which both journalists described with keen interest. Cook added the dates of his five visits to the reverse side of the cross, confirming his record of more frequent time ashore.

The return to Matavai Bay was shorter than earlier expeditions, just over a month, but it still afforded the captain and his crew plenty of time to renew old acquaintances, exchange presents, resupply the vessels, and set off fireworks. Many of the crew also took the opportunity to engage with the women despite Cook's protestations. There was a brief scare that the Spanish had returned to Oaitepeha Bay, but after an inspection that rumor proved false. Cook had never been to nearby Mo'orea, called *Immco* or *Eimao* in the journals, so he set out to the nearby island at the end of September. Unfortunately, the visit was marred by the theft of a goat and Cook's overreaction in tracking down the thief, including the rampant burning of homes and canoes. When the miscreant was finally found across the island, the commander had him punished by cropping his ears, a dreadful reprimand that disgusted the crew. Cook repeated this punishment for another thief in Huahine.

Mai established his permanent home in Huahine at a site he selected with the consent of the local chiefs. The ships' carpenters then built a stout wooden building for all his European possessions, and the structure was soon surrounded by a home built in the local style, pens for stock, and a large garden. When it was completed Mai settled into the compound with several servants, at least one wife, and the two young New Zealanders.

The homecoming at Huahine was marred by more theft and even desertions of a few seamen. Cook again reacted strongly, taking hostages in an effort to recover the stolen items and cropping another man's ears. This was a troublesome measure for the captain to take in Huahine, as it risked Mai's future from repercussions after the expedition's departure. The thief with cropped ears openly declared he would kill Mai, but he later relented. Despite these fears, when the expedition departed, Mai gave a celebratory dinner for Cook with the local chiefs. But he was apparently overcome with grief when Cook finally bid adieu. Burney explains that a signal was devised in case Mai was threatened after the expedition sailed for Ra'iātea, but he gave a favorable signal there was no problem after their departure, so the British left Tahiti assuming he was safe.[23]

Roberts records a growing number of punishments of the seamen, sometimes for uncertain transgressions, but always quite severe. When the ships sailed on to nearby Ra'iātea, they had to retrieve several deserters. Roberts was put in charge of one of the fruitless searches for a deserter. After other desertions, Cook had the local chief's family seized as hostages, so the Natives would help look for the deserters and secure their return. The local people apparently planned to capture Captain Clerke in retribution but, when their treachery was exposed, they instead redoubled their efforts and finally recovered the missing sailors.

Roberts also explained how the ships were fumigated to rid them of rats and cockroaches. The rats were driven down a plank fixed to the shore, presumably populating the islands with the vermin. The expedition finally sailed for Bora Bora, the last Tahitian island they visited. Opposing winds and seas kept them offshore, but they were able to ensnare and capture part of an anchor left behind by the French captain, Louis Antoine de Bougainville.

Journal of James Burney

Tuesday, August 12th At daylight Saw the Island of Olnaburgh bearing NE and at 7 Otaheite appears in Sight to the Westward. By Sunset were within 2 miles of the NE point of Tiarraboo, or Otaheite Etc. (i.e., little Otaheite, the name given to the SE division of the Island). Stood off and on all night.

Wednesday 13th In the morning made Sail for Oaitipeha Bay, where we anchord and moord, [Bearings omitted.] Distant off shore 1 mile.

John Webber, "A Human Sacrifice in a Morai in Ohteite [Tahiti]," circa 1781-83. Pen, wash, and water color showing a Tahitian sacrifice observed by Cook and Webber in early September 1777. A bound and prostrate man is in the foreground with a chief performing the ceremony at his feet. As part of the ceremony two drummers and other chiefs surround the spectacle, with the British observing at the right. Dixson Library, State Library of New South Wales, PXX 2, f. 10.

The first News we heard was of the Spaniards having been here. According to the Otaheitean accounts, they made their first appearance, shortly after Captain Cooks departure hence in the Resolution 1774. On hearing Captain Cook was at the Society Isles, they left Otaheite and ran down to Huaheine and Ulietea [Ra'iātea]; but missing the Resolution did not Anchor there. Some Months after this they again appeared at Otaheite and Staid a considerable time in Oaitipeha Bay, where they set up a wooden House, which they had brought in pieces numbered. This house we found here, with some Old Clothes and Lumber in it. Before the Door, a Cross was erected, with the following inscription.

CHRISTVS. VINCIT. CAROLVS III. IMPERAT. 1774

While they remained here, the Captain of one of their Ships died and was buried ashore. At their departure they took away 4 of the Natives whom they carried to Lima, and left a person behind called Martemo (according to the Otaheite pronunciation) who lived on the Island, till the return of the Spanish Ships with the 4 Otaheiteans.

The Spaniards left a great many Lima Hogs, which are now mixed with the Otaheite breed; some Goats, Dogs, a Bull and Cow, the latter of which died. They likewise planted Vines, which have been neglected. Omiah got some Slips [cuttings] and means to cultivate them where he fixes his residence.

Coming here immediately from the Friendly Islands, it is impossible to avoid taking notice of the difference of form and Shape in the People, and drawing a comparison by no means favourable to the Otaheitans. Nevertheless the Women, though not so perfectly well made, have in general, handsomer faces and a softness of feature, truly feminine; and which was only to be found in a few individuals at the Friendly Islands.

Thursday 14th All Ships provisions were stopped, great plenty of pork and Vegetable being procured. Spirits likewise were stopped by consent of both Ships companies, it being represented to them, that, as we had missed the Season this year to the Northward, there was great probability of our falling short in that Article, in which case, it was better to go without in a Warm Country than in a cold one.

We deferred doing anything with our Main mast till we should arrive at Mattavi [Matavai] Bay. Our only employment at present was getting the Ship caulked.

Omiah found one of his Sisters Married and Settled at Oaitipeha, and behaved in a very kind and generous manner to her and her Husband, who was a greedy Rascal, ever begging and never Satisfied. Indeed, Omiah's Vanity and extravagance was but too great an encouragement to people of this Stamp. He always went drest in the most tawdry manner he could contrive, and was constantly attended by a large train of Followers whose only motive was to profit by his profusions and carelessness. Omiah did not however forget his court to the great men: To Owyeduar, the Aree of Tiarraboo, he presented a fine piece of red feathers, and sent another equally good for Otu, the Aree at Mattavi.

Our Otaheite Friends we found as great Thieves as formerly. Any person caught in the fact, we Shaved half his Head, one Eyebrow, and took off half his Beard; which effectually rid us of his company till his Hair grew again, and at the same time made him an object of ridicule and contempt to his Countrymen: whereas a more serious punishment always created pity and compassion for the Offender. Before our departure, some fireworks were played off on shore. Captain Cook likewise made the following inscription on the other side of the Spanish Cross.

GEO. III. REX. AN. 1767. 1769. 1773. 1774. 1777.

Saturday 23rd Wind Easterly. This morning got under Sail and left Oaitipeha. At Sunset, the Resolution anchored in Mattavi Bay. Our Ship being 2 or 3 miles astern, and Night coming on, we were obliged to keep the Sea all Night.

Sunday 24th At 11 in the Forenoon Anchord in the Bay, in ¼ less 5 fms Sandy bottom and Moord, Small Bower to the NNW in 11 fathoms. [Bearings omitted.] Unbent our Sails, began to Strip the Main mast and raised Sheers for getting it out. The Tents of both Ships were erected near Point Venus and all the Cattle sent on Shore. Captain Cook gave to Otu, a Bull and 2 Cows, some Sheep, peacocks, ducks and Geese. It was now discovered that Otu had been cheated of the piece of red feathers sent him by Omiah; the Tiarraboo Chief with whom it was intrusted, having substituted a much smaller piece in its Stead. Otu sent a Messenger to demand restitution of Owyeduar, who would not be prevailed on to part with it. However to compromise Matters the Tiarraboo people we were informed, afterwards sent Otu a man they had devoted to Sacrifice and who was to Serve Otu as a Victim on the next occasion.

James Burney, "A View in Huaheine [Tahiti]," October 1777. A view of a bay or inlet surrounded by trees, including palm trees, and native huts. Burney stuck a Webber drawing into his journal of a cabbage plant at Kergulen's Island, but this image of the Tahitian landscape may have been produced by Burney himself. Burney Journal p. 94, Mitchell Library, State Library of New South Wales, Safe 1/64 and 1/79.

So great a Value was set on red feathers, that Otu gave 10 large Hogs for a Tongitabu head dress made of them. Here we found Odidde, the man who went with Captain Cook in his expedition to the Southward [in] 1773 [and] 1774 and for whom many things were sent from England as a present.

Tuesday 26th At 8 this Morning got out our Mainmast and sent on Shore to be fished and repaired.[24] Employed Watering, repairing the Sails and rigging, and Caulking the Ship.

Wednesday 27th This forenoon a report was raisd of 2 Spanish Men of War being arrived at Oaitipeha. This was afterwards backd by the testimony of an Indian, who affirmed he had been on board the Spanish Ships, and produced a piece of Spanish Cloth quite new. Captain Cook immediately sent Lieut. Williamson in the Resolution's Cutter, round for information, the Indian going with him. In the mean time we got all our Guns mounted and cleared the Decks. The Otaheitans all the preceding day had been very inquisitive to know whether Spanish and English Ships fought when they met.

Friday 29th In the Night the Boat returned with an account of no Ships having been seen or heard of. Their Indian informer jumped out of the Boat and made his escape before they got half way to Oaitipeha.

Went on again with our business as usual. On examining our Casks of Bread, found some damp: Got 13 Batts on Shore to be sifted and Aired. As the Ship was now considerably lighter than at leaving England, we took in 11 Tons of Stone ballast. Being rather overmasted makes it the more necessary to keep her well down in the Water.

September 5th Got in the Mainmast and began to rig it.

Sunday 21st These last 2 or 3 days a great many War Canoes have come into the Bay from different parts of the Island; and this morning was a Grand Review, the Fleet consisting of 65 large Canoes decorated with Colours and tricked out in all their finery in which were about 1300 men. This force was collected on account of a quarrel with the people of Immco [Mo'orea]. We were informed that 2 men had been sacrificed on this occasion. An Old Chief named Towhah, went over to Immco, with a Strong party, and was to have been joined by the rest. But Maheine, the Aree of Immco, managed matters so well, as to buy off Otu and soon after Towhah was obliged to return, not without leaving marks of his Anger. Some of the Chiefs were much displeased with Out's conduct, who acted without their concurrence.

The Otaheiteans in general, did not speak of Otu with any great veneration, except the inhabitants of Mattavi and Oparre, which two districts were more immediately under his jurisdiction. Some little things he was guilty of, in his intercourse with us, shewed him but poorly qualified to support the Dignity and consequence of an Aree. Old Towhah seemed to be the most gentlemen like Character of any of the Otaheite Chiefs. Of him Omiah bought a very good Sailing Canoe, chiefly for red feathers, and borrowed a number of Men to manage her.

Saturday 27th Being ready for Sea, Struck the Tent, and got the remainder of the Cattle on board. While they were ashore, a young Ram was killed by the Spanish Dogs, for which Captain Cook ordered all that were seen to be shot. This effectually Secured the Sheep from further Mischief, for the Otaheitans immediately tied up their large Dogs.

Monday 29th This Afternoon got under Sail and left Mattavi Bay, steering to the Westward for Immco. Whilst we were heaving the Anchors up, Otu came on board, to complain of the Girls going with us from Otaheite, several staying on board by their own desire. But in consequence of this complaint, they were all sent ashore. We afterwards learnt Otu was disappointed, and that we had mistaken his Errand, as he did not care about the Girls, but expected his consent to have been obtained by some considerable presents.

As we ran down by Oparre, Captain Cook fired his great Guns by way of Salutation to his Otaheite Friends at parting. After Sunset we brought too and lay with our Maintopsail aback all Night.

Friday 30th At Daylight made Sail. At 7 brought too off the North Side of Immco and sent Boats in shore to Sound. . . . Anchor'd in a good Harbour fast to the West Shore. [Bearings omitted.] On the North Side of Immco are 2 Harbours, that in which we Anchored is the Westernmost. As we came in, we saw the remains of several Houses that had been burnt by Towhah. Here we found plenty of Wood and employed a party of Men on shore cutting it. The days after our arrival most of the Otaheite Girls who had been sent on shore at Mattavi on account of Out's complaint, came on board to take up their quarters with their old Friends again.

Thursday, October 2nd Maheine, the Aree of Immco, visited the Ships this morning and received several presents. By the end of this Week, compleated Wooding & Watering.

Wednesday 8th The Indians having Stole 2 Goats belonging to Captain Cook, some Canoes were seized on by way of reprisal. The Resolutions Cutter was sent to the Eastward, and in the Evening returned with one of the Goats.

Thursday 9th The other Goat not being restored, the Boats of both Ships were Armed and went to the Westward, the Marines marching round by Land the same way. In the Evening the whole party returned without the Goat, after having destroyed some Houses and Canoes.

Friday 10th At Daylight, the Boats with the Marines went to the Eastward. In the Afternoon the Indians brought the Goat to the Ships. At Sunset the Boats returned. In these expeditions, Omiah secured for himself 2 good Canoes and a quantity of Plank was carried on board the Resolution, which Served afterwards to build his House.

Saturday 11th Hove up our Anchors and at Noon ran out of the Harbour, being bound for the Society Islands. Omiah in his Sailing Canoe leading the Van[guard]. His prize Canoes were hoisted into the Resolution.

Sunday 12th About 3 in the morning, Omiah fired a Musket which we imagined was intended as a Signal for Land. We learnt afterwards his Canoe has nearly overset in a Squall, by bad steerage and that his firing was meant to signify his distress.

At Daylight Saw the Island of Huaheine. At Noon Anchord in the Northern passage of Owharre Harbour with the Best Bower in 19 fms and got small anchors and Hawsers ready for Warping farther in. The Best Bower Anchor having hookd the Rocks, were unable to weigh it. After many unsuccessful efforts Slipped the Cable and left a Boat on the Buoy to prevent the Indians stealing it. All the Evening Employed Warping up the Harbour [Bearings omitted.]. The Tents were erected and the Marines of both Ships sent on shore for a Guard. Found part of the Cable damaged by the Rocks, which we cut off. Omiah, whose intention hitherto had been to settle at Huaheine, now declared he would fix at Ulietea. This new Resolution did not last above 2 or 3 days, when he resumed his former plan again, the Chief people of Huaheine allotting him some Land. The Carpenters of both Ships were sent on Shore to make a close wooden House, whilst Omiah with his people built a very good House after the fashion of the Country to live in, the Wooden being designed for a store house to keep his things safe.

The present Aree of Huaheine was a Young Boy named Territerrear. Aree who governed when we were here last Voyage, had dwindled into a private man, and retained none of his former consequence. The Mother of Territerrear had a great Share in the Management of Affairs and appeared very capable.

Wednesday 22nd A grand Heavah was performed on shore this Evening, at which several of our folks were present, the dancing part by a very pretty Girl just arrived from Bolabola [Bora Bora]. In the midst of this Entertainment, Mr. Baily missed a Brass Sextant out of his Tent, and soon after, Captain Cook entered the Heavah House and put an end to the performance. After much enquiry, Omiah seized upon a Ulietea man who was strongly suspected to be the Thief, and Captain Cook sent him on board the Resolution. A strict lookout was kept the remainder of the Night to prevent any Canoes from leaving the Bay, lest the Sextant should be carried off the Island. Some Canoes were seized paddling along shore and taken on board the Ships. Next Morning, however, the Sextant was brought back, the prisoner having given information where it might be found. The Canoes were released, but the Offender was punished with the loss of his Ears and Hair. This proved a very troublesome business to Omiah, for when the Man got on shore, he openly declared that as soon as the Ships sailed he would revenge the loss of his Ears with Omiah's Death, and as an earnest of his future intentions, he destroyed all the Vines, Omiah had brought from Tiarraboo and planted here, for which on the forenoon of

Saturday 25th . . . he was taken again and put in close confinement on board the Resolution. All this time we were employed examining the remainder of our Bread, which was sent on shore to be Aired and Sifted. 1856 lbs. (near 4 Weeks Bread at full allowance) was found bad and condemned, being damaged partly by damp, and partly by Vermin.

Wednesday 29th In the Night by the Centinel's neglect, the prisoner found means to escape. The next day a Reward of 20 Hatchets was offered by the 2 Captains for the reapprehending him, but to no purpose.

31st The Escape of this man obliged Omiah to be constantly on his Guard, and not without reason, for on Friday Night an attempt was made to burn his House, which he was fortunate enough to prevent, and with the Assistance of Some of the Huaheine Chiefs, caught one of the party, who was next morning taken into confinement on board the Resolution. The Principal, Omiah's sworn Enemy, got clear off.

The time of our departure approaching, and Omiah's affairs being settled, he gave several dinners, to which the gentlemen of both Ships and some of the Huaheine Chiefs were invited. As Omiah was Doubtfull how his Countrymen would behave towards him after the Ships were gone, many long Orations were made by the Chiefs with promises of friendship and protection in case he or his property should be attacked. Being bound to Ulietea from here, Omiah had private instructions that if things turned out to his liking, he was to send two White Beads. If indifferent, two Brown Beads. And if he was ill used or in distress, two Blue Beads were to be the Signal.

Sunday, November 2nd This morning the man taken in the attempt to burn Omiah's House was released at the request of Territerrear's Mother, she engaging for his future good behaviour.

In the Afternoon hove up our anchors and ran out of the Harbour.

Omiah at parting with his Old Friends Shed Tears of real and unaffected Sorrow. The two Young Zealanders who staid with him, both shewed great reluctance at leaving us. These Boys had quite shaken off that savage disposition so inherent in their Countrymen. Tibarua, the eldest, was remarkable for being of a placid modest disposition. The other was a fine lively Boy, somewhat given to Mischief. There was left with Omiah an English Boar and Sow, a Horse and Mare, and a pair of Goats.

We stood towards Ulietea under an easy Sail till 11 o'clock and then brought too for the remainder of the Night. Wind Easterly.

Monday 3rd At Sunrise Bore away. Soon after, sailed round the South End of Ulietea [Ra'iātea] stood alongshore to the Northward. At 4 in the Afternoon Anchord in the passage of Ohamaneno Harbour in 29 fms and warped up the Harbour.

Tuesday 4th Made the Ship fast close to the South Shore and fixed a Brow from the Ballast port to High Water Mark, in hopes some of the Rats would leave us. The Resolution for the same reason, having hauld close in to the Northern Shore. We found Ulietea still under the government of Oreo, the same Chief who managed for Opune when we were here before. Opune lived at Bolabola and never came near us. Oreo and his family gave us a hearty wellcome.

We were obliged to strip our Foremast here, the Foremast Bolt in the Trussel-trees being broke and the Fore Cap Split. On getting the Spare Cap out of the Hold, it proved rotten and unfit for service. We therefore made use of the Old Cap again, after Strengthening it with Iron Hoops and Bolts.

Wednesday 12th Sent our powder on Shore to be Aired and Sifted, at a Small Sandy Island near the Entrance of the Harbour. Some Canoes from Huaheine brought us an account of Omiah's being in good health and living in harmony with his neighbours. When they left Huaheine he was trying to catch one of his Horses that had broke loose. We were not a little surprized at the Stealer of the Sextant making his appearance here, who told us he was friends with Omiah. Probably an Axe or two might have helped to accomodate Matters. This News of Omiah was confirmed by the arrival of his Sailing Canoe with 4 White Beads to Captain Cook, and to acquaint him his She Goat had died in Kidding. To repair this loss 2 young Goats were sent by the return of his Canoe.

Thursday 13th One of the Resolutions Marines who was Centinel ashore at the Astronomer's Tents, deserted in the Night with his Arms and Accoutrements.

Saturday 15th The Boats of both Ships went to the NE Side of the Island in search of the Deserter and there found him.

Monday 24th In the Morning two of our Company were missing. On enquiry among the Indians were informed, they had set out the Night before in a Canoe for the NE part of the Island, intending thence to pass over to Huaheine. Captain Clerke in the Resolutions Pinnace and our great Cutter went immediately after them.

Tuesday 25th Having received intelligence of their being at Otaha, Captain Cook went thither, but returned in the Evening without them, they having escaped to Bolabola. There was reason to apprehend if these people got clear off, their success would encourage others who might be disposed to leave us. It therefore became necessary to take some effectual step, and that no person for the future might be long about without being missed, the Ships companies were Mustered every day at Sunrise and Sunset.

As Oreo, besides being of the first consequence, was the most active and Stirring of any of the Chiefs, it was judged, the most likely method for recovering the Fugitives, would be, to make it his interest to exert himself.

Wednesday 26th An opportunity offered the next morning, Oreo's Son Tioora, his Daughter, Poeduar, and his Son in Law Baidoe (husband to Poeduar) coming aboard on a Visit. They were informed, after having got safe down in the great Cabin, that they would be detained untill our people were brought back. During their confinement, we were most disagreeably serenaded every morning, by the female relations and dependents of the prisoners, who lined the Shore and surrounded the Stern of the Ship in Canoes, to perform the ceremony of Lamenta-

Henry Roberts, "Otaheite, When Point Venus bears S.W. by W. 5 miles distant [Matavai Bay]," circa 1775. Water color drawing prepared during Robert's visit to Tahiti during Cook's Second Voyage. Mitchell Library, State Library of New South Wales, PXD 11, f. 16.

tion, which consisted in striking their Heads with Sharks Teeth till the blood ran down over their face and Shoulders, at the same time Shedding Tears and repeating set words in a most dismal tone. Each after having thus mourned a decent Share, became easy and chearfull, as if perfectly satisfied they had done their duty.

Though the men exhibited none of these marks of Sorrow, yet they were not idle. A plan was concerted that would have procured the release of their Chiefs had it been conducted with any common degree of prudence, which was no other than to use our own methods against us by seizing on the Captains in their Rambles. This Scheme failed from want of secrecy and not waiting [for] a proper opportunity.

Thursday 27th Afternoon. We had Notice given us by the Otaheite Girls who had all along stuck by the Ship, that the Indians were laying in wait for Captain Clerke, then walking on Shore. This tallying with Several Suspicious circumstances that had before been remarked, a large party went in quest of the Captain, and arrived time enough to prevent their making the attempt. Oreo had all the morning been very importunate with Captain Cook to go with him to the fresh Water River to bathe, which hitherto he had daily done, but omitted then on account of some business.

This project miscarrying, Oreo seriously went to work about getting our people, as the only means of setting his family at liberty and for that purpose the next morning he departed for Bolabola. Struck the Tents and got everything on board.

Friday 28th Cast off from the Shore and Warped the Ship into the middle of the Harbour where we moored. Best Bower in 15 fms soft sandy bottom. Stream Anchor to the Westward. [Bearings omitted.] Do not imagine we have got rid of many Rats by laying close to the Shore.

Sunday 30th This afternoon, Our Stragglers were brought on board, and the Indian prisoners released. The next week employed Wooding, completing our water and getting ready for Sea.

Sunday, December 7th At Noon Sailed out of the Harbour [and] Ran towards Bolabola till dark, when we Shorten'd Sail and Lay too till daylight.

Monday 8th By Noon were off the Entrance of a good Harbour on the West Side of Bolabola but the Tide of Ebb made so strong out, that the Resolution after making several Trips, without gaining ground, brought too Main Topsail to the Mast. The Boats of both Ships were hoisted out and went on shore, to enquire after one of the Bougainvilles Anchors, which we were told, was brought hither from Otaheite. Iron, the most valuable article of Traffic in the South Seas, was by this time become exceeding scarce. At 6 they returned with part of a broken Anchor Captain Cook bought of Opune, hoisted the Boats in and made Sail. Soon after Sunset lost sight of Bolabola, which was the last we Saw of the Society Islands.

In the Night ran to the NW till we imagined ourselves past Tubai, some small Islands that lay 4 or 5 Leagues NNW of Bolabola and then hauld up to the Northward. Wind ENE. Continued our Course to the Northward with a Moderate Trade Wind and fair weather.

It has been generally imagined, the Language of Otaheite and the Society Islands, is confined to few words, and though easily learnt. For my own part, with the help of above 300 words got by heart, and those the most common in use, I could never understand the Natives when talking to each other. Sometimes by their gestures and catching a word or two, the meaning of a Single Sentence or the Subject of their discourse might be gathered. In their intercourse with us, they commonly adopted our mistakes and method of pronunciation for the better dispatch of business, but when any Strange party arrived, we were half lost again, till the old Standards gave instructions to the New comers.

Thursday, 18th [Bearings omitted.] Saw a great number of Gannets, Tropic and Men of War Birds.

Journal of Henry Roberts

August 12th Saw Osnaburgh Island, and the South Point of Otaheite.

Wednesday 13th Being frequently becalmed under the High Land, Hoisted out the Pinnace & Cutter & attempted to Tow the Ship into Oite Peha Bay. But a light land breeze springing up baffled us, that we were obliged to stand out for the Night. At Daybreak, stood in for the Bay. Boats a head towing. Great many Canoes with our old Friends and Acquaintances round the Ships.

Thursday 14th The Captain went to the Shore [and] found that the Spaniards had visited this Place and built a small House with a Cross erected near it, on which there was this Inscription: **Christvs. Vincit. Carrlvs. 111. Imperat. 1774.** Saw also some Goats and many other things which they had left. We Got the Cattle on Shore. The Natives informed us that the Spaniards had given them a Bull & Cow.

Friday 15th Put the Ships Company to ½ allowance of Grog. The Captain acquainted them all his reasons for so doing, making known the Intent of the Voyage and the Improbabilities of getting any kind of supply after leaving these Isles. [The captain explained] the Purport of the Act for Discovering the NW passage or the straights to the NE with the premium as also that of reaching within a Degree of the North Pole, and farther. [He] added how much better it would be (though he left it to themselves) if they gave consent for the whole [the allowance of grog] being stopped, excluding on Saturday Nights, that every person had liberty to purchase Cocoa Nutts, which were brought in vast abundance. It remained not a moment under Consideration but every Man gave his approbation to it.

Employed in the Main Hold, getting provisions out of the ground Tier, Launch bringing on board Ballast. Served fresh Pork to the people. Our Meat, which we cured at the Friendly Isles, was continued to be serv'd daily, 1 pound per man, which was just expended the first day of our arrival here. Natives bringing on Board Hogs & every other produce of the Island in great plenty.

Thursday 21st Employed watering and cleaning the Ship below. Carpenters as Yesterday. Great many of the Natives on Board constantly.

Friday 22nd Employed occasionally. Carpenters as before. Captain Cook took the Spanish Cross down and had this Inscription wrote on it: Georgis, Tertius, Rae, Annis, 1767, 1769, 1773, 1774, 1777. Erected it again.

Saturday 23rd Unmoored, weigh'd and Came to sail as did the Discovery, standing on for the Northern point in sight.

Sunday 24th Anchored at Point Venus, great Many of the Natives on board.

Wednesday 27th Employed at the Rigging. A report prevailed here [in Matavai Bay] amongst the Indians of two Ships being in Oite Peha Bay. The 3rd Lieut sent in the Cutter to examine into the truth of it.

Friday 29th The Cutter returned [and] found the report of the two Ships false. Otoo with his attendance, and many of the Natives continually with us, supplying the two Ships with every necessary that the Island produces.

Saturday 30th Carpenters began caulking the ships side. Cleared Hawser. Killed a Number of large Hogs Daily for salting.

Henry Roberts, "Chart of Moorea Harbour in Eimao [Mo'orea, Tahiti]," October 1777. Roberts Journal p. 125, Dixson Library, State Library of New South Wales, DLMSQ 151-52 and DLMSF 2.

Tuesday, September 2nd Otoo with his family and acquaintenances Daily visiting us with several blooming Damsels attending.

Monday 8th Displayed a Number of pieces of Fire works on Shore. Otoo with his family, and many other of the first Chiefs accompanying, with near 2000 of the Inhabitants present expressing their surprize & admiration with uncommon Shouts and acclamations.[25]

Wednesday 10th Employed making the spare sails up & bringing them on board. Scrap'd the Masts & painted the Top Masts with Varnish of Pine. Punished Will Doyle, Boats Mate, with a Dozen Lashes for Neglect of Duty & breeding Disturbances among the Natives.

Friday 26th Captain Cook presented Otoo with 2 Cows, a young Heifer and Bull, several Yews with a Ram, a pair of purfowls, Turkeys, Geese, and Ducks & we have the Happiness in seeing a very fine Bull brought by the Spaniards in a thriving Condition. The King appeared to be greatly pleased and very thankful for the present, promising to take particular care in copulating them & stocking the Neighbouring Isles.

Monday 29th Punished William Doyle, Seaman, with 6 lashes for striking an Indian Girl. A party on shore cutting Grass. Loosed sails to Dry. Captains Cook & Clerke generally backed the Horses every Evening during the stay here. From the time of our arrival here we have salted & cured 10 Puncheons and a Barrel of excellent pork, [but] for want of Salt we are obliged to Desist curing any more.

Tuesday 30th Our friends of Otaheite, waiting our departure and taking their last farewell, bidding adieu with a seeming unaffected sorrow. Otoo with several of the principle Chiefs on Board, taking a little trip too & from the Shore. During His Majestys presence we fired 8 Guns shorted. Afterwards he retired with his attendants bewailing our Departure. We then made sail for Eimao. At 6 in the Evening took a Reef in the topsails & brought too for the Night. At 8 saw two Entrances through the Reefs under the lee part of the Island. Hoisted out the Cutter & sent her to Sound the leeward Entrance for anchorage. She soon returned with a report of a very good Harbour. Stood in between the Reef & sailed up to the head of the Harbour & anchored with the small Bower in 10 fathoms.

Wednesday, October 1st Sent a party on Shore to cut wood. Natives bringing on board Hogs, Bread fruit, Cocoa Nutts etc. Carpenters repairing the Pinnace.

Thursday 2nd Employed in the After Hold. Hands on Shore cutting wood. Hauld the Ship to the Shore and secured her with Bow & Quarter fasts. Got hawsers out of the lower skuttles with Spars lashed on them, with an intention to Clear the Ship of Rats, being much pestered with those Vermin.

Friday 3rd Many of the Natives on board trading as before. Mahine, one of the greater Chiefs of this Isle, paid us a Visit & brought a small present to the Captain.

Tuesday 7th Found one of our Goats Missing, which was sent to the Shore to feed. Sent the Cutter to the Chief Mahine to seek after it.[26]

Wednesday 8th The Cutter returned, brought the Goat and the Man who stole it. Confined him in Irons. This evening we had the mortification of finding another was stolen. Sent the Cutter away again to the East, where we had information of its being Carried.

Thursday 9th The Cutter returned, but could not find the Goat. The Natives behaving insolent at our leaving the Shore. Captain Cook went with a party of Men under arms in order to get with the Boats from each Ship to meet the party on the Back part of the Island.

Friday 10th The Captain, Officers & Men returned, but could not get the Goat. [They] Burnt & Destroyed several Houses & War Canoes on the opposite side of the Island. In the Morning the Excursion was renewed to the Westward towards Mahine, and a Man was sent to acquaint him of our intentions.

Saturday 11th The Boats came back, having set fire to most of the Canoes on that part of the Island. Found the Goat was Returned, brought by the Messenger sent Yesterday to the Chief. At Noon, standing out of the Harbour, several Canoes round us with Cocoa Nutts, fruit etc.

On the NE side of the Island Eimao, are two very commodious good Harbours. The lee or most Eastern one (called by the Natives Moreea) is the best & may be known by a remarkable Peak resembling a pyramid appearing, when you are off the mouth of the Harbour. The Entrance between the Reefs is Narrow, but steep too, having 40 fathoms water Mid Channel and good anchorage. Immediately you are within the passage from 20 to 30 fathoms, with regular soundings & clear ground to the head of the Bay, sheltered from all Winds. The Valley abounds in great plenty of Wood & an excellent River of fresh Water, every thing suitable & convenient for recruiting & refitting a Ship in great safety. This Harbour is by far superior to any among the Society Isles, none having this quantity of Wood. Its Latitude 17°29′ South and Longitude East of Greenwich 210°10′.

Thursday 23rd [At Huaheine] In the Evening a Sexton [sextant] was Stolen out of William Bailey's Observatory. [We] detected the thief. Sent him on board and confined him. [We then] seized several of their Large Canoes until the Sexton was produced, which was the proceeding Morning, brought by one of Omai's servants, who found it lying under a Tree. Likewise released the thief, after depriving him of his hair & Ears. This partly was our constant punishment for every theft, to cut off the aggressors Hair, which in a great measure I firmly am of opinion prevented many petty offences. This was this first Villain who was bereaved of his lugs [Scottish slang word for "ear"].

Friday 24th Launch assisting the Discovery in getting their Bread on Shore. The Natives perfectly reconciled these matters, accommodated in very amicable manner & a perfect harmony of friendship subsisting between us, bringing their fruits etc to sale.

Thursday 30th An Indian prisoner we had confined on Board for these few last Days for threatening Omai's destruction, some time in the Night made his escape to the Shore. The Key of the Bilboas [shackles] being found near the place where this man lay, gave room for the Captain to suspect some person or persons assisted in freeing him (and am sorry to say) challenged some of his petty Officers & gentlemen in being privy to the affair (saying he heard) "several of them pity the fellow during his confinement". Its very hard that every one in that station should fall under this severe lash in a matter that's absolutely impossible to be cleared up. For myself I say this, I ever was a well wisher of Omais & no person could actually wish him happily situated & free from any kind of interruption & insult more than myself.

Punished Thomas Morrice, the Marine that was on watch when this happened, with a Dozen lashes for sleeping on his Post. Likewise, Thomas Harrison, for Neglect.

Sent all the Chests out of the Ship on Shore, to cleanse from Vermin being very much infested with Cockroaches, eating & destroying every thing belonging to the People. Hands scraping & cleaning the Ship fore & aft & giving her a good smoaking between Decks.

Friday 31st Struck the Tent & observatory [and] got everything off from the Shore. Punished Thomas Morrice, the Marine, with 12 lashes, for admitting the Bilboa Bolt of the Prisoner to be unlocked. I forgot to make mention that the Indian which made his escape was the same rascal that stole the Quadrant, his threats & abuses to Omai was owing to Omai being the person that detected him in the theft.

Saturday, November 1st Employed clearing all the Cabins out as Yesterday & smoaking. Punished Thomas Morrice, Marine, with 12 lashes for letting his prisoner escape, this being the last of his punishment. Released him to his Duty.

Sunday 2nd Punished James Carly, Marine, with 12 lashes for sleeping on his post, & William Bradley, Gunners Mate, for Insolence & Contempt. The Captains & Officers of each ship was invited by Omai to dinner on Shore during our short continuance with him.

Monday 3rd Here we took our long farewell & bid adieu to Omiah & the two young Zealand adventurers, the two Boys equally affected with their Master, weeping intolerably at our parting.[27] Omiah appeared to be very confident within himself that the Chiefs would continue their friendship & not suffer him to be disturbed or molested. However, he was advized to send some signal of their behaviour to us while at Ulietea. We left the two Horses with him in a very good condition. The Mare then thought [to be] with Fold [Foal]. Likewise an English Boar & Sow with a couple of Goats. While we lay here a garden was dug & several seeds sown & vegetables planted with several young Vines that were planted at Oite Peha Bay by the Spaniards, but the Indians made way with some of them, which Omai suspected the Native that was confined.

Wednesday 5th Opened the Ballast Port & run out a small passageway to the Shore with an intention to clear the Ships of Rats. Hauld the launch on Shore into a House to repair. Oreo with his daughter Paedua & many of the Indians constantly with us trading.

Wednesday 12th Hands on Shore making Brooms. Many Indians about the Ships trading as usual. Armourer continually employed at the Forge making trade [items] to purchase provisions.

Thursday 13th In the night John Harrison, Marine, then Centinel at the Observatories, absented himself with his Musket and accoutrements. In the Morning I was sent with a party in quest of him, accompanied by Oreo's son & several other of the Natives that had knowledge of his Route.

Friday 14th Hands on Shore Brooming and cutting Grass. [I] returned with my party, but could get no intelligence of the Deserter. The Indians after leading us up the Valley at the head of the Harbour & over the summits of the different hills, assuring us we should be brought to the Man, sometimes (declaring they saw him). They at length seated themselves down & absolutely denounced any further thought to assist us in getting him. I however both entreated and threatened them but all would avail nothing. We then continued our Route, directly over the Ridge of the Hills, flattering ourselves we should hear some tidings of him on the other side of the Isle, but the Natives there appear to be totally ignorant of the affair. We afterwards proceeded on our journey round the East of the Isle, but we could hear nothing of the deserter.

Saturday 15th Captain Cook went with two Boats in search of the Deserter.

Sunday 16th The Captain returned with the party, having secured & brought back Harrison. [They] found him in a house seated with several of the Indians round him, at a Bay on the other side of the Island, next to the Bay we examined yesterday. It seems he came down from the Mountains about an Hour after I had departed. Captain Cook was conducted to him by the Chief Oreo, having confined & carried him with him for that purpose.

Monday 17th Punished John Harrison with 12 lashes as part of his punishment for leaving his post.

Tuesday 18th Punished John Harrison with 12 lashes as the remaining part of his punishment and released him. Aired sails and overhauled the sail Rooms, smoaked the Bread Room with Brimstone. Natives trading as usual. The Indian that was deprived of his Ears & made his Escape from us at Huaheine was seen here making no manner of ceremony of coming near the Ship and conversing with us.

Wednesday 19th It has escaped me until this to make mention that we received intelligence of Omai's being happily situated with the principle Men of Huaheine, having distributed many of his unnecessary things to a great number of the Chiefs [and] by that means procured his friendship and attachment. We received this advice by his own people sent purposely. They likewise told us that Omai had lost his She Goat, having died in kidding. When they returned to Huaheine, the Captain sent him 2 Kidds to replace the loss of the former.

Monday 24th This Morning two of the Discovery's people were found missing. Boats went in Quest of them.

Tuesday 25th Captain Clerke returned with the Boats, but could get no certain intelligence of his people. [Then] Captain Cook went with a party to the Island of Etaha in search of them, the Natives saying that they were there. Punished Theopehilis Hinks, Marine, with 12 lashes for sleeping on his Post.

Wednesday 26th Captain Cook returned. [He] found that the people who absconded from the Discovery were gone off for Bolabola [Bora Bora].

Thursday 27th Hauld the Ship off the Shore. Struck the Observatory & got it on board. On Tuesday last the Captain thought it proper to confine some of the principle people, knowing it would be an inducement for the Indians to use their utmost endeavours to seize upon & bring back the 2 runaways. In the evening we were alarmed by some of the Indians that a party had seized Captain Clerke and some of our Officers. Our conjectures were not without foundation for every Indian were making off as fast as possible. The Ships Crews were immediately ordered to arms & partys dispatched to the Shore and Boats in Chase of the Canoes, but however we were presently deceived to find Captain Clerke return without having received any molestation, yet (he said) they appeared very suspicious & believed they only waited for an opportunity that seeing Captain Clerke provided (for them) with a pistol totally upset their design. The others that were with us no doubt thought the matter was executed [and] made off with all their Goods & Chattels, being alarmed & dreading the Consequences which might follow. Several Muskets were fired in an alarm, but [I] am pleased to say without any damages to the Natives, orders being given to fire wide.

The next Morning, the Chiefs finding we were satisfied, his delivering up their Canoes & other matters we had taken into possession, came to the Ship again & every thing conducted in a very amiable manner with equal the Harmony as before subsisted.

Saturday 29th The Chief Oreo went off for Bolabola in quest of the Discovery's people, expressing great anxiety for his family, which were under confinement, among which was the charming Nymph Paedua, his daughter.

Monday, December 1st Old Oreo returned with the two people that eloped. It seems they had got as far down as Tubai, where they were seized upon by the Indians and brought back to Bolabola to the Chief Opoonie, who immediately delivered them up to Oreo, who conveyed them hither without loss of time, wishing no doubt with great eagerness to see his Children sett free, which was instantly done at their arrival. The Natives seemingly pouring forth their congratulations at their prisoners release by assembling in crowds to the Shore where they first landed. This step of gaining our Countrymen again answered the intended purpose without any further disagreeables arising (this precaution was [n]ever used after the first Evening). No person [was] permitted to go on Shore, to directly throw themselves in their clutches, therefore would turn the Tables on us.

Smoaked the Ship with Brimstone to destroy the Cockroaches.

Tuesday 2nd Opened the hatches & finding many of the Vermin destroyed, smoaked a second time, the Cockroaches so damned numerous & destructive there's scarce a possibility of preserving an article of any sort from them; few things coming amiss, to the gentlemens pallets, several of the people being bit by them & places eaten on their legs as large as a Shilling. I have seen their hands, likewise mauled, but [I] am of the oppinion it was owing to the grease & filth grafted in them.

Sunday 7th Made the Signal and unmoored. The Chief Oreo with several of the principle people, taking a trip with us to Bolabola, a prodigious Number of Canoes filled with Men, Women & Children, round the Ships at our Departure, much afflicted at our leaving them.

December 9th [The peaks of Bora Bora in view on December 8.] Having knowledge of an Anchor being here in possession of Opoonie, belonging to Bougainville, (which he lost at Otaheite), the Captain went in with the Boats with an intention to buy it from the Chief. At 4 Peak of Bolabola EBS and the Island Tubai [in view]. At 6 the Boats returned with the Anchor, or rather part of one, they having taken off the palms & part of the Shank. Several Canoes came off with Cocoa Nutts etc. At 7 Bore away and made Sail, standing to the NW to clear the Islands. Then Stow'd the Anchor. Pleasant weather. Serv'd slops to the Ships' Company.

John Webber, "A View of the Harbour in Huaheine [Fare Harbor]," circa 1781-83. Pen, wash, and water color showing a sweeping view of Fare Harbor in November 1777. The *Discovery* is at anchor with many Native vessels plying around it in the harbor, with peaked mountains in the background. There are huts and an English observatory tent on shore. Dixson Library, State Library of New South Wales, PXX 2, f. 16.

6

Finding Hawai'i

December 1777–February 1778

Passing the Equator, the expedition entered the North Pacific, the first time Cook had been this far north in the Pacific. Since they only knew the world they had passed, they recorded longitude at 202°20′ East of Greenwich, more than twenty degrees into the Western Hemisphere. On Christmas Day they chanced upon an uninhabited island surrounded by a reef they called "Christmas Island." The weather was hot and humid, unbearable to most of the sailors, but they nonetheless collected coconuts and greens ashore. They also sent parties to kill as many turtles as they could find, probably two hundred in all, the largest weighing over three hundred pounds. The hunting was called "turtling" in the journals. Two sailors nearly died from heat exhaustion crossing the island pursuing the lumbering giants. At Christmas Island, they observed another eclipse of the Sun.

They soon chanced upon another series of islands, the leeward Hawaiian Islands. They saw the mountains of O'ahu in the distance, but they first approached Kaua'i, which both Burney and Roberts called "Atoui." There was no harbor, so they simply anchored offshore and adjusted their anchorage with the shifting currents and pounding surf. Cook issued an order prohibiting sexual relations with the Hawaiian women because, as Burney explained, many seamen caught the "venereal distemper" in Tahiti and the captain did not want it spread to the unsuspecting people of Kaua'i, who seemed to have no prior contact with Europeans. Cook's directive was not followed and, to his disgust, the captain discovered a year later the disease had been transmitted throughout the islands.

When crews first came ashore in Kaua'i, they were besieged by the inquisitive inhabitants. In the initial excitement a Hawaiian was killed, but the local chiefs soon arrived to restore order. The English traded for the island produce as they prepared for their trip to America, including hogs, fowls, yams, sweet potatoes, breadfruit, plantains, and salt. Even Cook went ashore. When he did, the people prostrated themselves in his presence, perhaps to recognize him as a god or, more likely, to acknowledge the superiority of his weapons and avoid another confrontation. The ships later stopped at the smaller Ni'ihau Island, which the sailors called "Oneehow," where they also anchored offshore. Burney and Roberts said it was a barren, desolate island and, although the landing was difficult, the ships were able to trade for fresh provisions at Ni'ihau before leaving for the northwest coast of America.

Journal of James Burney

Monday, December 22nd At Midnight Crossed the Equatorial Line, Longitude from Greenwich 202°20′ East.

John Webber, "An Inland View in Atooi [Waimea, Kaua'i]," circa 1781-83. Pen, wash, and water color depicting Cook's visit to the village of Waimea in January 1778. British sailors are bartering with Hawaiians and other people are carrying a pig strung on a pole, surrounded by Hawaiian homes and a panoramic view of the island interior. Dixson Library, State Library of New South Wales, PXX 2, f. 19.

Wednesday 24th At ½ past 7 Saw Land to the NE, which proved to be a low Sandy Lagoon Island [Christmas Island, a raised coral atoll which is now part of the Republic of Kiribati]. At 5 in the Afternoon Anchord to Leeward of the Island in 27 fathoms Sandy bottom [Bearings omitted.]

Thursday 25th At Daylight Sent our great Cutter in company with the Resolution's Boats to Sound, and one of our Small Boats in shore fishing. At Noon the Boats returned. Plenty of Fish, but no landing near the Ship. Hove up our Anchors as did the Resolution and made Sail to the Northward, a more convenient Anchoring place being found, and an Opening into the Lagoon, with good Landing. No Inhabitants here. In the Afternoon Anchord with the Best Bower in 17 fathoms Sandy bottom. [Bearings omitted.]

This Island is surrounded by a Reef, except the Entrances into the Lagoon. Within the Lagoon is Shoal Water and Rocks, that make it difficult Navigation for Boats. Where we Anchord had good clear ground about the Ship. The Tide rises between 3 and 4 feet perpendicular. High Water 4 H 30 M after the Moon passes the Meridian.

Friday 26th Our Boats away Fishing and looking for Turtle.

Saturday 27th Served biscuit again to the Ship's Company, our Stock of Ulietea Vegetables being expended.

Monday 29th At Noon, our great Cutter, which these 2 days past had been to the Southward within the Lagoon catching Turtle, returned to the Ship; leaving behind 2 men (Bart W. Lowman and Thomas Tretcher) who had straggled from the Boat the day before. This party had been in great distress for want of Water, as they Staid longer than was intended on account of the people missing. When they came away, one of the Resolutions Boats were Turtling near the same place, but as it was probable the Stragglers might lose their way, and perish for want of water, Mr. Hollamby, one of our midshipmen, with 3 men, were immediately sent on Shore in search of them, each carrying 2 Quarts of Water and a pint of Brandy. In the Afternoon the Launches of both Ships went round the South point of the Island to fetch the Turtle.

Tuesday 30th At 7 in the Evening, the launches returned and with them Bart W. Lowman, who had fell in with the Resolutions people in the Forenoon. Mr. Hollambys party got intelligence from him which way to look for Tretcher, whom he left the Evening before, unable to walk further. These 2 men had mistook their way in bringing Turtle across from the Sea Beach to the Cutter at the Lagoon Beach. They had made wells in 2 or 3 different places, but found the water quite Salt, and were reduced to the necessity of Cutting Turtle's Throats to drink the blood as it issued from the wound, and of plunging hourly into the water to cool themselves, on account of the excessive heat of the Sun on the open Sand.

Wednesday 31st At day break the great Cutter was sent within the Lagoon to assist in Searching, but returned at Noon for Signal, Tretcher being brought on board. Mr. Hollamby found him a few hours after receiving the intelligence from Lowman, and walked from the South end of the Island to abreast the Ship.

James Burney, "Sketch of Sandwich Islands [portions of Kaua'i, Ni'ihau, and O'ahu Islands, Hawai'i]," January 1778. Burney and the master of the *Discovery*, Thomas Edgar, were the only expedition members to sketch the island geography after the first visit to Hawai'i in January 1778. Burney Journal p. 116, Mitchell Library, State Library of New South Wales, Safe 1/64 and 1/79.

Thursday, January 1st, 1778 Called in all our Turtling parties and hoisted the Boats in. We have caught here 90 Turtle from 50 to 200 lbs weight each. The Resolution more. The longest extent of this uninhabitable Spot is about 7 Leagues. It produces nothing but Some Small Brush Wood and a few old Coconut Trees, that are blighted by high winds or long droughts. Rats here.

Friday 2nd At daylight got under Sail and Stood to the Northward. Before Noon lost sight of the Land.

Tuesday 6th Went to an Allowance of 2 Quarts of Water per day. Kept our Still at work every afternoon in fine Weather, which gave us about 11 Gallons of fresh water in 4 Hours. Our Outer Best Bower Cable being very much wore and no longer trustworthy, cut it up for Junk, and bent a new one. Till we past the 8th degree of North Latitude, the wind blew mostly from the ESE. Afterwards from the ENE and NE.

Sunday 11th Past a great many Turtle. Birds about the Ship. [Bearings omitted.]

Sunday 18th At daylight saw High Land [O'ahu] bearing NEB¼E and at 9 in the forenoon saw more Land to the NNW. [Bearings omitted.] Having a light Easterly Wind we ran on to the Northward all this Afternoon and Night.[28]

Monday 19th At ½ past 6 in the morning the Body of an Island [Kaua'i] bore NNW½W about 6 Leagues and Land in sight ENE½E 12 or 14 Leagues dis-

John Webber, "A Morai at Atooi [Heiau at Waimea, Kaua'i]," circa 1781-83. Pen, wash, and water color depicting the inside of the walled enclosure of the heiau (temple) at Waimea observed in January 1778. The principal features are the long house and oracle tower. Dixson Library, State Library of New South Wales, PXX 2, f. 17.

tant. From ½ past 6 to noon ran 14 miles North. [Bearings omitted.] The Land to the Eastward not in sight. At 1 [in the] Afternoon, some Canoes came off to us, being then within 2 miles of the SE end of the Island [Kaua'i]. Bore away along the South Side, keeping at the distance of half a League. Passed several Small Towns. At 5 having run 15 miles to the Westward, a Strait Shore all the way, brought too and Sounded. Got Ground and 20 fathoms Soft Black Sand. The Island then bearing from EBN to N60W distance off shore 2 miles. Another Island [Ni'ihau] in sight W ½ S 6 or 8 Leagues. Hauld off Shore upon a Wind and Stood backwards and forwards all Night.

Tuesday 20th At day light made Sail in shore. At 1/2 past 9 the Resolution made the Signal for our great Cutter, which was sent in Shore with their Boats to Sound. At 3 in the Afternoon they returned. In searching for a Landing place, the Resolutions Pinnace was attacked by the Indians, some of whom endeavoured to overset her in the Surf, whilst others were dragging her on shore. This Obliged our people to fire, and an Indian who had got in the Boat was Shot dead, on which the rest immediately desisted.[29] At 4 Anchord in 21fms brown Sand . . . off shore 1½ miles. [Bearings omitted.]

An Order was given prohibiting any intercourse with the Women here, to prevent our communicating the Venereal distemper, which many of the people had contracted at the Society Islands. No Women were admitted into the Ships and particular care taken that no person infected or recently cured Should be suffered to go in the Boats.

Wednesday 21st In the morning the Launches were sent for Water, with a large party of Marines for a Guard. The Indians were so much frightened by yesterdays quarrel that on our people's Landing, they all fell on their faces in token of Submission. A great many Canoes about the Ships all day, with Hogs, Fowls, Sweet potatoes and Plaintains, which they sold for Iron. A few Coconuts and 2 Heads of Bread fruit were brought on board. Of these, there is reason to supose they have no great Stock, almost all the Country we have hitherto seen, being open and laid out in plantations of Yams, Sweet potatoes and Sugar Canes.

This Island is called by the Natives, Atoui [and] that to the Westward Oneehow, and the one we first saw (to the Eastward) Wouahoua [O'ahu]. Besides these, they tell us of another Island to the SE, and one to the NW called Tummatta papappa. To the whole of them Captain Cook gives the name of the Sandwich Islands.

This day Grog was served again, it having been stopped by consent of the Ships Companies since the 15th of August.

Thursday 22nd The Weather Cloudy with rain. Too much Surf for Landing, but few Canoes came off.

Friday 23rd Smoother Water. At Daylight sent our Launch Watering. The Resolution having Anchord in foul Ground, weighd in order to Shift her Birth, but the wind dying away, and the current setting strong to the Westward, She fell to Leeward of the good Anchoring Ground, and was obliged to Stand Offshore. This afternoon completd our Water. Lost some casks by the Surf and one Stole by the Natives.

At Sunset the Resolution bore West, about 3 Leagues. The Swell setting on shore and not wind enough to keep the Ship under Command, prevented our getting under Sail to join her.

Saturday 24th At Sunrise, Saw the Resolution to the Westward. At 9 got under Sail, but the wind dying away, were obliged to anchor again. This morning, a great many Indians were about the Ship, till a large Canoe in which their Chief was, came and ordered them away. Those that were slow in obeying, he gave chase to and fairly ran over 4 Small Canoes, leaving the owners swimming by the wreck, after which he came alongside. This Chief was a tall young man. He came half way up the side but his attendants would not suffer him to enter the Ship. Captain Clerke made him several presents and received in return a very curious Bowl in which they made their Kava, a Liquor used by almost all the Indians in the South Seas.

In the Afternoon, an Indian, who had been very usefull in keeping his Countrymen orderly, when we were watering the day before, came alongside and desired us to Send our Boats on Shore for a present of provisions. This invitation could not be accepted, as we every minute expected a breeze and wanted to join the Resolution, who fell fast to Leeward and was now but just in Sight from the Masthead. At 5 o'clock we got under Sail with a light Air off Shore. At 8 it falling calm, were again obliged to Anchor in 44 fathoms, half a mile without our last Birth.

Sunday 25th A moderate breeze from the ENE. At Sunrise Saw the Resolution bearing SSW. Got under sail and at 9 Joined Company. At noon the Island of Atoui bore from E¾N to NBW distance 6 or 7 miles.

26th 27th & 28th Endeavouring to regain our Anchoring Birth.

Thursday 29th Finding the Westerly Current too strong to turn against. This morning, Bore away, and Stood close in to the South End of Oneehow [Niʻihau] and Sent Boats to sound for Anchorage. [Bearings omitted.] Sent Boats on Shore to Trade for Yams and Salt.

Friday 30th The Boats of both Ships on shore at a Small Town, trading for Yams and Salt. In the Afternoon our great Cutter parted from her Graplin and narrowly escaped being dashed to pieces against the Rocks. The Surf increasing, all the Boats came off, being obliged to leave some of the People on Shore.

Saturday 31st Cloudy weather with much rain and a very high surf. No Landing. The people remained on Shore.

Sunday, February 1st Smoother water. Got the people and every thing off. The Resolution filled 4 puncheons of Water at a Small Cove under a high Bluff point to the Eastward. No Water there in dry weather. Captain Cook gave the Inhabitants a He Goat, two She Goats, an English Boar and Sow.

At ½ past 6 in the Evening, the Resolutions Anchor came home and she drove out to sea. Hoisted Lights as a Mark for her during the Night.

Monday, 2d At Daylight saw the Resolution bearing WBS distant 4 Leagues. At 10 got under Sail and at 2 in the Afternoon Joined her. At ½ past 4 made Sail to the Northward and left the Land.

The Language of these Islands seems to be a mixture of the Otaheite and Tongitabu Languages which is the more extraordinary as they are 2400 miles distant from Otaheite and still further from Tongitabu.

A Man	—	Tongarta
A Hog	—	Bohah
Eyes	—	Marta
Belly	—	Opu
Teeth	—	Neo
Set down	—	Annoko
etc.		etc.

The Houses are thatched close down and Shaped something like our Cottages. The Walls lower. Their greatest fault is want of light, having no Window and but one small Door, which there is no entry without Stooping.

Their Dress in general is Cloth, beat out of the Bark of a Tree, but on extraordinary occasions they wear Caps and Clokes of red and yellow feathers, which seem to have been made in imitation of Spanish Dresses. We saw here a piece of a Sword, which they said came from an Island to the SE. The Red Feathers are inferior in brightness of Colour to those of Tongitabu.

Their Arms are Lances, Bows and Arrows, and Small Wooden Daggers, all well wrought, but, I think very innocent weapons. We have nowhere found more hospitable and friendly treatment, than amongst these Islanders.

The women, who are not much inferior to the Otaheiteans, have been more forward in their offers, which may be chiefly attributed to the backwardness on the part of our people, under the restrictions before mentioned.

Besides completing our Water, we procured at these Islands an excellent Stock of Pork, Yams, Sweet potatoes, Salt and Salted Fish.

JOURNAL OF HENRY ROBERTS

Thursday, December 25th Working up under the lee of the Island [Christmas Island], sent the Pinnace to look for land & Anchorage. The Discovery saw many fish near the break of the surf. In the morning, the Boats were sent a fishing. The master with the Cutter examining the shore to the Northward to seek for an Entrance into the Lagoon. The Boats returned [and] found an entrance through the Reef and a good anchorage off it. The Discovery's boat saw many turtle. Caught plenty of turtles, which were served to the people. At Noon got under way, not being able to land here.

Friday 26th Found a point with a cluster of Cocoa Nutt trees, which makes the Southern part of the Entrance into the Lagoon. Boats fishing & others examining the Lagoon. Served fresh Pork & fish to the people.

Saturday 27th The Boats came back [and] brought on Board 2 fine Turtle, the largest weighs 320 lbs. Saw many more in the surge of the Sea. In the afternoon the Boats sent with partys to catch Turtle & fish.

Sunday 28th Employed Fishing & Turtling. Serv'd fish to the people.

Monday 29th As yesterday employed, caught many Turtle, which was serv'd to the Ships Company.

Tuesday 30th The Launch sent with the Discoverys round the SW point to bring Turtle parties as before.

Wednesday 31st Employed as Yesterday. One of the Discoverys people being missing, having lost himself on this Island, sent Boats in quest of him & shortly was found by the parties.

Thursday, January 1st, 1778 Parties fishing & catching Turtle, which was serv'd to the people.

Friday 2nd Having found upwards of 150 Turtle, generally weighing 50 to 150 weight or 200—with many excellent fish, particularly the fine Cavalley, some of these weigh 80 lbs. At Daylight we got under weigh & made sail to the Northward. Discovery in company.

Christmas Island so called from our spending that Festival on it. The center of it is situated Latitude 1°57′2″ North and Longitude 202°30′ East from an Observation of the Sun Eclipsed. The whole Circuit of the Island is not more than 12 leagues, and may be properly numbered with the Lagoon Entrance. On the West side is an oppening into the Lagoon, with a small sandy Islet lying Midway, which forms two Channels for Boats only. The Water shallowing immediately, you pass the Narrows on either side, and the Ground resting. On this Islet the Observations was made of the Suns Eclipse.

From the situation of this remote spot without any Inhabitant, but the feathered Creation, and them chiefly of the Oceanic Fish, with a few Turtle, we were somewhat surprized to find that the soil was in some measure capable of producing the Cocoa Palm and other small trees, and appeared a lot to be in a state that in a few Years, would arise. In some perfection, the Mould [loose soil] in many places where the Trees lie in thickets, much surpassing that which was exposed to the heat of the Sun and never received the least benefits but from the dung of the Fowl, the leaves of the Trees therefore must doubtless contribute more to the enrichment of this soil than any other thing.

The birds on this Isle are the Gannet booby, Brown booby, Notty's, Black & White Peterals, and a dark brown Sea bird, which I never observed before, with a black semicircular Mark under its wings and lays an Egg, the Size and Collour of a Pidgeons. A small Bird the size of a lark and the plumage very similar also.

It seldom flies any great distance but runs very swift among the Tufts of Grass. While we lay at this place, the people who were on the Turtling expeditions, suffered extremely from the intense heat of the weather.

Monday 19th The extremes of an Island bearing NNW. At 6 the Island first seen and the peaked hill on the Western of a large isle. Saw an other island to the West offshore about 2 leagues. [First views of O'ahu, Kaua'i, and Ni'ihau.]

Tuesday 20th Many Canoes came off along side. ½ past 1 Bore away and sailed along the SE side of the Island, the land to the Northward appearing broken and seemingly would afford shelter. Continued our Route Down the Coast, many of the Inhabitants along shore looking at the Ship. Sent the Boats in Shore to look for anchorage and fresh Water. A great number of Canoes round the two Ships, bartering for Sweet Potatoes, etc with the Natives. Boats still on shore reconnoitering for anchorage. Purchased abundance of potatoes, small Hogs, etc.

Wednesday 21st The Boats returned, found good Anchorage and fresh Water. Many of the Natives on board trading with Hogs, sweet potatoes and roots, & were extremely sociable and friendly. AM sent parties on Shore watering & to trade with the Inhabitants. Served fresh Pork and Turtle to the people. Punished Samuel Bishop with 6 lashes for neglect. Served whole allowance of Grog to the people.

Thursday 22nd The wind coming in at SE sent a great swell into the road, which prevented our Watering. A great many of the Indians on board trading, with Cloth, Hogs, Roots, etc, which were served to the People. The surf not so great on the beach to obstruct landing.

Friday 23rd Sent the Boats on Shore to trade & water. Served Fresh Pork & potatoes daily to the people. Latitude Observed 21°57′ North

Saturday 24th The Boats returned with water and plenty of good Salt & plantains, with a quantity of potatoes. All the night plying to windward with little wind, endeavouring to reach our last anchoring place.

Sunday 25th All the night stood off to the SE and at day light stretched in for Land. Served Fresh Pork and sweet potatoes daily to the Ships Crews. At noon the West point of the Island about 3 leagues off the SE point.

Monday 26th In the night much lightning in the WNW. About 9 leagues distance found the tide or current setting strong to the West, the Ship drifting very much to leeward.

Tuesday 27th Employed the people making off slatts & nippers. At 10 Departed this life Thomas Roberts, seaman, after a long fitful illness. In the evening committed the body of the Deceased to the Deep.

Thursday 29th Standing in for the land, found we had drifted far to the west. On return to the west saw a small Isle [Ni'ihau]. Tacked Ship and stood off and on all the night. In the morning stretched in, close under the SE head or high hummock. At 8 AM Hoisted out the Pinnace and sent her along shore to sound for Anchorage and look for fresh water. Several Canoes came along side & bartered with Yams, sweet potatoes, etc. The Boats came on board, found but indifferent landing & no fresh water.

Friday 30th PM sent the boats to look for a landing & water. At 5 they returned, found tolerable landing, but no water within any convenient distance for the Ship. Hoisted the Boats in for the night. AM sent the Boats to the Shore to Trade, many of the Natives along side in their Canoes, bartering with Yams, Potatoes etc. Very peaceable & friendly.

Saturday 31st PM the Boats returned with a quantity of Yams and Salt, which was got off with great difficulty, the surf running very high. The party with the First Lieut were left on Shore. At 11 PM the wind coming immediately on those, hove the Anchor up & run farther out. AM sent the Pinnace to the Shore, but the surf beating very heavy [so] could not land. Found the Tide or Current sett very Strong to the Eastward, continuing its course near 15 hours, then changing & running to the WNW for about 4 hours, flood tide setts to the East.[30]

Sunday, February 1st Employed painting the ends. The boats were sent to a small Cove at the South End of the Isle close under the high bluff, in order to get the party off.

Monday 2nd At 4 the Captain returned with the boats & party from the shore. Brought a quantity of Yams, Potatoes & salt with 4 puncheons of fresh water, which was got from a Run occasioned by the Rain. Captain Cook presented one of the principal Women with a Ram & 2 She Goats, likewise a Boar & Sow of the English breed. During the Night plying to windward. Fired a Gun and made a signal for the Discovery to get under weigh and come down, standing off & on, repeating the Signal when we saw our Consort Standing before us. At Noon the Southern Bluff bore about 6 leagues off, the high land of the large Isle then oppen with it. The Land to the Northward much higher & more Cliffy than the part to the Southward were. We anchored. We were too great a distance to judge whether or not there was any Shelter or Anchorage, but seemingly to appearances its quite a steep Shore. The hilly parts were wooded.

Henry Roberts, "Views of the Anchoring Places of Atoui and Oneehow [Kaua'i and Ni'ihau, Hawai'i]," January 1778. Roberts offered these colorful first impressions of the Hawaiian coastline from the anchorages off Kaua'i and Ni'ihau during the expedition's first visit to Hawai'i. Roberts Journal p. 155, Dixson Library, State Library of New South Wales, DLMSQ 151-52 and DLMSF 2.

PART TWO
THE NORTHWEST PASSAGE

INTRODUCTION

For three centuries European navigators searched in vain for the location of an imagined short route from Europe to the riches of the Orient. Jonathan Swift placed the fantasyland of "Brobdingnag" roughly in the latitude of present-day Oregon and Washington in *Gulliver's Travels.* In 1745 the British Parliament offered a £20,000 prize for the discovery of a passage to the Pacific by way of Hudson Bay. While the search would prove futile, the theoretical geographers convinced the Admiralty that the passage existed because of tales of imagined and mystical voyagers passed down through the ages.[1]

Both Spanish and Russian traders had been sailing along the Northwest Coast of America for decades, but there were no maps until Jacob von Stählin published an account and map of two modest voyages conducted for the Russian Navy by Lt. Ivan Sindt (1764-67) and captains Peter Krenitsyn and Mikhail Levashev (1766-69). These did little to expand geographic knowledge of the Bering Sea or the Alaska mainland, but von Stählin's map suggested Alaska was a large island between the North American and Asian continents. Among other things the map showed Sindt's "new northern archipelago" with many other islands and a wide passage into Arctic waters between Alaska and North America, making it appear that the Arctic (even Hudson Bay) was relatively accessible from Southern Alaska.[2]

The detail of the third voyage instructions, particularly since the search was to begin in 65° North Latitude, suggest that the Admiralty assumed von Stählin's account and map were believable. After reaching the South Pacific, Cook and his men sailed for America to find Sindt's archipelago and claim the £20,000 prize. They came in view of the Oregon Coastline on March 7, 1778, sighting and naming "Cape Foulweather," before they were besieged by high winds and vicious seas that forced them south to Cape Blanco, near the California border.

After a considerable battering off the coast of Oregon and Washington, they sailed north along the coast, passing the outlets of the Columbia River and Strait of Juan de Fuca while far out to sea.[3] They could not find shelter until they reached modern-day British Columbia at a place they called King George's Sound. While they assumed the rocky, windswept shore was a part of the continental landmass, the anchorage, which soon became known as Nootka Sound, is located on the exposed west coast of Vancouver Island. They stopped in the inlet for water and wood, as well as to recaulk and refit the vessels after a perilous voyage from the tropics. They found the region densely forested from the water's edge to distant, snow-capped summits.

As soon as the sailors entered the inlet melodious whooping was heard from shore. In an instant a few hundred Natives came out in thirty or forty massive cedar canoes and surrounded the ships. The people were clothed with animal skins and smeared with paint, so they were not as attractive to the English as the exotic islanders the crew had seen in the South Pacific, but on first approach they stood in their dugout canoes and sang in wild chorus. Some held rattles and waved their arms, pointing at the sky and shore. Others threw colorful ochre into the sky and even danced in their excitement. It was an uncommon, raucous welcoming ceremony.

The English soon learned about the Nootka people and wrote at length about their customs in their journals. They were superb artisans and, instead of the unremitting thievery of Polynesians, the English were impressed with their insistence on trade and exchange, even for greens, wood, and water on shore. The people offered furs and skins, bark clothing, weapons, fishhooks, carved objects, and even human skulls and hands. The British responded with iron, axes, and cloth in return. Although the sailors tried communicating, Polynesian languages had little effect, and it was soon clear these people were distinct from Pacific Islanders.

The logs and journals vary in accuracy and details, sometimes retreating into racial generalizations to describe the local people in relation to Europeans, Polynesians, and other Americans. But they also carefully describe the local culture, particularly the people in the nearby village at Yuquot, who were from the Mowachaht tribe of the Nuu-chah-nulth nation. John Ledyard, an American who was corporal of marines on the *Resolution*, was from Connecticut, so he drew similarities of the Nootka people to other North Americans he had seen on the East Coast. "I had no sooner beheld these Americans than I set them down for the same kind of people that inhabit the opposite side of the continent," he wrote. "They are rather above the middle stature, copper-coloured, and of an athletic make . . . in their manners they resemble the other aborigines of North-America, they are bold and ferocious, sly and reserved, not easily provoked but revengeful; we saw no signs of religion or worship among them, and if the sacrifice it is to the God of liberty." He thought their language was "very guttural," and if written in English it "would very much abound with consonants."[4]

The oratory and songs of the people intrigued the sailors. Cook noted,

> On their first coming they generally went through a singular ceremony; they would paddle with all their strength quite round both Ships, A Chief or other principal person standing up with a Spear, or some other Weapon in his hand and speaking, or rather hollaring all the time, sometimes this person would have his face covered with a mask, either that of the human face or some animal, and sometimes instead of a weapon would hold in his hand a rattle. After making the Circuit of the ships they would come along side and begin to trade without further ceremony. Very often indeed they would first give us a song which all joined with a very agreeable harmony.

Burney was also impressed, writing they had an unusual ability to shout and hold a single note in unison until it echoed off distant mountains.

The English stayed a month in the sound, where it rained nearly every day. Once the ships were repaired and provisions secured, they pressed on. No sooner had they entered the Pacific than the wind shifted and they were enveloped in another storm, a whirlwind of crashing waves, high winds, and a drenching rain. The need to make up for lost time outweighed any other consideration, so Cook pressed on, unwilling to return to Nootka to wait out the storm. Clerke called it "a perfect hurricane." By nightfall the gale was tearing at the rigging, as the vessels pitched in the seas. The weather was so hostile that even at daybreak they could not see the length of their ships through the fog, mist, and screaming winds. The weather was "dark and rainy." They could only navigate by compass far out to sea, and not by coastal features.[5]

The storm finally passed after a week's fury. They were in the latitude of modern-day Sitka. There were no injuries, just weary agitation about the deplorable condition of the ships, especially the *Resolution*. In the meantime they passed a good part of the coast, six degrees in latitude, and all without sight of land. But when it cleared they saw the Alaska coast was even more rugged than the topography of Nootka Sound, a wild and tremendous landscape of towering mountains, deep valleys, and rocky shores. It was a stark and dramatic scene, teaming with wildlife. Steep, dense woodlands of spruce, hemlock, and cedar surrounded each body of water. They frequently saw whales, seals, and sea otters, even bird life.

Cook was aware the expedition was now in the area of Russian influence, so he began to refer to maps he carried that were supposed to come from first-hand observations of the Russian voyagers. But the maps, particularly von Stählin's, were woefully inaccurate. The coastline was solid, not a series of islands as portrayed, and it trended to the west, and then southwest, adding enormous distances to the pretended outlet with Hudson Bay. Soon the expedition entered another inlet on the Pacific, now called Prince William Sound, where Webber drew the striking and forbidding landscape at Snug Corner Cove.

In Prince William Sound the expedition came in contact with several dozen local people who came to the ships despite severe weather. They came all night and, after a time, some ventured on board. They reminded Cook of Greenland Eskimos he had observed in Canada years earlier. He had a copy of the *History of Greenland*, by the Moravian missionary David Crantz (1767), an illustrated book with chapters offering "a Description of the Country and its Inhabitants." Cook readily compared the people of the Sound to those in the book. Certain he had found Eskimos so far from Greenland, he speculated there might be a real opportunity to find the imagined water-borne connection to Hudson Bay.

Although far short of the parallel at which they were to begin investigating, Cook discharged the shore boats to look for channels and passageways. John Gore and Henry Roberts were sent to examine the northern arm of the sea, probably entering modern-day Valdez Arm before retreating. Gore reported he saw "the entrance of an arm which he was of the opinion extended a long way to the northeast, and that probably by it a passage might be found." Roberts was less enthused, advising Cook "they saw the head or end of this arm." William Bligh took another crew east, and returned with a similar discouraging report. Although Burney was less certain, Cook decided Prince William Sound was a great cul-de-sac. The only matter of consequence was that they found and named Bligh Island, later assigned to the nearby Bligh Reef, on which the oil tanker *Exxon Valdez* would famously ground two centuries later.[6]

Ever the optimist, Gore wanted to press on to examine these distant inlets, but Cook declined, speculating that it was unlikely any channel or strait could extend 1,500 miles to connect Alaska with Hudson Bay. Rather than get entangled in the shoals of a narrowing inlet, Cook chose to exit Prince William Sound and investigate to the west. Sailing along the Kenai Peninsula to the southwest, in a few days they reached the entrance of today's Cook Inlet. Burney and Gore were thrilled, assuming they had reached the western tip of America and they were entering a channel that would lead them to a temperate Arctic Ocean that would take them to Europe. But after a week of sailing with the tide, anchoring on the ebb, they soon discovered they were effectively embayed in a long, narrowing channel, with unpredictable winds and extraordinary tides that confound sailors even to this day. When they reached the apparent end of the channel at today's Fire Island, it divided into two smaller arms. Bligh investigated the northern route and soon found its end. Efforts to explore the eastern channel were frustrated by adverse tides and winds, so the search was abandoned. In exasperation, Cook called it "Turnagain Arm," the name still in use today.[7]

On June 1, 1778, Lieutenant King led a party to take possession of the region for King George III at a nearby point of land, today called "Point Possession," where the local Dena'ina people first met Europeans. The ritual claim of British possession was similar to the routine performed by Europeans in new lands. The shore party displayed the flag, turned the turf, buried a bottle with some coins and papers, and drank some port wine to the health of the king. The Natives observed the ceremony with a touch of wonder and amusement. As Midshipman George Gilbert explained, "We . . . took possession of the Country in the name of His Britannic Majesty. . . . About a dozen of the Natives were present and behaved very friendly but had no idea what we were doing."[8]

Cook assumed the inlet was a wide river, but he was so frustrated with the two-week delay that he gave it no name. "If the discovery of this River should prove of use, either to the present or future ages," Cook wrote, "the time spent in exploring it ought to be the less regretted, but to us who had a much greater object in View it was an essential loss; the season was advancing apace." Undeterred, Gore had Roberts prepare a chart for his journal, where he called the inlet "The Gulf of Good Hope." Prominent features on this chart later encouraged the Admiralty to believe there were prospects for finding the elusive passage to the Atlantic, including "Cape Hope," "Mount Welcome," and the "Land of Good Prospect." The island of the cape that enters the inlet was "Hopes Return."

Residents of present-day Anchorage, Alaska, take pride in knowing that Captain Cook was the first European to visit the region, now with the largest population of all the places he visited that summer, but few are aware that Cook despised the place. Ironically, the British Admiralty later named it after the Captain. When Cook's third voyage journal was published in 1784 the Admiralty called it "Cook's River." After Vancouver's definitive survey a decade later, it was changed to "Cook's Inlet."[9]

The expedition sailed southwest for nearly a month before it found a passage to the north in the Aleutian Islands. In late June the expedition had a close call. They were still on their westerly course weaving though islands in fog and mist. Cook wrote, "Daylight availed us little as the Weather was so thick that we could not see a hundred yards before us, but as the wind was now very moderate I ventured to run." Throwing caution to the wind, he spread the sails to run with the wind, but no sooner had they unfurled the sails than they took them in. When the fog cleared they found themselves in a deep bay surrounded by rocks. They might have perished in an instant. "The sound of breakers had been the sound of salvation," Cook wrote. "The ships had been running straight for the shore, which was only three quarters of a mile off, the head of a bay guarded at each side by a high rock, with lesser ones attendant." He was candid about their luck, "Providence had conducted us through between these rocks where I should not have ventured in a clear day and to such an anchoring place that I could not have chosen a better." John Ledyard clarified their good fortune, "when the fog cleared up, and we found ourselves embayed with rocks, reefs, and an island, all within two cables length. We were not only amazed to find ourselves in such a frightful situation, but were still more astonished to conceive how we got there, as the least accidental deviation from the course we had steered would have been fatal."

After finding a passage through the Aleutians near Unalaska, the voyagers sailed north, finally achieving the Admiralty's assigned 65° North Latitude. Shallow water at the Yukon Delta forced the expedition to cross to Siberia, where they had a brief and peaceful encounter with Chukchi warriors. Stretching north again, they passed Bering Strait, and by August 16 the ships were above the Arctic Circle. They saw walrus, several flocks of birds, and sea ice. Cook spent much of the second voyage sailing in and out of the ice approaching Antarctica and, as he passed the Arctic Circle the northern horizon had an unmistakable brightness that warned him they would soon reach the Arctic ice pack. "We perceived a brightness in the Northern horizon like that reflected from ice, commonly called the blink," he reported "it was little noticed from the supposition that it was improbable we should meet with ice so soon, and yet the sharpness of the air and Gloomyness of the Weather for two or three days past seemed to indicate some sudden change."[10]

They reached the ice pack as they neared 71° North Latitude two days later. Cook said it was "as compact as a wall," where he found solid, impassible sea ice ten or twelve feet high that seemed to extend from the shores of Alaska to Asia. When the weather cleared they could see land three or four miles to the east, which Cook dubbed "Icy Cape," a significant coastal feature southwest of modern-day Point Barrow, Alaska. The crew was alarmed when the ships were forced against the shore in a sudden gale, trapping them between ice and rock. When it appeared they were embayed, the winds just as suddenly reversed direction and the ships escaped. Alaskans today know the ice pack frequently moves far off shore at this time of year, exposing open water leading past Point Barrow to the Canadian Arctic. Fortunately the pack ice was solid that year. Had they been able to follow the coast any further north, changing winds would have almost certainly ensnared them, blocking any hope of retreat.

As the vessels ran alongside the ice, the crew frequently came in contact with walrus or "sea horses," as Cook called them, and they shot several for fresh meat. Cook said this "marine beef" was "as sweet as Marmalade." He wrote, "we had got on board the Resolution Nine of these Animals . . ., so that we were not a little disappointed, especially some of the Seamen who for the Novelty of the thing, had been feasting their eyes for some days past . . . we lived upon them so long as they lasted and there were few on board who did not prefer it to salt meat." Clerke was equally effusive. "For my own part," he wrote, "I declare I think them pleasant and good eating; and they doubtless must be infinitely more nutritive and salutary than any salt Provision we can possibly have in store, or I believe any in the World."

But most of the crew found the meat repugnant. Midshipman George Gilbert wrote:

> the flesh disgustfull as it was we eat thro extreme hunger . . . the quality of which will be best described in the several preparations it went through before it was possible to eat it; in the first place we let it hang up for one day that the blood might drain from it, which would continue to drop for four or five days, when permitted to remain so long but that our hunger would not allow of at first; after that we towed it overboard for 12 hours then boil'd it four hours and the next day cut it into stakes and fry'd it; and even then it was too rank both in smell and taste to make use of except with plenty of peper and salt and these two articles were very scarce amongst us.[11]

After sailing the length of the ice pack from Alaska to Russia, the expedition turned south past the Siberian coastline, then back to Alaska at Norton Sound before returning to Aleutian Islands. Recollecting the voyage after forty years, Burney said the explorers were in a collective congratulatory mood. "And here closed our first season of northern discovery, a season of unremitting activity. The ability and diligence exercised will best appear by comparing the Map of the World drawn immediately after and by keeping in mind that the addition of so large and extent of intricate coast, before unknown, was effected by the labour of a single expedition in a little more than half a year."[12]

They spent much of the month of October in Unalaska with the local Aleut or Unangan people. Unlike the people encountered further east, these people were already under the influence of Europeans, the Russian fur hunters or "promyshlenniks." The English journals offer an account of the society under stress from commercial exploitation. In three voyages spanning a decade at sea, Cook encountered dozens of cultures in the far reaches of the Pacific. He had spent eight arduous months in the North Pacific since the landfall at Oregon, and his only other substantial contact was with the people at Nootka Sound. Yet these Aleuts held a special place in the journals. These were "the most peaceable inoffensive people I ever met with" Cook wrote, "they are remarkably cheerfull and friendly amongst each other and always behaved with great civility to our people."[13]

When word spread of their arrival, the principal Russian factor for the region, Gerasim Grigorovich Ismailov, turned up with twenty or thirty Aleut hunters in kayaks. Although they did not share a common language, he and Cook spent hours poring over Russian maps and compared them to Cook's recent discoveries. Ismailov had been with Sindt and confirmed that the published Russian maps had nothing to do with the voyage and that Alaska was not an island. Instead, he confirmed the Alaska landmass was impassible and that the mainland to the east was called "Alaska." "I have already observed that the American Continent is here called by the Russians as well as Indians *Alaska*," Cook observed, "which is the proper Indian name for it . . . [they] call the whole by that name and know very well that it is a great land."[14]

Cook could only speculate about how the Russians controlled the local people, or how long they had been in control of Unalaska, but he knew the Aleuts were not hunting solely for profit. "I never thought to ask how long it was sence they got a footing upon *Oonalaska* and the neighbouring isles, but to judge from the great subjection the Natives are under, it must have been some time." The Russians had been in control of Unalaska for about three years when Cook arrived. When the Russians reached the Aleutian Islands after Bering's voyage in 1741, the Aleuts inhabited all of the major Aleutian Islands and much of the Alaska Peninsula to the east. The estimated population at first contact was as many as 18,000. By 1799, when the Russian-American Company was formed, probably half of all Aleut males between eighteen and fifty years of age were hunting for the Russians, enslaved to pay tribute in furs to protect their families. The population was reduced by as much as eighty percent during the first and second generations of Russian contact.[15]

When he left Unalaska, in the event his expedition was lost at sea, Cook gave Ismailov a chart to be forwarded to the Admiralty depicting his discoveries to date. Sketchy as it was, it showed "all the Northern coasts I visited" and for the first time put New Albion, Nootka Sound, Prince William Sound, Cook Inlet, the Alaska Peninsula, and Bering Strait in their correct locations. It arrived in London in March 1780, six months before the expedition's return, and offers Cook's assessment of the expedition's achievements that grueling summer along the Northwest Coast. Like many of the chart makers on board the two ships, Burney and Roberts included similar charts in their journals, revealing the actual trend in the Alaska coastline for the first time.

Although Cook provided thoughtful descriptions of his meetings with the inhabitants from Nootka Sound to Unalaska, the expedition's relations with the people of the Northwest Coast were relatively detached and formal. Instead, during this time of intense exploration, Cook concentrated on seafaring and discovery, not interpersonal relations. As the expedition left Unalaska in late October, Gilbert wrote "This ended a very hazardous and disagreeable Season; wherein we surveyed an extent of Coast of 1200 Leagues which is far more than ever any navigator had done before." Cook and his crew longed for a long rest in warmer climates. "My intention was now to proceed to the *Sandwich Islands* to spend a few of the Winter Months," Cook wrote, "and then proceed to *Kamtschatka*, endeavoring to be there by the Middle of May next."[16]

1

NOOTKA SOUND
FEBRUARY–APRIL 1778

The expedition left Hawai'i to begin the search for the Northwest Passage in early 1778. There were few entries in the journals except when they confirmed the ships were approaching a colder, more forbidding shore. The coast of Oregon was first observed on March 7, 1778. Burney claimed the Oregon coast was covered in snow, but Roberts said it was really sand with patches of snow. A gale soon arose with constant wind, rain, sleet, and high seas that drove the expedition southward and out to sea. Roberts was alarmed when the storm blew them within a few miles of the coast before the ships could safely get away. It was an alarming prospect. Roberts said they even saw a water spout, suggesting a tornado.

After two weeks fighting the miserable storm, the ships rejoined the coast and followed it to the north. In desperate need of wood, water, and refreshment, Cook chose his first entry along the west coast of Vancouver Island (although he did not know it was an island) where the expedition made first contact with people of the Northwest Coast at Nootka Sound. It was a pleasant, melodic welcoming, followed by periods of intense trade. While both writers described the regional topography and shipboard routine in detail, Burney's journal offers the more precise portrayal of the people of the region and their interplay with the sailors. His observations are a welcome complement to the captain's journal, particularly the description of their language and customs, as well as the revelation that the people had two silver tablespoons from an earlier Spanish visit. The British apparently exchanged the spoons for a pewter wash basin.

Roberts was consumed by the repair and replacement of the masts of the *Resolution*, many of which were ruined in the previous weeks at sea, and the confounded weather, as it seemed to rain in Nootka Sound every day. He was not as concerned as Burney about the interplay with the local people, although he was alarmed about a confrontation between two neighboring tribes over the right to trade with the British.

In a month the voyagers completed their chores, struck the tents, bid farewell to the local people, and sailed back into the Pacific. They had not been in the open ocean long when they were confronted by another storm that forced them well out to sea. They did not return to the coast until they reached the latitude of modern-day Sitka.

JOURNAL OF JAMES BURNEY

February 1778 Till we passed the 30th degree of North Latitude the Wind continued Easterly and after became Variable. Made the best of our Way to the North and Eastward.

John Webber, "A Man of Nootka Sound" and "A Woman of Nootka Sound," circa 1781-83. Companion pen, wash, and water color images depicting Nuu-chah-nulth man and woman observed in April 1778. The man has a squared pattern on his forehead and a ring through his nose and wears ornaments suspended from his right ear. The woman is wearing a cedar bark rain cape with a sea otter fur collar and a basketry rain hat decorated with scenes of whale hunting. Dixson Library, State Library of New South Wales, PXX 2, f. 21 and 22.

As different Weather was to be expected from what we had lately been used to, a great part of our running Rigging was shifted with new Cordage. The Old Sails unbent and put by, and other necessary preparations made.

Saturday 14th At 8 this morning thought we saw Land to the WSW. [Bearings omitted. No land observed, just a cloud bank in the mid Pacific.]

Friday 28th Thomas Goodman, Seaman, fell out of the Fore Shrouds and broke his Collar Bone, which was set and he soon in a fair way of recovery.

March 6th Saw Drift Wood, Sea Weed & many Divers.

Saturday 7th At Daylight the Resolution made the Signal for seeing Land, which proved to be the Continent of America. At 8 had Soundings at 95 fms, the Land bearing from NNE to ESE distant about 9 Leagues. Latitude at Noon 44°32′ North/Longitude 235°10′ East. Variation 17½° East.

Sunday 8th Wind Westerly. The Weather unsettled and a Swell setting in from the Sea, stood to the SSW to Clear the Land.

Wednesday 11th Wind North. At 7 in the morning Stood within 4 miles of the Land. [Bearings omitted.] From the Northernmost Land in sight which bore N½W about 10 miles distant, to a point 6 Leagues SE from us, a Straight Shore. Around this point the Land bends in and we saw a continuation of it as far as SSE per Compass. The Country woody in many places covered with Snow. Saw Smokes. Tackd and ran off, the Wind veering round to the Westward with dirty Weather, were obliged to keep an Offing.

Saturday 14th Saw the Land bearing SE. A fresh Gale from the NW with Hail and Sleet.

Sunday 15th Our Stock of Yams being expended, served Biscuit again at 2/3rd allowance.

Sunday 22nd Made the Land again, having Moderate Weather. [Bearings omitted.] The land bearing from NNE to East, distance 6 Leagues. Ran to the NNW (wind at West) till Sunset 7 Leagues when the Land in sight . . . and an appearance of a Harbour . . . 7 or 8 miles distant. Night coming on, we Tackd, expecting to stand in, the next morning, but the bad weather again obliged us to keep the Sea on which account we went to a daily allowance of Water 2 Quarts each man.

We saw no more of the Land till the 29th in the Forenoon, . . . [when we] stood in for the shore with a fresh breeze . . . for an appearance of a Harbour to the ENE. At 1/2 past 4, the Resolution made the Signal for Anchoring and soon after we got in the Entrance of a deep Sound and past a Town on the Western Shore [Yuquot in Nootka Sound]. Some Canoes came alongside, shaped not unlike Norway yawls, No Outriggers. Being pretty well within the Sound, tried Soundings and got bottom at 55 and 60 fathoms. Ran to the NE farther up in hopes of Shoaler Water, but at dark were obliged to Anchor in 67 fathoms, 3 or 4 miles within the Entrance of the Sound and within a quarter of a mile of the South part of an Island. The Resolution having Anchord further up to the NE in 86 fms [Bearings omitted.] Found the Tide drained out all Night. Some Canoes kept watch round the Ship.

Monday 30th At Daylight, Boats were sent from each Ship to look for better Anchorage. At 1 they returned, having found a good Harbour about 6 miles to the Westward [Friendly Cove] whither we should have gone, but in the Evening, discovered a Small Cove not half a mile distant in the Island [Bligh Island] near us with good Anchorage, Wood and Water. Up the Sound to the NE and Northward, the Water deepens to above 100 fathoms.

Tuesday 31st Shifted our Birth and Moord Head and Stern in the Cove, the Small Bower out in 17 fms muddy bottom, and Hawsers fast to the Shore . . . East Shore of the Sound about a mile distant.

Captain Cook names this King George's Sound. It is between 2 and 3 miles wide at the Entrance, and opens one way to the NNW, the other to the NE. How far it runs up was not discovered.

The Head of the Resolutions Foremast being sprung, it was stripped and on examination found necessary to be got out to be repaired. Her lower Rigging being in the same state, they were obliged to fit new Main Shrouds.

Wooding, Watering, repairing Sails and Rigging, Caulking and other necessary Jobs were carried on as usual. Both Ships fixed additional Rudder Chains to secure the Rudder in case of getting intangled in the Ice.

We Brewed Spruce Beer and were supplied with plenty of Fish by the Indians, with whom we were soon upon familiar terms, they visiting us every day, and for the first week, never failed leaving two or three Canoes to watch us during the Night.

Wednesday, April 1st This morning, 2 Indians had a Quarrel whilst alongside the Ships. The occasion we could not make out. The Disputants who were in different Canoes, seized each other by the hair with both hands, and held their foreheads close joined together, probably for fear one should dash his head against the others face. All the other Canoes hastened to the Spot and the Hubbub became general. Several Indians stripped themselves naked ready to join in the quarrel, which however ended in words and the plunder of 2 or 3 Canoes.

Their Language though not in general guttural, is harsh, and when they are in a passion, or very earnest in discourse, seems insufficient to express their feelings. This they make up in Action, jumping at each other and nodding their Heads in a manner that much resembles Punch and the Devil [puppet show of the era]. While any Single person is Speaking no one seems to attend or to take the least notice, yet when he has finished another will begin, whilst the former, however violent during his Oration, sits down with the same apparent indifference. Listening without looking.

We did not on our first Arrival discover the Inhabitants to be a white people, so disfigured and besmeared were they with paint and dirt. Of those who were clean enough to distinguish, some few had a colour equal to our Country people in England.

Their common Dress is either a Skin, a Blanket of their own Manufacture, or a Cloth made like the New Zealand Hahoo, but of much coarser flax, which is thrown loose over their Shoulders. They wear besides a Wicker or Straw Hat and a short Cloke of the flax Cloth made with a hole in the middle to put the Head through, and hangs down equally all round. This last is chiefly worn by the women.

Saturday 4th At 11 this forenoon, all the Indians about us, went ashore to the Watering place and hauld up their Canoes on account of another party they said were coming. Soon after a Number of Canoes from the outer part of the Sound, made their appearance off the South Point of the Cove, armed with pikes, Bows and Arrows, Knives, and a Weapon of the same size and intention as the New Zealand patow, but in various Shapes. Most of them were dressed in long loose Buck Skins doubled and made up like a Womans Shift without Sleeves, being sewed at the Sides, with separate openings for the Head and each Arm.

Both Ships turned all Hands to Small Arms and those who were at work ashore assembled on a Rock where the Astronomers Tents were erected. In this Situation we dined under Arms, the new Comers all the while remaining off the South point of the Cove and the other party on shore. After Dinner we went on with our work till 3 in the Afternoon, when they drew near the Watering place and we took to our Arms again. A parley ensued between the 2 parties, which ended in a reconciliation, the Canoes separating and the Indians taking off their War Dresses.

Their pikes are Stout Sticks headed with a large bone, well Sharpened at the End. Their arrows are likewise headed with bone, and bearded, the inner end feathered. Their Knives are in form of a Semicircle, the outer part being the Edge, and made of Iron, which we found them well stocked with. They had copper, but in no great quantities. Besides the Arms above mentioned, they brought a Cargo of Stones. In the Evening, several of the larger Canoes Saluted us by making a Circuit round the Ships and giving 3 Halloos at their departure. They paddle in most excellent time, the foremost man in every 3d or 4th stroke making flourishes with his paddle. The Halloo is a single note in which they all join, Swelling it out in the middle and letting the Sound die away. In a Calm with the hills around us it had an effect, infinitely superior to what might be imagined from any thing so simple.

These Indians are rather quarrelsome, and though not over cautious in their own conduct very apt to take offense at the slightest indignity. But to do them justice, when they are angry, any little degree of submission immediately pacifies them.

In stature they nothing exceed Mediocrity, the men rather lean. The Women are in general broad faced with high Cheek bones, and Jolly, likely Wenches, but they most filthily ornament themselves with a mixture of Paint and Blubber over their Hair and Face. Yet are they more modest and Coy than the Women we met with between the Tropics.

The Men daub their faces with Tallow in which they scratch different kind of figures, and powder their Hair with the finest down of Birds, which is thrown out of a Machine like a powder Puff. The Noses and Ears of both sexes are bored to hang any thing by way of ornament.

Sunday 5th The Canoes from the outer part of the Sound visited us at daylight, leaving a canoe without the Mouth of the Cove to watch.

At 7 the Guard Canoe made Signals, on which all the rest left the Ships and paddled as fast as they could round the South point of the Cove to prevent being cut off. At the same time the party from the Northward, which was now the strongest, made their appearance. They stopped abrest the middle of the Cove and single Canoes passed and repassed in consequence of which the flying Canoes returned, and after a short parley, erected their Pikes and began a Song, beating Time with the lower end of the Pikes against the Sides of the Canoes. Having finished, they laid down their Pikes and the other Party who had during the performance Sat still, now reared theirs and gave a Song in return, which being ended, the Southern Canoes Saluted them with the parting Halloo, and went off, leaving the Market to the quiet procession of the Northern Party for that day.

Their Song was composed of a variety of Strange Placed Notes in a solemn stile: all in Uniform and well in tune. The first words were given out by one man as a Parish Clerk gives out the first Line of a Psalm.

This Afternoon a Canoe alongside, treated us with a Song of a different kind, which was very laughable. Three people Sung, beating Time with their Paddles, whilst one with a Deer Head Mask on, made motions resembling that animal. They have great variety of Masks not ill executed, in likeness of different Animals and Birds, which they probably use for Decoys. They have Snares and all kinds of Bird Calls, and are excellent at imitation, as well in Voice and Action as in Carving. The Shyness of the Game here is a sufficient proof of their being Good Sportsmen. They parted willingly with any of their Masks, except those of the Human Face. When any of these were Sold, it was done in a clandestine manner, as if ashamed of being seen.

Tuesday 7th The Resolution's Foremast was taken out and got on shore to be repaired.

The 8th and 9th had a very heavy Gale of Wind from the Eastward, on which account we carried out another Anchor. In this Gale, the Resolution Sprung the head of her Mizen Mast, which they afterwards got out, and were obliged to make a

John Webber, "A View of the Habitations in Nootka Sound," circa 1781-83. Pen, wash, and water color sketch depicting the Nuu-chah-nulth people and their homes at Yuquot observed in April 1778. Groups of people are clad in skins standing on the beach with flat-roofed houses in the background interspersed with drying racks for fish. Dixson Library, State Library of New South Wales, PXX 2, f. 23.

new one, here being plenty of good Trees for that purpose. Each Ship provided themselves with a Spare Topmast and what other Sparrs they wanted.

Saturday 18th The Resolution got her Foremast in, and 2 or 3 days after, her new Mizen Mast.

Monday 20th An Indian who was admitted into Captain Cooks Cabin contrived to carry off his Watch, and left the Ship before it was missed. His Canoe being seen alongside of us, Notice was sent, and on search the Watch found in a Chest of the Canoe.

Captain Cook went this morning with both Ship's Cutters up the Sound and returned in the Afternoon. This same day, 2 old fashioned Silver Table Spoons, suposed to be Spanish, were bought of the Indians alongside the Resolution for a Pewter Wash Hand Basin.

Wednesday 22nd The Resolution's Pinnace and our great Cutter went to the Town on the West Side of the Entrance into the Sound to cut Grass.

This Town stands at the back of a Sandy beach in the bottom of a fine little Cove, where is good Anchorage, and consists of 2 Rows of Houses, one behind the other, in a line with the Water Side. Their Houses are built of Wood, each being one large Room, 7 or 8 feet high on the inside. One Side is somewhat higher than the other and covered with loose broad planks laying across, that reach from side to side, and move occasionally, to admit light or shut out the weather. The Entrance is in a nook, formed by a break in the Side, one part projecting out a little and continued, so as to overlap the other, making a short narrow Lane. Over one of the Houses was placed lengthways 3 large Sparrs, the middle stout enough for a great Ships Mainmast. This was supported at one end by an enormous Image of a Man's Head.

Within Doors they are as uncleanly as in their persons, heaps of stinking fish bones and dirt lying in every corner. At this time they were drying great quantities of small fish, that hung up in their Houses for the benefit of the Smoke. On the beach were stages for drying larger Fish, at present unoccupied. They boil their Victuals in wooden boxes by throwing in red hot Stones. At the back of the Town was a large Plantation of Cherry Trees, Gooseberry and Currant Bushes, Raspberries and Strawberries, unluckily for us, none of them in season. The Indians were very hospitable, and seemed to take more pains to avoid giving offence, than when alongside our Ships.

Our opinions concerning the number of the Inhabitants at this Town differed widely, from 500 to 2000. The Canoes on the Beach were counted 95.

Besides this we saw 4 other Towns in different parts of the Sound.

Friday 24th Being ready for Sea, Struck the Tents and got every thing on board. The wood here is all pine and being full of Turpentine, consumes away very fast, on which account we took as much as we possibly could.

This forenoon an Indian alongside the Resolution was shot in the backside for some unfair dealing. Four Canoes of the same party immediately left the Cove, threatening that they would soon return. The Indians in the other Canoes gave themselves no concern about the matter.

With respect to Traffic: Iron, Brass and Copper were the Articles on which the Indians set the greatest Value. Lead, Pewter and Tin went off well at the beginning, but soon fell into disrepute. Any Crack or flaw in Iron lowered the value of it considerably, which makes it probable they beat it out cold. On their part they brought Deer, Wolf, Fox and Bear Skins, and Furs which we supose to be chiefly of the Sea Beaver. They likewise supplied us with Fish, and a quantity of Oil for burning was brought, sufficient to serve both Ships a Twelve month. They keep their Trade in double Boxes, one going over and inclosing the other. Many of our people provided themselves with Bear Skin Coats, which are excellent for keeping out rain.

Saturday 25th Took up the Best Bower Anchor and cast off some of our Shore fast. As we hove up the Anchor, all the Canoes in the Cove assembled together, and sung us a parting song, flourishing the Saws, Swords, Hatchets and other things they had got from us.

One man was mounted on a Stage of loose Boards, supported by the Indians nearest it, and danced with different Masks on, at one time, resembling a man, and at others, a Bird or a Beast.

The wind being unsteady were obliged to lay fast till next day.

Sunday 26th In the Afternoon having light Variable winds, Towed the Ships out of the Cove. At 6 a breeze sprung up from the NW. At 8 were abrest the western point of the Entrance into the Sound. The Wind soon after Shifting to the ESE with squally Weather, Stood to the Southward all Night for an Offing. Next morning seeing nothing of the Land, Bore away to the NW.

28th and 29th A Strong Gale from the SE.

30th Moderate Weather. Wind the same. Still continuing our Course towards the NW.

Journal of Henry Roberts

[Six weeks of ship duties, bearings, coordinates, wind and weather. The *Discovery* in company.]

Monday, February 9th, 1778 Saw a Grampus [whale] and some flying fish and sheerwaters about. People employed picking of Oakum and working up Junk. Sailmakers mending the worn sails & Carpenters on the Boats, which received much damage from the surf at the late Islands.

Tuesday 10th Found a very sensible difference in the Weather, the wind veering round to the North, renders the air much cooler as the thermometer.

Wednesday 11th Served a Cask of spruce beer to the people brewed from the Essence that we brought from New Zealand.

Monday 16th Found one of the Starboard Iron Threads broke, owing to the strain occasioned by the main Topmast Staysail Tack. Knotted the Shroud, & fixed a slight spare (athwart the whole to make each Shroud to have an equal strain) with a Thimble to haul the Tack down by. People employed picking of Oakum.

Thursday 26th Saw the Aurora Borealis shooting very strong between the NNW and NE.

Friday, March 6th Many porpoises about. Passed the stump of a Tree. Saw 2 seals and several Grampoises or Whales.

Saturday 7th A swell from the NW. Passed much sea wreck or rock weed. A number of seals and birds about, chiefly Gulls. A number of whales seen. At day-break saw the land [and] made the signal to the Discovery. The low land shew itself first, the High points being covered with haze, which soon cleared away & appeared very hilly & Mountainous but could not perceive any parts covered in the snow. Many seals and large flocks of birds around us.

Sunday 8th A heavy swell from the NW. A number of Seals and Porpoises about the Ships and many Birds, Gulls, Gannetts and the large kind of brown Peterel. The Extreme of the land from NNE to SE¼S offshore about 5 leagues [West Coast of North America]. The weather being very squally & unsettled & much the appearance of Dirt & blowing hard. Likewise we perceiving no Bay or Harbour to shelter us, we Tacked and stood off, carrying a press of sail to help ourselves from being embayed. Distance off shore 6 or 7 leagues.

Monday 9th The weather very unsettled, Strong Gales and hard Squalls. At 1 a severe squall of wind came in & continued about ½ an hour, obliged us to take the Double Reefs in each topsail. No land in sight.

Tuesday 10th No land to be seen, very few birds about and no seals.

Wednesday 11th Squally weather with Hail and Sleet. A heavy swell at NW. Passed a large log of Wood. Saw the Land the Extreme bearing from NEBN to SE¼E. In the Morning stood in for the land, making in a bluff head with Sharp Cliffs, with a fresh Gale from Northward. At 7 Tacked Ships being within 3 leagues of the Shore. The Land near the Sea in general is of a Moderate height, most parts well covered with Trees resembling the tall Ash Tree. The Hills inland were extremely wooded with patches of Snow, but the summits of the risings near the Skirts of the shore appear to be white sand, which at the Distance might be taken for white Cliffs.

There alarmed us much, just before break of Day, by one of the sailors calling out Breakers! But proved to be nothing more than white sands appearing thru the haze. This part of the Coast has nearly North & South true, being straight, without the appearance of Bay or Inlet.

Thursday 12th Fresh winds & squally, with Hail and Sleet. At ½ past 11 taken aback with a squall of Wind [with] unsettled weather in the NW. Split the Main Top Staysail. The Squalls, extremely severe, got downwind. Saw a Water Spout. Heavy Squalls came on very suddenly.

Friday 13th Hard squalls with Snow and Sleet. Very unsettled weather. Saw a Seal.

Saturday 14th Fresh Gales and Squally with Rain. Heavy Squalls with Hail and Sleet. Very severe Squalls with Wind.

Sunday 15th Strong Gales and heavy Squalls with Hail and Rain.

Friday 20th A number of Whales and porpoises round the ship. Smoaked the Bread Room with Brimstone and killed a vast Number of Cockroaches. These cursed vermin are not so destructive as when we were in the Hot Climates.

Sunday 22nd Fresh breezes and Hazy with hard Rains, the weather unsettled. At 9 the Extremity of the Land seen from the Masthead from N to ENE 12 or 14 leagues, a low point under the highest part of the land. We find the Coast to begin to take a Western Current.

Monday 23rd Fresh breezes and Squally with Hail. At 6 the extremes from NBW and W to ESE. The Northern part (which appeared to be a detached Island or a Deep inlet) was about 9 leagues off. A high Rock making like the Mewstone about 5 leagues, a high round Hill inland offshore about 6 leagues. The land well covered with Wood and to appearance very fertile many levels and gradually rising to the summits of the Hills. No Snow to be seen. A heavy Sea and Showers of Hail.

Monday 30th Saw two appearances of Inlets and bore away for the latter [Nootka Sound]. At 3 had Soundings from 24 to 17 fathoms, then abreast of some sunken Rocks about 2 miles off shore. We now found ourselves in the Mouth of a Deep Sound with 40 and 50 fathoms water and little wind. Hoisted the Boats out to tow her farther in. Several Canoes at this time, round us, immediately offering their few trifles they had with them for sale. At 6 were obliged to Anchor in 90 fathoms, being becalmed between an Island and the West Shore. The Indians continued with us the greatest part of the Night, entertaining us with their Songs which are musical and observe excellent time with the beat of their paddles against their Canoes.

In the Morning the Boats were sent in search of a Convenient place for the Ship. Carpenters over the side caulking. Many Canoes along side.

Tuesday 31st The Boats returned, having found a very commodious Harbour on the Western Shore of the Sound, sheltered well by several small Isles. The Cove is not more than ½ or ¾ of a mile in Breadth, secure from every Wind. Being little winds with Calms, we warped the Ship into a small Cove on the Island abreast of us. Carpenters caulking the upper works. Many of the Natives along side trading.

Wednesday, April 1st Employed securing the Ship. Sent the observatory on Shore, which was fixed on a Rock very near us. Parties sent out to cut wood. Many Natives with us.

Thursday 2nd Found the Top Mast sprung & the larboard Trussletree also sprung. Carpenters employed on the Defects and caulking the sides. Partys wooding and watering. The Natives trading with us bring Bear, Skins, Sea Beaver, also with the Wolfes, Fox, etc. etc.

Friday 3rd Employed wooding, Watering & about the Fore Rigging. Carpenters as Yesterday. Sent hands to brew Spruce Beer. Set the Forge up to make Hoops for the Trussletree. Not so many Canoes with us to Day.

Saturday 4th Punished Patrick Whelon with 6 lashes for Neglect. Got the People from the Shore, being alarmed by the Natives, who armed themselves very precipitously with Stones and lances etc, but it soon appeared to be quarrels among themselves, by a Number of Canoes, which came off round the Southern point of the Cove, well peopled. They afterwards ventured farther in the Cove, and advanced nearer us. After gazing for a little time they continued their rout up the Sound, leaving our few old friends without any molestation. Found the starboard Chunk of the Fore Mast decayed.

Sunday 5th Sent our People to the shore again. Many Canoes were round each point of the Cove, appeared to be two different parties, threatening each other, with brandishing Weapons.

John Webber, "The Inside of a House in Nootka Sound," circa 1781-83. Pen, wash, and water color sketch depicting the inside of a Nuu-chah-nulth home at Yuquot observed in April 1778. More than a dozen men, women, and children are situated in groupings about the home, with fish hanging from poles in the roof and two large carved wooden images in the back. Dixson Library, State Library of New South Wales, PXX 2, f. 24.

Monday 6th Found the Cheeks [Chocks] of the Fore Mast so bad as to oblige us to get it out. Unbent the Main Topsail and Top Gallant Sail and got ready for unrigging the Main Mast. Punished Thomas Hereford, Marine, with 12 lashes for sleeping on his Post.

Tuesday 7th Unrigged the Main Mast & erected the Sheers for the Foremast. Carpenters on shore making Cheeks for it. Got the Mast out.

Wednesday 8th Hauld the Fore Mast on Shore. Got the Tent fixed on Shore to Shelter the Carpenters. Found the Fore Rigging much damaged & the greatest part unfit for service & overhauled the main rigging & fixed it for the Noses. Very few Canoes in the Cove.

Thursday 9th Strong Gales and very severe Squally and Rain. Carpenters on Shore about the mast [finding] the head of the Mizzen Mast sprung. Got the Yard and Topmast down. Employed fitting the rigging.

Sunday 12th Cloudy with showers of Rain. Got the Main Rigging overhead. Cut some spars and erected a Deck Crane and Sheers in order to get the Mizzen Mast out. Carpenters about the Mizzen Mast. Few Canoes about us.

Tuesday 14th Fresh Gales & Squally. Sent Hands on Shore to cut a spar for a Mizzen Mast. Haul'd it on Shore for the Carpenters to work at it.

Wednesday 15th Rainy weather with Thunder and Lightning in the latter part. Got the Fore Mast along side, a small number of the Natives with us.

Friday 24th Got the Observatory on board and a spare Topmast. Cleaned below, set the Main Rigging up. Punished Thomas Dermot with 12 lashes for theft.

Saturday 25th Got on board some Spars and Timber for converting into Plank. Carpenters sawing, hands cutting brooms and others employed about the Rigging.

Sunday 26th This Inlet, which obtained the name of King Georges Sound, in honor of the present Majesty, lies in the Latitude of 49°30′ North and Longitude East of the Meridian of Greenwich 233°17′. It may be known by a remarkable sound, Notu [Nootka]. Situated on the Northern side of the Entrance, from this the land falls slopingly to quite a level and forms a Rocky point within which is a Village of the Natives at the bottom of a very Commodious small Harbour [Yuquot]. The whole of the Country is overrun with wood, chiefly the Pine and Spruce Trees. The Harbours that this Inlet affords are to be found in almost every part, and fresh water generally to be met with. The principle Arms seem to have a great extent and may possibly connect with other outlets, particularly those to the NW and a farther indication is that the immense depth of water before them. The Tides run with no great Rapidity, the utmost was 2½ Miles in the Middle of the Stream, but this small Motion might be occasioned by the great depth of water.

The Habitations of the Inhabitants are but few and those but insignificant, roughly built, of broad Boards, the Roof Flatt, and will admit either wind or water. Several Families live together in one house, which are large, uncouth Dwellings. These people are Filthy & lousy in their person, dirty in their Houses, nor have they in any one respect, the least pretensions to Cleanliness. They were friendly, Courteous and affable in their disposition, but when provoked, it with difficulty, to pacify or form any kind of reconciliation.

The Articles of Trade they putt the most Value on, is all kind of Metal, particularly Brass, which serves them for Ornaments. Iron or Brass, Kettles, Pewter Plates, and in short everything consisting of Metal, they highly esteem. In return for these we got Skins of Bears, Wolves, Moose deer, Foxes, Raccoons, Marlins & Sea Beaver. The two last afterwards proved to be the same found at Kamtschatka and which are so much coveted by the Chinese to that degree that a single Beaver Skin will sell for upwards of one hundred Spanish dollars.

Monday 27th Weighed the small Bower & Towed the Ship out of the Cove. Several Canoes following us. Squally and hard Rain. The Jib split & blew to pieces.

Fresh Gales and Squally with Lightening in the North. Brought too to [exchange] the Mast for the Discovery. Bore away, unbent the Jibb. Strong Gales and thick hazy weather. Carpenters employed making a spare topmast. Sailmakers fixing a new foot cap rope for the Main Top. Bent another Jibb.

Tuesday 28th Strong Gales with heavy Squalls of Rain. A great Sea. Found a great quantity of Water in the Fish Room, upon searching the after parts, we heard the Water sent in the larboard Buttock. Employed the Hands getting the Bread close aft, fearing it would damage & bailing the Water out the most part of the Night. Cleared the Fish room of the Water & find it drain through but slowly. Got the Sails out of the Fore sail room to Dry & made fires between Decks to air the Ship.

2

Prince William Sound and Cook Inlet

May–June 1778

After battling a storm along the coastline of northern British Columbia and Southeast Alaska, the expedition enjoyed the first clear weather in the area of Mt. Edgecumbe, a prominent dormant volcano near modern-day Sitka. A few days later they observed the lofty Mount St. Elias, one of the tallest coastal peaks in the world. On May 12 they entered Prince William Sound, where they met local people in kayaks and looked in vain for the mythical passage to Europe. It was still late winter and the land was covered by snow.

Both Burney and Roberts offer careful descriptions of the Native encounters. While the journal writers were frustrated by petty thievery, they offered a more thorough report on local customs and how these people were distinguished from the people of Nootka Sound. They were captivated by the stone labrets worn by the women in their lower lips, as well as the construction of their water-tight kayaks. Roberts explained the kayaks "never admits a drop of water, although they [were] frequently upset." The *Resolution* had been so badly damaged after leaving Nootka Sound that, during the visits, it was careened on a beach for repairs.

On May 17 two shore boats from the *Resolution* and the *Discovery* were sent to explore and chart the inlets of Prince William Sound, called Sandwich Sound by Cook. They soon returned, finding many islands and inlets surrounded by high peaks, but no sea lane to the north. Relying on the brief foray and the recollections of the local people, Cook concluded there was no sea lane into the interior and that any passageway would be found further west. Burney struggled with the captain's decision to abandon further exploration in what he called a "little Mediterranean Sea," but Cook took advantage of favorable winds to sail out of the sound and resume the voyage westward.

The ships passed the Kenai Peninsula and were soon at the mouth of Cook Inlet, which seemed to be the long-sought opening to the north. Burney and Roberts each described the struggles of the two ships as they sailed against the strong tides, anchoring with each tide to avoid losing ground. The inlet at first offered a promising opening, possibly the imagined passageway, but mountains soon came in view, surrounding the near shore landscape in most directions, and the water was found to be fresh. They turned around at the inlet Cook called "Turnagain Arm" southeast of modern-day Anchorage.

Before leaving Cook Inlet, Roberts apparently joined Lt. King, who took formal possession of the area for the British crown. Both journals recorded the encounter with the local Dena'ina people, then they followed the ships in the cautious, laborious journey returning down the inlet. Roberts described with considerable alarm the grounding of the *Resolution* in mid-channel and the substantial effort to free the ship on the next tide. By June 7 they were sailing west again, the two most promising inlets proving to be dead ends.

John Webber, "A Man of Prince William Sound" and "A Woman of Prince William Sound," circa 1781-83. Companion pen, wash, and water color sketches of Chugach Sugpiaq man and woman observed in May 1778. The man wears a conical basketry hat decorated with geometric designs and a sealskin frock, with a beaded ornament through his nose. The woman is wearing a close-fitting skin jacket with a sea otter fur slung over her shoulders and various bone and beaded ornaments attached to her nose, lips, and ears. Dixson Library, State Library of New South Wales, PXX 2, f. 26 and 27.

Journal of James Burney

Friday, May 1st At Sunset, the Resolution made the Signal for seeing the Land to the NNE. Ran to the Northward all Night.

Saturday 2nd At 4 in the morning, within 3 Leagues of the Land, . . . an Uneven Mountainous Country, the Hills covered with Snow, the Lower parts Woody. Running alongshore all day, . . . passed many deep Bays. Saw large flocks of Geese, Ducks etc. [Bearings omitted.] At 2 in the afternoon were abrest a remarkable flat-top'd Mountain, standing on a point that projects into the Sea [Mt. Edgecumbe].

Sunday 3rd At 4 in the Morning, passed an opening that appeared like the mouth of a River. This forenoon the Resolutions Boat came on board. Learnt they had sprung a Leak, the Night after leaving King Georges Sound, which made them keep their Hand pumps constantly at work for 2 Days, when it stopped of itself. Had Soundings at 4 Leagues off shore 60 fathoms. [Bearings omitted.]

4th 5th 6th & 7th Running alongshore to the NW, with light Variable Winds & Clear Weather. The 7th at Noon, a High Mountain which we take to be Mount

Elias bore NWBN distant 18 Leagues. This was first seen at 4 in the morning on the 4th being then 46 Leagues distant. Latitude observed 59°25′ North, Longitude in 219°11′ East. From Mount Elias the Land trends more Westerly.

8th and 9th Got very little forwards.

Sunday 10th [Bearings omitted.] An Island in sight to the Westward between which and a low point of the Main Land to the NW of us, we attempted to pass [Kayak Island]. Not getting near enough before dark, Stood backwards and forwards all night. Had Soundings from 60 fathoms at 4 Leagues off shore, to 30 fathoms at 2 Leagues distant. Soft muddy bottom.

Monday 11th At 4 in the Morning Mount Elias bore NE½E distant 33 Leagues. This was the last we saw of Mount Elias, being afterwards hid by the Clouds. But from its height above the Horizon, there is reason to conclude, it might be seen in clear Weather at not much less than 60 Leagues distance. Made Sail towards the Channel between the Island mentioned yesterday and the Main Land. The Wind baffling us, at 5 Bore away for the South point of the Island, off which, at half a mile distance, lays a high Rock. The Resolutions Boat went on Shore at the Island, and our small Cutter was out shooting Sea fowl all day. Being little wind, did not get abrest the South point till 8 at Night.

Tuesday 12th [Bearings omitted.] At ¼ past Noon found this point and the back Land separated. The North part of the back Land when in one with the point, bearing West per Compass. Stood for the opening. At 3 past a Small Island on the West Side of the passage. It coming on foggy dirty Weather, hauld up for a Harbour in the Eastern Shore, where at 6 we Anchord near the South point off the Mouth of a Cove in 12 fathoms, muddy bottom. [Bearings omitted.] The outer points of the Harbour lay NWBN and SEBS distant asunder about 4 miles.

At Sunset 2 large Canoes came over from a low point of Land on the opposite side of the Harbour. They stopped at some distance from the Ships and gave us a Song in much the same kind of stile as the Singing we heard at K. Georges Sound. On coming nearer a man whom we suposed to be the Chief of the Party, stood fronting us with his Arms extended strait out. They remained with us about 2 Hours. None of them ventured on board, nor did we understand any thing they said except the Word Toquay, which signifies Beads both here and at K. G. Sound. In the Night, a Small Canoe with two men kept paddling round the Ships and departed before Sunrise.

Wednesday 13th At 10 in the forenoon got under Sail, being directed by Captain Cook to run up the Harbour, he intending to look for a more convenient place to examine his Leaks. Wind SW. Stood backwards and forwards, waiting for the Resolution, whose Anchor held so fast, that they found it difficult to get out of the ground. At Noon she got under Sail. The Wind coming round to the SE, Captain Cook altered his plan and we stood out of the Harbour and steered to the Northward. A fresh Gale with thick hazy Weather and rain, which prevented our seeing whether or not we were running into a Clear Sea.

At 3 Saw more Land to the North and NNE. At 5 having run 9 Leagues to the Northward, Hauld up to the NE between 2 points that bore nearly WNW and ESE of each other per Compass, distance asunder 8 Miles.

At 6 Saw the Land ahead and on each Bow, that appeared broken and disjointed, forming deep Bays and Inlets till 9 Turning up into a Bay near the Southernmost of the 2 points, under double Reefed Topsails, when we Anchord in 12 fathoms, muddy bottom. [Bearings omitted.] Some Canoes came into the Bay from the SW and went alongside the Resolution [Snug Corner Cove].

John Webber, "A View of Snug Corner Cove," circa 1781-83. Pen, wash, and water color sketch of a cove inside Port Fidalgo in Prince William Sound observed in May 1778. Framed by dramatically rendered peaks and glaciers, the *Resolution* and *Discovery* are at anchor, with Chugach Sugpiaq men and women from nearby villages approaching in two large canoes to trade with the British vessels. There is also a smaller kayak with two occupants to the right. Dixson Library, State Library of New South Wales, PXX 2, f. 25.

Thursday 14th Early in the Morning, we were visited by 2 Indians in a small Canoe who seeing only 2 or 3 people on Deck went to the Resolution, where were many other Canoes, who immediately left her and all repaired to us. On entering the Ship, one man begun by throwing the Jolly Boats Rudder over board to those in the Canoes. Our people offering to lay hold of him, he drew a long Knife from under his Jacket and very composedly walked towards the Gangway, seizing a Tin pot that lay in his Way. Whilst his Companions equally willing to profit by so fair an Occasion, were endeavouring to knock the Iron Hoops from off some Casks.

The Alarm was immediately given to our People below, some of whom appearing with Cutlasses, the Indian relinquished his second prize and hastened into his Canoe, as did the rest, describing how much longer our Knives were than theirs, by holding one of their Arms at full length. They all left the Ship carrying the Rudder with them, which was not thought worth making a bustle after, and we had not a single Canoe about us the rest of the day, although the Resolution was surrounded with them, and there they broke all the Glass Scuttles round the Ship that were within reach of their Paddles.

It continuing dirty weather, Moored the Ship. The Resolution on a Careen, examining her Leaks. Saw some Animals running along the Beach, barking, but could not distinguish whether Dogs or Wolves.

Friday 15th The Resolution continuing on a Careen, hoisted out the Launch and compleated our Water. This forenoon saw Land to the Westward, which the foggy Weather had hid from us when we came in. Since leaving King Georges Sound, the Resolution has out sailed us, which we attribute to being too deep by the Head. On this account we got 2 of our Guns down the After Hold and scrubbed the Ships bottom.

In the Afternoon, some Indians visited us, who mindfull of the late quarrel, threw a stick with Birds Wings tied about it into our Boat alongside, and till it was taken into the Ship, would not venture to fasten their Canoes.

This Custom is mentioned in the Account of the Russian Voyages. The stick so bedecked, being there called a Calumet and said to be a peace offering. These Indians all come from the SW, no one inhabiting the Bay we are in.

Their Canoes are only slight wooden Frames, covered with pieces of Whale Skin neatly sewed together. The large Canoes are open for carrying a number of people. The small which are for fishing, carry only one or two men and are close covered all round except where the people sit, which is a round hole hooped. And to prevent any Water getting in, they wear Jackets made of Bladders, which tie close round their Necks and the bottom tucks under the Hoop. They paddle very fast and are well provided with Fish Spears, etc.

The Inhabitants of this part of the Coast differ greatly from those of King Georges Sound. Their Language is even more unintelligible, the words being so muddled upon one another, that it is difficult to catch them. Their Dress is partly the same, viz, the flax Cloth and Wicker Hats. At King Georges Sound they wear the Skins loose; here they make Jackets with Sleeves, Boots and Handskoons [gloves]. But what distinguishes these people from any we have hitherto Seen, is, their under lips being all slit in a line parallel to the mouth and about ¾ of an Inch lower. Through this they thrust their Tongues, or pieces of bone in imitation of Teeth. We found plenty of Iron amongst them, and blue European Beads, which were more valued than Iron or any thing we could produce.

They gave us to understand that there were two ways to the Sea. The one South and the other North, which latter would take us 2 Days and Nights before we came into the open Sea. Their Method of communicating this intelligence was by turning round with their Hands closed and opening them only in the direction of the Passages. The Northern passage they described to be round a point of Land bearing N78°W per Compass from where we lay.

Saturday 16th The Resolution Righted, having repaired her Leaks. Boats away Shooting all Day. Wild Geese and Ducks here in great Numbers but not easy come at. The Country hereabouts produces plenty of Wood, chiefly Firs, and of a very moderate Size. The Ground as yet is nowhere cleared of the Snow.

Sunday 17th At 5 in the morning, got under Sail and stood over to the Westward. A light Easterly Wind and fair Weather. Having run 5 miles out, Saw Land in every direction except the opening we entered at, bearing SSE½E, and the appearance of another outlet, bearing from S½E to S¾W. The Land on every side full of deep Bays and Inlets. At 9 were abrest the point past which, according to our Indian intelligence, we were to find a Passage to the Northward. It falling little wind, the flood set us towards a point half a League farther to the WNW, with Rocks just above Water, laying off ¼ of a mile.

The Resolution being in S of us, sent our Cutters to a point in towing her off. A Light Breeze springing up, Shot past the Rocky Point and deepened our Soundings from 5 fathoms hard bottom, abrest the point, to 15 fms half a mile to the westward. Opened a deep Sound, up which we kept Turning with variable baffling Winds, till 2 in the Afternoon, keeping a Boat a head. Soundings irregular from 46 to 12 fathoms. At 2 Anchored in 19 fathoms muddy bottom in a Bay formed by Islands on the East side of the Sound. [Bearings omitted.]

At 3 our Cutter was sent with the Resolution's Boats to Search for a Passage. At Midnight they returned, having been several miles without seeing the end of the Sound. The Eastern Shore near the Entrance was found to consist of Islands, with passages through towards the Bay we last came from. Further up, the Sound divided into branches leading in different directions. The Tide was tried in Shore, and in the middle of the Stream and at both places the Ebb found to set to the Northward. Though it is certain, this morning when we came in, the flood set us to the North. However no fair conclusion can be drawn from the Course of a Tide amongst such broken Land, where point projects beyond point and so many different Channels communicate with each other.

Nevertheless the report of the Indians and our Boats not finding the End, makes a thoroughfare highly probable, which after all may perhaps lead to the Southward again. If into the North Sea, we stand a fair chance of finding a wider passage more to the Westward; in it is hardly to be suposed that two large Tracts of Land are seperated only by a Labyrinth like this.

A passage directly to the North would be of great advantage to us, for besides hastening our arrival to the scene of business, our stay there might be lengthened with the less hazard, from having so short a Cut to return by. The Wind coming Northerly, which was fair for running out to Sea, this business was given up for fear of expending too much time.

Monday 18th At 3 in the morning Weighd. Stood to the Southward for the Westernmost of the 2 Openings. To the whole of this little mediterranean Sea, which we have been examining since the 12th, Captain Cook gives the Name of Sandwich Sound.

In the Afternoon the Wind came round to the SSW. At Sunset were abrest a Bluff Head, the Northernmost part of the Land between the two openings. About 6 miles to the Westward of this, are a Cluster of low Rocks. Between the Rocks and the Bluff we, stood backwards and forwards all Night, having Soundings from 53 to 95 fathoms, muddy bottom.

The Land between the Openings is a long Island. The East Side is the West Shore of the Opening through which we Entered Sandwich Sound, and the West Side of the long Island makes the Eastern Shore of the passage we are now going out by.

Tuesday 19th At ½ past 4 in the morning Stood to the Southward. Wind ENE. Kept within 2 or 3 miles of the Eastern Shore past a low Island that lays nearly in midchannel to the South of which is a smaller Island with a number of Rocks. Many lesser Islands in different directions. The Land to the Westward [is] broken and full of Inlets. At Noon little wind [so] our Cutter ahead towing. Soundings all morning from 30 to 22 fathoms mud. [Bearings omitted.] Light Airs all the Afternoon. At ½ past 8 Anchord, having gained by 3 miles since Noon. 25 fms mud. Our distance from the nearest of the East Shore 2 miles.

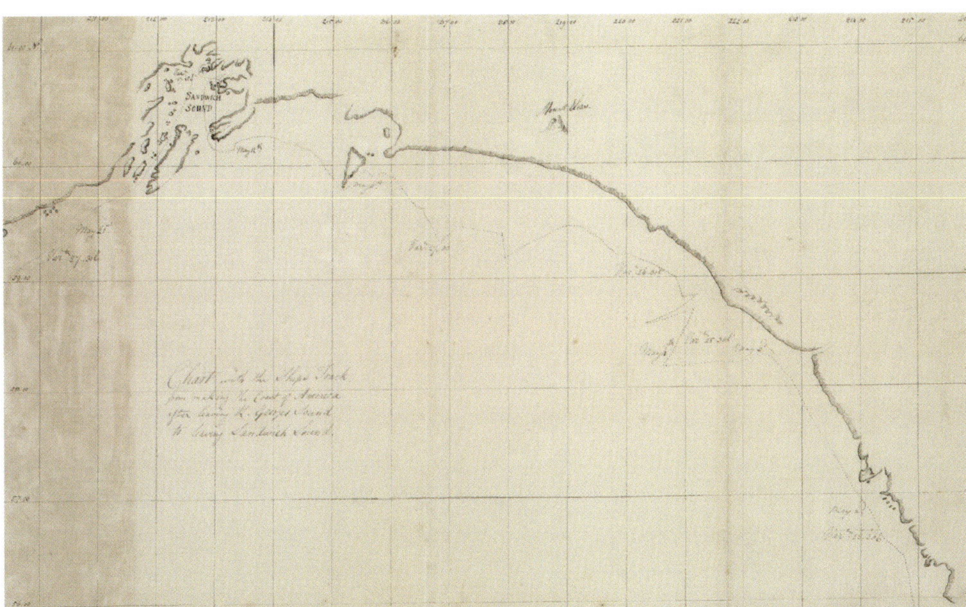

James Burney, "Chart with the Ships Track from Making the Coast of America after Leaving K. George's [Nootka] Sound to leaving Sandwich [Prince William] Sound," May 1778. Burney was the only one to prepare a map of the vessel tracks in the initial months sailing along the coast, drawn after the ships sailed west from Prince William Sound. The chart incorrectly assumed solid land where storms prevented the expedition from observing the coastline of British Columbia and Southeast Alaska. Burney Journal p. 147, Mitchell Library, State Library of New South Wales, Safe 1/64 and 1/79.

Wednesday 20th It continuing little wind with rainy weather, lay fast till 10 in the forenoon, when a breeze sprung up from the NNE and we got under Sail. At 2 in the Afternoon were abrest the high Island in the Entrance between which and the East Shore, the Channel is about 5 miles wide. At 7 were clear out in the Open Sea again. Saw a continuation of the Main Land to the Westward, as far as SW¾S per Compass, which has the same broken appearance as the Land in Sandwich Sound. Stood to the SSW along shore, not coming nearer than within 6 Leagues.

Friday 22nd The Wind having come round to the westward, had thrown us off shore. At Noon were 14 Leagues distant from the Main Land. More Land in sight to the SW, which appears detached from the Main, distant from us 8 or 10 Leagues. [Bearings omitted.]

23rd and 24th Turning to Windward, endeavouring to get in with the Main. Wind Westerly with Squally Weather.

Monday 25th Wind NE. At 8 in the Morning were within 2 Leagues of the SW Land, which proves to be an Island, with Land to the West and South of it that has much the appearance of Islands. Stood to the NNW. [Bearings omitted.] At 4 in the Afternoon, were amongst the Small Islands endeavoring to pass through between them. The Wind baffling us, and a Strong irregular Tide running, were obliged to bear away to the Westward of them. Saw more Land to the WNW, in which direction we Stood all Night.

Tuesday 26th Wind Northerly, a fresh gale and clear Weather, with a great Swell. At 8 in the morning were within 7 or 8 miles of a Mountain that stands in the North point of a Bay in the Western Land. By the South point of this Bay are 2 high Mountains. Tackd and Stood to the Eastward. At Noon latitude observed 59°06′ North. The Cluster of Small Island bearing from East to ESE per Compass. distance about 5 Leagues. Land to the Eastward, which is a continuation of the Land we coasted from Sandwich Sound, . . . [with] Mountainous Land in sight to the Westward . . . From NNW to N27°East no Land to be seen, which with the Swell from the North makes us hope to find the Continent end here [entering Cook Inlet].

Stood over to the NE till 6, when we were in the Mouth of a Bay whose outer points bear of each other NW and SE about 5 miles asunder. Being in a line between these points, at half a League distant from the Southernmost, had soundings at 23 fathoms, Sand. Tackd and kept Turning to Windward all Night.

Wednesday 27th Had light variable winds. Got but little to the Northward. Latitude at noon 59°21′ North. In the Afternoon, Saw Land all round to the Northward except from North to NNW which yet keeps the appearance of a fair Sea. In the Night, saw Fires on the East Shore [Kenai Peninsula].

Thursday 28th At 6 in the morning, finding we lost ground considerably, having but little wind, and the Tide which in the night had set us to the North, now against us. Both Ships Anchord, we in 25 fathoms black Sand and broken Shells. Luckily with our Best Bower Anchor, as we found the Tide running 4 Knots. The Resolution having let go their Stream Anchor, the Cable parted, and they were obliged to Anchor with one of their Bowers. [Bearings omitted.] The Eastern Shore, Low level Land, about 7 miles distant . . . to the South of this falls in a deep Bay, behind which, High Land in sight . . . Our Distance from the Western Shore, 6 or 8 Leagues. The Northernmost part in Sight . . . makes a greater extent of clear Horizon to the Northward, by two Points, than we had Yesterday.

At 10 Slack Water. Weighd and came to Sail. At 11 the Resolution Anchord again, her Boats endeavouring to recover their Stream Anchor. At Noon we Anchord in 25 fms, Sand and broken Shells, half a League to the North of the Resolution . . . distant 8 or 9 miles from the Eastern Shore.

It being doubtfull whether we might not be in the entrance of a large River, the Water was weighd at ¼ past 10 in the forenoon, when the Tide from the North Slacked, and found not to differ from the Water at Sea. [Bearings omitted.] In the Afternoon the Tide from the South Slackd at 4H45m. The Resolutions Boats creeping for the Stream Anchor, but without Success. At 8 a Breeze from the Eastward. At 9 got under Sail. At 10 the Wind Shifted to the Northward, a fresh Gale. All Night turning to Windward.

Friday 29th At 5 in the morning Anchord, in 25 fathoms, Shingles [gravel or pebble bottom]; having gained about 6 Leagues to the NNE this Tide. The Channel here, about 10 Leagues across. The East Shore, a low level Country, . . . distant 7 or 8 miles. High Mountainous Land beyond the low Land. Northernmost Land in sight on the West Shore. N28°West.

At 7 the Tide running 4½ Knots. Slack Water not till near Noon, which may be owing to the Strong Northerly Wind. At ½ past Noon, got under Sail. Working to the Windward till ¼ past 6, when we Anchord in 19 fathoms black gravelly bottom 8 or 9 miles distant from the East Shore. Rocks half way . . . [Bearings omitted.] Latitude 60°22′ North.

Saturday 30th At 2 in the morning, Weigh'd and Turned till 7, when we Anchord in 14 fathoms, Shingly bottom, 7 or 8 miles from the East Shore which continues a level flat Country. [Bearings omitted.] Some Canoes came half way off from the East Shore, but were carried astern by the Tide. At 2 Afternoon got under Sail. Wind Still Northerly. At 4 were between 2 points where the Channel is but 3 Leagues broad. All the west Shore to the North of this is low Land [and] both Sides covered with Wood.

At ¼ past 8 Anchord a League from the West Shore, in 20 fms, bottom of hard Clay. The East Shore about 4 Leagues distant. The Northernmost continuation of either side NE, distant high Land in sight to the NE. Latitude 61°01′ North.

Sunday 31st From 3 in the morning till 9 [we were] under Sail, when we Anchord in 19 fathoms 5 or 6 Leagues to the NEward of our last birth. . . . Land in Sight all round the NE and NW quarters of the Horizon, except a small opening in the High Land to the Eastward. [We] find the Course of the Tide very irregular, shifting NNE to E. Latitude observed at Noon 61°12′ North.

At 2 in the Afternoon, both Ships Cutters were sent to the NNE, where is some appearance of a Passage between the low Land and the high back Land. At ½ past 3 Slack Water. A Ripling with 2 different coloured waters crossed the Ship. A bucket full of each being drawn, the clearer Stream of the two was found salt and the muddy water fresh and drinkable.

At 4 Weighd, and at 7, Anchord, 3 Leagues East of our last birth in 19 fathoms black Sand. The opening in the High Land bearing N80°East. Several Canoes about us. Much the same kind of people we saw at Sandwich Sound. Their lower Lips Slit and ornamented the same. They are likewise well stocked with blue Beads, Iron Knives and Copper. Some of their Small Canoes were managed by double paddles.

Monday, June 1st At 1 in the morning the Cutters returned, having found an Inlet in the low Land, which they entered but saw not the end of. This Inlet [Knik Arm] first runs to the North 4 or 5 miles and then turns to the NE. The Water when they first entered was somewhat fresh, but salt as they advanced, occasioned probably by the rising of the Tide, which then run strong up with them. At the highest part they went, which was about 3 miles, the depth of water was 18 fathoms, and the Channel near 2 miles broad.

At 4 Weighd with little wind. At 7 having drifted 6 or 7 miles in a direct line for the opening in the High Land, the entrance of the Inlet in the low Land bore N29°E being then in one with the North End of an Island about a League distant from us.

At 8 The Cutters were sent towards the Eastern Opening [Turnagain Arm]. A fresh breeze Springing up at NE . . . [and] the Cutters making but little Ground, a Signal was made and they returned.

In the Afternoon, the Weather becoming much clearer than it has been these 2 or 3 days past, Saw more plainly into the Opening in the high Land, which now has the appearance of a deep narrow Sound. The Entrance is not a League in breadth and does not seem to widen within. This, by its direction, may probably communicate with Sandwich Sound. As to the opening in the low Land to the Northward, the narrowness of the Channel forbids any great expectations. Yet there was in its favour, besides the depth of Water, this Circumstance, that from the NBW to the NW points of the Horizon, no High Land was seen at the back of the low Land, which was a swampy flat. Though in almost every other direction, there was Land in sight of a height sufficient to be seen at 15 or 20 Leagues distance.

Lieut. King was sent with the Cutters of both Ships to the low East Land, which he took possession of for his Majesty.

At 4 got under Sail, being bound back for Sea again. Tried soundings as we hove up and found 6½ fathoms, which is above 4 fathoms less depth than when we Anchord. Stood to the Westward. Against the young Flood till ½ past 6, when finding we began to lose Ground . . .

At 7 the Cutters returned. They met several of the Natives, of whom was bought a small Quantity of fresh Salmon and a Dog. Half an hour before Midnight, Weighd with the Ebb, a light breeze Southerly.

Tuesday 2nd At ½ past 4 the Ebb being quite spent, Anchord in 17 fathoms . . . about 5 miles from the West Shore. At 10 ¾ Hours High Water, got under Sail. At Noon Latitude Observed 61°00′ North. Till 2 Turning to the Southward, when the Resolution got aground on a Shole, and we Anchord in 17 fms, black Sand, nearly in mid Channel. [Bearings omitted.] The Resolution bearing East 2 miles.

At 6 the Resolution floated, and came to an Anchor in clear ground. We Saw nothing of the Sholes coming up . . . Stood over to the West Shore to keep clear of the Flats, having before kept that side close on board in this Reach.

Wednesday 3rd At 6 in the Morning, Anchord in 21 fathoms Stoney bottom, being half a League distant from the South point of the continued Low Land on the West Shore . . . Many Canoes came off to us with Salmon, and Fish somewhat resembling but larger than Smelts. Bought some of their Bows and Arrows. The Bows are strengthened with the Sinews of Animals and the Bowstring made of the Same. Their arrows are headed, some with Slate and some with Copper. [Bearings omitted.]

At 1 Shoaled from 13 fathoms to 6 fathoms Rocky bottom. The low Island then bearing South . . . 5 miles. Many riplings and smooth patches in the Water that looked suspicious. Bore away to the North and afterwards to the NE. Kept a Boat ahead sounding till we deepened to 15 fathoms, then hauled on a wind. At ½ past 6 Anchord in 18 fathoms, Stoney bottom, the flood having made strong against us. At Midnight Weighed. Turning to the Southward with the Ebb.

Thursday 4th In the morning, observed Smoke to issue from a mountain bearing SW of us [Augustine Volcano]. This from the Mistiness of the Weather had escaped our notice as we came up. [Bearings omitted.]

Friday 5th Stood to the South, with light Variable Winds till 6 when we Anchord 7 or 8 miles distant from the East Shore, about half a mile South of our first Anchoring place the morning of the 28th when the Resolution lost her Stream Anchor. Most part of the forenoon, the Resolutions Boats looking after the Anchor . . . but without success. At 1 gave it up & made Sail to the Southward. [Bearings omitted.]

Saturday 6th At 8 in the Morning ran by the East of the Cluster of Small Islands, and stood for the broken Land to the Southward. In the Evening, little wind. Caught a great many Halibut.

Sunday 7th At Noon an Island off the South Cape of the Inlet we have been examining . . . This is the Easternmost of the Land we first Saw to the SW [on] May 22d. [Bearings omitted.] All the ensuing week, had contrary winds, with much foggy weather. Turning to the Southward [leaving Cook Inlet].

James Burney, "Sketch of Track Along the Coast of Alaska from May 21 - June 15, 1778 [Cook Inlet, Alaska]," June 1778. Burney kept careful records of the track of the vessels as they sailed in Alaska waters, including this sketch chart of Cook Inlet, offering marginal notes on the high water and tides encountered. Burney Journal p. 158, Mitchell Library, State Library of New South Wales, Safe 1/64 and 1/79.

Journal of Henry Roberts

Saturday, May 2nd At 8 Squally weather with hail & sleet, the Northern Extremities in sight off shore about 2 to 4 leagues. Sailing past some small Islands which seemed to abound with Seals & Sea lions from the number we had about us, with large flocks of Birds. The land here takes a NW & SE direction nearby [and] is very mountainous, covered in Snow even to the waters edge. The Shore is bold & steep too. We passed several Inlets to appearance afforded Shelter and good Harbour. At noon a fresh Gale & Squally weather. A remarkable round mountain, distance from the NW Land 3 or 4 leagues [Mt. Edgecumbe].

Sunday 3rd Sailing past a deep Bay formed by the west point, the land to the East of the Islands seemed to trend to the NNE, our sight about 7 leagues. Many flocks of birds passing us, among which were geese. The Land extremely high and mountainous & intirely covered with Snow.

Monday 4th At Noon the High Mountain set for the Northernmost extremity in the morning off shore about 11 leagues. Another mountain we take to be Mount St. Elias, seen by Behring, the point of the Bay being the Southernmost land in sight.

Tuesday 5th A number of Whales & Seals about, with large flocks of Birds. Mount St. Elias NW, the Northernmost point of land we judge to be Cape St. Elias.

Friday 8th The Land [is] still carrying a most inhospitable aspect, being much covered with Snow, rocky and very Mountainous.

Monday 11th Many Whales blowing & Seals about. The Captain with some of the officers landed in the pinnace, saw many patches of Trees in the Valleys, the Hills barren [Kayak Island]. [Later] the Captain returned from the Shore, hoisted the Boats in. A number of Whales and Seals about.

Wednesday 13th Standing in for an oppening [in Prince William Sound]. Close in with the East Shore, thick weather coming on. Hauld close in for an anchorage, discovered an Inlet or oppening about 5 miles distant stood in for it. Shortly after the weather clearing up we found ourselves at the Entrance of a Deep Bay in a small Cove on the East side, distance from the Shore ¾ of a mile. Sent the Boats in the Cove to haul the Seine upon a fine sandy beach. The Net being rotten met with no success. Caught a few Cod along side with Hooks & lines.

Towards the Evening two or 3 Canoes came into the Cove, near the Ships, & paddled round them several times. In each of these Vessels were a dozen or fifteen people, to appearance which resembling the Natives or Inhabitants of Georges Sound. The night intervening they left us & saw no more of them. This Cove is in Latitude 60°19′ North and Longitude 203°16′ East.

Thursday 14th Standing on for some high land ahead appearing like Islands. We sailed past a small Island & oppened a Bay carrying 25 & 26 fathoms water.

Hauld to the eastward to get Shelter for anchorage but the weather at this time very thick and hazy with frequent Showers of Hail and Rain. It therefore obstructed our sight of the land, but shortly after it grew somewhat clear & shew us the Land intirely round us forming deep sounds or Arms [Snug Corner Cove].

A few Canoes came along side with a single Man in each. They had no Articles of trade with them but seemingly came to gratify their Curiosities & with an intention to pilfer what things they could conveniently lay hands on. In heaving the Anchor out of the Boat one of our seamen unfortunately stood in the Way of the boring rope and was carried to the bottom. But, having the presence of mind to clear himself, he came up with one of his legs broke.

Friday 15th Healed the Ship to port to enable the Carpenters to stop the leak under the Starboard Buttock. Many Canoes along side, some of which were the Baiders [baidarka], carrying from 20 to 30 people, these as well as the small ones, are justly described by people that has been in Hudsons Bay. Answering every description, both large and small, [the boats] are composed of a slender frame with a skin covering sewed over it.

The Inhabitants were of a swarthy Complexion, with black hair, their cheek bones rather prominent, small Eyed in general and an Aquiline Nose [Roman nose]. The most commonly perforated the under lip, especially the Women, in which they stuck small bits of Ivory and blue beads, which Article the most have had from the Russians. We had at this time but few of these beads in the Ship, one of which would have purchased a large Sea Beaver skin that are so much in esteem in Europe.

Their clothing chiefly consists of this with the addition of other skins of different Animals, such as Bears, Wolves, Foxes and Deer, etc. The Garment of both sexes are made in a kind of Jackett and Trowsers. The women indeed often wear the skin loosely thrown over the shoulders, accompanyed with a Bone and appeared to be extremely Modest. The Men besides these wear another Jackett made of Fishes Gutts neatly sewn together, and answer the purpose in wearing to our Oil Skin. One of these they wear in the single canoe which lashes close round the whole of the boat in which they sat, and never admits a drop of water, although they [were] frequently upset.

Saturday 16th The Carpenters employed stopping the leak, which they found to be chiefly occasioned by the Oakum being rotten in the Seams, and part of the wood decayed. Several of the Natives with us, and were extremely peaceable and friendly, but not one of them without their Arms, which they most commonly carry with them for taking Game are for their own security. This Harbour is situated immediately to the North of Cape Hinchinbrook, the Eastern Cape of the Eastern Entrance into this Sound.

Sunday 17th At 3 hove up the Stream Anchor & sailed out of the Bay or Cove, standing across a large Arm running in a NNW direction, the upper part about 5 or 6 leagues from us. The Land, very high & steep, much covered with Snow.

At 10 we shoaled the water suddenly to 7 & 5 fathoms, then abreast of some rocks which lie to the southward of a small Island. Hauld off to the Southward and hoisted the Boats out to Tow ahead, deepened the water to 15 & 10 fathoms. The Land to the NE of us was much broken, forming several small Islands to the distance of about 3 leagues. When we could perceive the Main Land at the back surrounding the whole, the tops of the Mountains [were] very barren & covered in Snow, many of which were extremely high. The Latitude observed was 60°57′ North and Longitude 212°03′ East.

Monday 18th At ½ past 2 (PM) came too in 11 fathoms under the Western part of the Inlet. The pinnace & great Cutter was sent with the first Lieut to the North to examine an Arm which bore NWBN from the Ship. The Master with the Discoverys Cutter to reconnoiter to the NE. At 9 the boats returned, hoisted them on.

The Latitude of [our] anchoring place being the most Northern situation of the Ship in this Arm was Latitude 60°50′ North and Longitude 212°54′ East and the most Northern extremity of any Channel that was seen Latitude 61°09′ North and Longitude 213° East. This Sound, which received the Name of Sandwich, occupies 1½ degrees of latitude and 1¾ degrees in Longitude. The Shores in general steep & well clothed with wood, the higher hills buried in snow.

Wednesday 20th Many Grampoises, Seals and divers about the Ship. The East point of the Entrance SBW offshore 4 miles. The boats ahead towing. Upon this shore there are several small sandy Coves, or Creeks, but not of a sufficient size to admit shipping upon. The low ground is a great plenty of wood but the Hills are wholly covered with snow. Our Boats went on Shore with some of the Officers. At 8 a breeze springing up making for the boats to return, when we weighed Anchorage and stood through the passage.

Thursday 21st Standing through the South through the passage, distance from Entry Isle 2 leagues. We were at this time clear of the Inlet, which was listed with by the name of Sandwich Sound. The land is much broken, forming deep inlets and several Small Islands. The inlets are not wide, but many appear to make separation & afford good Shelter, a barren, rocky, desolate appearance. A number of Whales, Seals & prodigious flocks of birds flying to the Westward. The large island that's been mentioned was honoured with the name of Montague Island.

[In his journal entries from May 22 to May 27, Roberts painstakingly describes the course of the ships as they sail up Cook Inlet, struggling with the wind and tides until the sea narrowed and finally split into two lesser inlets. The *Resolution* lost and searched for its Stream Anchor, which could not be found. It also frequently tacked against the wind to avoid losing ground in the fluctuating tide.]

Thursday 28th At 5 found a strong tide to the North setting against us. When the tide slacked sent the Boats to Creep for the Anchor.

Friday 29th The Boats sweeping & creeping for the Stream Anchor. The Stream Sett to the Northward at 4 O'Clock, which we found to be the flood by the lead line. Sent the Boats again to search for the Anchor but met with no success. At 8 Weighed & made sail to the North with the Tide.

Saturday 30th At 1 Weigh'd and made Sail under double reefed Topsails. At 3 Tacked within 3 leagues of the low land of the Western Shore (which we suppose to be an Island), the low land on the Eastern Shore extending about 3 leagues. Two small Canoes with 2 of the Natives came off to us. At ½ past 6 the Flood ended. Tacked & anchored in 19 fathoms and veered ½ a Cable.

Sunday 31st At ½ past 1 Weighd & made sail with the flood tide. Two small Canoes came along side within Inhabitants in each. At 8 the flood being done, came too in 15 fathoms sand & stones. At ½ past 2 Weighd and Came to sail with the Tide in favour. At 3 we were abreast of the sandy hill [Fire Island near modern-day Anchorage, Alaska] about 2 miles off. The shores on each side being extremely low & well covered in trees, as much as the appearance of banks on a river, besides the strong flood tides setting to the North with thick muddy water and no Sea Weed, but much Drift Wood floating about.

Monday, June 1st At 3 the Weather cleared when we could perceive from the masthead (by the help of our Glasses) the lowland stretching across the Northern part of the supposed channel, nearly encircling the whole. The Inlet formed by the High land to the Eastern hills open. The large Cutter from each Ship sent with the Master to examine further up the oppening. At the pitch of low water we found it quite fresh & intended filling some Casks, but before we could get ready the flood made, which prevented us. At 4 Weighd & sailed up with the Side but we soon saw some Shoals, which were dry.

The Inlet formed by the High Land bore NE. We were visited by many of the Inhabitants in their Canoes bringing Skins and other Curiosities to trade. At 3 the Boats return'd from their search, found that the Arm closed to the westward & only a small inlet running to the Northward [Knik Arm], the stream [tide] running in great rapidity, in the middle of which they had 10 fathoms. The other oppening [Turnagain Arm] to the NE we could perceive was clear from low land. At 4 Weigh'd & made sail in the flood tide to the Eastward opening. Sent the Boats ahead to sound. At ½ past 10 the tide having done, anchored in 10½ fathoms.

Tuesday 2nd The tide very strong from the Inlet to the Eastward. The 2 cutters went with the second Lieut. to the only point of low land on the Eastern Shore to take possession of this part of the Country [Point Possession, Northern Kenai Peninsula]. At our landing we saw several of the Inhabitants. They at first retired seemingly, rather timorous & fearful, but on presenting them with a few things it gave them encouragement & they immediately grew quite reconciled & behaved extremely civil and friendly. Most of them were Armed with Bows and Arrows, & others with Spears or lances. We purchased a few Skins from them & a Small

Quantity of fresh salmon. When we expressed a desire to go into the Country or, rather, up the rising hill, they shew a seeming dislike. But not paying any attention to their noncompliance & immediately ascending the hill, they left us abruptly. On our return to the Boats we found they had increased their Number & every man of them equipped for Battle. Before we left the Shore Mr. King presented them with a few more trifles & we parted on very amicable terms.

Wednesday 3rd Plying down the River carrying sounding at 20 & 40 fathoms. At 2 we were close over to the West Shore, with regular soundings at 17 fathoms. The Ship struck on a bank suddenly & went some distance on it. On sounding we found we had only 2 fathoms and 2½ at a considerable distance from us. The Ship heeling with the Tide, but seem to lay very quiet & easy. This Shoal we saw in coming up the River, but were deceived in judging it to be the supplying & meeting of two Tides, but this time there was no break or nipple to point out the danger. At low Water we could perceive the Shoal dry in many places to the Southward of us, yet never had less that 2¼ fathoms where the Ship lay. Before the flood made, we saw a clear passage to the South and East of the Shoals. At 5 the Ship floated off with the Tide, sent the Boats to sound round her, found deep water nearer the west Shore of 14 fathoms and at 6 came too in 16 fathoms. At 12 weigh'd & made sail, stood on within the Shoal, regular sounding of 13 & 10 to 20 fathoms.

Many of the Inhabitants paid us a Visit in their Canoes, most of [them in] large Vessels covered with Skin, each carrying between 20 & 30 people. We bought great quantity of fresh & dried salmon (a certain proof of their having a vast plenty) and for further argument of <u>this</u> being only a large River, our people purchased many of their Bow & Arrows, with numbers of the Sea Beaver Skins & Martins. They are fond of old cloaths, Glass Bottles, & all kinds of Iron. Their complexion is of a light copper colour, tolerable features & coarse black hair. Most of them were clothed with Skins with the Furs inwards. Several stripped themselves stark naked & sold us their garment. At 11 AM the Flood being done, hove up with a light breeze from the SW & turned down the River.

Thursday 4th Plying down the River with a light breeze from the Southward. a high Mountain issuing forth smoak [Augustine Volcano]. To the Northward of this there is another high Mountain [Iliamna Volcano]. The Volcano distance from nearest Shore 6 miles. The low land of the Eastern Shore in many places is covered with Ash Trees and Birch. It gradually rises to a middling height, having an even summit to the Eastward or at the Back of this, level land at some distance is a Chain of Mountains trending to the Northward. On the west side (to the Southward of the low Island is covered with Trees) the shore is steep & very Mountainous. At Noon weigh'd with the Tide.

Friday 5th Turning down the River with the Ebb tide & a Gentle Gale from the southward, shifted the courses with the old ones. At 7 the Stream being done, anchored in 20 fathoms & veered ½ a cable. At 12 hove up & drifted with the

Ebb sounding 24 fathoms, being near the place we lost the Stream anchor. The Boats were sent at slack water to sweep & creep for it. At 10 Weighd & made sail, stood off & on till noon, waiting for the Boats, which met with no success.

This Extensive Arm occupies at least 12 degrees of Latitude and extends 45 leagues from the Entry Isles in an NBE direction, its breadth at any part, before you reach the head, is not less than 4 or 5 leagues. The banks are low on each side after entering the Arm, about 6 leagues, and wooded with mostly the small Ash Tree & Spruce. The Soundings in general are regular and danger persisted by strong ripplings sufficient to give warning. The Natives are but thinly dispersed here & these from the few smokes we ever saw on either shore. The Mountains on the East rise at a Considerable distance from the low lands which trends to the very foot of them, a space of 6 or 8 leagues level, and capable of Cultivation and offers the best prospects of any other land on this Coast for establishing a Settlement.

Saturday 6th Hoisted the boats in. Several Canoes came off, bringing fish to trade with us. After tacked & stood to the Southward and passed near some small Isles or Rocks lying around the Southern shore.

Sunday 7th [Leaving Cook Inlet.] The West end of the Entry Isles bore N60°W & the large Island to the Southward SEBS about 6 leagues. To the Eastward of this Island are some dangerous rocks, only some of which are above water. Caught a number of fine Halibuts.

Monday 8th The land here very high and mountainous but most parts free from snow.

Henry Roberts, "Chart of Sandwich Sound and River Turnagain," June 1777. This manuscript map was prepared after Cook's ships left Cook Inlet. It is probably the earliest European map of the southern Alaska coastline, naming Sandwich Sound (Prince William Sound) and Turnagain Arm, establishing the basis of the engraved chart published in the third voyage journal. Roberts Journal, Dixson Library, State Library of New South Wales, DLMSF 2, Chart 2, Vol. III.

3

Finding Arctic Ice
June–August 1778

Reaching the open sea south of Cook Inlet, the expedition sailed in fog and rain to the southwest. They passed Kodiak Island but decided not to examine the strait that separates the island from the American Continent, fearing another dead end. Stretching further west to the Aleutian Islands, on June 26 they luckily avoided disaster while under sail in a thick fog as described in the introduction to this chapter. Roberts described this narrow escape.

They sailors were more cautious as they continued west. The constant rain and fog did not abate and they did not want to risk another close encounter with the rocky shoreline. The weather was so thick they could not see the other ship in company and sometimes could not even clearly view the far end of their own ship. Creeping forward, they soon found an opening to the north, today's Akutan Pass, that took them through the broken chain of islands to the Arctic.

The expedition briefly passed a village of Unangan people on what the sailors variously called Samgonuther or Shamganooda Harbour, situated on the eastern part of Unalaska Island. Because of the visit by Cook's expedition to this place, it is known today as English Bay. It was a provident pause after harrowing days at sea, as they searched for a route through fog bound islands. The stop was essential to refresh greens, wood, and water for the ships. Both journals described the contact with the local people, who were among the friendliest they met, particularly since they seemed to be so loyal to the Russian fur hunters in their midst. Burney compared them to the Siberians described in Steller's book from the earlier Bering voyage and Roberts was again fascinated by the construction and use of the skin canoes.

Sailing north of Bristol Bay the ships were successful in landing salmon during the height of the annual salmon run. Running to the northwest they soon encountered shallow water and hidden shoals as they approached the outlet of the Yukon River. Each journal documents the ships' struggles to avoid grounding as the smaller shore boats were taken out to tow ahead. But they were unable to continue their course along the shoreline, so in late July the ships abandoned the coast and sailed west into Bering Strait, first crossing over to St. Lawrence Island, then Siberia, where they had a brief interchange with Chukchi warriors on the Russian coast.

Returning from Siberia, they sailed in and out of thick, foggy weather to the northeast, returning to the Alaska coastline above the Diomede Islands, finally reaching packs of irregular ice near Icy Cape. They had a close call when they were nearly embayed, as shifting winds trapped them between the ice and shoreline for several hours before they could escape. On August 18 they achieved the farthest north on the voyage, 70°44′ North Latitude according to the official record of the journey. Burney and Roberts each gave slightly different coordinates.

Burney wrote they had "apprehensions of being closed in" as they assaulted the ice pack during the next three days. Cook then steered the two ships away from the Alaska coast, periodically testing the pack as they sailed west, looking for a northern opening. When they reached the Asian coast, they abandoned the search and headed south again. There are memorable journal entries about the dismal weather, difficulties with ice, and the regular encounters with walrus. Many of the creatures were killed and consumed, part of Cook's strict dietary regimen for the crew. The taste of the walrus was hotly debated, but the officers were more cautious with their remarks, unwilling to offend the captain. Burney said the crews "cured them of their rank fishy taste, that they were by many thought preferable to the Ship Salt Meat."

John Webber, "The Tschuktschi and Their Habitations," circa 1781-83. Pen, wash, and water color sketch depicting two Chukchi men armed with bows and arrows observed in August 1778. A third figure with a dog is at right. Their summer skin huts are in the background. Dixson Library, State Library of New South Wales, PXX 2, f. 31.

JOURNAL OF JAMES BURNEY

Sunday, June 14th At Noon were 2 or 3 Leagues to the SE of an Island [Kodiak Island], the Easternmost of a Groupe laying about 5 Leagues distant from what we imagine to be the Continent. [Bearing omitted.] In the Evening, the Wind came to the Southward, and after to the SE. Ran all Night to the Westward keeping an offing of 4 Leagues South of the Islands.

Monday 15th At 3 in the morning [we sailed] past a low Island, the Westernmost we saw of the Groupe. After 4 the Weather became hazy, and we lost sight of the Land. The Wind freshened. From 4 in the morning to 3 in the Afternoon, ran 23 Leagues to the Westward, when the Resolution, being a mile ahead of us, saw Land to the NW about a League distant. Shortened Sail, and hauld on a Wind to the Southward. At 9 it fell little wind. Saw more Land bearing SWBW. Light Airs with Calms all night.

Tuesday 16th At 3 in the morning, saw Land in each Quarter of the Compass, having in the fog, passed between the Land seen yesterday afternoon and 2 Islands now bearing E½S.

The Land to the Westward, bearing WNW to SW½S, from its extent and Mountainous appearance, is likely to be a continuation of the Land we have all along been coasting. Directed our Course to the SWward along the Shore. Many Islands within us. [Bearings omitted.] Distance off Shore 7 or 8 Leagues.

17th and 18th Had very little wind.

Friday 19th A breeze from the NE with fair weather. Running through between the Main and a large Groupe of Islands. Latitude at noon 55°19′ North Longitude 200° East. At 6 in the Afternoon were past all the Islands, and abrest a Head Land to the SSE of which (per Compass) lay a small cluster of Rocks at 4 miles distant. Having run through within the Rocks, saw a large Fire on the Head Land, and soon after some Canoes came off and delivered us a Note, which we imagine to be in the Russian Language, dated at the beginning 1778 and in the last line but one was written 1776. We immediately brought too and made Signals to speak with the Resolution. The Note was sent to Captain Cook, but no one in either Ship were able to make out the meaning of any part except the dates. At 8 Bore away and made Sail again.

Saturday 20th Wind Northerly. Running along the Coast to the SW. Many Islands, Rocks and Breakers laying a considerable distance from the Main Land.

Sunday 21st At Noon were becalmed 4 or 5 miles distant to the South of a low Island. This part of the Coast is remarkable on account of 4 high Mountains on the Main being all at once in sight, the Easternmost . . . distant 22 Leagues, and the westernmost, which is a Volcano, . . . distant 19 Leagues. [Bearings omitted.] The Calm continued most of the Afternoon and we caught a great many Halibut, having Ground at 34 fms black Sand. The 3 following days, had light Variable Winds with hazy weather.

Wednesday 24th [Bearings omitted.] The Main Land bearing from NNE to NWBN and Islands in sight from WBS to SWBW.

Thursday 25th Wind Easterly. In the forenoon saw the 2 Westernmost of the 4 Mountains, they having all been hid by the Haze the 3 last days. At noon were about 2 Leagues from the Easternmost of the Islands seen Yesterday. [Bearings omitted.] All the Afternoon, running along the South Side of the Islands, which lay in a Range NEBE and SWBW per Compass . . . our distance from the nearest 7 or 8 miles. Foggy weather coming on, with Rain. At 11 hauld on a Wind to the Southward.

Friday 26th At ½ past 1 in the morning, having as we imagined, increased our offing 9 miles, bore away again to the Westward. At 5 heard a noise to the SW, like a Surf beating against Rocks. Tried Soundings, and fortunately finding Ground at 20 fathoms, both Ships, being within Hail of each other, immediately Clewed all their Sails up and came to an Anchor. Bottom black Sand. At 7 the Fog clearing up a little, found ourselves near the East Side of a large Island, . . . our distance from Shore ¾ of a mile. A Small Island bearing NBE a League distant. Rocks and breakers from S¼E to S39°E half a League and 2 Rocks N89°E distant 2 or 3 miles.

We must have passed very close to these last, it being a dispute whether we came to the North or South of them. Our Course Steered us in favour of the first. The next days Observations make the latter probable, as we found the Ships set by the Tide to the Northward. Whichever way we got here, certain it is, we could not have picked out a safer birth than the one we so providentially hit upon. [Bearings omitted.]

Wind from the SSE with a continuance of the dirty weather, lay fast all this day. The Resolutions Pinnace and our small Cutter were Sent on Shore to cut Grass. Tracks of Foxes were Seen but no signs of Inhabitants.

Saturday 27th The Weather more moderate and clearer. At 7 in the morning, got under Sail and ran to the Northward along the East side of the nearest Land. At 9 falling Calm, Anchord in 30 fathoms black Sand and Shells, being about a League North of last Anchoring Birth and a mile to the ENE of the Eastern point of a large Sound . . . Saw a Number of Canoes towing a Whale into the Sound and soon after, some came off to us. Latitude Observed 53°52′ North.

At 1 afternoon got under Sail. Light variable winds and fair Weather. Stood to the NW towards a Channel formed by the Land to the North of the large Sound . . ., finding a Tide against us, Anchord in 38 fathoms Sand and Shells, 5 or 6 miles to the NWward of our last birth, and half a League distant from the western point of the Sound . . . The Tide very irregular all Night.

Sunday 28th At 3 in the morning got under Sail with little wind. Boats ahead towing. At 5 a fine breeze having sprung up at SSE, were in the Channel before mentioned, which is about 2 miles wide . . . At 6 found the Tide strong against us and that we began to lose ground. At ½ past 6 the Resolution Anchord, being to the NW of a ledge of Rocks that lay along the Larboard Shore, which we were then abrest of. Finding the bottom under us Rocky, sheered over towards the NE Shore for better Anchorage, but before we reached mid channel the Stream carried us into a Strong Race that almost instantaneously hurried us back into the entrance of the Sound we had passed, in Spite of a Breeze with which we were then running 4 Knots through the Water. Our great Cutter very narrowly escaped being dashed to pieces against the Ships side by the violence of the Ripling.

The Race Shifting, stood over to the NE, and at ½ past 7, Anchored under the South Side of an Island in Smooth Water and Sheltered from the Tide. Depth

32 fms, Sand and Shells . . . Then the Resolution at an Anchor between this point and the ledge of Rocks, distant from us about 5 miles. At 10 got under Sail. The Tide from the North not being quite Spent Stood backwards & forwards under the Island.

At Noon slack water and little wind, the Resolution towing for a Harbour that turns Short in round the ledge of Rocks. At ½ past 1 we were nearly in the same place where the Resolution last Anchord. The Tide having made strong, Anchord in 24 fathoms Rocky bottom, in a great Measure Sheltered from the Tide by the Ledge of Rocks, the outer part of which we brought to bear ESE. [Bearings omitted.] The Entrance of the Harbour . . . distance off shore about half a mile.

At 2 the Resolution having Anchord in the Harbour, Sent her large Cutter to our Assistance. At 4 a breeze from the North and no Tide where we lay, though very Strong in mid Channel, Weighd and made Sail with Boats ahead Towing. At 6 Anchord in the Harbour 11 fathoms, Sandy bottom, and Moored. [Bearings omitted.] Distance from the West Side of the harbour 3 Cables length.

This Island is called by the Natives Nowan Alascha and the Harbour we are now in Samgonuther. [English Bay, Unalaska Island.]

Monday 29th Employed all day in compleating our Water. Many Canoes about us. These people do not paint their Faces, which makes them appear more cleanly and decent than any Indians we have yet seen on the American Coast. Their Lips are Slit like the others, their Canoes and fishing Gear in the same fashion. We found them well acquainted with the Russians, some having Notes similar to the one we received the Afternoon of the 20th. They imitate the manners of Europeans in taking their Hats off and bowing when they come alongside, and in the whole of their behaviour observed a degree of modesty we have long been unaccustomed to meet with.

Tobacco, Snuff, Beads and Otaheite Cloth was here the Current Mony, for which they gave fish, Spears, Lines, Hooks and a few other things of their own manufacture. Furs we saw none. Perhaps the Russians had taken care of them.

Tuesday 30th At 5 in the morning, Unmoored and Warped toward the Mouth of the Harbour. Wind at North. The Resolution got under Sail, intending to Turn out but was obliged to Anchor again, it coming on foggy. Lay fast. Our people ashore in the afternoon gathering the Tops of Wild Pease, Water Cresses & Scurvy Grass. No Trees here, nor have we seen any since leaving the Inlet the beginning of this month. Some pieces of drift wood in the Harbour.

Wednesday, July 1st At ½ past 6 in the morning weighed, it being Calm and began to Tow out of the Harbour. A breeze springing up from the NNW with thick foggy weather at 7 Anchord again. [Bearings omitted.] The people on shore all day gathering Greens. A Party walked over the narrow Neck of Land that makes the East Side of the Harbour, and found a small Indian Town, the only Houses we have met, since leaving King Georges Sound.

They are much in the same plan with those of the Kamschadales as described by Steller. The Shape is nearly that of the Longitudinal section of an Egg. The floor is 2 or 3 feet lower than the Ground without, the Sides and Tops are well thatched with Straw and covered with Earth, which makes them appear as so many little hillocks or Mounts. The Entrance is at the Top, by a post with Notches in it, and the whole is supported by a few Slight pillars on the inside. One House generally contains 3 or 4 families or more, according to its size. They live in by the sides, which is made a kind of broad Trench, being a foot lower than the rest of the floor. In the middle part are holes dug for sinks, where they empty all kinds of nastiness. This is soaked up by the Ground, and, besides occasioning an intolerable stink, breeds large Maggots, with which, together with Lice and Fleas, their Houses swarm. The largest House we saw measured in length 56 feet, in breadth 45, and its height in the middle 13 feet.

In the Afternoon a Fox den was discovered and dug out. One young one was killed and one taken alive. The rest got off. Some Grouse or Moor fowl were shot.

Thursday 2nd At light breeze SSE, with fair Weather. At 6 got under Sail and ran out of the Harbour. The Tide without being strong from the South, [we] soon got through the Channel on the West Side of which is the Harbour we now leave. Stood to the NNW. At ½ past 8 Saw very high Land to the NE which we found to be a continuation, or rather the Western Extremity of the Land we have suposed the Continent. Latitude 54°16′ North. Altered our Course keeping to the NE. In the afternoon the weather became Hazy.

3rd & 4th Running to the ENE now and then through the Haze getting a sight of the Land to the SE of us. The 4th at Noon being little wind, lay too, and caught Cod, having Soundings at 32 fathoms black Sand. [Bearings omitted.]

Sunday 5th At Noon were to the Eastward of the 4 Mountains seen the 21st of June, having run by the North Side of them within 15 Leagues distance. The thickness of the weather having prevented our seeing them. [Bearings omitted.] The Land in sight to the SE offshore 5 Leagues. In the night little wind. Caught a great many Cod fish. Soundings between 35 and 40 fms black Sand.

Monday 6th Went to 2/3rd allowance of Beef and pork on account of the Fish lately caught.

7th and 8th Clear Weather. Running along shore to the NE past many deep Bays, the Land making much like a Cluster of Islands. The forenoon of the 8th Calm. Caught a great quantity of Cod and flat Fish, having bottom at 26 fathoms black Sand. [Bearings omitted.] The Surface of the Water covered with feathers.

Thursday 9th This forenoon were abrest a large Sound, past which the Coast trends more northerly. Latitude at Noon 57°47′ North Longitude 201°49′ East. Our Track to the NE from Nowanalascha, makes the Land we have coasted since the middle of June, either a long narrow neck or a range of Islands.

All the afternoon a fresh Westerly breeze with Clear Weather. Standing to the North, along a low level Coast at 3 Leagues distant from the Shore. At ½ past 9 saw Land all round the NE & NW Quarters of the Horizon. A point of low Land NNE½E 6 or 7 miles, round which was seen a continuation of the Sea, running in to the Eastward, which we imagined to be a River. Takd and Stood to the SW, the wind veering round to the NW. Sounds in the Night 9 to 16 fathoms black Sand.

Friday 10th At Daylight 3 or 4 Leagues off the Shore, which here runs in a Westerly direction, a low flat Country. Steered SW till 11 in the forenoon, when we shoaled our Water from 13 fathoms to 7 fathoms and after to 4½ fathoms. Hauld our Wind to the NE and made the Signal of danger to the Resolution. [Bearings omitted.] . . . Found a Tide setting to the SW at the rate of 2 Knots per Hour. Land in Sight . . . about 4 Leagues distant, which is low Land with distant Hummocks behind it. 2 hills to the Eastward . . . the body of the Land to the Eastward not in Sight.

At 3 in the Afternoon the Course of the Tide changed, running SBE. At 4 got under Sail. Many Salmon Swimming near the Surface, it being thought the last quarter of the Ebb Tide, some water was taken up, and on trial, found lighter and fresher than Sea Water. These Circumstances with the low Land amount nearly to a proof of our being in the mouth of a large River [called "Bristol River" by Cook, this is now Kvichak Bay, the outlet of the Kvichak and Naknek Rivers].

From 4 to ½ past 7, standing mostly to the Southward to deepen our Soundings. Kept Boats ahead. Soundings irregular, from 5 to 18 fathoms, black Sand . . . Anchord in 17 fathoms about 7 miles South of last Anchoring place . . . Tide running to the N and NNE.

Saturday 11th At 1 in the morning Slack Water, having increased our depth by the Leadline 1 fathom. At 2 got under Sail, wind SW. Turning to the Southward, Soundings between 13 and 24 fathoms . . . [and] Anchord in 24 fathoms. Thick foggy weather. No Land in Sight. Caught Fish. At 1 in the Afternoon, got under Sail, a light Southerly wind with hazy weather. . . . No land in sight.

Sunday 12th Fair weather. In the forenoon saw the Land to the NW. [Bearings omitted.] A Round Hummock bearing NW, which we have found to be one of a number of small Islands along shore. The remainder of this, and the 2 following days, had light westerly winds with fair Weather. Kept Turning to windward, without losing sight of the round Hummock . . . Cod and flat Fish in abundance.

Tuesday 14th In the afternoon, sent the small Cutter after 2 Sea Cows, but before the Boat got near enough for Harpooning, they both went down.

Wednesday 15th At 4 in the morning being foggy, anchord in 17 fathoms black Sand. No Land in Sight . . . Stood to the Westward. At Noon, just got a glimpse of the Land bearing NW and a Sight of the Sun. Latitude Observed 58°21′ North. A thick Fog all the afternoon. . . . At 7 lost Sight of the Resolution. At 8

Tackd per Signal and Stood to the Southward. At ½ past 10 Saw her again and both Ships came to an Anchor, we in 17 fathoms . . . Sea Cows, Seals and Sea Lions about the Ship. No Fish.

Thursday 16th Between 3 and 4 in the morning the Course of the Tide veered round, coming from the NW and after from the NE. The Fog clearing, Saw the Land, . . . a small Island . . . 3 or 4 miles distant. At ½ past 5 got under Sail, having fair weather and a light Westerly wind. Turning to Windward till Noon, when we Anchored . . . about 3 Leagues West from last Anchoring Birth, and 8 or 9 miles from a point of Land, the Westernmost in Sight. [Bearings omitted.] Past this point, the Coast turns to the Northward again and we lose the low Land. The Country being hilly and uneven, all the Land we have coasted since leaving the Inlet, June 6th, appears quite destitute of Wood. The Resolutions Cutter on Shore all the Afternoon. Saw Deer and Foxes, but no signs of people. At ¾ past 5, the Tide slacked, being low Water by the Shore . . .

Friday 17th Running to the Northward alongshore. . . .

Saturday 18th Wind Southerly with fair weather. At 8 in the morning lessened our depth to 5 fathoms, being about 3 Leagues off shore. Brought too and got Boats out, . . . both Ships Cutters a head Sounding. White Water towards the Offing, that had much the appearance of Sholes. Stood to the NE in shore. . . . At ½ past 3 the Boats ahead made the Signal for Shoal Water. Anchord in 6 fathoms, . . . distance from the nearest Shore, about 8 miles. [Bearings omitted.] A Shoal, dry at low water, NWBW 2 or 3 miles. Appearances like Shoals to the NNE, NW and SW. Found the Tide running from the NBW 2 Knots per hour.

The Resolution having Anchord with her small Bower, the Cable parted and they let go another Anchor. In attempting to recover the Small Bower at Slack Water, the Buoy Rope broke . . .

Sunday 19th At Sunrise 2 Canoes came within a quarter of a mile and after looking some time at the Ships paddled for the Shore again. Boats of both Ships sweeping all Day for the Resolutions Small Bower Anchor. In the morning, Saw an appearance like distant Land to the WNW.

Monday 20th This day taken up in sweeping for the Resolution's Anchor. Our great Cutter Sounding to the Westward and SW. [We] find a Bank with not more than 2 and 3 fathoms, running in a direction nearly South per Compass from the Shoal, dry at low water, to the NW of us. In the Evening hoisted the Launch in, the Resolution having recovered their Anchor.

Tuesday 21st At 4 in the morning got under Sail and Stood to the Southward again for deep water. Four Boats sounding before us. At ½ past 7 the Boats making the Signal of Danger, Anchord in 6 fathoms, 10 miles SSW of last birth and about 3 Leagues from the Land.

A Fleet of 27 Small Canoes, with only one man in each, came off; and after much speechifying on their Side and invitation on ours, ventured alongside the

Ships. These have the dirtiest appearance of any Indians we have yet met with. In our little communication together, we found them unfair dealers. In other respects they seem to be the same kind of people as those of Sandwich Sound and the Inlet.

At ½ past 10 got under Sail again, and Stood to the Southward till 3 when the Wind not being Strong enough to Stem the Tide of flood then running, Anchord in 7 fathoms. . . . Distance off shore about 7 miles . . . At 6 under Sail, wind SSE. Turning to Windward with Boats ahead. Soundings between 8 and 13 fathoms . . . At ½ past 9, being hazy, Anchord again, being the 3d time since getting under Sail this morning.

Wednesday 22nd At 5 in the morning weighed and stood to the SW with Boats ahead. Soundings from 9 to 17 fathoms. At 10 The Boats making the Signal for Shoal water, Tackd and Stood to the Eastward. At Noon Anchord in 15 fathoms 5 or 6 Leagues distant from the Land, . . . the point we Anchord near the 16th at Noon and which Captain Cook names Cape Newingham. [Bearings omitted.] At 5 in the Afternoon Weighd, Wind East. Stood to the Southward with Boats Sounding ahead. At ½ past 9 hoisted in the Boats [and] continued our Course to the South all Night under an easy Sail . . .

Thursday 23rd At Noon the Land but just in sight to the NE . . . All the afternoon ran to the SW. At 6 having deepened to 26 fathoms, kept away to the westward for a clear Sea.

Friday 24th At Noon, depth of water 28 fathoms . . ., our distance from the Land 36 Leagues. Continuing our Course to the westward, Wind at ENE. [Bearings omitted.]

Saturday 25th Thick foggy Weather. Wind NE. At Noon, [Bearings omitted] Distance from Cape Newingham 58 Leagues. Having gradually increased our Soundings to 35 fathoms, hauled up to the NW. In the evening it fell calm . . . found a Tide or Current from the WNW about 8 Knot . . .

Sunday 26th At 7 in the morning weighd and Steered to the NW. Wind NE. Moderate and foggy.

Tuesday 28th Soundings these two last Days between 26 and 31 fathoms . . . Depth decreasing as we hauled towards the North. The Fog clearing away had an Observation. [Bearings omitted.] In the Afternoon a fresh Gale from the Northward and foggy . . .

Wednesday 29th At ½ past 4 in the Morning, the Weather moderate and tolerably clear. Saw Land bearing WBN about 6 Leagues distant. At 11 were within a League of the Land, which has the appearance of a barren, rocky Island. Shoald our Soundings to 26 fathoms Small Stones, which is the only alteration in the bottom since we left Samgonuther Harbour (July 2nd) having till now constantly sailed over a bottom of black Sand. Tackd and Stood off. At Noon, the East point of the Land bore N¼W 4 miles distant. The Western part of the Land hid by a fog Bank. Latitude 60°22′ North, Longitude 187°30′ East. Foggy all the afternoon. The Land in sight at times . . . Continued our Course towards the NE with Variable Winds.

Monday, August 3rd At 6 in the Afternoon Saw Land bearing WBN distance 7 or 8 Leagues. Hour Latitude in 62°50′ North, Longitude 192°30′ East. Since the 30th our Soundings have gradually decreased to 15 fathoms. At 8 lost sight of the Land, having a fresh breeze from the ESE and not altering the Course.

Our Ship has lately Sailed worse than the Resolution, which we imagine is owing to want of weight in the Bread room. Having expended from thence 16000 lbs. weight of Bread since leaving the Cape of Good Hope, which being from the very extremity of the Ship, must have the greater effect. This cannot at present be remedied without danger of damaging the remainder of the Bread.

Tuesday 4th Weather Hazey with rain. Wind Easterly. At ½ past 2 in the Afternoon, Saw Land about 3 Leagues distant, extending from WNW to NE. Latitude 64°18′ North, Longitude 194°15′ East. At ½ past 3, having Shoaled to 7 fathoms, stood off shore, it falling little wind and coming round to the Southward with a swell setting towards the Shore . . . The Extremes of the Land, which from its extent we imagine to be part of the American Continent, bearing WNW and NEBE and a small Island . . . 3 or 4 Leagues distant. [This is the first view of St. Lawrence Island.]

Wednesday 5th At 9 in the forenoon Weighd, and ran between the Small Island and the Main, where at Noon, we Anchord in 7½ fathoms muddy bottom . . . Tide setting 2 Knots to the Westward. A number of Small Clumps on the Main Land that have a good deal the appearance of Houses.

Received information of the death of Mr. Wm. Anderson, Surgeon of the Resolution, who departed this Life the Evening of the 3d, having some months past been in a decline.

Mr. John Law was appointed Surgeon of the Resolution, and in his room, Mr. David Samwell, before Surgeons first Mate on board the Resolution, to be Surgeon of the Discovery.

All the Afternoon Boats ashore on the Island to the South of us, cutting Grass and Sallad. An Indian Snow Sledge and the remains of old deserted Houses were seen, and some Foxes.

This Island lays in Latitude 64°27′ North, Longitude 193°38′ East distant from the Main Land about 3 Leagues . . . The Rise or fall of the Water ashore was scarcely perceptible.

Thursday 6th At 3 in the morning got under Sail and stood to the Westward. Having Shole Water, were obliged to keep a good offing. Soundings all day, between 7 and 13 fathoms . . .

Friday 7th Early in the morning, Boats were sent to Sound towards the NW. Found Shoal Water in that direction. At ½ past 7 Weighd and stood to the

Westward till Noon. All the Afternoon, Wind Northerly with Hazy Weather. Kept turning to Windward to get in with the Land . . .

Saturday 8th At 3 in the morning, the Weather clearing up [we] found ourselves nearer the Land than was suposed. The Wind soon after dying away, at 6 Anchord in 13 fathoms about 2 miles from the Land . . . Hazey to the Eastward . . . The Haziness of the Weather, together with the Shoal Water, having prevented our making it certain that this was being one continued Land, Stood towards the ESE on a wind. At 10 more Land appearing in sight to the NE and the depth of water decreasing, Tackd and Stood to the Westward . . .

Sunday 9th Wind Northerly. At ½ past 8 in the Morning, Weighed the Anchor, which was done with much difficulty, a great Swell setting from the Northward, occasioned by the Wind and Current in opposition. This forenoon, turning to the Windward. At 9 the Wind freshened to a Gale, with thick hazey Weather, which hid the Land from us. At 11 Standing to the ENE, saw the low West point of the Main bearing SEBE, within a League of us, with Breakers laying off it. Put about and Stood to the Westward. At Noon a high Rock bore SWBS and Land which was afterwards found to be two Islands from West to WSW distant 4 Leagues. The Main Land to the Eastward hid by the Haze . . . At 4 in the Afternoon ran by the South Side of the 2 Islands. At 7 Saw Strange Land to the Westward. Made the Signal to the Resolution. Stood backwards and forwards all Night . . .

Monday 10th Stood in for the Land to the Westward. At 10 in the forenoon Anchord in 12½ fathoms . . ., an Indian Town . . . 2 or 3 miles. [Bearings omitted.] Boats were hoisted out and Captain Cook went on Shore to the Indian Town [Chukchi village on St. Lawrence Bay, Northern Siberia]. Many Indians were seen running in Land over the Hills, which we suposed to be Women and Children, for as the Boats approached the Shore, the Men to the Number of about 60 Came down Armed with Pikes, Bows and Arrows.

Captain Cook landed by himself and was met by two of them to whom he made presents, and they all Soon after laid aside their Martial appearance and became sociable and friendly. A Number of Dogs were laying on the Ground that appeared just killed. Meant perhaps as a Sacrifice, on the Suposition of an Attack. Their Pikes were headed with Iron and inlaid with some Metal. They had blue Beads, and took Tobacco and Snuff in exchange for some of their Clothes, which shows they are not unacquainted with the Russians, though unwilling to acknowledge them Masters.

They sold us Salmon, of which here is plenty, a small River running close at the back of the Town, but no consideration could prevail on them to part with any of their Arms.

They have 2 kinds of Houses; the one for Summer and the other for Winter. The former are Rib Bones of Whales, stuck in the Ground, circular at the bottom and meeting at the Top in a Peak, the Whole covered with Whale Skin. The latter are part under Ground on the plan of the Kamtschadale Houses. Some of them floored with plank. In several places were Stuck up a number of the Rib Bones of Whales, making a kind of scaffolding, but for what purpose was not discovered. They have Snow Sledges and a great many Dogs.

This Land we supose to be part of the Island of Alaschka. (We afterward found this to be the Coast of Asia and the people the Tschuktschi.) The Indians here have not like those we have been lately accustomed to, holes cut in their Lips to Stick Ornaments through.

At 2 the Boats returned. At 4 got under Sail. Wind Southerly with fine Weather. Stood all Night to the NE, running by the West Side of the 2 Islands . . .

Tuesday 11th In the Morning kept more Easterly to get in with the American Continent. At Noon Latitude Observed 66°06′ North, . . . ran 4 Leagues to the Eastward, gradually Shoaling till we came into 7 fathoms. The Wind dying away Anchord . . . The Easternmost point of what we supose to be Alaschka . . .

Wednesday 12th Turning to the Northward all day without losing Sight of the 2 Islands.

Thursday 13th In the Afternoon, the Wind shifted to the SSE. Steered NE per Compass. Before Night, lost Sight of the Land . . .

Friday 14th At 4 in the morning hauld to the Eastward. At 9 Saw Land to the NE . . . distance 5 or 6 Leagues, depth 16 fathoms. Latitude 67°25′ North, Longitude 194°38′ East. All the afternoon thick hazey Weather. In the Evening it blew strong at South. Hauld our Wind to the Westward to keep clear of the Land, which we soon lost sight of. This we imagine to be part of the American Continent.

Saturday 15th At Noon, having deepened to 25 fathoms, Bore away, making good nearly a North Course . . .

Sunday 16th Steering towards the NE on which Course our Soundings gradually shoaled. A soft sticky bottom, the Lead coming with difficulty out of the Ground . . . thick foggy weather.

Monday 17th Land Birds about the Ship all the morning. Foggy Weather. At ½ past 10 having Shoaled to 11 fathoms, hauled our wind to the NW. At Noon, Latitude 70°31′ North, Longitude 197°34′ East. In the Afternoon at 2 Saw a Field of Ice to the Northward. At ½ past 2 were close in with the Ice, on which were great numbers of Sea Horses [walrus]. Soundings 21 fathoms. Clearing up a little, Saw more Ice to the SW and Westward. Kept Turning all Night, Wind Westerly with a thick fog. As we ran to the Southward, decreased our Soundings to less than 12 fathoms and deepened on the Northern Tack to above 20 fms, near the Ice, which stopped our run that way. The Weather being squally, lost Ground.

Tuesday 18th At Noon close in with the Ice. Wind west. Latitude 70°49′ North, Longitude 198°24′ East. In the Afternoon standing to the Southward. At ½ past 5, the fog clearing away, Saw Land, a low point . . . 3 or 4 miles distant.

At 6 lessened our depth to 6¼ fathoms. Tackd and made the Signal of danger to the Resolution. At 7 Tackd and Stood to the SWward again. At 8 clearing up a little, got another sight of the Land bearing ESE and Ice from NNW to NEBN, which must have drifted from the NW within this 24 hours, our Track having crossed where the Ice now is. Kept to the SW all night . . .

John Webber, "Shooting Sea Horses [Walrus] on Arctic Ice," circa 1781-83. Pen, wash, and water color sketch depicting one of a series of encounters with walruses in August 1778. The journals offer lengthy accounts about the quality and taste of the meat and how it should be prepared. Because of their antiscorbutic value, Captain Cook required his crews to eat fresh provisions instead of stores of preserved, salted meat. Dixson Library, State Library of New South Wales, PXX 2, f. 32.

Wednesday 19th Wind still Westerly. At 8 in the morning Tackd and ran to the Northward. At 2 in the Afternoon were near the Ice. The Weather moderate. Hoisted out the Boats and sent them after Sea Horse. The Resolution Caught 9, we 4. The flesh very indifferent eating, fishy. The Blubber was used for making Lamp Oil. At 8 made Sail to the Southward from the Ice. Soundings this last 24 hours, from 14 to 17 fathoms.

Thursday 20th At ½ past 2 in the morning saw Land to the Eastward about 5 miles distant, which was soon hid by a thick fog coming on. Kept Turning between the Land and the Ice, trying to get to Windward, but without gaining Ground, till the Afternoon, when the wind came round to the NE and we steered to the Westward. Having these 3 days past been pent up by a Shoal Coast on one side and Ice on the other, forming a deep Gulf, which by the drifting of the Ice has been continually growing narrower, and kept us under some apprehensions of being closed in.

At 9 in the Evening heard the noise of Sea Horses. Being a thick fog, steered to the SW to keep clear of the Ice. At ½ past 10 found ourselves close in with [ice]. Hauled on a Wind to the SE in which direction we ran the remainder of the Night.

Friday 21st At ½ past 10 in the forenoon the fog cleared up. Saw Land to the ESE high and uneven. At Noon Latitude 69°35′ North, Longitude 195°34′ East. The Land in sight from South to ENE about 5 Leagues distant. Soundings these 2 last Days, 14 to 20 fathoms. This we take to be part of the American Continent . . .

Saturday 22nd Foggy Weather setting in again. We left the Land and Steered to the Westward for the Coast of Asia. In this passage, which took up a Week, we kept between the 69th and 70th degree of North Latitude, sometimes falling in with the Ice, which could not be so coasted as to tell whether it joined across, by reason of the foggy thick Weather and unsteady Winds. As we left the American Main, our Soundings gradually deepened to 29 fathoms and afterwards decreased as we approached the Coast of Asia.

Friday 28th Little Wind and close in with the Ice. Our Boats were out the greatest part of the day after Sea Horses, of which we caught 4. Cutting the throats of these and letting them bleed immediately as they were caught, so far cured them of their rank fishy taste, that they were by many thought preferable to the Ship Salt Meat. Tried and found no Current. At Noon Latitude 69°23′ North, Longitude 183° East.

Saturday 29th Wind WNW. Standing to the SW at 9 in the forenoon, Saw Land ahead, having lost Sight of the Ice 2 hours before. At Noon within half a League of the Land which bore from WBN to S61°E, depth 10 fathoms. Latitude in 68°45′ North, Longitude 181°24′ East of Greenwich.

The Coast low and level [with] Land behind Mountainous. This we find is the Continent of Asia. Till the 2d of September running to the SE along the Coast, having Soundings constantly between 10 and 24 fathoms. The Land bends in Bays here and there, with some appearances like openings but on coming near the Shore, the Water is so Shoal as to exclude any chance of a Harbour fit for Ships. Saw no Wood all along.

Journal of Henry Roberts

Thursday, June 11th No land to be seen. The Weather very thick and misty. [Rainy weather passing Kodiak Island.]

Tuesday 16th Saw the land appearing through the haze not more than 3 or 4 miles. This last head land obtained the Name of Foggy Cape. Saw a high bluff head bearing NBS & more land to the Westward, which we judge to be the Continent. A heavy Sea setting on the Shore with little or no wind, Sounded 72 fathoms.

Saw land bearing SBE½ (an Island), Behring's Foggy Island. Latitude 56°07′ North and Longitude 202°42′ East. Distant 4 leagues a remarkable point, making like spires, is obtained the name of Pinnacle Point. Extremes of the Continent in sight, offshore about 6 leagues. At noon here appeared to be several good Harbours & many Bays or Inlets to offer Shelter. The land much broken & very mountainous & equally covered with Snow as the land in 60° or 61° [Cook Inlet, now sailing 5° south in 56°N latitude].

Thursday 18th The land near the Main appears to be much broken and makes like several distinct Isles. The cluster of Islands to the Southward (which we suppose to be Schumagins Isles) seen by Behring, about 8 leagues.

Friday 19th Standing through the passage between Schumagins Isles & the Continent to the NE of those Isles. The land is much broken & to appearance many Islands & deep Inlets.

Saturday 20th At 7 the Discovery made the signal to speak. Brought to & haul'd out the Boat & sent an Officer on board. At 8 the Boat returned, hoisted her in & made sail. About 4 leagues to the West of Schumagins Islands.

Monday 22nd Being Calm put over our Hook & Lines and caught a great number of very fine Halibuts, the largest weighing about 140 pounds. A Canoe came off with one of the Inhabitants. By his deportment & being dressed partly by European Clothes, we conjectured the Russians have had a communication hereabouts.

The peaked Mountain we now perceive to be a Volcano. The high hummock on Halibut Isles is situated in Latitude 54°23′ and Longitude 197°00′ East, opposite which we afterwards learnt from the Russians was a passage which divides the Great Isle of Oneemak from Alaska [Unimak Pass]. Very large flocks of birds about the Ship.

Tuesday 23rd Very large flocks of Sea parrots [puffins] flying round us. No land in sight.

Thursday 25th At 10 saw more land at the back of the Islands & the Weather coming in Foggy, hauld out, to clear the Islands. Great many birds and Whales about. Distance from the nearest island 3 leagues.

Friday 26th The Weather extremely thick we were suddenly alarmed by the noise of Surf, when upon getting a cast of the lead, found ourselves in 20 and 25 fathoms. We immediately hove her head to the Northward. The sound being to the Southward of us & dropped the Best Bower Anchor & veered a whole Cable. The Discovery at anchor near us. About 7 the fog faintly clearing at intervals Shew us the nearby land was very high & steep, with much snow on it, & not more than 1½ miles from us. On our looking about us, we perceived a high Rock lying to the West of the westernmost Head & a prodigious surge breaking on its reef. It was this that first apprised us of our danger. It bore SEBS about 2 miles, some other Rocks just above Water. We sailed between the high Rock

& these (which are both detached. The Northern part of this land, which we suppose to be an Island) about 2 miles. This place formed a kind of a Bay, at the bottom of which is a sandy beach that bore SW about 2 miles. Hoisted out the pinnace & sent her with an Officer to the Shore.

At noon, a continuance of the Fog, scarcely able to see the Discovery, which was within a Cables length of us.

Saturday 27th At daylight we hove the anchor up and stood for the channel [and] opened more land to the Eastward, the Western parts appearing like Islands. The land to the West and Southward seemingly formed a deep Bay. Several small Skin Canoes came off to us with a single Man in each boat. We purchased a quantity of fresh and dried fish from them, salmon & Halibut chiefly. At the spot where the pinnace landed there was no Inhabitants or structures. They found a bush similar to angelica & wild celery. Saw but few birds & those extremely shy.

Sunday 28th Saw several fine Coves on the Eastern side of the Bay, which we are crossing, and habitations of the Inhabitants. By the help of Glasses we could perceive great quantities of Halibut drying on stages, many of the small Canoes towing a dead Whale to their Settlement.

Monday 29th The Harbour's mouth was from the West to NNW, not more than 2 Cables length from the Shore. Great many Canoes alongside with the Natives trading with dried Fish for Tabocco & other Curiosities. At daybreak began to Water, having 26 Tons empty.

Tuesday, July 7th The land here is in general very high & cover'd in many places with snow. It appears at a distance to form in deep Bays but in going to the Mast head & by the help of our Glasses could easily distinguish that low land connected each particular range of Hills that occasioned this description. [Outlet observed offshore 3 leagues, named River Bristol on July 10.]

Thursday, 16th The Cutter sent to the shore with the third Lieut. to take possession of the Country. [Cape Newenham]

Friday 17th The boat returned from the shores, the officers having climbed one of the Hills near the western Promontory [and] saw the direction of the Coast, which trended NNW, and likewise from every appearance judged that part to be the Continent which he landed on. This western point obtained the Name of Cape Newenham, its Latitude 58°41′ North and Longitude 197°36′ East. Our people saw a few deer, which were shy, & brought on board several teeth, or Tusks, of the Sea Horses [walrus]. [Boats out sounding and finding shoals and shallow water, the *Resolution* losing an anchor on July 19. After a considerable search, the anchor was recovered on July 20, but difficulties continue when the ships incur shallow water north of Bristol Bay, stalling progress eleven leagues after leaving Cape Newenham.]

Sunday 26th Many whales blowing around us. Large flocks of birds upon the water, which was taken to be sea parrots. Fired a Gun as a Signal to the Discovery in a fog. Bore down to her.

Wednesday 29th The sea covered with Divers and sea parrots. At 8 the Land made like an Island, distance 4 leagues, the Eastern point making in a remarkable high bluff. The land appearing like several islands but probably not near enough to distinguish the low land that might join the Hills. The whole element darkened with birds of the Gull & petteral kind. At noon we had but an imperfect sight of the Islands, the weather being thick.

Friday 31st Fired 2 Guns as a Signal to the Discovery. [Large tree and other drift wood in the water. Geese observed both days. The surgeon William Anderson died from the lingering effects of tuberculosis on Tuesday, August 4. The crews committed his body to the sea the next morning.]

Wednesday, August 5th Made the Signal for the Discovery to keep more ahead. Passed by great quantities of drift wood. At 2 the Discovery made the signal for seeing land, the shores appearing very low. The Weather being very thick and the Ship drifting on the Shore, Came too in sight of the Land, a high round Island bearing WBS 3 or 4 leagues. The weather being very hazy to the Eastward, could not see any land in that quarter.

Thursday 6th At 2 hoisted the boat out. The Captain with some of his officers landed on the Island. At 8 they returned on board with a quantity of Grass, Celery & herbs for the people. The Inhabitants from the continent regularly Visit this Isle by the number of recent fires we saw & several decayed hutts, which are entirely under ground. We likewise saw a Sledge that they use in crossing the Ice. By the assistance of our glasses we could perceive several Villages on the Main & other places erected which we took to be fish stages. The Country here is a pleasant appearance, many plains, & the land in general lying in gentle ascents, gradually rising to the Hills. The interior parts are not so mountainous as the most of the coast we have seen nor does the snow lie so thick. At noon the weather frequently hazy, which covered many parts of the Land.

Friday 7th Hoisted the pinnace out and sent her to sound. Found a regular depth of water at 7½ & 8 fathoms to the distance of 2 miles within the Ship. The weather extremely thick. No land in sight.

Saturday 8th Shoald our Water, bore away to the Northward. At 10 having shoald the water to 7 fms Tackd & bore away to the Westward. The Weather very thick & gloomy.

Monday 10th Out all Reefs & bore away for the Bluff Point, it appearing from a deep bay [crossed to Kamchatka]. Saw habitations of the Natives on the Shore with several of the latter near them. The Coast in general hilly but not Mountainous and with little Snow, no Wood & sun. The Captain and some of his officers and Gentlemen landed near a Village abreast of the Ships. The Inhabitants greeted them under Arms, their Weapons consisted of lances, Dirks, & bows & arrows, but were presently reconciled to their new Visitors.

Tuesday 11th At 2 the Party returned from the Shore, having purchased a few Curiosities from the Indians [Chukchi], who behaved extremely friendly and affable. Our people saw none of their Women or Children, the Men not more than 30 in number. They had many Sledges and dogs in them. Their summer houses [were] built in the Sea Horse hide & their winter habitations under Ground, supported by wooden rafters & lined with long, shaggy Grass. At half past 2 we weigh'd the Anchor & made a trip to Clear the Shore with a light breeze from the Southward, then stood on to the Eastward.

Wednesday 12th At 5 shoaled the water suddenly to 7 fms. Hauld the wind but it falling little wind obliged us to anchor in 6½ fms on a hard sandy bottom. The breeze reviving, hove up and stood on the Westward, gradually deepening the Water.

John Webber, "Resolution and Discovery Beating Through the Ice, 1790." Pen, wash, and water color aquatint drawing showing the peril of the *Resolution* and *Discovery* as they attempted to find a way through the ice pack at Icy Cape, in wind, fog, and shallow water near the Northwest Alaska coastline. The *Resolution*, in the foreground, is in clear water, but the *Discovery*, in the distance, is apparently trapped in the ice and "in the most eminent danger." Dixson Library, State Library of New South Wales, X989/1.

Saturday 15th This coast not mountainous, but Hilly with little Snow. The Northernmost part forming a point in Latitude 67°45′ North and Longitude 194°52′ East. Found the Ship very leaky & a great quantity of Water in the Spirit & Fish rooms. Employed bailing it out with buckets.

Sunday 16th The weather coming on Foggy, hauld the wind. At 5 fired a Gun as a Signal to the Discovery, which was answered.

Monday 17th A Number of Sea Horses about the Ship. Shoald the Water gradually to 11 fms. Hauled the wind and deepened it again.

Tuesday 18th Tacked Ship close in within the Ice, the edges of it broken, but at a small distance we could perceive that it connected & form'd a solid field, totally impossible for any Vessel to penetrate. We saw a number of Sea Horses on the Ice. Made a stretch off & stood in with an intention to kill some of those animals but the sea coming in directly, Tackd and stood to the Southward within ¼ miles of the Ice. A number of Sea Horses on it. Latitude 70°03′ and Longitude 198°56′ East. Saw the Ice ahead.

Wednesday 19th Saw some low land extending from East to SEBS, distance from the nearest part 3 miles. The weather being very thick & hazy, it was impossible to identify high land or inland mountains, as we have reason to conjecture this to be part of the Continent of America, by the regular ice showing off the water whenever we advanced to the NE. The Shores appeared to be much encumbered by the Ice. The Discoverys putting about, meeting we apprehended with some Shoal Water, obliged us to do the same. In 6½ fms we made a stretch to the Northward and at ½ past 7 Tackd again and stood to the SW, shoaling the Water to 10 fms afterwards. The Northern extremity of this land was in Latitude 70°28′ North [Burney reported they were at Latitude 70°49′ North; in his journal, Cook said the expedition reached Latitude 70°44′ North. This is the northern most point reached by the expedition.] and longitude 198°16′ East and obtained the name of Icy Cape, which proved to be the most Northern part we saw in either Continent.

Thursday 20th Tackd close to the Field Ice, many parts of it covered with the Sea Horses. Hoisted the Boats out & parties sent to kill some of those animals. Stood off and on with the Ships while they were employed. At 7 they returned on board & brought with them 9 Sea Horses. Hoisted them in & made sail to the Southward. A very thick fog.

Friday 21st Saw the Ice, the Southernmost part bearing WBS. Many large flocks of birds flying to the Southward. Heard a number of the Sea Horses to the Northward of us. The weather extremely thick, passing much drift Ice & many of the Sea Animals abreast. Heard the surge of the Sea Breaking on the Ice. At ½ past 10 the fog cleared away [to] show us the land, from the nearest part 7 leagues. The land appeared to be of a moderate height & very free from Snow. The Chains of hills seemed to denote its Continentals.

Saturday 22nd No land in sight.

Sunday 23rd We heard a noise like the surge beating on the Ice to the Northward of us. Wore & stood off and passed some loose pieces. [Two punishments recorded on August 27 against sailors for theft and sleeping on duty.]

Friday 28th Tackd Ship amidst much broken Ice. Farther on it appeared to connect & form one solid field. Saw prodigious number of Sea Horses in clusters on the Ice. Hoisted the Boats & sent parties to kill some of them. The weather came on thick & foggy. The Boats returned on board with only one of these animals. Hoisted them in and stood off from the Ice. Much loose Ice about.

With little wind and thick, clear at intervals, stood in among the Ice and sent the Boats to kill Sea Horses. The Boats returned with 7 of those Sea Animals. They killed many more but lost them by their getting off the Ice and into the Sea. [Another punishment recorded, this time for drunkenness.]

Saturday 29th At ½ past 9 saw land. We take this to be part of the Coast of Asia. The land near the Sea is very low and at the back of it could perceive large swamps or lagoons. Inland the Mountains appeared lofty. The coast seemed to take a turn to the west beyond the Northern point seen.

Sunday 30th At 2 Tackd & stood in for the Land. This proved to be the Northernmost part of the Asian coast we ever saw and is in latitude 68°56′ North & longitude 180°45′ East. The weather being extremely thick gave us but an imperfect View of the land. The whole Coast covered with Snow.

John Webber, "Inhabitants of Norton Sound and Their Habitations," circa 1781-83. Pen, wash, and water color sketch depicting a family in Norton Sound in September 1778, while the expedition returned from the Arctic. The woman is carrying her child in a cloak over her shoulder in customary fashion. A man with the family's log hut, canoe, and fish drying rack are shown in the background. Dixson Library, State Library of New South Wales, PXX 2, f. 33.

4

Return to Unalaska
September–October 1778

After testing the ice pack along its front eastward from Alaska to Siberia, the expedition returned to the Alaska coast to see if it could complete charting the coast from the north. Earlier in the summer, they had abandoned the coast just north of Cape Newenham because of shallow water, obscuring fog, and hidden shoals. Now they retraced their route, crossing the Bering Strait to the American Continent to complete their survey of Alaska.

On September 16 they reached and named Norton Sound. This was the first landing after transiting the ice pack, so their principal objective was to secure wood, water, and other provisions after a weary month in the Arctic. They also encountered several people, finding their customs and habitations similar to Alaskans they met earlier in the year. Like many other Alaskans, the women cut a slit below their lower lips and wore bone labrets as a facial adornment, which Burney found especially unsightly. They also observed the sleds, shore boats, and subterranean homes of the people and found a great deal of driftwood and fresh water to replenish the ships. Roberts and King investigated a small hill that overlooked the coast, where Roberts described the tundra landscape and ground cover well-known to this part of western Alaska.

Stretching south from Norton Sound they came again to shallow water and hidden shoals, preventing further progress. Since they could not trace the coast further, Roberts lamented that they missed almost three degrees of latitude between this point and Cape Newenham. Burney said this left sixty leagues of coastline uncharted, a distance of about 200 miles. But he was likewise sure from regular soundings that there could not be an inland passageway of any distance. As it turns out, the shallow water concealed the outlet and delta of the 2,000-mile Yukon River, one of the longest rivers in North America.

Returning west to the central Bering Sea, the sailors struggled to identify the breadth and topography of St. Lawrence Island, which Roberts thought was as many as four separate islands. But they had little time to study the islands, as a terrible gale arose that drove them south, preventing further investigation. Within hours the *Resolution* was leaking again. Roberts reported, "we could hear the water sent through." He then described the flood in the ship's spirit and fish rooms, which required endless bailing and pumping before the torrent subsided.

The ships were soon in Unalaska again, where they spent three weeks, the longest stop since Nootka Sound. They spent their time repairing the *Resolution* after the horrific flood at sea. Roberts reported the planks were decayed, requiring a major overhaul. The crews also resupplied the ships, trading vigorously with the local people, especially for fresh fish. Burney noted some of the local language and both journals offered a comprehensive description of the people, their kayaks, habitations, and customs.

The sailors learned from the Natives that Russian fur hunters were stationed nearby. Gerasim Grigorovich Ismailov, the local factor of the station, described the Russian presence in the region and pored over his maps of the islands with Cook. They agreed that the Russian maps Cook carried from England were grossly inaccurate, if not fabricated. Burney concluded von Stählin's chart was "very incorrect and almost unintelligible." The British also deduced that the local people were enslaved by the Russians to hunt for sea otter. This might have explained their inoffensive nature and friendliness, as all their furs and weapons had been taken away.

At the end of October the ships sailed from Unalaska Island, but it took more than a week for them to find favorable winds to get away from the island. Once at sea another fall storm sprung up, causing great alarm, as the ships were driven back toward the island, where they feared being driven ashore. There was constant wind, rain, and hail. In the fury two masts were dislodged on the *Discovery*, killing one seaman and injuring three others. After several more harrowing days the winds subsided and the ships cleared the islands, making their way south to winter in Hawai'i.

Journal of James Burney

Wednesday, September 2nd In the Night passed by a Headland which (August 11th) we suposed to be the Eastern point of Alaschka, but which we now find to be the East point of Asia, laid down in Behrings Chart by the name of the Serge Kamen. The Land we then suposed to be the American Continent, must, according to the Chart prefixed to Heydinger's Translation of Stahlin's account of these Seas, be Alaschka.

From what we have already seen, the Chart last mentioned may be pronounced [to be] a very incorrect and almost unintelligible Chart. From the Serge Kamen the Coast trends towards the SW. Latitude of the Serge Kamen 66°07′ North and Longitude 190°13′ East.

Thursday 3rd Running alongshore to the SW. In the forenoon passed by the Indian Town near which we Anchord the 10th of August. The Land to the South of this appears full of Openings but no great depth of Water.

Friday 4th Wind Northerly and fair Weather. In the forenoon passed another Indian Town, Latitude at Noon 64°38′ North and Longitude 187°50′ East distance off Shore 6 miles . . . Stood towards the South all the Afternoon, without Seeing any more Land again. At 8 Hauled off to the Eastward and left the Continent of Asia, having seen no Trees all along the Coast . . .

Saturday 5th At 6 in the morning and again at 6 in the Evening saw distant Land to the Southward which we passed without going near, continuing our Course to the Eastward.

Sunday 6th In the morning saw the Coast of Alaschka to the Northward, and by Evening were abrest the Island under which we Anchord the 5th of August at Noon, but at a great distance from the Shore.

Monday 7th Running to the Eastward along the Coast of Alaschka [we found] a Strait Shore. Soundings these 2 last days, 19 Shoaling to 10 fathoms. In the Evening some Canoes came off towards the Ships for whom the Resolution brought too, but the Canoes paddling to the Shore again, made sail. A little after Midnight Anchord in 10 fathoms muddy bottom, about 3 Leagues from the Land . . .

Tuesday 8th At 4 in the Morning got under Sail and continued our course to the Eastward alongshore, having fair Wind and Weather. Soundings between 7 and 12 fathoms. At 7 in the Evening were abrest the East point of a Bay, past which the Coast falls back, running in a NE direction. This point is the Southernmost of Alaschka . . . [Bearings omitted.]

Wednesday 9th Wind SSW. Fair Weather. At ½ past 4 in the Morning Weighd and made Sail to the NNE per Compass, nearly in a line with the Coast. Saw Land to the Eastward making like Islands. Found the depth of Water decreasing. At 9 Sent Boats to Sound ahead . . . distant from the Shore of Alaschka about 7 Miles. Latitude Observed 64°36′ North. Wood in many places, which is the first we have seen in growth since the beginning of June. Land like Islands in sight to the Eastward.

At 3 in the Afternoon Shoaled to 4 fathoms. Hauled on a Wind. The Land to the Eastward which made like Islands, was seen to be one continued Body, extending North and NWward to the back of the Northernmost part of Alaschka in sight between the two, having the appearance of a Shoal Inlet or River [Norton Sound]. Kept Turning to the Southward all Night . . .

Thursday 10th The Wind came round to the North. At 8 in the morning were within 2 miles of the West Land (Alaschka). Sent Boats on Shore in search of Wood and Water, both which were found, but very indifferent Landing for the Surf. In the Afternoon at 3 made Sail from the Alaschka Shore, standing towards a Bay in the Eastern Land where more convenient Wooding and Watering was expected and better Shelter for the Ships. Soundings across 7 to 9 fathoms . . . about 5 miles South from a Head Land that makes the West Side of the Bay to which we are bound.

Friday 11th At daylight Weighed. All the forenoon turning into the Bay. At Noon, Anchored in 6½ fathoms mudd [bearings omitted] a Continuation of the Eastern Land in Sight, as far as S49° East. High and Mountainous. This Land from its extending towards the South, we supose to be the Continent of America, being now nearly due North of that part of the Coast where we got intangled amongst the Sholes (July 16th to 22nd).

Sent all the Boats on Shore to the West Side of the Bay. Canoes came from the Eastward who Sold us dried Fish and Berries. There seems but little difference between these and the Indians we have before met on the Coast of America. Their under Lips are slit under each corner of the mouth. A Snow Sledge was seen on shore and some of their Houses, which were built above ground of thick pieces of Timber laid close together, the interstices filled up with Moss and the whole thatched over. They are small and in different Shapes: some Square and roofed, others like the Roof only of a House, having no Walls, but the Timbers resting on the Ground and meeting in a Ridge at the Top. Some were floored with plank on the inside and a large hole dug in the Ground for Fireplace.

At 3 in the Afternoon got under Sail. Stood backwards and forwards waiting for the Boats. At 9 they returned, the Launches laden with drift Wood of which there is great plenty, but no good Watering place. In Boats and made Sail to the Westward for the place we left Yesterday on the Alaschka Shore.

Saturday 12th Anchord within 2 miles of the Alaschka Shore, abrest a Sandy Beach where was plenty of drift Wood and good landing . . . Latitude Observed 64°31′ North and Longitude 197°17′ East. Sent our Boats for Wood and Water. The Wood taken by us here is all drift, which being dry, was better for use than any other. The Trees here, mostly Firs and Birch, plenty of Currants, Hurtleberries [huckleberries], Crow and partridge Berries, and a plant which drinks well as Tea, known in Newfoundland by the Name of Indian Tea. Some Canoes came from the Southward with Trout and other Fish.

Monday 14th Having completed Wooding, and taken in 6 Weeks Water, at 3 in the Afternoon Weighed, wind NNE. Turning to Windward till 8 when we Anchord in 6½ fathoms about 2 Leagues from the Alaschka Shore. Lieut. King was sent with both Ships Cutters to the Northward to examine whether there was any passage between Alaschka and the Land to the Eastward.

Tuesday 15th At daylight got under Sail and Stood over for the Bay to the Eastward, where in the Afternoon we Anchord in 5 fathoms muddy bottom. [Bearings omitted.]

Wednesday 16th The greater part of both Ships Companies ashore gathering Fruit, cutting Spruce and Broom stuff. In the Afternoon Lieut. King returned, having seen the Land of Alaschka to join with the East Main. This Inlet Captain Cook names Norton Sound.

Alaschka being part of America, makes the two Continents not 14 Leagues apart. The West point of Alaschka, which is likewise the Westernmost of America, laying in 65°43′ North Latitude and 191°35′ East Longitude and the Serge Kamen which is the Easternmost point of Asia being in 66°07′ North [Latitude] and 190°13′ East [Longitude].

Thursday 17th Got under Sail and Stood to the Southward. In the Afternoon attempted to run through betwixt the Main Land and a small Island that bore SE¼S at Anchor [but] finding the bottom too Shoal were obliged to keep out again. The greatest part of the Night Standing alongshore to the Southward with Soundings from 9 to 11 fathoms at 5 Leagues distance.

Friday 18th Running alongshore to the Southward, at ½ past 10 Steered for a passage between 2 low Islands that lay near the main. Our Soundings decreasing, the Resolution hailed us to go ahead. Hoisted the Cutter out and sent her to sound before us.

At Noon Latitude observed 63°35′ North and Longitude 197°46′ East. At ½ past Noon being in 4½ fathoms and the Boats Making the Signal of Shoal Water, hauled off and ran round by the West side of the outermost of the 2 Islands, having soundings from 5 to 7 fathoms . . .

Saturday 19th Wind ENE. At 4 in the morning made Sail to the SW . . . kept to the Westward to deepen our Soundings. At 10 having run 7 Leagues, found the Water Shoaled, being in 6 fathoms at about 12 Leagues distant from the Land. The Wind freshening, hauld up to the NW. At 4 in the Afternoon, having deepened to 9 fathoms, kept away to the Westward and after to the SW, leaving the Continent of America.

In tracing the Coast from Norton Sound, the Southernmost Land seen was in 63°00′ North [latitude], high mountainous Land extending towards the South. The farthest Land seen by us to the North of Cape Newingham was nearly on the same Meridian and in 60°00′ North Latitude, being obliged then to leave the Coast for the same reason as now, i.e., on account of the Shoals. This makes a Gap of 60 Leagues, by much the greatest length of Coast unseen, from making the Land after leaving King George's Sound to the Northernmost part seen by us. This deficiency is in a great measure made up by Soundings, got constantly at no great depth, and always regular, except when in sight of some Island. Ran all Night to the SW per Compass, increasing our depth to 17 fathoms.

Sunday 20th Wind Northerly. Running to the SW. In the Morning the Land of Alaschka in Sight to the Northward. At Noon Saw Land bearing SWBS 10 or 12 Leagues distant. Latitude observed 63°38′ North and Longitude 192°40′ East. This is the Land we saw the Afternoon of August 3rd [St. Lawrence Island].

At ½ past 5 were within 4 miles of the Land, which at first made like a number of separate Islands, but now appears to be all joined by low Land except some Rocks that lay about 5 miles South from the East End. Bushes and Shrubs in great plenty but no Trees. Ran along the East End till 8 and then Brought too with our Head to the ENE.

Monday 21st At 5 in the Morning made Sail towards the Land. All the forenoon, running along the SE side. At Noon were within 2 or 3 miles of a point on which stands an Indian Town. [Bearings omitted.] This Island extends in length from NE to SW 15 or 16 Leagues.

Tuesday 22nd Steering between the South and SW . . .

Wednesday 23rd At 5 in the morning Saw Land to the SW, which like the other Island at first makes like several separate Small Islands, but on coming near proves to be so many high Clumps joined by low necks of Land, except a Rock or Small Island to the South of it. This likewise was before seen by us (July 29th), when there were about it a prodigious number of Sea parrots and other Sea Birds, but now scarce any. It appears ragged and barren. [Bearings omitted] the

East point of the Island bearing South 2 or 3 miles distant . . . Steered to the SE and left the Land, being bound towards Nowan Alaschka.

Thursday 24th The Wind came round to the Southward, and in the Night freshened to a Gale, which continued till the 27th when it abated and we had Variable Winds. Carried Soundings as far to the Southward as 56°25′ North Latitude, having then 55 fathoms, black Sand. Longitude 193°20′ East. After this we got no bottom till we made the Land again, the Ship always Sailing too fast to get more than 50 fathoms of line up and down.

Friday, October 2nd At ½ past 5 saw the Island of Nowanalascha, from NEBE to South, which was mistaken for an Island NE of Nowanalascha, being deceived by a low point to the Westward making like the West End of an Island we had before seen. In this error we continued till the Noon Observation set us right, by which means we got near the NW End instead of the East End of the Island. At 1 bore away to the Eastward. At 3 hauled up for a large Bay. Canoes came off to us. [We] knew some of the Indians for the same we had before seen in Samgonuther Harbour.

Coming into the Bay had light baffling Winds. On the West Side is an Indian Town near to a low point, off which runs a ledge of Rocks. Saw Whales blowing within the Rocks. Here we wanted to get but were overtaken by the Night. At 6 being well in the Bay, found no bottom with 40 fathoms of line. It growing dark made Sail out of the Bay again . . . At 9 lost sight of the Resolution. Stood backwards and forwards all Night. Wind Westerly.

Saturday 3rd At daylight saw the Resolution in shore of us. Made Sail and at 2 Anchord in 9½ fathoms in Samgonuther Harbour, having been kept out all the forenoon by the Tide from the SE running through the Straits between Nowanalascha and the next Island. Moored with our Stream Anchor up the Harbour. Bearings Latitude 53°56′ North Longitude 193°38′ East . . .

The Astronomers Tents were erected at the Watering Place. The Resolution busied in examining and repairing her Leaks, and we in Watering. The Indians every day brought us Fish, which with what we caught ourselves, proved more than Sufficient to serve every body. The Fish here are Salmon, Trout, Halibut and Rock fish. Found plenty of berries and wild Herbage which served for Sallading.

Wednesday 7th This afternoon 2 Indians brought a present to each of the Captains of Salmon and a Rye Loaf with Fish baked in the inside. Captain Cook imagining from this present there were Russians on the Island, sent his Corporal of Marines back with the 2 Indians with some Rum, English Bread and a few other things.

Saturday 10th The Corporal [John Ledyard] returned and with him 3 Russians from a Factory at the bottom of the large Bay. We attempted to Anchor in the Evening of the 2nd, and which is called Egookshue. This Settlement consists of 60 Russians and 20 Kamschadales. They have a Sloop here. Besides this, there are other Settlements in these Seas in which by their accounts are 400 Russians besides Kamschadales. This Island, by the Russians is called Ooanalusch.

Wednesday 14th The Chief of the Russian Factory, whose name is Erasm Gregori Sin Ismiloff, came to an Indian Town on the other side of the neck of Land that makes the East Side of this Harbour. Next morning he came on board the Ships attended by many Indian Canoes. He received several presents from the Officers of the Resolution, for which he afterwards made returns.

Many of our Gentlemen after this walked over to the Russian Factory 12 or 15 miles distant from us, where they met with a hospitable reception. Some of the Russians brought Boots, the Legs made of Whale's Guts, and the Soles of Seahorses hide; and Bladder Jackets for Sale. The Purchase being Rum, which is a very scarce article amongst them. They drink it unmixed. The Natives will drink none.

A few days after this, Ismiloff brought a Russian Chart of these Seas for Captain Cook to take a Copy of. This Chart extends not much more than a degree North of Nowanalascha. The Coast to the Eastward towards Mount Elias is from Behrings Chart, so that no information was gained with respect to the American Coast.

Samgonuther Harbour is laid down 30°East from the Harbour of St. Peter and St. Paul. Several Islands are laid down to the WSW and within 80 Leagues

John Webber, "A Man of Oonalaska" and "A Woman of Oonalaska [English Bay, Alaska]," circa 1781-83. Companion pen, wash, and water color images depicting Aleut or Unangan man and woman observed in October 1778. The man wears an eyeshade or visor adorned with whiskers and a walrus ivory carving, as well as a seal gut frock with a hood drawn around the neck. The woman is wearing a close-fitting sealskin coat with her hair tied in the back. There are tattoo lines across both cheeks, as well as nose and chin ornaments and a perforated lower lip. Dixson Library, State Library of New South Wales, PXX 2, f. 28 and 29.

of Nowanalascha, and 2 or 3 about half way to Kamtschatka. The Island of Seduction, mentioned in Behring's Voyage, the Russians say has been searched after, but no Land found in the direction that it is laid down. [Bearings omitted.]

The Natives of Nowanalascha are kept under great Subjection by the Russians, who have taken away all their Spears, Bows and Arrows, and left them no other weapons but Darts for Striking Fish. Whether it is owing to this their defenceless condition or to their natural disposition, they are the most quiet inoffensive set of Indians we have any where met with, and apparently as contented.

Their living is chiefly Fish, Sea Animals, Sea Birds, Berries and some Roots they use as Bread. The Russians themselves here live very little better. For boiling their victuals they have large Pots, the bottom being a smooth flat stone and the Sides unburnt clay. Straw serves for firing, the Island producing no Wood, and what drifts here can be but barely sufficient for the purposes of building or repairing their Houses, Canoes, Fish Gear etc. They strike Fire with 2 Common beach Stones rubbed over with Brimstone. Like the Indians on the Continent they have their under lips slit, some in the middle and some under each corner of the Mouth besides holes in the middle of their Noses, through which they stick ornaments, mostly pieces of Seahorse teeth carved. The Women are tattowed on the Chin, across each cheek, and some in the Arms. They are not niggardly of their favours nor the Men Jealous.

Thursday 22nd Wind Easterly. In the morning unmoored. At ½ past 10, the Resolution got under Sail, intending to run out of the Harbour, but the Wind Shifting, she got aground and being Ebb Tide, lay there till near Midnight, when she hove off without damage.

Friday 23rd Wind NW. Were obliged to lay fast.

Saturday 24th Some Russians came from an Island to the SW called Humanak.

Monday 26th Wind SE. At 7 in the Morning got under Sail and ran out of the Harbour. The Wind being Easterly, ran to the Westward intending to go round the West Side of Nowanalascha, and from thence to the Southward for Sandwich Islands. In the Night the Wind came to the South.

Tuesday 27th A strong Gale from the SW which obliged us to hand the Topsails. Thick hazey Weather. Stood backwards and forwards without seeing anything of the Land all day. [Bearings omitted.]

Wednesday 28th At 1 in the morning the Fore and Main Tacks broke in a heavy Squall of Wind, by which accident John Macintosh, Seaman, was killed on the Spot. The Boatswain and 2 other of the people much hurt. In the morning standing to the SSE to make the Land. At ½ past 7 it clearing up a little, saw a point of the Land bearing ENE 4 or 5 miles, and more Land extending to the South and SWward, but whether a continuation of Nowanalascha or part of Humanak could not tell for the thickness of the Weather. At ½ past 9 wove round and stood off Shore [only to] Find by the Land we have lost ground since yesterday. In the Evening the Wind abated and became Variable. Ran to the SW all Night.

Thursday 29th The Wind came again to the Westward and blew strong. At daylight found we were within 2 Leagues of the Shore, contrary to our expectations, as we suposed ourselves far enough to the Westward to weather the Land. There being no likelihood of the Weather moderating, at 9 bore away for the Streights of Samgonuther. At Noon a Rock which we had taken all the forenoon for a Sail bore NW½W 2 miles. This Rock is about 6 Leagues distant from the nearest part of the Land. Its Latitude 53°56′ North and Longitude 192°1′ East. Not being able to reach the length of Samgonuther Streights before dark, at 3 in the Afternoon, hauled on a Wind and stood backwards and forwards till next morning.

Friday 30th At day light Bore away. At 1 were in the Streights. Ran down along the East Side of Nowan Alascha. In the Evening lost sight of the Land, steering to the SSE for Sandwich Islands. Wind still Westerly.

As this may properly be called the finishing of the first Season, I have collected into one Chart all the Land seen by us from first making the Coast of America, March 7th, to our present leaving Nowanalascha. In this, no part laid down but what we have seen ourselves: What might have been added from other Maps is left out, as another Season may perhaps afford an opportunity of filling up some of the Vacant Spaces from our own Observations.

Journal of Henry Roberts

Saturday, September 5th At 2 high land to the westward at some distance appended with the Southern point [East Cape, Siberian mainland]. On the low land which juts off the south extreme we could perceive the Habitations of the Natives & other buildings which we took for fish stages [deep bays observed but not approachable]. The SW part of this Land lies in Latitude 64°13′ Longitude 186°33′ East and may be the SE promontory of the Great Gulph of Anidar [Kamchatka].

Sunday 6th This land is near that we Discovered on the 4 of August to the westward, probably the same group of islands [St. Lawrence Island].

Tuesday 8th The Mountains just appearing above the Horizon appear like so many distinct Islands [West coast of Alaska]. At 8 saw two Canoes coming off from the Shore, brought too for them. They paddled near the Ship but would not venture alongside. There appeared to be a dozen or 20 people in each boat. On the Shore we saw several fires. Made sail again.

Wednesday 9th The land at the head of the Bay, low & flat encircled by a fine sandy beach, carrying 7 & 10 fms. About 2 miles distant land opening at the NE. Hauld round the point, the Shore being steep, we deepened the water to 15 & 13 fathoms. The weather dark & Squally. We perceived that the Coast under which we had anchored was well Clothed with wood, seemingly small pine or Spruce Trees.

James Burney, "NW Coast of America from Cape Foulweather to Bering Strait," October 1778. Most of the cartographers prepared a final map of the voyage results after returning to Unalaska. Burney's chart was unique because it only showed parts of the coast observed from the ships, leaving a gap where the storms kept the expedition to sea along the coast of Canada and Southeast Alaska, with another gap when they were forced offshore because of shallow water at the broad mouth of the Yukon River. Burney Journal p. 223, Mitchell Library, State Library of New South Wales, Safe 1/64 and 1/79.

Thursday 10th Sailing on to the Northward, gradually decreasing our depth of Water, we saw the land to join from the barren hummock to that to the westward & more land projecting to the NE of the Hummock. The haze clearing sometimes gave us a perfect sight of the land, being a high range of Hills with low land on its shores [Norton Sound].

The breeze freshening and night coming on, with very much shoal water to encounter with, our situation was rather alarming. We kept beating and plying to windward during the Night, towards morning the Gale favourved us by veering round to the West & North. We stretched over to the west shore. Sent the Boats to the Shore & stood off & on while they were absent.

Friday 11th Waiting for the Boats. At 2 they returned with a Quantity of Spruce, hoisted them in and made sail. Our people saw on the shore only one hut which appeared to have been some time deserted. There is a good river of fresh water with a fine sandy beach covered with driftwood, some of which is large & good Timber. The spruce trees are in general small. The country abounded in berries.

We now find the supposed Island join with the high land to the Eastward by a narrow neck of low land (making a peninsula) and formed a good Bay. We ply'd to windward, endeavouring to get into the Bay. About 2½ miles from the Eastern Shore made the Signal to the Discovery to Tack, hoisted the boats out to Sound.

Saturday 12th At 2 the Cutter came on board, found the water very shallow within 1½ miles of the Shore. Saw a great quantity of driftwood on most parts of the coast. Hoisted the launch out & sent her with the pinnace to a small Cove on the east side of the peninsula to cut up some and the Cutter with the Discoverys sent to sound & examine the Bay. At 6 the Cutter returned, having found the Bay very shallow, not being able to approach the Coast by 1½ or 2 miles without shoaling the water to 3 fms. At 8 the pinnace and launch came on board loaded with wood. Cleared the Boats & hoisted them in, the Launch towing, made sail & stood over for the western shore again, soundings of 5, 6, 7 and 4 fms. Sent the Boats to the sandy beach where they before landed with party's to Wood & water. By noon we received two boat loads of wood & a launch load of water, standing off & on picking up the boats.

Monday 14th Made the signal for all persons to repair on board the Sloops, having completed wooding & got 13 Tons of water on board with a quantity of Spruce, when we began to brew beer. During our stay here we only saw one family of the Natives, who were extremely friendly and peaceable. We purchased abundance of small Herrings and Trout from them, made up in bundles with grass. Our people gathered plenty of Hurtel [seal], partridge, heath & Cranberries, of which the land is covered with.

Wednesday 16th Working into the Bay to the eastward of the peninsula, we anchored in 5 fms offshore 2 miles. In the morning several small Canoes came off to us from the Villages on the East side of the Bay that appeared to be pleasantly situated. We bought a quantity of both fresh & dried salmon with other small fish. Sent the Launch on Shore with a party to cutt broom and spruce, as this side of the peninsula is only lone patch of Trees which are near the sandy cove where the boats landed. Sent one half of the people on shore to refresh themselves on the Berry's etc. At noon the Liberty men called on board & the other half sent to the Shores.

Thursday 17th In the evening got all the people on board with a quantity of broom stuff & spruce. The two boats returned from their expedition to the Northward. We landed about 1½ miles to the Northward of the barren hummock in a fine sandy Cove, but it being a flat shore, rendered it awkward landing, obliging us to tow the boat for a considerable distance before we reached the beach. We attempted to land in many places but found them still worse. William King & self ascended a hill near the point that was seen from the Ship,

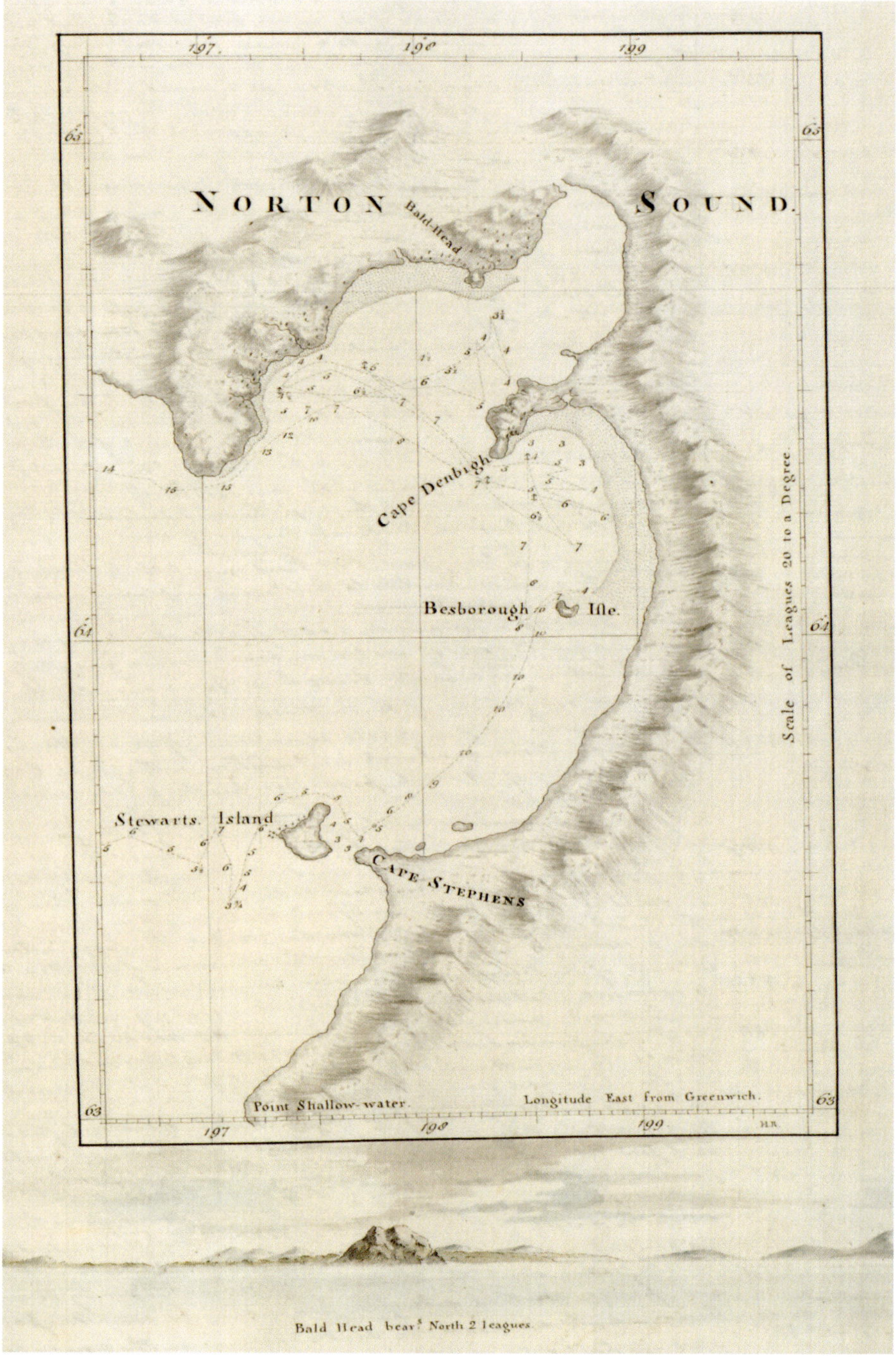

Henry Roberts, "A Chart and View of Norton Sound," September 1778. Many of Roberts' charts show precision and careful penmanship. Here he presents the ships' tracks as they traversed Norton Sound, drawn in detail, with a modest water color drawing of a coastal view below. Roberts Journal p. 249, Dixson Library, State Library of New South Wales, DLMSQ 151-52 and DLMSF 2.

projecting from the barren Hummock where we commanded the whole range of the Coasts, which we found to join within 12 miles, that seemed to form a small rivulet with sand banks above water at the mouth of it. The opposite shore to us about the same distance when we could trace this range of mountains to connect with those of the western shore. The Valley here is very fertile, well clothed with the spruce tree & luxuriant grass. The sides of the hills equally flourishing, abounding with berrys of all kinds that are generally found in these climates. The low land near the sea is marshy & full of swamps. We saw prodigious numbers of the Turkey buzzards on these flats, but could never get within shot at them.

Friday 18th Stood onto the Northward of the Island, intending to pass between it & the Main, but shoaling the water to 4 fms abreast of a low point which runs off to the East of the Island on which are several decayed houses. We were obliged to haul the vessel & Tack and sailed round the West part of it, increasing the depth of water to 10 fms.

Saturday 19th At ½ past Noon, the Boats ahead, made the signal for shoal water when we had no more than 4½ fms. When the Ships hauled off for the west part of the Island, a Canoe came off to the Boat, but in their firing a Musket as a signal, made him retreat to the shore again. We sailed around the Island carrying regular soundings of 5 fms. From this point runs a reef of rocks & flats to the distance of 2 miles. We could perceive on the Shore a number of the Natives with several of their habitations, making a number of fires as we passed them. By 10 we had shoaled the water as before. Hauld off again but not increasing our depth of water & weather looking finally like an approaching Gale. This point in Latitude 63°00′ and Longitude 197°15′ East and is distant 60 leagues from Shoal Ness.

Sunday 20th Saw the Continent to the Eastward of Sledge Island distant 13 leagues. At noon the weather being very thick with snow showers could not see the land.

Monday 21st [Because of shallow water along the coast, the expedition was forced to sea, regaining the southern coast of St. Lawrence Island in the central Bering Sea.] Bore away sailing along the Eastern side of the Island, some high land to the westward came on with the Northern end off shore 2 miles. Soon after we saw more land to the Southward of this, which appeared like another Island [with] high snowy land to the west between the two. Stood in for it, the land appearing like three different Islands. On this spot are the dwellings of the Inhabitants. We made all the land to join by low land forming a Bay. Bore away round the Southern end we could perceive many houses of the Natives with other buildings, like fish stages, but saw no people on the Shore or even fires. This Island is situated in Latitude 63°15′ North and Longitude East of Greenwich 190°30′.

Wednesday 23rd The land appeared as 4 distinct Islands. We attempted to weather the westernmost, but the wind coming short we gave it up & stood in shore. The high tower rock to the Southward, we soon made the hills, like the last land we left, to connect with each other by low land. The Ship probably frequented this Island [before]. When we first fell in with this Island we saw immense flights of Birds, but now not one to be seen. We could perceive no signs of Inhabitants [but there were] several sea horses about.

Thursday 24th Strong gale and squally with heavy seas. Found a great quantity of Water in the Spirit Room occasioned by leaks in the starboard buttock, where we could hear the water sent through. Put the people to watch & watch to attend bailing it out with buckets. At 6 a heavy Sea. Employed bailing the water out of the Spirit Room and pumping. The Ship very leaky. [In the following two days, the gale decreases and the bailing and pumping gains on the flood with little new water aboard. Another punishment recorded for a theft.]

Passed a dead Whale, which was much eaten by the birds and very offensive. Several whales blowing.

Friday, October 2nd At ½ past 5 saw the land [Unalaska]. The Island we watered at in the beginning of July off shore 4 leagues. We had little wind & baffling for the most part of the fore noon, endeavouring to sail round the west point. Several of the Natives came off to us in their single skin Canoes.

Saturday 3rd Sailing round the Northern part of the Island, we opened a deep bay, haul'd in for it, the West point making in a high bluff. [We were] not more than ½ miles from the rocks. From this shore is a low point projecting out with a reef of flat rocks extending at some distance athwart the bay. At the back of this, the Inlet appeared oppen & the shores bold. Sent a boat to sound near the reef [but] called the boat on board and stood out again. On the low point was several dwellings of the Natives where a great many of them had assembled to look at the Ship, with a number along side in their Canoes trading with dried fish, etc.

At day light Bore away for the Harbour we watered at in June [English Bay], it bearing SSE 6 or 7 miles. It falling little wind, hoisted the boats out & sent them ahead to tow. At 11 a breeze sprung up, weighed again & stood in for the Harbour, all the Boats ahead towing. By Noon we had entered it & sailing further up, many of the Inhabitants along side in their Canoes. The Discovery some distance astern.

[End of volume one of two Roberts volumes. Signed by "Henry Roberts, Mate."]

The Harbour of Shamganooda, situated on the Northern part of the Island of Oonalascka, it may be known by the east point of the entrance being low and cliffy with several rocks at a little Distance from the Shore. The land from point rising in a gradual ascent to the summit of the hills, or by a remarkable peaked hill on the west side at times covered with snow. There is good anchorage in any depth between 12 and 4 fathoms. The east shore is the boldest. The opposite having a shallow bank running off it, with not more than 2 & 3 fms water. The best anchorage is above the Shoal in 7 fathoms where you lye land locked by the Midd Channel Island and secure from all winds. The banks of the harbour above this is low on each side with a stony beach until you come to the head of it, where its sandy & flatt water. This low land produces very luxuriant Grass, with

Wild Celery, Scurvy Grass, and a root called by us Angelicka, & wild peas. The land from these shores rises rather precipitously to hills of a middling height that form deep Gullies or Chasms, which afford great plenty of fresh water. The outer part of the harbour is steep, cliffed & rocky. The sides of the hills, well clothed with Grass but no wood.

Here are great abundance of berries, among which variety is a peculiar kind of a bluish bloom, much superior to the others. The Valley at the head of the harbour abound with them, growing thickest nearest the sides of fresh water upon small bushes. Among the high grass & heathers [are] many grouse or a kind of partridge, and on the hills we saw a great plenty of Eagles, Ravens & plovers, with several foxes. The sea game consists of Geese, Ducks, Curlews, Snipes, and Shags, etc, all of which are extremely shy, although the harbour is filled with them at times. Our seine afforded us but a small supply of fish, but the hooks & lines made up for it generally, catching a sufficient quantity of Halibut to serve the people daily as much as they could consume. Here are also some few seals.

The Inhabitants are not numerous [but] very peaceable, courteous & friendly. Neither sexes are clothed with furs, the Russians most probably depriving them of this article. The men wear an inner garment made of birds skins, the feathers near their skin, over which they put on a foul weather jacket. This was thought to be the bladder of a Whale, first cutt into a long narrow slip & then sewed together with a degree of ingenuity & excellence. They likewise wear a kind of hat or bonnet made of wood & adorned with beads, etc. The women are in general well made & comely, though their cheek bones lay high with small Eyes. They wear nothing more than a Covering made of Seals Skin. Both sexes are fond of snuff & the men chew Tobacco, both of which articles are good trade. They have contracted the Veneral Disease.

Sunday 4th Came too with the Best Bower in 7 fathoms at the upper part of the bay, about 12 cables length from each shore, and steadied the Ship. Got on board a launch load of Water. The Carpenters, with the Discoverys, ripping the sheathing off under the starboard buttock searching for the leak which was found to be occasioned by the seams being entirely oppen & many of the Trunnels decayed. Began to clear the Spirit and fish Rooms to get at the timbers to cleanse them in order that the water might have a free passage to the Well. A third part of the Ship's Company sent on Shore daily to refresh themselves. Several of the Natives along side, trafficking, with fish and berries.

Monday 5th Hauled the Seine on a stony beach near the head of the Harbour and caught some salmon trout, with a large Hallibut. Got the forge up and the armourers employed at it.

Tuesday 6th Such constant rain as prevented the people from working. A few Canoes in the bay, but several of the Natives sleeping on board all night.

Wednesday 7th Taking stone ballast into the fish room, scuttled the bulkheads of both it and the spirit rooms to give water intercourse to the pumps. Hauled the seine. Caught but few fish.

John Webber, "The Inside of a House in Oonalashka [English Bay, Alaska]," circa 1781-83. Pen, wash, and water color sketch depicting the inside of an Aleut or Unangan home observed in October 1778. The homes were sunk partially underground and covered with earth, with the entrance provided in the center, using a ladder to the top. There are five people seated and two others standing in conversation. Around the walls are shelves with baskets, mats, fish, and other provisions. Dixson Library, State Library of New South Wales, PXX 2, f. 34.

Thursday 8th The Carpenters finished on the buttock, stowed the fish room up and got more stone ballast into the spirit room. Sent a boat with hooks & lines to fish off the rocks at the entrance of the harbour. They caught three Hallibut of a middling size. The Natives trading with us as usual for Tobacco & beads.

Friday 9th Sent a boat fishing. Caught some Hallibut sufficient to serve 2 pounds per Man. A small number of the Natives with us.

Saturday 10th Employed getting some ballast in the fore hold. The Captain understood and having received some intimation of there being Europeans near this place he dispatched a man (with the Indians that he got his intelligence from) to these unknown people with a present.

Sunday 11th The messenger that was sent returned with three Russians, who came on board, at present residents on this Island.

Monday 12th The boat returned from fishing with 20 Hallibut, which was served to the people, as much as they choosed to take.

Thursday 15th Compleated the fore hold, having stowed 15 Tons of stone ballast before the births. Began to clear the after hold to get at the timbers and stowing the spirit room up, having 6 or 8 Tons of ballast in it & the Fish Room. This morning another Russian visited us, whom we had not seen before. He appeared to have more authority than the others being attended with upwards of 50 Canoes with the Natives. The latter trading with us as usual. The boat fishing & caught 5 Hallibut.

Tuesday 20th Compleated with the after hold. Received 3 puncheons of Oil from the shore, which we extracted from the blubber of the Sea Horse.

Friday 23rd At 5 am the Ship floated off when we warped further down the Harbour & endeavoured to sail out, but the wind failing us, we were forced to anchor near the East shore in 10 fms.

Saturday 24th Fresh Gales and Squally. We attempted to heave the ship further off, but having severe gusts of wind from the high land, we let go the Best Bower and veered on both cables to a half when we were within ½ a cables length from the rocks. Came on board 5 Russians, some of whom we had not seen before.

Tuesday 27th Sailing past some deep Inlets lying to the Westward of the Harbour. At the head of one of these the Russians have an Ostrog or Village, where they reside. At 2 met with baffling breezes off the high land, the west part of the Island South distance 3 leagues. The Discovery fired a Gun which was answered. The Gale increasing, wore the Ship with a strong Gale, close reefed and handed the Topsails. Got down the Top Gallant Yards.

Wednesday 28th Strong Gales & squally. A hollow sea, the Ship labouring very much. The Hail exceedingly large. The Discovery fired a Gun which we answered. The west part of the Island about 4 leagues distant. Very hazy over the other parts. Latitude 53°59′ North and Longitude 192°05′ East.

Thursday 29th The weather being very thick & deceitful & fearing we could not avoid the land, we bore away to the Northward for the streights. This land was very mountainous, cliffy and much covered with Snow. At ¾ past 10 we perceived through the haze a high rock bearing N ¾ E, no shoal or breakers near it, 3 leagues. The Gale increasing.

Friday 30th At 2 past Wore Ship and bore away for the Streights. The high steep head (which makes the West Point of the Sound we stood in for on the 3rd of this month) offshore 3 or 4 leagues. At Noon, the Gale continuing with severe squalls, sailing through the Streights. [The journal describes the periodic firing of cannons to keep the ships together through November 3, 1778, due to constant gales, squally weather, and high seas, when the risk of the ships being dashed against the land finally subsides and the expedition sails south for Hawai'i.]

PART THREE
REVISITING HAWAI'I AND THE DEATH OF COOK

INTRODUCTION

After grueling months sailing in and out of storms along the Northwest Coast, then pushing through fogbound coasts to the Arctic ice pack, the expedition steered to the tropics to rest and overhaul the ships, particularly the *Resolution*, as well as explore the far reaches of the new-found Sandwich Islands. Leaving Unalaska in late October, for several weeks they only saw the constant frenzy of thick fog, torrential rain, and turbulent seas. The storms were so frightful that one sailor fell to his death from the rigging of the *Discovery* and three others were injured. Occasionally they would see a few birds or a solitary dolphin, but the weeks devoted to reaching the middle latitudes and temperate seas were frightful and exasperating.

By mid-November they finally found warm trade winds that took them to Hawai'i. On November 26, at 20°55′ North Latitude, an unknown island rose in the horizon. It was Maui, large and well wooded, dominated by a ten-thousand-foot saddle-shaped peak, Haleakalā Volcano. Native canoes came out as soon as the ships were in view and trading was soon brisk, seeming to exhaust the supplies on shore. Midshipman George Gilbert summarized the sentiments of the men:

> The joy that we experienced on our arrival here is only to be conceived by ourselves or people under like circumstances; for after suffering excess of hunger and a number of other hardships most severely felt by us for the space of near ten months, we had now come into a delightfull climate where we had almost every thing we could wish for, in great profusion.[1]

Soon a chieftain came aboard the *Discovery* to welcome the sailors to Hawai'i, leaving Captain Clerke a gift of a red feather cloak. A week later an elderly, scaly-skinned chief the sailors called Terreoboo, better known today as Kalani'opu'u, arrived with a great entourage on board the *Resolution*. The young warrior Kamehameha, who later conquered many of these islands to establish the Kingdom of Hawai'i, was one of the chief's attendants. Kalani'opu'u gave Cook presents of pigs, sweet potatoes, roots, and an even more magnificent feathered cloak.

The voyagers could not find a safe anchorage in this part of Maui, so continued to sail south. Soon another, even larger island came into view, today's "Big Island" of Hawai'i. Dominated by two snow-capped peaks, Cook was mesmerized by the length and breadth of the island, but he was still unable to find a place to anchor. Tacking in a zig zag pattern around the island, the sailors spent over a month in view of the island and its peaks, frustrated by storms, currents, winds, and pounding surf.

When the weather permitted, the local people came out in canoes to trade on a regular basis and, to the captain's chagrin, the women frequently stayed on the ships overnight. Cook at first attempted to prevent friendly relations between the women and his sailors, but he found strictures impossible to enforce. "It was not possible to keep [the women] out of the Ship," he wrote, "and no women I ever met with were more ready to bestow their favours." He noticed the Hawaiians had already been infected with venereal disease, probably from the expedition's first contact at Kaua'i and Ni'ihau a year earlier, so at length he concluded there was no reason to keep the women away. They came on board and spent many nights below decks, even though the rolling ships often made them seasick.[2]

The miserable seas waned after the ships rounded the south point of the island in early January at 18°55′ North Latitude. At the same time the coast turned from a lush green to a devastated wasteland covered with lava. Sailing north along the island's western shoreline, they came upon a village along the beach within a curving bay and steep cliffs. The master, William Bligh, was sent to investigate, and he soon returned with the recommendation that the ships anchor inside the bay, Kealakekua Bay. While exposed to storms from the southwest, it was the best anchorage they had yet seen in the islands.

As the expedition anchored, thousands of Hawaiians came to the ships, many in canoes and even more swimming from shore, overwhelming the crew in a tumultuous welcome. Thousands more watched the spectacle from shore. "The decks both above and below were entirely covered with . . . men, women and children," Gilbert wrote, "so that when we wanted to work the ship we could not come at the ropes without first driving the greatest part of them overboard; which they bore with the utmost cheerfulness and good nature." The following day there were so many people aboard the *Discovery* that it began to keel over.[3]

Amid the excitement two chiefs came aboard to restore order and welcome the sailors to the bay. They guided Captain Cook and the other officers to shore, where the captain was entertained in an elaborate ceremony. Everywhere he went the Natives prostrated themselves, much like his experience in Kaua'i, as they seemed to adore him in the manner of a god they called "Lono." Cook arrived at a propitious time. Each year during the winter months Hawaiians worshipped the god of peace and prosperity, *Lono*, and, at least from the British perspective, Cook seemed to be the incarnation of the god. Ceremonies offered by the priests featured the productivity and fertility of the islands, a central theme of the *Makahiki* season then underway. They wanted to honor Clerke in the same way, but he would have none of it.

There was brisk trade on the ships. It seemed the Hawaiians were willing to provide all the island could produce for a nail, bit of iron, or other English treasure. Like other Polynesians, the people were also prone to theft. Anything not tied down or under close observation might be pilfered in the daily frenzy aboard the ships. As the whirlwind continued, the sailors set up the astronomer's tents on shore and found a place to refurbish the sails and spars nearby. Unfortunately for them, they chose a site next the *heiau*, the most sacred part of the cove. Soon the *Resolution* was under full renovation, the carpenters and other crew oblivious to the evident conflict with island religion.

A week after the ships arrived in the bay, the aged king, Kalani'opu'u, whom they met off Maui, arrived with stately formality in three elaborately-carved outrigger canoes. More ceremonies were staged in Ka'awaloa, the king's residence, where the ruler of Hawai'i soon became Cook's fast friend. Although they probably depleted the plentiful countryside of virtually every article, this did not diminish the goodwill of Kalani'opu'u or his people. There seemed no end to the boundless enthusiasm for the visitors—the priests even acquiesced when the sailors uprooted the wooden railing from the *heiau*, including its treasured carved images, to be used as firewood for the journey north.[4]

After a bounteous three weeks, the ships were repaired and Cook announced their departure. A host of canoes followed the ships out of Kealakekua Bay on the morning of February 4 and Cook set sail to the north. Kalani'opu'u offered one final gift and they parted forever—or so they thought. In a few days a gale sprang up, with turbulent seas and heavy offshore winds, and the foremast of the *Resolution* split. Cook faced a dilemma: should he continue north to find another harbor to repair the mast, or return to Kealakekua Bay? He knew of no other Hawaiian port. So even though he anticipated a cool reception, he concluded his only choice was to return to the Big Island.

There was no grand reception when the ships returned to the bay; in fact, there was no reception at all. To make matters worse, the *Makahiki* season was now over, replaced by the worship of *Ku*, the god of combat and war. The people could not understand why *Lono* had reappeared so quickly to challenge the sovereignty of Kalani'opu'u. In the days that followed the priests placed a *tabu* on the ships, and thievery, mistrust, and growing hostility erupted on several occasions. The problem with pilferage was especially great on the *Discovery*, in part because Cook might still be revered, but more likely because Clerke, weakened by tuberculosis, ran a much looser ship.

On February 13 Cook, who was ashore with the carpenters, heard shots fired from the *Discovery* and saw Natives paddling franticly away from the ship with two midshipmen, Edgar and Vancouver, in hot pursuit. Armorer's tongs had been stolen in a daring daylight raid. When the two midshipmen caught up to the fleeing thieves on shore, an angry mob assembled and pelted them with stones, then the oars of the canoes. Although the two midshipmen were badly injured, a chief advanced into the crowd and stopped the fracas.[5]

Shocked by this sudden change in temperament, Cook confided that night to King, "I am afraid that these people will oblige me to use some violent measures, for they must not be left to imagine that they have gained an advantage over us." Yet the troubles only escalated the following morning when Burney learned a shore boat from the *Discovery* had been spirited away overnight. Cook quickly reacted as he did in Tonga and Tahiti. He sent some of the crew to the outlets of the bay to ensure none of the thieves could leave with the stolen boat and then he set off for Ka'awaloa to take the king hostage as security for the boat's return. While this strategy might provoke the Natives, as it had before, Cook was confident any opposition would melt in the face of British firepower. It was a fatal miscalculation.

So at seven o'clock in the morning, Cook took three boats to shore, a small pinnace, or tender, and two larger boats loaded with marines. Cook and Lieutenant Molesworth Phillips, the marine sergeant, were in the pinnace, which was commanded by Henry Roberts. While Roberts waited in the shallows, Cook and Phillips went to seize Kalaniʻopuʻu at his residence. Once awakened, the old chief quickly agreed to accompany Cook on board and sent one of his young sons ahead, who gladly climbed into the pinnace with Roberts.[6] But soon two other chiefs and one of his favorite wives objected. The chief dallied and, as he did, a crowd gathered. In a few minutes the uproar was so overwhelming that Cook and Kalaniʻopuʻu abandoned the plan and the chief deserted Cook to the multitudes.

Although he may not have understood it, Cook was in grave danger. The boats sent to blockade the bay had just fired on an escaping canoe and unwittingly killed a chief. When the crowd learned of the chief's death the mood turned ugly. They blamed Cook for the murder. On shore with Lieutenant Phillips and just a few marines, the captain had little more than his own musket to protect himself. He shot the first warrior who charged him but, filled only with small shot, the charge struck the Native's heavy body mat harmlessly, emboldening the crowd. He fired again, as did the marines, but they were vastly outnumbered. Although several warriors were killed, the crowd advanced.

Cook was struck from behind, fell in the shallows, where he was stabbed and clubbed to death. Four marines also died. Although more than two dozen Hawaiians were also killed, the crowd of warriors stood their ground despite another volley from the marines. Vastly outmanned, the British hastily retreated, leaving the bodies of the commander and four marines where they lay. A short distance away, Roberts sent Kalaniʻopuʻu's son back on shore. Seriously injured, Phillips struggled into Roberts' pinnace and the vanquished soldiers retreated to the ships.[7]

Shock overcame the people on both sides, who were horrified by the tragedy. The crews lost their "father" and commander and the Hawaiians their British adversary, as well as many husbands and friends. "When on the return of the boats informing us of the Captains Death," Gilbert wrote, "a general silence ensued throughout the ship for the space of a near half an hour; it appearing to us somewhat like a Dream that we could not reconcile ourselves to for some time. Grief was visible in every Countenance, some expressing it by tears, and others by a kind of gloomy dejection, more easy to be conceived than described, for as all our hopes centered in him, our loss became irreparable and the sense of it was so deeply impressed upon our minds as not to be forgot." As they returned from the skirmish, the retreating marines were heard to say, "We have lost our father! Our father is gone!"

Watching from the deck of the *Discovery*, Clerke and Burney viewed the incident with clarity, and later saw the Natives take the bodies of the dead inland to be dismembered and burned. In the afternoon canoe loads of Natives came out from the crowded shores to shout insults at the English. By nightfall screams of rage could be heard from the villages and the British fired cannons aimlessly in return. Soon cooler heads prevailed as Clerke, now in command, simply sought to recover Cook's body. He concluded nothing could be gained by further bloodshed and, using King, Burney, and Vancouver as emissaries, spent the next several days urging peace and moderation while the carpenters hurriedly completed repairs to the broken mast.

One evening two Natives came to the ships under the cover of darkness with a bundle containing part of Cook's body. Later another procession yielded the Captain's thigh bone and perhaps some body parts from the dead marines. With these few remains, Clerke performed a burial service for the fallen and they were committed to the bay. Clerke wrote, "I had the remains of Captain Cook committed to the deep with all the attention and honour we could possibly give it in this part of the World." With nothing remaining for them in the bay, in the late evening of February 22 Clerke gave orders to hoist anchor and cast off from the scene of the tragedy.[8]

In the years since the disaster, there has been considerable analysis of the melee and its aftermath. At the time Clerke decided the death occurred simply because Cook used his weapon at the wrong time, electrifying the mob. Later missionaries and more recent scholars have assigned the death greater meaning, speculating on Cook's role in the Pacific, insisting the death was the explosive outcome of colonialism and nationalism that exposed British indifference to local culture. Given Cook's growing temper and insensitivity to his crew, as well as the people ashore, it was clear he was unable to give a measured response to the theft of the cutter. As Beaglehole concluded, "At the fatal moment, the strained cord snapped."[9]

The expedition's remaining time in Hawai'i was anticlimactic. They retraced their course to the north in the face of contrary winds, observing Kahoolawe, Maui, Lanai, and the mountain mass of Moloka'i, taking observations and charting the islands from the decks, but they did not land. They then rounded the west end of Moloka'i and coasted along the eastern shore of O'ahu. Ironically the only island coastline left unexplored was the south side of O'ahu, so they missed the anchorage at Pearl Harbor. Instead they observed the well-populated windward shore of the island and its abundance, anchoring a short time in a promising bay. They were warmly received with supplies and the seeming endless prostration of local people, but only found brackish water, so they did not stay long.

They returned to their former port at Kaua'i, where they anchored outside the surf of Waimea for several days. It was unclear whether the hostilities on the Big Island were already known in Kaua'i, but the reception on shore was uneasy. Even though the trustworthy Lieutenant King was in charge of the shore party, another warrior was shot, but this time the local chiefs restored order so trading could continue. The sailors exchanged nails, other iron bits and trinkets for hogs, sweet potatoes, fruit, and yams. There was also plenty of salt, so pork was cured for the journey north. In a week the ships crossed to the island of Ni'ihau to trade for yams, but few were available.

Despite the experience at Kealakekua Bay, King, Burney, and Roberts each made careful and far sighted observations about Hawai'i, each time favorably comparing the people and the climate to Tahiti and Tonga. In concluding his comparison of the Polynesian islands, King wrote, "If Otaheite is called the Queen of the South sea Isles and the Society Isles the most amiable group, Owhyhee may be termed the King of the South sea, and these Islands the most capable of being made useful." King estimated the population of the archipelago to be about 500,000, compared to just 120,000 at Tahiti.[10]

On March 15 they weighed anchor, sailing southwest for rumored "turtle islands" to find more provisions. When the islands could not be found, they changed course for Kamchatka. After the drama of Kealakekua Bay, Clerke resolved that he would follow Cook's plan to test the Arctic ice pack a second time. In a month the temperature dropped from 82° to 29° as they returned north, reaching Avacha Bay while it was still choked with ice. Overwhelmed by tuberculosis, Clerke was rarely on deck and never again in active command of the expedition.

1

IN HAWAIIAN WATERS
NOVEMBER 1778–JANUARY 1779

Leaving stormy Unalaska in October, the expedition sailed to the Sandwich Islands, first encountered the previous January. Burney wrote, "We had mostly fair Winds and no bad weather the rest of the Passage." Cook speculated there would be more islands to the windward of Kaua'i, so they fell into latitudes further southeast and were rewarded by sighting the islands of Maui and Moloka'i on November 26. The winds were against them so they tacked and coasted in along the eastern shores of Maui.

The time rounding Maui, and later the Big Island, was a slow and tedious shipboard routine, with the monotony broken by visits from the Natives in canoes from shore. Although they did not know it, the king of the Big Island, Kalani'opu'u, visited from Maui on the last day of November. There also were continuous visits from the women. The journals said the Hawaiians showed signs of venereal disease and speculated this was caused by the visit to Kaua'i a year earlier. Burney wrote that about three-quarters of those who came aboard from the canoes had signs of the disease. He also was aware the current visitors knew of the skirmish at Kaua'i that resulted in the death of one Hawaiian.

Roberts kept a straightforward log of the progress of the expedition from frigid Alaska to tropical Hawai'i, with each journal page committed to two days of bearings, coordinates, ship duties, winds, and weather. As they left Alaska the *Resolution* struggled to keep the *Discovery* in sight by firing guns and burning false signal fires on board. Usually the consort replied, but sometimes the signals were not answered. Roberts also observed nearly continuous thick and rainy weather in the week after leaving English Bay, with gales and high seas. The logbook comes to life at the end of the month when the ships see dolphins and tropical birds, and then the genial splendor of Maui, with its imposing central volcano and cultivated plantations.

The ships continued a clockwise pattern around the Big Island, the largest island seen by Cook in the South Seas. They stayed close to shore to trade for provisions with the local people, who frequently arrived in canoes, but there were no signs of a harbor. Rounding the southern tip of the island, the landscape changed from cultivated plantations to stark, barren lava fields. Burney said it was a field of "burnt and melted Stones." Roberts compared the wasteland to the barren volcanic summits of Ascension Island in the South Atlantic Ocean. He explained, "This part of the Island is much inferior to any that we have before seen, having certainly received some very severe eruptions from Volcanoes, the whole face of the Country being a mass of Cinders and Lava."

They finally detected the modest anchorage at Kealakekua Bay. It was by no means protected or commodious, but Roberts said it was passable, explaining "it affords good anchorage but receives little or no Shelter from the Easterly trade winds."

Journal of James Burney

Monday, November 2nd, 1778 Had a hard Gale of Wind from the Southward. About Sunset lost sight of the Resolution, and soon after our Foresail Split. Fired Guns and burnt false fires as a Signal for the Resolution to bring too. Saw the flashes of 2 Guns in answer. Lay too all Night firing Guns and shewing false Fires, none of which were answered.

Friday 3rd The Wind veered round to the Westward. At ½ past 7 Saw the Resolution bearing SBE. Set the Courses and joined her. In the afternoon the Gale abated; Set Topsails and continued our Course to the South and SSE. We had mostly fair Winds and no bad Weather the rest of the Passage.

Wednesday 25th Having run as far to the South as 21°10′ North Latitude, our Longitude being 205°52′ East of Greenwich. Steered to the Westward, Captain Cook having gone so far to the SE in hopes of falling in with some Island to Windward of those we have already seen. Ran all day, keeping abrest of each other and at the distance of 7 or 8 miles asunder, that we might be less liable to pass any Land without seeing it. At Sunset joined Company and after Midday Lay too.

Thursday 26th At daylight Saw an Island to the Southward towards which we made Sail. At 8 were within 5 miles, when we bore away to the Westward and ran along the North Side [of Maui]. Some Canoes came alongside with Fish. They knew of our having been at Atoui [Kaua'i]. A Small Iron Tool made in imitation of their own Hatchets, which they call Tae, was given to the first Indian that came on board, who held it up to shew his companions, calling out Tae no Atoui. They mentioned to us the Fray we had at Atoui in which an Indian was killed.

The Ships going too fast for the Canoes to keep us with us, at Noon we brought too, Maintopsail to the Mast, to trade for Provisions with the Natives, who brought us Hogs, Sugar Canes, Bread fruit, etc. Had Soundings 52 fathoms. Latitude Observed 20°58′ North and Longitude . . . 204°09′ East. Extremes of the Island which is called Mowwhe [Maui] S86°E to N79°W distance from the Shore 3 miles. The North End of another Island [is] called Morotai [Moloka'i]. The Island of Mowwhe rises by a gradual ascent from the Shore to the Mid parts, which is very high Land. From the Sea side to half way up the Mountains is laid out in Plantations. At 2 in the Afternoon made Sail and kept turning to the Eastward till next morning, gaining very little ground.

Friday 27th Most part of the day laying too off the North Side of Mowwhe, trading with the Natives for Hogs and Vegetables. A Chief came on board with a present of a Hog and red featherd Cloak to Captain Clerke. He had 2 long pieces of Iron shaped like Skewers, well pointed, which we supose to have been got from the Spaniards. One of the Indians held his 2 fore fingers across each other and pointed to the Land, which we construed into the Spaniards having set up a Cross on Shore. These circumstances, however, fall short of a Proof. In the Evening made Sail and kept turning to Windward.

Saturday 28th Stopped serving Ship provisions, fresh Pork and Vegetables being procured in plenty. Spirits likewise were stopped by Captain Cooks order. Another Order from Captain Cook was read to the Ships Company containing Rules to be observed in our intercourse with the Natives, in which the buying curiosities before the Ships should be properly supplied with provisions, was prohibited and those of our People suspected of any Venereal Complaint forbid to go on shore, or to have any connection with the Women. Nevertheless, this same day several Indians told us they were infected with the Venereal Distemper, and which on examination we found to be true. As further confirmation, the people of a large Canoe that went on board the Resolution were searched and not more than 3 out of 12 were without some symptom of infection. Whether this disorder was communicated to them by us at Atoui last Year or that they had it before, we could not understand them at this time well enough to determine.

Tuesday, December 1st Having turned round the East End of Mowwhe, Saw another Island to the SE, by the Indians called Owhyhe [Big Island of Hawai'i], towards which we stood, but did not get in shore till Night.

Wednesday 2nd [We were] laying too off the North Side of Owhyhe, trading with the Natives for Provisions. Sounded and found bottom at 42 fathoms, brown Sand & Shells, distance from the Shore half a League. This was the only time we found bottom on this side of the Island . . .

All the first part of December continued cruizing off the North Side of Owhyhe, now and then laying too in Shore, to trade for Provisions. This method of recruiting from time to time well enough answered the purpose of a present Supply, except that 2 or 3 times, unsettled weather kept us off Shore longer than was intended, and obliged us to have recourse again to the Ship provisions, till we could get near the Land.

The latter part of December was taken up in attempting to Weather the East Side of Owhyhe, which we could not effect in the course of this Month. Owhyhe is much larger than any Island we have as yet seen between the Tropics this Voyage. It is higher Land than Mowwhe. The Tops of the Mountains are flat and level and covered with Snow.

Wednesday 23rd Many Canoes alongside with Provisions. An Indian swimming alongside narrowly escaped being surprized by a Shark before he was aware, but being called to and advertised of his danger, he immediately turned round and with his hand Struck the Shark on the Head, which frightened him away. Other Indians continued in the Water without taking further notice of this than now and then looking round to see if any Shark was near. When the Canoes went away in the Evening one of the Indians was left behind, who remained with us till we came in Shore again, which was almost a fortnight afterwards.

At 10 in the Night, being astern of the Resolution, the Strap of the Foretopsail Sheet Block broke, and the Main topmast Staysail Sheet, by which accidents the Resolution got out of sight before the Sails could be set again. The next morning she was not to be seen. [We] continued turning to Windward to get round the East End of Owhyhe.

Tuesday, January 5th, 1779 Having weathered the East part of Owhyhe, this morning bore away and ran alongshore by the South Side of the Island. Some Canoes came alongside with sweet Potatoes, Bread fruit, Sugar Canes, etc., which we had been without these last 6 Days. The Indian who had been on board from the time of our parting with the Resolution went on shore. The first week he was with us he scarce eat anything and was so ill that we were under great apprehensions of his dying, which would have been an unlucky circumstance and created suspicions in the Natives.

At 2 in the Afternoon, seeing an appearance like a Harbour, brought too and sent our Cutter in to examine. At 5 She returned, having found no good Anchorage. The Shore being Rocky and Steep close in. Most of the South Side of Owhyhe is covered with burnt and melted Stones, as if, produced by the eruption of a Volcano, though we saw nothing like Smoke rising from any part of the Mountains. This part of the Island is very thinly inhabited in comparison with the North and East Sides. In the Night, stood off and on.

Wednesday 6th At Daylight, bore away to the Westward. At 11 in the forenoon, were abrest a Bay which falls in just to the Westward of the Southernmost point of Owhyhe, and by its appearance promises fair for good Anchorage. Stood in towards it, when soon after, we saw the Resolution to the WNW and immediately bore down. At 1 joined her again, being then off the SW part of the Island. Both Ships continued cruizing near the SW and West Sides of Owhyhe, the Natives coming off to us every day, of whom we bought besides Provisions, a good quantity of Small Cordage, made of the Bark of the Cloth Tree, which we used for running Rigging. [We] found a Current setting to the SE against the Wind.

Journal of Henry Roberts

Thursday, November 26th, 1778 At day break we discovered land Coursing from SEBS to WBS [Maui]. Made the Signal to the Discovery, the land is appearing as two Islands. We bore away for the westernmost part, distance from Shore 2 leagues. In sailing along Shore several Canoes came off to us with many of the Natives, who appeared to be of one race with the Sandwich Islanders seen [before]. Their Canoes of the same built & the whole face of the Country equally fertile & many parts well cultivated, the sides of the hills being lay'd out in different plantations. At Noon we brought too to trade with the Natives, abreast of an Isthmus, which joins the high land that first appeared to be two different Isles.

This day orders and restrictions were read to the Ship Companys concerning Trading with the Natives. Latitude 19°48′2″ North, Longitude 203°31′ East.

Friday 27th Tackd about 3 miles from the Shore [in] 35 fathoms. Stood off & on during the night & at Daylight stood close in Shore to trade for provisions, when we were presently surrounded with Canoes, most of which was loaded with Roots of the Country & hogs. Trading with the Natives for provisions, served fresh Pork & roots to the People.

Tuesday, December 1st Saw more land, which appeared to be another Island bearing SBE [Big Island of Hawai'i]. Latitude 20°51′ North, Longitude 203°56′ East. Many Canoes came off from the Shore, in one which was an old man who appeared to have much authority. Began to trade for provisions & purchased several hogs & roots. The Island extended offshore 2 leagues. At ½ past 5 made sail & stood off with a Canoe towing astern & several of the Natives on board, and a Chief, who's name was Maiha-Maiha. In the morning, the Natives perceiving our intents were to reach the other Island, left us. The Natives name it Mowee.

Wednesday 2nd The Extremes of the Island [Big Island of Hawai'i] 5 or 6 miles distant. At 9 Wore Ship & Brought too to trade with the Natives for provisions. Many Canoes along side & others coming off the Shores, covered with people, looking at the Ship, throwing out white streamers as imploring peace.

Thursday 3rd At 6, having purchased a quantity of provisions from the Natives, such as Hogs, Fowls, Bread fruit, Tarro roots & potatoes, etc., made sail and stood. The Western point of the Island (called by the Natives Hawyhee) SWBW, distance offshore 3 miles. Standing off & on all Night at the Distance of 4 or 5 leagues from the Shore. At Noon the Island of Mowee extending N46°W to N77°W and Hawyhee from S55°E to S59°SW, distance 8 miles, the highest part of the Land covered with snow. At Noon 79° [Fahrenheit] and at Midnight 75°.

Friday 4th In the afternoon saw several Canoes coming off. Stood in for them, 4 leagues from the Shore.

Sunday 6th Tack'd within 12 miles of the Shore. The sides of the hills covered with plantations, with many dwellings of the Inhabitants interspersed among them. The Valleys and the summits of the hills well clothed with wood, having the most fruitful appearance, which afforded a pleasing prospect. The shores are steep too, with many falls of water, [and] by Noon we were within 3 miles of the Island.

Monday 7th At 2 past Noon we brought too and traded with the Natives for provisions, having a number of Canoes along side. By 9 we were close in when many Canoes came off loaded with Hogs, roots, etc, which we purchased for Iron, sounding with 75 fathoms no Ground.

Tuesday 8th At 2 made sail & stood off, distant 4 leagues. Stood off and during the remainder of these 24 hours, the high land of Hawyhee and the snowy peak bearing SBE off Shore 11 leagues.

[In mid-December Roberts again limits his journal entries to bearings, coordinates, ship duties, wind, and weather. Temperatures rarely fluctuate, staying between 73° and 79° from morning to night. The ships sail and tack in view of the Big Island with views of the island's dominant snowy mountains for bearings. They also endure a sizeable storm that shredded sails and disconnected the ship tiller, too far off shore to maintain contact with any inhabitants. On Thursday, December 10 he reports Latitude 20°29′ North, Longitude 204°34′ East.]

Monday 14th A fresh trade wind with a few squalls of rain. At 2 we made sail to the Northward, having purchased near 130 hogs, mostly large, with a great supply of roots & fruit and quantities of Salt. Employed salting and curing pork. Stood off & on for the remainder of the 24 hours.

Saturday 19th At 6 AM, having had thick weather for most of the night, it cleared away and showed us the land, when we found ourselves in an alarming situation, not being above 12 miles from the Shore, near the East point, and a heavy swell setting directly on. Fortunately a stiff breeze sprung up from the Eastward which just enabled us to clear the point to the Northward, having carried away the Main Topmaststaysail stay & split the Main Topsail and Main Top Gallant Sails, [and] bent others. Offshore 5 PM the tiller rope broke, unhung it & seated a new one. At 8 the weather still squally & unsettled. The Discovery some distance to leeward. At Noon, hazy weather that we could not see the land. Latitude 19°56′ North, Longitude 205°20′ East.

Thursday 24th The Discovery not to be seen. The East point of this Island is to be known by a remarkable range of rocky hillocks, a little within the point. The point itself being very low, with a heavy swell from the Eastward, generally rolling on it, and breaks with great Violence, which renders it very difficult and hazardous in attempting to Weather it. Latitude 19°35′ North, Longitude 205°72′ East.

Friday 25th The East point of the Island bore SWBS 7 or 8 miles, oppen'd more land to the Southward of it. At 2 AM we Wore & Stood to the Northward, tack'd & hove too, to wait for the Discovery. [Later] the Appearance of the Discovery.

[After Christmas Day the *Resolution* tacked repeatedly to negotiate the southern tip of the Big Island, using the snow-capped Mauna Loa and Mauna Kea, the earth's largest volcanoes, as its bearing points. The vessels are 7 miles from shore on January 1, 1779.]

Saturday, January 2nd, 1779 Trading with the Inhabitants as usual for provisions. At 3 made sail to the Eastward, having purchased but few hogs in consequence, most probably, of our refusing to buy them the other day. We however got a good supply of roots and vast quantities of Salt made up in neat packages.

Sunday 3rd PM several Canoes along side trading. At 4 the East end of the Island bore NNW 3 or 4 leagues from the nearest shore. Many Canoes along side Brought too & traded for provisions, the Natives bringing off large hogs, roots, fruit, etc, with immense quantities of very fine white salt. Employed salting & curing the pork.

Monday 4th At 10 Brought too to trade, purchasing great supplys of every article before mentioned. The shores here are rather barren, nor have they by any means that fruitful appearance with the Northern parts of this Island.

Tuesday 5th Running along shore and lying bye, trading with the Natives. In the evening, several Canoes came off from the Southern point with fish, which was purchased for the Ships Company. These fish were bonneatoes & one of them the largest that most of our people had ever seen. Punished James Dermot, Seaman, with 6 lashes for defrauding the Natives. Standing off and on & lying too all night.

At Daylight bore away for the Southern point, which is very low. On it stands a Town of the Natives. We hauled close round to the westward of this point in a small kind of Bay & sounded, but had no ground. There appeared to be good landing for boats near the Village and seemingly there was fresh water by a high cliff, forming a Gully which was likely to afford a rivulet. We brought too & soon after many Canoes came off, loaded with the produce of the Country. We drifted along shore trading with the Indians at the distance of 2 & 3 miles. This part of the Island is much inferior to any that we have before seen, having certainly received some very severe eruptions from Volcanoes, the whole face of the Country being a Mass of Cinders and Lava.

Wednesday 6th PM we kept drifting along shore until 3 O'Clock, when we bore away for the SW point. At ½ past 4 we sounded with 160 fths but could get no bottom within ¼ mile of the rocks. This point may be known by three remarkable sandy hillocks, between which stands a small Village for fishermen. The Country here appeared to be in a worse state than that part before taken notice of, in resemblance much like the Island of Ascension in the Atlantic Ocean.

At 8 in the morning we were close in with the SW point when many Canoes came along side, trading with us as usual. Hoisted the Pinnace out & sent her in shore to try for an anchorage, brought too & drifted along shore.

Thursday 7th Discovery joined Company [and] the pinnace returned from the shore. [The pinnace] found no anchorage and no Ground within two Cables length of the Shore. Lying bye, trading till 6, when we stood off, the nearest point NNE 3 miles. In the morning [we] came in shore to trade, meeting with great supplies of large Hogs, the pork of which is very good, salting great quantities daily. The Natives called this Large Island Hawyhee.

Friday 8th A Moderate Gale. At 5 made sail under single reef'd topsails. Stood off with several of the Natives on board, being dark & could not land them. Standing off & on, until 8 AM, when we brought too & traded again, distance 4 or 5 miles from the SW Shore.

Tuesday 12th A light baffling wind under the Land, standing off and on, & lying bye, trading with the Natives, but got indifferent supplies. We ran into the Eastward of the Southern point, which forms a bight with another bluff point, off which lies a reef of rocks. In this Bay are several small detached Villages. It affords good anchorage but receives little or no Shelter from the Easterly trade winds.

John Webber, "A View of Kealakekua Bay," circa 1781-83. Pen, wash, and water color giving the artist's impressions of the view from shore with the *Resolution* and the *Discovery* first anchored at Kealakekua Bay. It was estimated that over 1,000 canoes and 10,000 local people swarmed the bay when the ships first arrived on January 17, 1779. They are surrounded by Native craft, including double-hulled canoes with upright lateen sails, and Native habitations seen along the shore. Dixson Library, State Library of New South Wales, PXX 2, f. 39.

2

KEALAKEKUA BAY

JANUARY–FEBRUARY 1779

Bligh went ahead in a pinnace to reconnoiter Kealakekua Bay. Although exposed to storms and winds from the southwest, Bligh concluded it was the best anchorage they would find in Hawai'i. There were a number of villages around the bay, which the British called "Karacacooa Bay" after the local pronunciation, including the seat of Hawaiian royalty, Ka'awaloa or "Kavarooa" in the journals. The great heiau, a nearby religious temple, which the British likened to a morai of the Society Islands, extended along the beach southwest to Hikiau.

The local people observed the ships circling the island for weeks, so when the ships finally anchored there was an overwhelming reception. Burney said they were greeted by a fleet of eight hundred canoes. Roberts counted six hundred canoes around the *Resolution* alone. An equal number of people swam to the ships and thousands more crowded the shores. Until some chiefs came to restore order, dozens of sailors were assigned to the decks to simply clear the crowds on board.

Theft was rampant, particularly in such a multitude. Anything not tied down was taken, and women were escorted below decks to spend time with the crew. Iron was in demand, particularly nails and daggers. Roberts described an ingenious method where local divers would pry nails off the sides of the ships underwater. It was a frenzied scene captured effectively in the journals and, despite the periodic firing of canons and muskets, it could not be controlled.

Burney also wrote of the reception given by the priests to Captain Cook when he first came ashore, including the abject submission of the people toward Cook, as if he were a god. The crew was familiar with the concept of a "tabu" from Tahiti and learned the priests placed a tabu on the bay after these ceremonies, lifted on the arrival of Kalani'opu'u, whom the sailors already met off Maui. He was called "Terrioboo," "Kerrioboo," or "Keree-Oboo" in the journals. Burney then offered an extensive, erudite account about the behavior, language, and traditions of the Hawaiians, frequently relating them to his earlier experiences with the Polynesians from Tonga and Tahiti.

When the king came to the *Resolution* after a week at anchor, there was another large procession and splendid ceremony, attended by many chiefs. Cook was given an elegant, flowing feathered cape. The tabu placed on the ships was lifted and the crowds, especially the women, returned in earnest. Even Kalani'opu'u and his sons came aboard the ships frequently, as the chief and Cook became fast friends. The journals also reported the results of several expeditions into the interior of the island.

Roberts kept a log of punishments, including one sailor for not fairly trading with the Natives, and another for having sexual relations when he knew he had venereal disease. But attempts to respect the islanders were uneven. At the end of the month Burney noted two auspicious events that would soon haunt the voyagers: the destruction of the wooden fencing around the heiau, which the sailors took aboard for firewood, and the death of a seaman,

William Watman, of a "nervous fever." He was buried at the heiau in a ceremony jointly performed by the local priests and his countrymen. Both actions suggested the British were human and foretold the looming crisis when they returned to the bay two weeks later.

The British traded for hogs, many of which were salted for later use, fowls, breadfruit, coconuts, sweet potatoes, taro roots, sugar cane, bananas, and plantains. They did not find yams, which the British considered a substitute for their dwindling supply of bread, so they planned to pick up yams as they investigated the other islands to the north. They left the bay in early February after just three weeks, refreshed and ready to return to the north. They participated in boxing ceremonies and the British displayed fireworks, typical of earlier Polynesian visits. The observatory tents were struck and the spars reattached. Kalaniʻopuʻu and his principal chiefs came aboard to wish them farewell, and hundreds of canoes accompanied the ships out of the bay.

Journal of James Burney

Saturday, January 16th, 1779 In the forenoon, Boats were sent from each Ship to try in Shore for Anchorage. A greater number of Canoes about the Ships this day, than has been seen by us at one time during the Voyage. At Night the Boats returned, having found a Harbour with Water Somewhat brackish but clear. Turning in Shore with a light Land Breeze all Night.

Sunday 17th At 10, a Breeze sprung up from the Sea, and about ½ an Hour before Noon, we came to an Anchor in Karacacooa Bay (so called by the Indians) in 17 fathoms black Sand. Glad to find ourselves in a safe Harbour, after so long a Cruize in sight of Land, it being almost 8 weeks since our making Sandwich Islands.

The Ships were accompanied into the Harbour by an immense Fleet of Canoes, near 800, according to those who took the pains to count. The people on board these, were not more numerous than those who having no Canoes swam off to us from the Shore as soon as we Anchord. The Numbers being too great to admit all Visitors, none but females were at first allowed entrance and with those the Ship soon became so thronged that many hundreds were obliged to be drove overboard to make room for carrying on the necessary duty of the Ship, and it was constant employment for a fourth part of the Ships Company to keep the decks clear.

On the NW side of Karacacooa Bay is a large Town called Kavarooa, and on the East Side another that extends to the South point of the Bay or rather a number of small Towns close together, each having different names. The Easternmost called Karacacooa and the Southernmost Ka-hi.

The Space between Kavarooa and Karacacooa is filled up by a Mountain quite steep towards the Sea. The Watering place is at the Town of Karacacooa where is a pond at the back of a large Sandy Beach, with brackish Water and a Well with better Water, just to the left hand of the Beach and close to the Sea Side. This well is sufficient for one Ship, but not for two Ships to water at the same time.

The Winds were generally from the Land in the Night and from the Sea in the daytime. The best Anchorage is in the North Part of the Bay, where we Moored with the Best Bower to the NW in 17 fathoms, the Outer points of the Harbour bearing the one South, and the other West. Distance from the nearest Shore ¼ of a mile. Latitude 19°27′ North, Longitude 204°02′ East.

Our present business, besides Watering and procuring Refreshments, was to repair the Sails and Rigging, Caulk the Ship and take in Ballast. From the length of our late Cruize the Ship was in a most tattered condition and her upper Works so leaky that we had been obliged to leave off washing Decks for the last 3 weeks.

The Chief of Owhyhe, whose Title is Aree Tabu, we learnt was named Kerrioboo, at this time on an Expedition against the Island of Mowwhe the occasion as follows: The last Aree of Mowwhe, named Cumeamea, dying, left behind a Widow and Daughter. This Widow Kerrioboo took to Wife and by her had a Son named Koorao, who when arrived at age, was married to his half Sister, the Daughter of Cumeamea, and laid claim to the dominion of Mowwhe. Another Claimant was Tahitirre, a younger Brother of Cumeamea, and who had power enough almost to drive out his competitor, on which account Kerrioboo went over to support his Son's Cause.

Monday 18th Early in the Morning, an Indian Chief named Parrear, came on board and with a long white stick drove all the Indians out of the Ship. This Man, we were told was a great Favourite of Kerrioboo, and the principal person here at this time. He proved of great service in keeping the Crowd of Indians off for turning them away ourselves, was hardly to be effected without affronting many and beating some. Besides this service, Parrear made himself useful in recovering some things that were stolen, the Owhyhe people being as dexterous and as little conscientious in that respect as any Islanders in the South Seas.

The Night before our getting here, the Resolution lost the Lids of the Ships Coppers which were conveyed out of the Ship by some Visitors who were allowed to Sleep on board. The Morning we Anchord almost all our Backstay Tackles were cut out of the Chains, for the Sake of the Iron Hooks and Thimbles, and carried off. Several other things which were part of the Ship's Furniture went the same way. On occasions of this kind, some that were detected in the fact were flogged, and some in making their escape, fired at with small shot. Parrear was always Zealous in advising and assisting to punish the Offenders, and several instances happened of his beating those whom we excused and let go, and taking their Canoes from them. Indeed, on all Occasions, Parrear was proud of displaying his Authority, which he frequently did, without much feeling for his Countrymen. Another Chief who visited both Ships and performed the same kind of services, was named Kanine, a much more moderate Man than Parrear.

In the Afternoon Captain Cook went on Shore for the first time and landed at the town of Karacacooa on the East Side of the Bay, where he was received with great ceremony by an Old Man, said to be the Chief Priest. All the people, except those of the Priesthood, laying prostrate or rather on their Hands and Knees with their Heads bowed down to the Ground.

Captain Cook was led to a large flat pile of Stones (like the Morai of the Society Isles), the Top making a Square Platform, which was enclosed with Wooden Rails. Within the Railing on one side was a Scaffolding with a number of Strange Carved Images in a Row before it, and several human Skulls. He was desired to mount the Scaffolding and a piece of red Cloth tied round him. Being seated at the Top, a dead Stinking Hog that had been an offering to the Morai, some time before, was held over him, whilst a Song or Incantation was pronounced. After this, a Barbecued Pig and Sweet Potatoes were brought, with which Captain Cook allowed himself to be fed, the Victuals being put into his Mouth by one of the Priests. A Cup of Yava or Kava (a Liquor used at all the Islands in the South Seas) was brought for him to Drink and the Ceremony ended with his making presents to the Chief Priest.[11]

Tuesday 19th This forenoon the Astronomers Observatories and Tents were erected on a piece of Ground adjoining to the Morai, and Captain Cook was complimented with more formalities in the same Stile, with some Variations, as

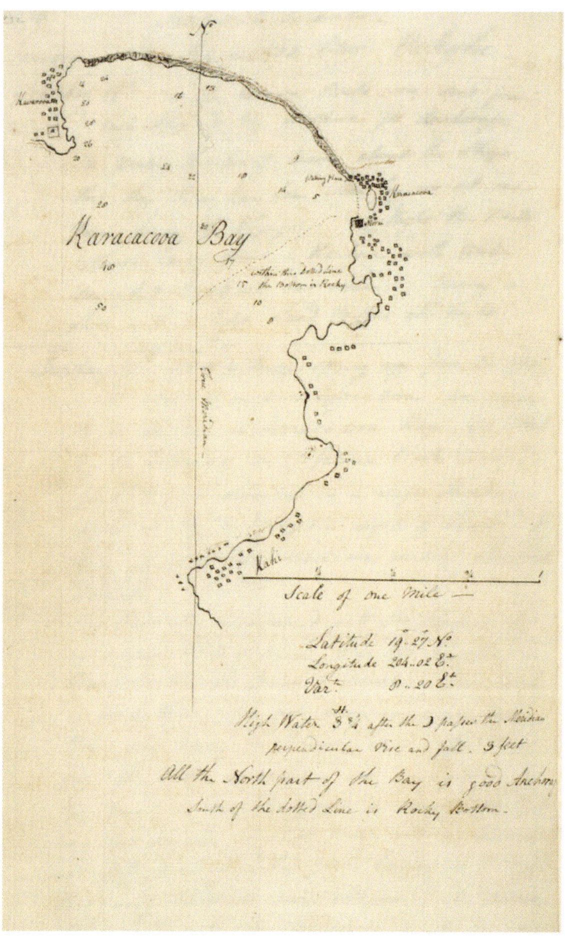

James Burney, "Chart of Karocacooa Bay [Kealakekua Bay, Hawai'i]," January 1779. Burney was one of several cartographers to sketch the perimeter of the bay with locations of principal structures and communities. He also offered marginal notes giving the bearings and details of high water and preferred anchorage. Burney Journal p. 232, Mitchell Library, State Library of New South Wales, Safe 1/64 and 1/79.

those of yesterday. Among other Strange Ceremonies, He and the Gentlemen with him were anointed with Oil expressed from chewed Cocoanut Meat. A Young Pig was sacrificed before him by the Head Priest, who held it by the hinder Legs over a Fire and burnt it to death. Afterwards a drest Hog was brought, the first Mouthful was chewed by the Priest and put into Captain Cook's Mouth. Another Pig was going to be sacrificed which Captain Cook declined and a Cocoanut was Substituted. At the conclusion Captain Cook of his own accord made an offering of some Beads and Iron to an Image before which these formalities had been acted.

Restrictions and Prohibitions are laid on the Natives in the same manner here, and by the same name as at the Friendly Islands: i.e. Tabu. All the Ground about the Tents for a considerable distance was put under the Tabu, which kept them from being crowded, none daring to come except those of the Priesthood.

The remainder of this Week passed without any remarkable Occurrence. We continued busy in refitting the Ships, Salting Hogs for a Sea Stock, and Watering. Took in near 20 Tons of Stone Ballast to keep the Ship by the Stern.

Sunday 24th A little Accident happened this morning that gave much offence to our Friend Parrear. An Indian had sold a large Hog on board the Resolution and taken the price agreed on, when Parrear happening to pass by, advised the Man not to part with the Hog without an advanced price, for which he was pushed away and somewhat sharply spoke to. Soon after a Tabu was laid on the two Ships and all the Indians went on Shore, which at first was suposed to be in consequence of Parrears being offended, till we were informed it was on account of Kerrioboo being expected, he having returned victorious from Mowwhe.

Monday 25th Continued under the Tabu and no Kerrioboo appeared.

Tuesday 26th About 2 in the Afternoon some Canoes ventured alongside and traded with both Ships, till a large Canoe, in which was an Elderly Chief, came off and drove them away, Chasing and running over them. A Musket was fired from the Resolution over the large Canoe, which made them desist.

Towards Sunset a large sailing Canoe, in which was Kerrioboo attended by many Chiefs, came into the Bay from the Northward and went on board the Resolution. He was remembered to have been on board the Resolution in a large Canoe when cruizing off Mowwhe. He is a tall thin Old Man, apparently more worn out with Debaucheries than with Age, his Skin being intirely covered with a Kind of Scaliness, the Marks of a great Yava drinker and his Limbs trembling under him, though in walking he still carries himself upright and erect. The Old Chief staid on board till after dark and then went on shore, having received many presents from Captain Cook.

With respect to his success at Mowwhe, we were informed he had left that Island wholly under the Subjection of his son Koorao, and that Tahitirre was allowed to govern in Morotai and two or three lesser Islands thereabouts. Koorao, though not his only Son, is next in succession to the Government of Owhyhe, Kerrioboo's other Children being by Women of inferior condition.

John Webber, "Tereoboo [Kalani'opu'u], King of Owyhee, bringing presents to Capt. Cook," circa 1781-83. Pen, wash, and water color showing the formal arrival of the king and his chiefs to Cook's ships after they anchored in Kealakekua Bay in late January 1778. The large double canoes came from shore, with the leading canoe carrying the king with a large, upright lateen sail, all manned by Hawaiian warriors in religious procession. Dixson Library, State Library of New South Wales, PXX 2, f. 35.

Wednesday 27th The Tabu was taken off the Ships and the Indians flocked about us again as usual. A great number of large Sailing Canoes arrived in the Bay, most of them from Mowwhe, where they had been with Kerrioboo. Towards Noon the Old Chief went with 3 large Canoes to visit the Astronomers Tents. All the Indians in sight except those of his own Retinue prostrated themselves, as they did likewise for Captain Cook, who landed soon after. Kerrioboo made Captain Cook a Present that was ushered in with great Ceremony and Song Singing. The Present was 7 or 8 very elegant feathered Clokes and Caps and a number of Hogs with Cocoanuts and Breadfruit. Afterwards Kerrioboo and one of his Sons (a Boy named Kaoowa) went with Captain Cook on board the Resolution.

An Indian died this morning in a House near the Tents. That it might be known how they dispose of their Dead, a Man was appointed to visit the House every 10 Minutes to get intelligence when they removed the Body. This kind of Lookout was kept till dark and the Indians gone to sleep. Next morning when the lookout was directed to be renewed, it was found the Body had been carried away during the Night.

Thursday 28th Kerrioboo visited the Discovery and brought a present for Captain Clerke of the same kind as what Captain Cook had received. All the Indians in the Canoes about us, Bowed down before him, both at coming and going. In the Afternoon he came with less State in a Small Canoe that had but 3 paddles, one of which he managed himself. The Indians omitted the ceremony of prostrating themselves, making a difference between his coming in a Public and a

Private manner. However they were not negligent in their Attentions to their Chief, keeping their Canoes out of his way, helping him up the Side and shewing a readiness to assist him on every occasion.

Saturday 30th The Wooden Rails that surrounded the Morai Captain Cook made a bargain for with the Indian Chiefs and it was taken on board, being 2 Launch Loads of Firewood for each Ship, a Seasonable Supply, it being above 4 months since we wooded, and none growing here within 2 miles of the Sea Side.

Sunday 31st This Evening, William Watman, an old Seaman belonging to the Resolution, departed this Life. He was in the Resolution the last Voyage, and left Greenwich Hospital, of which he was a Pensioner, to come this. In the Night some Houses caught Fire at the NW Town (Kavarooa) and burnt down in a few Minutes.

Monday, February 1st The Body of the deceased was buried at the Morai and an Inscription on a wooden Post fixed over him. In the Afternoon we were entertained with Boxing Matches by the Indians, the Spectators forming themselves into a large Ring. Their fighting was only trials of skill, none lasting long enough to deserve the name of a Battel. If a Man was knockd down, the affair was decided. If the Match appeared unequal, a Friend of the weaker party commonly Stepped between and supplied his place, by which custom one Engagement would sometimes be kept up a considerable time by a constant succession of fresh People on either side. On first entering the Ring, they approach each other with the most laughable and ridiculous gestures imaginable, clenching their Fists, distorting their Features and straining every Sinew to make themselves look formidable. They Strike hard but never Aim their Blows, and have no other Guard or way of fending off than by holding their Arms strait out before them and retreating. On the whole, their method of Boxing is much inferior to the Boxing of the Friendly Islanders, nor is the same good order or Moderation Observed.

Tuesday 2nd The Indians gave another Entertainment, which, like that of the preceding Evening, consisted wholly of Boxing. After dark, Captain Cook ordered some Water Rockets and Sky Rockets to be played off, which had their usual effect.

Wednesday 3rd Being ready for Sea, the Tents were Struck and taken on board. In the Evening a House near the Morai, in which our Sails had been repaired, caught fire and was soon burnt down with 2 or 3 others near it. This Accident was occasioned by their looking with Lights after a Knife one of our Sail makers had lost in the House and which at leaving the Shore he told them to keep if they found it.

During our stay here, several Expeditions or Rambles were made into the Country. All this part of the Island near the Water Side is Rocky Ground, full of large Cavities and covered with Lava or burnt Stones, in many places run like Glass. About 2 miles back is good Land, laid out in Woods and fine Plantations, which extends a considerable distance towards the Mountains. One Party was sent to see if there were any other appearances of there having formerly been a Volcano, but after 5 Days absence, they returned without having reached more than half way to the Snow Mountains. No Towns were seen inland, and but few Houses, wherein those who looked after the Plantations lived.

The Provisions we got at Owhyhe were Hogs (great Numbers of which were Salted for Sea Use), Fowls, Breadfruit, Cocoanuts, Sweet Potatoes, Tarro, Sugar Canes, Bananas and Plantains, all in great abundance. Yams, which we most wanted, they had very few of, nor were they much cultivated at any of the Islands, they told us, except Atoui [Kaua'i] and Neehow [Ni'ihau]. The Ships were shorter of Bread than of any other species of Provisions, and Yams were the only proper substitute for a good Sea Stock, as no other Roots or Vegetables here are capable of being kept good any length of time.

Besides the Similarity of Language, the Natives of Owhyhe have many customs which are common with the Southern Islanders, and but few that may not be found either at the Friendly or Society Islands. The Tattow or marking of the Skin, the Tabu, the Tuggituggi, the Women not eating with the Men, their being forbid Pork or Turtle, and many other particularities are practiced in nearly the same method as to the Southward. Their Dancing, though in a ruder fashion, is much like their musical Instruments are, Conk Shells and Drums like those of Otaheite, no Flutes. Their Common Dress is Cloth made of the bark of a Tree, which they paint in very fanciful and sometimes elegant patterns. This is just fastened round the middle. They have no covering above the Waist or below the Knees.

John Webber, "A Man of the Sandwich Islands, Dancing," circa 1781-83. Pen, wash, and water color showing a dancer, whose necklace is made of seaweed and with dog's teeth ornaments around his legs. In his right hand he is holding a rattle. A Hawaiian house with stone enclosure is in the background. Dixson Library, State Library of New South Wales, PXX 2, f. 36.

Their Ornaments in Dress are chiefly red and yellow feathers made up into Clokes, Caps and large Rings to wear round their Necks and Heads. All the Women have their Hair cut quite Short behind and the fore part kept turned back. Those of the better sort are commonly distinguished by wearing Ruffles made of Boars Tusks round their Wrists, and the Chief People of either Sex by carrying a Fly flap. The Houses of Owhyhe are like those we before saw at Atoui, dark and unpleasant.

The Natives are a stout active people, less cleanly in their Persons and I think more Savage in their appearance than the Natives of the Southern Islands. It is remarkable that at the Friendly Islands, the Island which governs and protects the rest is honoured with the Title of Tabu, i.e. Tongitabu, and here the Chief of the largest and most powerful Island is called Aree Tabu.

The Arees here are great drinkers of Kava and many of the old Chiefs from an excess of drinking, are marked all over like the Scales of a Fish, and this is reckoned an honourable distinction. These Islanders equal any people in lewdness and uncleanliness, there are no kind of impurities but are allowable and in daily practice amongst them, and that without reproach or Shame.

Though there may be reason to supose they are obliged to us for the Venereal Distemper, yet they never charged it upon us, neither did they seem to know themselves how they first caught it, nor could we learn when.

On our first arrival, the best articles of Trade were Beads or Buttons sewed on slips of Cloth to wear about their wrists, and Iron wrought into Small Adzes in imitation of their own. Latterly Iron Spikes from 18 Inches to 2½ feet long, worked in the form of their own wooden Daggers, were given. These were called Pahooah and few things that we set any value upon could be procured without them.

Thursday 4th At Daylight, hove up our Anchors and Sailed out of Karacacooa Bay, steering alongshore to the Northward, for Mowwhe. Had light variable Winds and fair weather. Many Canoes followed us out of the Bay. An Indian stole one of our Tackle Hooks, but being close pursued, was obliged to abandon his own Canoe and get into another in which he went clear off with his Prize. The Canoe we took on board.

In the Afternoon, Kerrioboo's Canoe came out to us loaded with Cocoanuts and Hogs.

Journal of Henry Roberts

Saturday, January 16th, 1779 Light breezes and pleasant weather, trading as usual. AM made the Signal for the Discovery's Cutter & sent her with the pinnace to a part of the Shore that appeared to afford shelter to examine it & try for anchorage. At 8 both Ships were surrounded with Canoes. We could count upwards of six hundred round the Resolution, each bringing their Cargo to market. We purchased a vast number of very large Hogs & quantities of Salt

& Roots. One of the Indians, having stolen the large Cutter's rudder, we fired several Musketts at the Canoe, which had it in and sent the boats in pursuit of her, but to no effect.

In order to give the Chiefs (many of these being on board) a proper sense of our dislike to those petty Thefts & likewise to convince them of our power, we fired a four pounder over the Canoes. When they perceived the shot fall, it struck them with a degree of terror & excitation. But being told beforehand that it should not hurt them, they were presently pacified, but several of them paddled off with the fright. Latitude 19°20′30″ North, Longitude 203°49′ East.

Sunday 17th About 8 the boats returned, having found good anchorage and a convenient place for watering. Stood in shore all night, with several Canoes round us, many lights upon the shores. In the Morning we were surrounded as Yesterday, the Canoes being full of Men, Women & Children. We had baffling winds for some time off the Land, but soon after a breeze sprung up from the seaward, the boats ahead towing. A prodigious number of Canoes along side with hundreds of the Natives swimming off and the Shores crowded with Spectators. The Discovery anchored near us.

Monday 18th The northern part of the Bay, which is low and rocky, and on it is a Town of the Natives, bore WBS. The Southern point, which is somewhat higher, but rocky and several houses scattered about on it, bore S¼W, and a sandy beach at the bottom of the Bay, East about ½ a mile. Sent the observatory on shore on a rising ground near the sandy beach. It was errected. The launch sent for a turn of Water for present use. The watering place is at a large pool at the back of the beach, where theres a large Town with Great Numbers of the Inhabitants.

Tuesday 19th Many Canoes about us, loaded with the produce of the Country. Found a butt of brandy leaked out to 7 gallons since leaving the Cape. The strength of the spirit having sprung one of the Staves.

Wednesday, 20th The Natives along side as usual in their Canoes & others swimming. Some of these swimmers were equipped with a short stick & a flint stone fixed in one end of it, which served them for a Tool in drawing the failing nails out of the Sheathing. To put a stop to this, we were obliged to fire small shot at them, but some would get out of our reach by diving under the bottom. The Natives informed us their O-ron-no, which signifies their King, whose name was Keree-Oboo, would visit us in 3 or 4 Days. We had daily on board several people of Distinction, the principle names were Kanina, Parai-ah, & Tee-wa-rua.

Friday 22nd The launch watering from a well among the rocks on the North side of the sandy beach, which water the Natives make use of, as being the best. But its bad getting off, particularly when there is any great surf rolling in, which was the case now, having stove several of the Casks. The well lies below the surface of the sea, therefore must admit the salt water when the surge is violent. It appears to be a spring by its filling nearly as fast as we could bail it with buckets.

Natives about us as before. Thermometer Midday 73°, Noon 78°.

Monday 25th Punished John Grant and Benjamin Lyon with 12 lashes each for absenting themselves from the boat when on shore, and William Bradly, for disobeying orders, with 2 dozen, and having connections with women knowing himself to be infused with the Venereal disorder, and Will Nash with one dozen for disobeying the orders.

Tuesday 26th Thermometer Midday 72°, Noon 79°. PM the Chief Keree-Oboo came on board in a large double Canoe without any other attendants. When we were much surprised to find this, [he was] the same old man who visited us off the east end of Mow-wee. In the morning he came off in great state with three very large Canoes, being the only Vessels upon the water, the others being forbid, or what they term Ta-bood, which had been the Case several Days before his arrival. The procession was in great form. After paddling around the 2 ships excessively Slow, with the Caps & Cloaks of red feathers, exposed in most splendid manner. The Priests, which was in one of the Canoes, singing in a slow tone. They landed at the beach near the Observatory.

John Webber, "A Canoe of the Sandwich Islands, The Rowers Masked," circa 1781-83. Pen, wash, and water color showing a double canoe with an upright lateen sail holding ten rowers wearing gourd helmets. Two others hold small images and another, presumably the helmsman, blows a conch. The northwest shore of Kealakekua Bay and the king's village of Ka'awaloa are shown in the background. Dixson Library, State Library of New South Wales, PXX 2, f. 37.

Wednesday 27th PM Captain Cook went on Shore to meet the Chief Keree-Oboo. Soon after they came on board together, the Captain having been presented with several Caps, Cloaks, Cloth & other curiosities, with a number of hogs and every production of the Island. The whole given with great Ceremony and a Pig burnt alive as a sacrifice, which we took for a peace offering. This was performed by their Priests with many prayers and songs upon the occasion, and at times joined by the whole in Chorus. In the evening, after he returned on Shore, a few Canoes were suffered to come off, but their Women, not permitted to enter the Ship. Temperature Midday 70° by Noon 80°.

Thursday 28th Temperature Midday 72° by Noon 82°. Parties were made daily by the Officers and Gentlemen making short excursions in the Country, when they received the greatest civilities of hospitality from the Natives. The Chiefs, sending people with supplies of provisions and water with them, and at our return would perform the ceremonies before related. The Country here [h]as suffered very much by the overflowing of the Lava, still continuing in perfect waves & a very hard cement. Other parts were heaped up with loose rocks, like Cinders, but in many places it has recovered itself very much. The Natives take great care to cultivate every little patch that's capable of production, even so much that I have seen the Cloth Tree planted among the Cinders, where they have been obliged to clear away far above 8 feet in depth before they could reach the surface of the soil, which in general is sandy. But on the summits of the Hills, it's a rich brown earthy mould, capable of producing every Tropical plant.

Sunday 31st The Natives along sides as usual and the Taboo taken off the Women. Most part of the Ships Company on Shore with liberty, the Natives treating them with the greatest friendship.

Monday, February 1st The Captain purchased two launch loads of Wood from the Inhabitants, which was stakes that were a fence to a Morai or burying place. At 10 Departed this life William Watman, Seaman, of a Nervous fever.

Tuesday 2nd The Deceased was buried on Shore at the Morai, when the Natives sacrificed a pig & other ceremonies after the Corpse was interred. AM bent the Sails and were ready for sea, but the Discovery was not.

Wednesday 3rd In the evening a few fireworks were displayed for the entertainment of the Chief and Natives, who were highly delighted and astonished. AM got the Observatory and party on board.

Thursday 4th PM got everything off from the Shore & ready for unmooring. At 3 AM unmoored and at 6 came to sail with the land breeze in favor. The Discovery in company standing out of the Bay, with a great number of Canoes round the Ships. During the time we have been among the Islands have salted and cured upwards of 25 puncheons of pork & purchased 18 Drums of salt, exclusive of the quantity thats been used in pickeling.

The evening before we sailed the Captain received a great present from Keree-Oboo, which consisted of Cloth, a number of Hogs & vast quantities of roots and fruit, with bundles of sugar cane, the largest and finest we had ever seen.

Friday 5th Light breezes with Calms and fair weather. Many Canoes towing and following the Ships, with the Chief Keree-Oboo on board. In the evening he left us & went to the Shore with several of the others.

John Webber, "The Death of Captain Cook," circa 1781-83. Oil on canvas. There were many pictorial accounts of Cook's death prepared after the event, but only John Webber was in Hawai'i at the time. He was not an eyewitness, but his later drawing closely follows the first-hand accounts. Cook is about to be stabbed in the back while Lt. Phillips, who has fallen to the ground, fires at an assailant. Cook is holding his hand up to the marines, presumably to tell them to stop firing, but it is too late. Dixson Library, State Library of New South Wales, DG 26 and PXD 59-2.

3

Return to Kealakekua Bay
February 1779

During the fourth night, February 7, 1779, before they even reached Maui, a gale arose that split the rotten foremast that had been replaced at Nootka Sound. While carefully splinted in the past weeks in Kealakekua Bay, the repairs did not hold in their first test, a modest storm in comparison to what they could expect was ahead in the Arctic. The officers consulted on what to do, knowing if they returned to Kealakekua Bay the Hawaiians would not understand the problem. "All hands much chagrined," King reported, "and damning the foremast." Aboard the *Resolution*, Roberts tells a dramatic story of the gales that overwhelmed the ship and how they saved as many as a dozen Natives in nearby canoes swamped by the storm.

In stark contrast to their first arrival, this time a less enchanted island people coolly received the captain and his crew. Burney said Kalani'opu'u was "dissatisfied" with their return. There seemed to be a taboo about the ships and no women or chiefs came aboard. The reverence accorded the strangers had now turned to contempt and, when the people came to the ships, it was usually with theft in mind. A Native who had been caught stealing armorer's tongs was punished with forty lashes. Some of the people were insolent and for the first time the Natives carried weapons.

Burney described the theft of the tongs on the afternoon of February 13. Midshipmen Edgar and Vancouver gave chase. They could not recover the stolen item, but were instead attacked and beaten by a mob when they reached shore. Bloodshed was only averted when a chief emerged to restore order. At dawn the next morning, Burney told Clerke that the cutter, the large shore boat critical to coastal explorations, had been taken from its mooring alongside the *Discovery.* Cook was enraged. It was a matter that Clerke should have handled, as the boat was stolen from his ship, but "Clerke was then in a deep decline in his health," Ledyard wrote, "and too feeble to undertake the affair." So Cook took over, responding as he did in Tonga and Tahiti. His plan was to take the king hostage until the craft was returned.[12]

Unfortunately for Cook, the plan backfired after an angry mob assembled. Burney quoted the captain as he formulated the plan. He wrote, "Captain Cook, who was then leaving the Ship, seeing the Canoe ashore, said he was sure she could not escape, and being asked how the Cutter was to get her if the Natives made resistance, he answered there could be no great difficulty, for he was very positive the Indians would not stand the Fire of a single Musket. Indeed, so many instances have occurred which have all helped to confirm this opinion that it is not to be wondered at, if every body thought the same."

Burney and Roberts were among the few journalists who witnessed the death of Cook, Burney through his glasses on the deck of *Discovery*, and Roberts in the pinnace he commanded a few yards from shore. Phillips was the only one on shore who gave a formal report, which was recorded in Clerke's journal.[13] But Burney and Roberts offer gripping eyewitness accounts. In shock from the death of the captain, Roberts described Cook as "equaled by few and excelled by none, justly stiled father of his people from his great good care and attention, honored and beloved by those who knew, or ever heard of him." Today there is a memorial to Cook on the volcanic rocks where he fell. Four marines and, by Burney's report, twenty-six Hawaiians were also killed in the melee.

The narratives continued in the aftermath of the clash as the hostilities gradually subsided and Clerke, who took command, first considered retribution, then decided on a more cautious approach. He engaged King, Burney, and Vancouver in shuttle diplomacy between the two ships and the shore to secure the remains of the dead captain and four marines for a proper burial. It took nearly a week, as the bodies were apparently distributed to the chiefs all over the island, but some body parts were returned. Clerke had them buried at sea in a solemn shipboard ceremony. Burney and Roberts wrote of the quiet observance at sunset on February 22.

Roberts concluded, like Clerke, that Kalani'opu'u played no part in the melee or its aftermath. The king was just as overwhelmed as the sailors by the captain's death and, after he recovered his wits, urged peace. Soon after Cook's few remains were returned, they learned the stolen cutter and captured firearms had been destroyed. Meanwhile, the broken mast was finally repaired and brought on board and the ships sailed for Maui a second time on February 23.

Journal of James Burney

Friday, February 5th, 1779 The light Winds continuing, made very little progress. In the Evening were becalmed and near the Shore. Hoisted our Boats out to tow off.

Saturday 6th At 4 in the Afternoon, a fresh breeze suddenly sprung up from the NE. The Canoes all left us, making towards the Land which was about 10 miles distant. In less than an hour the wind increased to a Gale and we lost sight of the Resolution to the Northward of us. At Midnight were within 3 Leagues of the South Side of Mowwhe. Stood backwards and forwards till Morning.

Sunday 7th At Daylight not seeing the Resolution and the Gale continuing, stood back to the SE to get under the Lee of Owhyhe. At 1 after noon saw the Resolution. Towards Evening the Weather Moderated. All Night Standing off and on near the NW part of Owhyhe.

Monday 8th In the Morning, being to Windward of the Resolution, took all the Sails in and set our Rigging up afresh.

Afternoon, running to the Southward along the West Side of Owhyhe. Find a Current against us. In the Night the Resolution hailed us that they had sprung their Foremast.

Tuesday 9th The Resolutions Boat came on board and informed us the Head of their Foremast was so badly sprung as to make it necessary to get the Mast out and that their Old Leak had broke out afresh, on which accounts Captain Cook was bound back to Karacacooa Bay again, there being no certainty of finding a Harbour at Mowwhe, and the Road at Atoui too exposed a place for getting a Mast out. The Indians likewise have been Sufferers by the late Gale. On the afternoon of the 6th, when we lost sight of the Resolution, their Pinnace had been sent to Sound near the Shore. In her return to the Ship they found a Canoe upset and the people trying to bale her out, which they were unable to do, the Sea running high. The Indians were taken into the Pinnace and carried on board of the Resolution, glad to escape with the loss of their Canoe. The next morning they picked up another Canoe in which was 3 men and a Child, whom they took on board and hoisted their Canoe into the Ship. In the Night, a fresh breeze from the NE with Squally Weather.

Wednesday 10th At 2 in the Morning, the Resolution having made too free with the Shore, found themselves very near Breakers and made the Signal of Danger. Both Ships hauled off till near Daylight and then ran along shore again. In the Forenoon being moderate Weather and in sight of Karacacooa Bay, many Canoes came off to us with Provisions. The Indians told us that 8 Men in a double Canoe were lost in the bad Weather.

Thursday 11th At 6 in the Morning the Resolution anchored in Karacacooa Bay, as did we 2 hours after, nearly in our old Birth and Moored the Ship. The Natives flocked about us with Hogs, Vegetables, Curiosities, etc. as formerly.

Friday 12th The Astronomers Tents were erected at the same place as before. A great many Canoes arrived in the Bay from the Northward, Kerrioboo with his followers amongst the rest. He was very inquisitive, as were several of the Owhyhe Chiefs, to know the reason of our return, and appeared much dissatisfied at it.

Saturday 13th The Resolutions Foremast was taken out and hauled up on the Beach between the Tents and the Watering Place. All the Carpenters of both Ships were set to work to repair it. This Morning, an Indian snatched away a pair of Tongs from the Armourers Forge, with which he jumped overboard and put them into a Canoe. Our Boat was so quick after him that he had not time to get in himself but was seized and brought on board, though the Canoe escaped. He was severely flogged and kept in Irons till the Tongs were sent from the Shore to procure his release. Our Launch Watering on shore this forenoon was much disturbed by the Indians who threw Stones and played other Mischievous Tricks, which made it necessary to have a Guard when she was next sent.

In the Afternoon the same unlucky Tongs were again stolen and in the same manner by an Indian who jumped overboard and got into a Canoe with them. They were fired at with Muskets from the Ship but without execution, whilst Mr. Edgar, our Master, [and Midshipman George Vancouver] in the Small Cutter pursued them to the Shore near the South point of the Bay. Parrear, the Indian Chief before mentioned, was in Captain Clerkes Cabin when the Theft was committed and immediately left the Ship, promising to get the Tongs restored.

At the same time the Resolutions Pinnace, which was at the Tent, seeing the Bustle, rowed along shore and joined in the Chase. The Thief got first on Shore and immediately put the Tongs with a Chissel and the Lid of a Harness Cask, that had been stole but not missed, into another Canoe, which came out and delivered them to the Small Cutter. Mr. Edgar then thought of returning to the Ship satisfied with what he had got, but seeing the Resolutions Pinnace at hand and Captain Cook walking that way from the Tents, he thought he might safely venture to seize the Canoe in which the Thief had landed. For this purpose he got on Shore and was pushing her off, when Parrear, to whom it seems the Canoe belonged and who probably was the contriver of the Theft, laid hold to prevent him, which was resented by one of the Pinnace's men striking Parrear with an Oar.

A Crowd of Indians, who had been by the water side all the time, and till then quiet, immediately began to throw Stones. There being no Arms in either Boat, the Pinnace men were so roughly handled that to avoid the Stones they all jumped into the Water and swam to some Rocks at a little distance. Mr. Edgar and one of our midshipmen, Mr. Vancouver, who were on shore, fared very little better, till Parrear ordered the Indians to desist, and told our people to go on board with the Boats. This they would gladly have done but all the Pinnace's Oars had been taken away. Parrear said he would fetch them, but he was no sooner out of Sight than the Mob began to throw Stones again.

Mr. Edgar on this, attempted to walk towards the Tents, expecting to meet Captain Cook, but was prevented by some Indians who said they would lead him to Parrear. He followed these people and soon met Parrear and another Man with an Oar and a broken one. He was conducted back to the Boats and put off, rowing towards the Tents. In their way thither, Parrear overtook them in a Canoe and brought Mr. Vancouvers Cap, which had been lost in the Fray. He then asked if he might come on board the next morning and whether we should hurt him for what had happened, being promised he should suffer no harm if he came. He went away paddling towards the Town of Kavarooa, where Kerrioboo lived.

Captain Cook, who at the beginning of the disturbance was at the Astronomers Tents, ran round alongshore towards the Boats with Lieutenant King & 2 of the Marines, but was misled by some of the Indian Chiefs, and did not know any thing of the ill usage of the Boats till he returned to the Tents, by which time it was dark and too late to take any notice of it.

Sunday 14th At daylight our great Cutter, which had been moored to the Buoy of the Small Bower Anchor, was missing, and on examining, the Rope which fastened her was found to have been cut. This Theft was the more easily committed as the Boat was left full of Water to preserve her from the Sun, which made the upper part of her Gunnel even with the Water's edge.

Captain Clerke having informed Captain Cook of this, Orders were given for our Launch and small Cutter to go armed to the South Point of the Bay and prevent any of the sailing Canoes going out, but not to molest the small ones. The Resolution's great Cutter was sent in chace of a large Sailing Canoe that was making off, their small Cutter was dispatched to guard the West point, whilst Captain Cook himself prepared to go with his Pinnace and Launch to the Town of Kavarooa with an intention to bring Kerrioboo on board.

The Canoe chaced by the Resolutions great Cutter was not overtaken, but her retreat cut off in such a Manner that she was forced to the nearest Shore within the South point of the Harbour, where the Indians hauled her up, the Cutter not being able to follow for the Rocks. Captain Cook, who was then leaving the Ship, seeing the Canoe ashore, said he was sure she could not escape, and being asked how the Cutter was to get her if the Natives made resistance, he answered there could be no great difficulty, for he was very positive the Indians would not stand the Fire of a single Musket. Indeed, so many instances have occurred which have all helped to confirm this Opinion that it is not to be wondered at, if every body thought the same.

A little before 8, Captain Cook landed at the Town of Kavarooa with the Lieut Philips of the Marines, a Serjeant, Corporal and 7 privates, in all, reckoning himself, 11. The Indians made a Lane for him to march along, having always shewed great respect to both Captains, however insolent they may have been at times to others. Captain Cook had scarcely got on Shore when the Boats near the South point of the Harbour fired several Muskets at some large Canoes that were trying to get out, by which an Indian Chief named Nooenemar was killed. The first notice we had of this was from 2 Indians that came off to the Ships in a Small Canoe to complain of it, but finding they were not attended to, they enquired for Captain Cook. Being told he was at the Town of Kavarooa, they went thither.

About half an hour after this, we heard the firing of Muskets on Shore, which was followed by the Resolutions Pinnace and Launch firing. With Glasses we could see Captain Cook receive a Blow from a Club and fall off a Rock into the Water. The Ships then fired, but at too great a distance to make certain of any particular Mark. The Boats soon after came off with an account that Captain Cook and 4 of the Marines were killed and their Bodies in possession of the Indians.

The particulars of this Misfortune gathered from those who were on the spot, are as follows. When Captain Cook with his party landed, the Indians made a Lane and some of them brought Hogs which they offered him. He enquired for Kerrioboo and his 2 Sons. The Indians immediately dispatched Messengers and the Boys came, who conducted them to Kerrioboo's House.

Having waited some time without, Captain Cook doubted his being there. Lieutenant Philips went in to see and found Kerrioboo just awakened. He came out to Captain Cook who after some enquiries appeared perfectly satisfied that Kerrioboo was innocent of the Cutter's being stolen, and desired he would go on board with him, to which Kerrioboo readily agreed, and they walked down towards the Boats. Kaoowa, the youngest of Kerrioboo's Sons, who was a great favourite of Captain Cooks, went before and got into the Pinnace.

When Kerrioboo came near the Water Side, 2 Chiefs and an old Woman who was crying, Stopped him, and made him sit down. He then seemed irresolute and frightened. At this time our people began to suspect Mischief. The Marines were stationed on a Rock close to the Water Side that they might not be surrounded by the Natives, who were seen to be arming themselves whilst an Old Man, who seemed to be one of the Priesthood was singing to Captain Cook and Kerrioboo as was thought to prevent suspicion. Captain Cook then let Kerrioboo go and said he was not to be forced on board without killing a number of People.

The Old Chief was immediately taken away and no more seen. Captain Cook likewise was about to give orders for embarking, when he was provoked by the insolence of a man armed with a thick Mat and a long Spike, at whom he fired with Small Shot, which neither penetrated the Mat nor frightened the Indians as was expected. Another Man with an Iron Spike came near Mr. Philips who, suspecting his intentions, drove him back with the Butt end of his Musket. 2 or 3 Stones were then thrown and one of the Marines knocked down. Captain Cook who had a double Barrel Gun immediately fired with Ball. The Serjeant said he had shot the wrong Man, on which he told the Serjeant to Shoot the right. The Indians gave a general Volley of Stones and began to close on our people. Captain Cook therefore gave orders for the Marines to fire, which they did amongst the Crowd and were seconded by the Boats. The Indians at first gave back, but directly after, before the Marines had time to load again, advanced.

Captain Cook called out to take to the Boats. The Pinnace was near the Shore, but distant from the Rock where the Marines Stood 10 or 12 Yards and this Short Space was uneven Slippery Rocks, so that being pressed upon in their retreat, they were obliged to take to the Water. Captain Cook in coming down was Struck by an Indian behind him with a Staff on which he turned and beat the Man back with his Musket. He was again followed and received at the same instant a Blow on the Head and a stab with a Spike in the Neck, which tumbled him into the Water. Being no swimmer and stunned with the Blow, he turned towards the Shore again and a Number of Indians Surrounded and dragged him on the Rocks, where they Beat and stabbed him in several places, snatching the Daggers from each other out of eagerness to have their Share in killing him. Four of the Marines were killed, one of them on shore (Thos Fatchet) whom nobody knew what became of, the other three in the water, viz. James Thomas, Corporal, John Allen and Theophilus Hinks, private. The Corporal had loaded again and received a stab in the Belly when up to the middle in the Water. He fired at the Indian who gave it and directly after fell dead. They were all dragged on shore.

Of those that escaped the Lieut of Marines was wounded in the Shoulder by a Spike, the Serjeant received a slight wound, and one of the Marines, [John] Jackson, was struck in the Face with a Stone, but which he is in danger of losing an Eye. Being unable to swim he would probably have been drowned or fell into the hands of the Indians, had not Lieut Philips jumped overboard out of the pinnace and assisted him. The People in the Boats, at first had so little apprehensions of any danger from the Indians, that when the firing began on Shore, the Pinnace [Henry Roberts in command] put close in to the Rocks to let Kaoowa Land, as he was much frightened and asked to go.

The whole of this affair, from Captain Cooks leaving the Resolution to the return of the Boats, happened in the Short space of one Hour. 9 Stand of Arms with Iron Ramrods, besides Captain Cooks double Barrel Gun and Hanger, fell into the hands of the Indians.

On Notice of our defeat, the Boats stationed near the Points of the Harbour were recalled and a strong reinforcement sent to Lieut King at the Tents and Soon after Orders to Strike them and get the Resolutions Foremast off. Many Indians being seen assembling to the right of the Tents, kept firing with our great Guns to disperse them, and a large Party of our People were posted on the Morai, which overlooked that part of the Beach where the Mast lay, to protect those who were busied in launching it.

About 1 every thing came off from the Shore without any other molestation from the Indians than a few Stones, in return for which, some of them were shot who ventured nearer than otherwise they would have done, from an Idea that their Armour (thick Mats Soaked in Water) were Musket proof. Notwithstanding this, an Indian of the priesthood named Kerrikaer, well known amongst our People, remained with them till the Tents were struck and supplied them with Drest Hogs, Cocoanuts and Water.

The Indians were observed to be very carefull of conveying away their Dead. Proofs of great courage were shewn by 2 Men in carrying off a dead Body from within reach of our Fire.

At 4 in the Afternoon the Boats were sent to the Town of Kavarooa to demand the dead Bodies. On approaching the Shore, Stones were thrown which fell short. Lieut King went in with our small Cutter waving a white Flag, whilst the other Boats lay on their Oars. The Indians left off throwing and waved a white Flag in return. They had already made a number of little Stone Breastworks to screen them from our Fire Arms, and during the conference they several times counted our numbers. In answer to the Demand, some Chiefs said that tomorrow the Bodies should be brought, of which, word was sent to Captain Clerke.

An Old Man named Kooaha, whom we have all along taken to be the Chief Priest, had the confidence to swim off and get into the Boat, where he remained some time. He had an Iron Dagger in his Hand. This is the same man who performed the Strange Ceremonies when Captain Cook landed at our first coming here. The reason given why the Bodies were not Delivered to Night was that they were carried some distance up into the Country.

At another part of the Town, however, the Indians made Motions which we thought Signified they were cut to pieces, and one Fellow came to the Water Side flourishing Captain Cook's Hanger with many tokens of exultation and Defiance. Orders soon after came for the Boats to return.

After Dark, a Guard Boat was stationed to row round the Ship, lest any of the Indians should swim off and attempt to cut the Cables. They were very busy on shore all Night, making much noise, running about with Lights, and Howling, as we suposed over their Dead.

Monday 15th In the Morning Kooaha, the Chief Priest, came in a Small Canoe alongside the Resolution, and desired that Captain Clerke or Mr. King would go on shore for the dead bodies. He was answered we expected they would bring them. He came off 3 or 4 times in the course of the day and always with the Same Message.

It being suspected the Indians were collecting a number of Canoes behind the NW point of the Harbour, the Resolutions pinnace was Sent to look but found none. The Indians threw Stones at the Boat as She went alongside.

In the Afternoon Lieut John Gore was appointed to command the Discovery, Captain Clerke having taken the command of the Resolution. Likewise, Mr. William Harvey was appointed 3rd Lieutenant of the Resolution.

At 8 in the Evening, 2 Men came off in a Canoe, one of them Kerrikaer, who was with our people in the Morai when the Mast was getting off. He brought with him a Small bundle in which was the flesh of one of the thighs of our late Commander. He said the body had been burnt and the limbs distributed amongst the Arees or Chiefs as trophies; that what he now brought was secretly and without their knowledge. He advised Captain Clerke to give no credit to Kooaha, the Chief Priest, none of the Indians being inclined to peace except those living in the Towns round the Bay, who were most likely to be the sufferers. The account he gave of the loss sustained by the Indians was 20 killed at Kavarooa and 6 from the Morai at Karacacooa, besides many wounded. Amongst the dead were 6 Chiefs, 2 of whom were Kanine and his brother, the former of greater consequence than any of the rest. He had been a constant visitor to the two Ships, in particular to the Resolution, where he exercised his authority in keeping his countrymen orderly, the same as Parrear had formerly done on board our Ship. At 10 Kerrikaer was conducted past our Ship by the Resolutions boat, lest we should fire at him in his way to the Shore.

Tuesday 16th About 2 in the Afternoon, a Small Canoe came from the town of Kavarooa and stopped near the Resolution. After looking at her some minutes, an Indian in the middle of the Canoe stood up and put Captain Cooks hat on, making many flourishes and antick gestures expressive of defiance and derision. He was fired at and a boat manned to chace him, on which he made towards the Shore, where he was received with great Shoutings by a crowd of Indians. 3 great Guns were fired which dispersed them.

Notwithstanding this, the Old Chief Priest came from the town of Kavarooa almost directly after and paddled several times about the Ships, asking for somebody to go on Shore. Two boys likewise swam off from the Town of Karacacooa, each of them holding a Spear and singing or rather repeating a set prayer. Being permitted to come on board, they delivered their spears and asked to stay with us. Not understanding the meaning of their errand, they were sent on shore again.

Wednesday 17th In the morning, carried out small Anchors and warped the Ship nearer to the town of Karacacooa so as to command the Watering place. At 9 the Launches of both Ships were sent with the Resolutions Casks and with them the other boats Armed.

At their landing and during the whole time of watering they were pelted by the Natives from their houses and from behind Stone walls with which many of the houses are surrounded. Although a constant fire of Musketry was kept up at every man that was seen and several great guns fired from the Ships, all this did not prevent Kooaha from coming off to the Ships with the same pretext as before. From the Ships he went to the beach near our waterers to whom he offered a Pig. Being turned away, he landed at the houses beyond the Morai and was afterwards seen amongst the Stone throwers.

At Noon the boats returned with 2 launch loads of water. Our Stock of fresh pork and vegetables being out, Served Salt provisions and biscuit again.

During dinnertime, our small Cutter was stationed near the well to keep off the Indians lest they should play tricks with the water. In the Afternoon, Lieut Rickman was sent again for water, with orders in case of Molestation to set fire to the Town.

The Indians beginning with their Slings, the boats were directed to keep out of the way of the great Guns and a constant firing was kept up from the Ship for about 15 minutes, after which our people landed and set fire to the houses between the watering place and Morai (about 60). 7 or 8 Indians were killed and one taken prisoner, who was sent on board the Resolution and afterwards released.

The well where we watered being at the foot of a Steep hill, a Crowd of Indians got on that part right over the waterers and rolled large Stones down, some of which came very near and made our people run to get out of the way, which always produced a loud Shout. Among these people we saw Parraer and none appeared more busy. A wall piece was fired from the Ship but would not carry the distance. Except this, the Waterers met with very little disturbance the rest of the day, scarce an Indian appearing within reach of a Musket. The inhabitants of the Town beyond the Morai were seen carrying their things away inland.

At 5 in the Afternoon, the Indians on the hill having been for some time quiet, about 12 of them walked down to the Waterers, each holding a white flag and a Sugar Cane. At the head of these people was Kerrikaer with a very small pig. He said he was sent by Kerrioboo to desire peace. One of our boats took him off to the Ships. At Sunset, the waterers came on board and soon after Kerrikaer was landed again. We learnt from him our great Cutter had been Stole by Parrears people and that she was broke to pieces the day after Captain Cook was killed. In the Night Canoes came off to the Ships with Bread fruit, Sweet potatoes, etc.

Thursday 18th At daylight the Indians struck up white flags in different places round the Bay and on the Hill. At 7 the boats were sent for water. All quiet, the Indians keeping at a distance. Whilst the Casks were filling, Kerrikaer came and asked leave to make an offering of a roast pig to one of the images on the Morai, which was granted.

In the forenoon, Kooaha, the Old Priest, came alongside in a small Canoe with a Hog and some plantains. He was turned away from both Ships, after which he went on Shore to the waterers, who likewise turned him off. He then went on Shore among the houses to the Southward and came near the Morai, on which a Small party of our Men were stationed, at whom he threw Stones. 2 Muskets were fired, which missed him. After he was gone, A Number of Indians came one at a time with Sugar Canes and breadfruit, which they laid on the beach and went away. These were sent off to the Ships.

In the Afternoon an Indian Chief named Eapoo came down the hill to the waterers and asked to go off to Captain Clerke, being sent, he said, from Kerrioboo. He was carried on board the Resolution where he remained about an hour and was landed again. At Sunset, the waterers came on board. In the Night some Small Canoes came, and several Indians swam off to the Ships with breadfruit to Sell.

Friday 19th Employed Watering. Eapoo made another visit and brought some hogs, plantains etc. as a present from Kerrioboo.

Saturday 20th Employed Watering. This forenoon the Resolution stepped her foremast and began to rig it.

At Noon a great many Indians with white flags, sugar canes, hogs, etc., marched in procession down the hill to the watering beach, beating drums and uttering loud yells. At the head of these people was Eapoo, who came off with Captain Clerke in the Resolution's Pinnace, bringing a parcel wrapped up in Indian Cloth, which contained part of the bones of Captain Cook. Some time after, a boat was sent on shore to fetch off a present of provisions.

Sunday 21st At 10 this forenoon, Eapoo came down the hill in the same kind of order as yesterday and bringing the remainder of the bones of Captain Cook and his double barrel Gun. With Eapoo came on board Kaoowa, the youngest of Kerrioboo's Sons.

In the Afternoon, Canoes came off to the Ships with provisions to Sell. At Sunset the Resolution fired 10 minute Guns with the Colours half staff up, when the remains of our late Commander were committed to the deep.

Monday 22nd At Noon, a present of provisions came on board from Kerrioboo. In the Afternoon, our water being complete and the Resolution ready for the Sea, Unmoored.

Received a four oar'd Cutter from the Resolution to supply the place of our large Cutter. At 8 Weighed and Sailed out of Karacacooa Bay, with a light land wind.

Tuesday 23rd Standing to the Northward along the West Side of Owhyhe. Some Canoes came off to us with provisions to traffic.

Journal of Henry Roberts

Saturday, February 6th, 1779 We saw several fires along shore at dark. A gentle land breeze came off [and] in the morning found we had opened an extensive bay. [We are] offshore 3 leagues. We now had a view of all the high land in one prospect, the high snowy peak bearing EBS immediately over the bottom of the

Bay. The Master was sent in Shore with the pinnace to look for fresh water and anchorage. Bending Mainsail, we had but few Canoes along side. At Noon a fresh breeze from the NE with squally weather. [We are] off shore 5 or 6 miles. The snowy mountain is much more covered with snow than when we first saw it. Latitude 20°08′ North, Longitude 203°58′ East.

Sunday 7th A little after Noon a heavy squall of wind came off the Land and continued in those violent gusts till the evening, obliging us to close all up & bring too under the Main Staysail. Most of the Canoes that were with us endeavoured to reach the Shore. At 4 the wind abated to a Moderate Gale when the boat returned from sounding, having found no water nor anchorage, the bottom being shoal & rocky at some distance from the Shore. The Pinnace in her return on board took up 3 of the Natives who were just perishing, their Canoe having upset. They slept on board the Ship with several others, who were fearful of attempting the Shore. We stood off to the Northward all the Night with a Stiff Gale from the ENE. Tack'd and stretched in to the ESE, we had at this time single reefs out, when the wind came on more violent.

Monday 8th Strong gales and Squally weather with baffling winds under the land. At 6 AM close reef'd the Fore Topsail, when we found the head of the foremast dangerously sprung. Towards the Noon, struck the fore Top Gallant Mast and got it down with the Rigging. The West point SBW. Several Canoes came off with a few roots etc, when we sent the Indians on Shore that were wind bound. This Morning we took up 2 Men and a Child, who had been blown off, since the first hard gust having suffered extremely by hunger & fatigue [and] the Child being almost lifeless.

Tuesday 9th Light breezes and hazy for the most part, with baffling winds off the land. Some Canoes [came] along side. Sent the pinnace in shore to look for water, being several deep Gullys, which seemed likely. The boat returned when they found no fresh water. The Country here is very barren near the Sea, nor are the hills so richly cloathed as the more western parts, very thinly inhabited with a few scattered dwellings only, the plantations equally thin. At 7 fired a Gun as a signal to the Discovery. At 9 repeated the signal, both answered.

Wednesday 10th Found the head of the Foremast so bad as to oblige us to take the mast out & not knowing any place so secure for that purpose as the last harbour, we now make the best of our way there. At 1 a strong Gale from the NNW with hard squalls, and at ¼ past we were close in with the breakers to the Northward of the west point, the weather at this time being very thick [and] our situation was rather alarming. We immediately hauld off & fired several Guns & burnt false fires as a Signal to the Discovery, which was answered. At 2 we bore away again, and at ½ past run on under an easy sail till morning, when we made all sail again with a moderate breeze from the SE with rain. At 8 the west point bore NBW, distance off shore 5 or 6 miles, and the Westernmost high land NEBN. At Noon Carricacooah Bay 3 or 4 miles, turning to windward with a light breeze, endeavouring to get into the bay. Many Canoes [came] round the Ship laden with provisions, equally plenty as before.

Thursday 11th The first and latter parts [of the afternoon] fresh breezes and Cloudy, the Midday Fresh Gales, lightening and hard rain. In the Morning at Daybreak stood into the Bay and anchored with the best Bower in 24 fms. The Discovery in company. [There are] many Canoes along side.

Friday 12th Got the Foremast unrigged and the two Main topmasts ready for erecting as Sheers. AM raised the Sheers and cleared the fore hold for getting the Mast out. Carpenters employed repairing the fore top. The Chief, Kerree-Oboo, came on board with several of his followers.

Thursday 13th Got the Sheers secured, the purchases save and hard taught, and already for getting the Mast out. AM Got the Mast out and hauled it up on Shore for the Carpenters to work at it near the Observatorys, which were fixed at the same place as before. Sent Sails on Shore and the sailmakers to repair them. Found the heel of the Mast much decayed and the spring at the head in a bad condition. The carpenters of the Discovery employed. Many of the Natives along side as usual, bringing Hogs, Fowls, plantain, Tarro root, Bread fruit, sweet potatoes, & sugar cane etc etc to market. Employed salting and curing the largest Hogs.

Sunday 14th PM The Natives having stolen something from on board the Discovery, a canoe suspected was pursued by one of the boats without arms in her. The crew landed and the things stolen was brought them. Afterwards our pinnace joined them and by some means occasioned a dispute, which rose to a quarrel, when they got themselves ill used & beat by the Natives, breaking the pinnaces Oars & endeavoring to have the boat but no other mischief.

In the morning the Discovery's large cutter was missing from the buoy where she was moored. Boats sent from each ship in search of her, with orders to keep every Canoe in the Bay from paddling off till there was a likelihood of her being returned, as it was well known that the Natives had taken her away. In order to make it more severe, Captain Cook went in the pinnace, manned and armed with the launch under the command of the Third Lieut, in company to the Village on the Northern point of the bay, with an intention to get the Chief Kerree-Oboo on board, for which purpose he landed with the Officer of Marines, the Sergeant, and 8 of his people.

After a little time they found the Chief and he would have willingly come off, but was hindered by his Wife and those about him, who offered presents of Hogs etc but were rejected. They afterwards were very troublesome and began to be exceedingly insolent and at last obliged the Captain to fire on them. This occasioned a great rumour among the Whole, who began to arm themselves.

Shortly after the Captain fired a small Muskett, which was seconded by the Marines and boats. The Captain immediately gave orders to cease firing, and come in with the Boats. The pinnace pulled in. The Natives on their parts had begun the attack, when the stones showered down with great Violence. The whole body, pressing in on our people, armed with spears, clubs, daggers & slings, forced them into the water. The Captain fell in the Conflict with four of the Marines. The officer, Sergeant and others reach'd the boats with great difficulty, three of the number being wounded.

The Boats, after keeping a warm fire for a while, returned on board, not being able to get the body of our lost Commander, whose death occasioned concern & sorrow in every countenance, such an able Navigator, equaled by few and excelled by none, justly stiled father of his people from his great good care and attention, honored & beloved by those who knew, or ever heard of him. The body's of the Marines also could not be taken, but exposed to the mercy of these savages, who were truly desperate and intrepid. Hands were immediately sent on shore to protect the Observatory & Foremast, which was at the inner part of the Bay. Here was a rising ground, which the party took possession of, being a most convenient place, as the Indians here, who had been quiet before, began now to be very troublesome, slinging stones at a considerable distance. But a few pieces of our Musquetry kept them at bay.

The Discovery, keeping a constant fire with their great Guns on a Village where the Natives were gathering in a great body, just to the Southward of our party. It was now thought advisable to get the Mast off, which was accordingly done, with the Tents & every thing from the Shore after this. The party embarked on board, after killing 8 or 9 of the Indians. At our leaving the Shore many of them followed us, shouting & slinging stones, one of these daring fellows I saw stand the fire of above 50 Musketts, within the distance of 40 Yards & drag the body of his companion away that had been shot. We were now under the necessity of getting the Mast, along the booms, for the Carpenters to work at it. Three of the Natives in a small Canoe put off from the point where our accident happened and came ahead of the Ship, throwing several stones, using menaces of Deffiance. We fired several shot at them, when they retreated with the utmost precipitation.

Monday 15th The boats from each Ship well man'd & arm'd went inshore with a white flag as a Truce to demand the bodies by fair means, but with no other success and satisfaction than a promise of their being brought the next morning. The boats then returned, a few stones were thrown at their first approaching the Shore, but afterwards tolerably peaceable. The Ships company quartered very advantageously, taking every necessary precaution in case of an attack on the Ship. During the Night many large fires were burning on Shore & by the help of the night Glass could distinguish great numbers of the Natives crowding round them, others running along shore with lights. Loud lamentations were heard at times and at others, prodigious shouts.

The morning came without any signs of the Bodys being returned. An old priest named Go-ah-sty came off in a Canoe with white flags, deceiving Mr. King to accompany him on Shore, saying the body's were brought down but was refused. Great numbers of the Inhabitants coming from over the Hill, stopping at the place where the largest fire was, still burning, & seemingly gazing with much attention. The numbers killed on the Northern Portion of the Bay, we are informed by the Natives, is seventeen among which was three of their principle chiefs, whose names were Ka-pa-na, his brother, Tee-wa-rua & Ka-aw-ve. Carpenters employed on the Mast.

Tuesday 16th The Carpenters employed about the Mast. From the fast concourse of people assembling on the hill over the Northern Portion of the Bay, we had reason to suppose an attack would be made on the Ship & from our situation it judged necessary to carry a small Anchor out as a spring to bring her broad side to bear on the Town. From the beginning of this fray with these people we have found two supportive divisions among them, those in our favor, where the priest, who performed the great ceremony to Captain Cook at the first arrival of Kerree-Oboo, whose name was Ka-ow. [He] and his party, who has ever been steadfast and faithful, even sending his people with water & refreshments to our party while we were attacking their countrymen from the Morai.

Two of them this night at the risk of their lives came on board the Ship and brought us a part of the sad remains of our unfortunate Captain, being a piece of his flesh from off the thigh. This no doubt was meant as a friendly act and as such it was considered. Their apparent openness and sincerity gave us no room to think otherwise. They informed us of the ill designs of their countrymen against us, strictly cautionary, us against them placing in them any confidence or truth. It's impossible to express the feelings that every Officer & seaman suffered on this occasion a sight so horribly shocking. Distraction & madness was in every mind and revenge the result of all. We inquired after the remaining parts and were told that they were burnt.

These people refused sleeping on board out of dread of its being known and which the night only could prevent. The next morning the old priest renewed his visit, requesting Mr. King as usual to go on Shore. He was told to bring on board hogs & roots, being much destressed for these articles, being obliged to issue out the Meat that was cured & flour in lieu of bread. He made answer that we should be supplyed the next Day. Our work forwarded as much as possible. Captain Charles Clerke took command of the Resolution and Mr. John Gore, first Lieutenant, appointed to the Command of the Discovery.

Wednesday 17th A little after noon, two daring fellows ventured off in a single Canoe ahead of the Ship & one of them slung a number of stones, producing a hat, which he waved with all the insolence conceivable with the most threatening nuances. At this time a prodigious crowd had collected on the Shore to see the event of this piece of deffiance. These provoking insults were not to be borne with. In order therefore to give these people their deserts, we fired 6 great Guns among them, the first two Guns that were well pointed, the shot falling in the midst of them, cleared the place instantly, some taking to the hills, retreating with the utmost precipitation, and others hastening behind the rocks.

The old priest notwithstanding came off in the evening with his usual arrant [errand]. He told us that Mai-a-mai-a was wounded & 2 or 3 others killed by the Great Guns. This Chief was a Son of Keree-Oboo's. Being thought necessary to compleat our water here, it was resolved that the Discovery, being the inner Ship should haul further in & cover the people, which was accordingly done. This next morning, with a strong party on shore, & the boats from each ship man'd and arm'd to lie off the water place, to secure a retreat, we got on board one turn of Water, not without molestation from the Natives. [They were] heaving stones, which we could not totally prevent by firing on them, having stone walls in many places, behind which & the houses they lurked. Mr. William Harvey appointed 3rd lieutenant of this Ship.

Thursday 18th The Boats & party sent to the Shore again, the Discovery having poured in two broad sides to clear the place of the stone throwers. Afterwards, the boats landed, when they received fresh insults from these people. [T]o prevent [further insults] made it absolutely necessary to burn & destroy their town and accordingly set fire to their houses & [we] killed five of them. When they fought us at a greater distance, rolling stones of immense size from the tops of the hills [while] we were watering, but the brow of the hill luckily turned them in a different direction. Towards the evening, a large party came down the hill with white streamers & green boughs to our party, bringing a small Hog etc as a ratification of peace. The Chief of this party was grandson to the old priest Ka-ow, whose name was Ke-nay'co'ahe, [who] came on board. The ships & people on shore [were] no longer insolent.

AM the waterers were sent on shore again. The old priest from the opposite Shore came off with a pig & a few plantains, but was refused admittance. Several white flags were also put up on the Shore, most doubtfully dreading the same fate of the other Village. A muskett or two being discharged by our party on Shore, on which a man servant of Sha-ow who brought on board a piece of flesh. [This man], having slept on board, went immediately to quell the rioters. When it appeared that the old priest, when he made a peace offering, had been objected too, had thrown several stones at our guard when they fired to chastise him for his insolence. By Noon got on board another turn of water without any interruption.

Friday 19th A canoe from the North point came along side with three men loaded with Sugar Cane, Bread fruit, Tarro roots etc, which were accepted. Got on board 3 Turns of water without any disturbances. Carpenters employed about the mast. Many of our people at this time have contracted the Venereal Disease from the women of this Island.

Saturday 20th The Carpenters finished the Mast. A great many of the Natives came down at the Watering place with white flags wishing peace, when Captain Clerke & Mr. King went to the Shore with two Boats & returned with a Chief from Keree-Oboo, bringing on board the bones, the only remains of Captain Cook, with a present of Hogs, Roots, etc.

Sunday 21st Got the Sheers down & Rigged the Main Topmast. AM Rigged the foremast, sett the Main rigging up & swayed the Topmast & Top Gallant Mast on end. The preceding evening a number of small Canoes came along side after dusk, loaded with hogs & roots, which were purchased. In the morning the barrels of Captain Cooks Gun was brought on board by the Chief, who came Yesterday. When inquiries was made after the Discoverys cutter and the arm's belonging to the Marine, the former, they told us, was broken to pieces for the iron work & the latter, the common people had got among them. Keree-Oboo was innocent of the whole of their proceedings, entreating to see some of the Officers & most earnestly desiring peace.

Monday 22nd Having the greatest part of the remains of our lost Captain returned, it was committed to the Deep, with all the Decency in our power and the usual Ceremony. Fired 10 minute Guns. AM set the fore rigging up. Got the Topmast & Top Gallant mast's on end. Set the rigging up, & bent the after sails.

Tuesday 23rd Bent the head sails, employed getting ready for sea. Hoisted in the launch. Many Canoes came off from all parts of the bay, bringing provisions, which were bought. Among the Number was the old treacherous Priest, who was refused admittance, nor even suffered to come near the Ship. The Chief who brought us the presents from Keree-Oboo, whose name was Yah-po, came to bid us farewell with our friendly priest Ke-nay'eo'a. At 8 a light breeze springing up from the Shore, weighed and stood out of the Bay, the boats ahead towing, and the Discovery in Company. Latitude 19°54′ North, Longitude 203°42′ East.

Caricacooah Bay is situated on the Western side of the Island of Hawyee, its Latitude 20°27′ North, Longitude by several Observations 204°00′ East of the meridian of Greenwich. The best anchorage is in 20 fathoms over a bottom of fine sand. The Northern Shore is steep & hilly but the SE parts are low and the ground very foul and rocky. This Bay is well sheltered, oppen only to the 8 points of the Compass, as appears by the plan, yet a northerly sett in a great swell. The dotted line denotes the limits of bad Ground and the figures the depth of Water in fathoms.

This Bay might be known by the high land on its Northern boundaries, which is the only remarkable steep land on the western parts of the Island. To the Northward of this Bay at the distance of about 2 leagues is another which appeared to be more oppen, its shores are fine sand at this place is a large Town, well shaded with Cocoa nut Trees, which is the residence of the Chief Keree-Oboo.

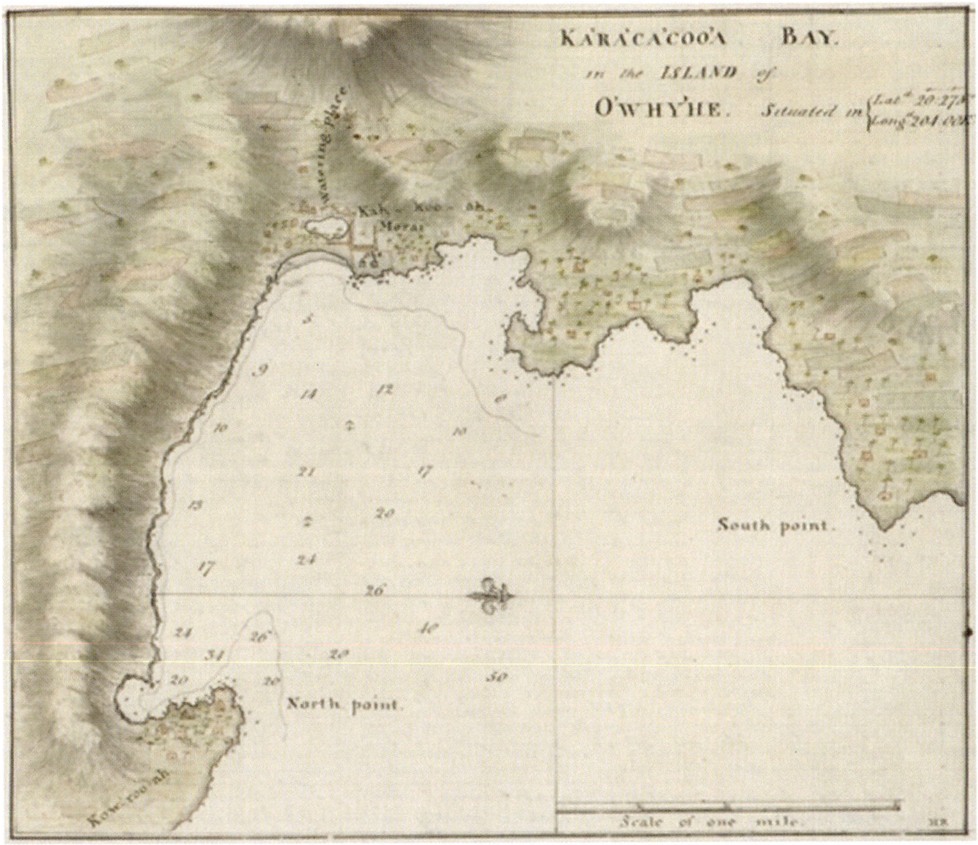

Henry Roberts, "Ka'ra'ca'coo'a [Kealakekua] Bay in the Island of O'why'he [Hawai'i]," February 1779. Roberts drew his charts of bays and harbors with precision and careful penmanship, but this is probably his most well-known, as it formed the basis of the official chart of the bay published in the third voyage journal. Roberts Journal p. 45, Vol. II, Dixson Library, State Library of New South Wales, DLMSQ 151-52 and DLMSF 2.

4

LEAVING HAWAI'I
FEBRUARY–MARCH 1779

For three weeks the expedition sailed to the north, past Kahoolawe, Maui, Lanai, and Moloka'i. There were frequent visits from canoes of local people offering provisions. The expedition anchored briefly on the north shore of O'ahu, where Clerke went ashore. Roberts reported a well-populated, rich island with broad, verdant plantations on the surrounding hills. Clerke was received by the local people with presents of hogs and the usual prostration, but the crews could not reach water without considerable trouble, so they decided not to stay. The people along the route were apparently already aware of the melee at Kealakekua Bay.[14]

The expedition left the north shore of O'ahu after only a few hours, sailing for Waimea Bay, Kaua'i, a familiar prospect. When they first arrived on shore, there was another confrontation with an unhappy mob. A rock thrower was shot, but the incident passed without recriminations. Given the death of Cook at Hawai'i, Burney speculated the people assumed the best way to deal with the English was belligerence. But after the arrival of some chiefs and cautious diplomacy, Clerke was able to restore order and the usual trade, maintaining high alert and a heavy guard for those who ventured ashore. It was a bountiful place. Clerke called it "the most extraordinary Hog Island we ever met with." The journals report that they salted about seventy hogs, each weighing one hundred pounds, for the journey north.[15]

Roberts offered an unreserved perspective of Kaua'i, impressed by their customs and language. Despite the initial hostilities, warm relations ensued and a crowd estimated at eight thousand people assembled to see them off. He also learned the people of Kaua'i and Ni'ihau were at war, fighting over goats and other gifts left by Cook the previous year.

The ravages of venereal disease were also evident. When first ashore, King reported "One Man without any putting questions to him on our beginning the conversation told us that we had left a disorder amongst their Women, which had killed several of them as well as Men; he himself was infected." Burney and Roberts likewise reported these sad circumstances, confident the English sailors "were the Authors of this disease in this Place." Roberts concluded in Ni'ihau, "Its with sorrow that these poor innocent people universally accuse and condemn us in leaving the Venereal Disease among them. It appears to have made great ravages from the most part of our Crew, who has at this time contracted it from the Women."

The expedition spent its final week at Ni'ihau in stormy weather, then cruised several days looking for a rumored island that was supposed to be overrun with turtles, Burney's "Tomogoopapappa" and Roberts' "Tamatta-papapa." The inhabitants of Kaua'i and Ni'ihau said it could be found southwest of Niihau, but the elusive island did not exist. On March 17 Clerke stretched from the Sandwich Islands for Kamchatka. The winter in Hawai'i had lasted three and one-half months, but it had been anything but a holiday.

Journal of James Burney

Wednesday, February 24th, 1779 Wind Easterly. A Moderate breeze all the morning. Ran by the West Side of an Island called Kahowraowe [Kaho'olawe], which is about 8 Leagues in Circuit. This Island looks ragged and bare of trees, making much such an appearance as Neehow.

At Noon were Standing to the Northward between Mowwhe and another Island called Oranni [Lana'i]. The South Sides of each being in direct opposition . . . Latitude 20°44′ North, Longitude 203°12′ East. Most part of the Afternoon light Winds and Calms. Canoes alongside with vegetables. After Dark the wind coming from the South, hauled to the Westward to pass by the South Side of Oranni.

Thursday 25th At Noon were becalmed about 4 miles distant from the South End of Oranni [Bearings omitted]. Towards Evening had a light breeze Easterly. Steered to the NW for the West part of Morotai [Moloka'i]. Oranni is 5 Leagues in length from NW to SE. It appears ragged and without trees. The Indians say it abounds in Roots.

Friday 26th Ran by the West Side of Morotai. Had Soundings at 2 miles distance from the SW end, 19 fathoms corral bottom. This part of Morotai appears naked. On the East Side (which we have seen) are Trees. In the Night Stood backwards and forwards between Morotai and Wouahow [O'ahu]. Wind Easterly.

Saturday 27th At daylight bore away for Wouahow. At Noon, the North end, which is a low Sandy point . . . 3 miles distant . . . From this point for near 4 Leagues to the SW is a Sandy beach, along which we ran at about a mile from Shore, having Soundings between 20 and 13 fathoms. At ½ past 2 Anchord in a Bay on the NW side of Wouahow . . . 1 mile off Shore [Bearings omitted].

All this part of Wouahow appears very pleasant and fruitfull. Boats were sent to look for a Watering place, but returned at Sunset without finding any, the River being brackish for more than half a mile up and too Shole for a Boat to get so far. We saw very few people here. Some Canoes came off with provisions to traffic. They brought great quantities of a large sweet root which they call Tee. The Chief of Wouahow we were told was gone to Morotai with which Island he was at war. Some Women that came in the Ship from Owhyhe, were sent on Shore, that the news of our late misfortune might not go to Atoui with us. At ½ past 7 got under Sail and left Wouahow.

Sunday 28th At Noon, saw Atoui. At Sunset were within 4 miles of the SE End. Stood off and on all Night.

Monday, March 1st At daylight bore away. At ½ past 8 Anchord near the Island of Atoui in the Same road where we lay last year, and Moored. Latitude 21°56′ North, Longitude 200°20′ East . . . The Island of Neehow in Sight to the Westward. Canoes came alongside with Hogs, Yams, and Sweet potatoes. In the Afternoon the Resolution's Boats on Shore watering, were insulted and robbed of several things by the Natives. As they put off from the Shore, the Indians threw Stones [and] in return a Musket was fired, which killed one man. We find they are not ignorant of what has happened at Owhyhe, which I believe they consider as a reproach to themselves for being frightened into submission by us last year.

Tuesday 2nd At daylight, the boats of both Ships were sent to get Water and a Guard of about 50 Men landed to keep the beach clear. The Indians remained quiet and at a distance. At 4 in the Afternoon the boats and Guard came off. Many Canoes alongside all day, trading with Salt and provisions.

Wednesday 3rd Boats watering with the same Guard as yesterday. Completed the Resolutions Water.

Thursday 4th Some of the Atoui Chiefs came on board the Ships, who promised that the Natives would be more friendly and peaceable ashore than the first day, attributing their riotous behaviour to quarrels amongst the Chiefs, which occasioned a general want of Order. The Sovereignty of Atoui is at present disputed for between Tawmehanno, the Chief who governed when we were here before, and a Boy named Kaavie. They are both Grandsons to the Chief of Wouahou. Among those who visited us to day was an Old Lady, the mother of Kaavie.[16]

The Goats left by us at Neehow have suffered from their unsettled State, having been a bone of contention and occasioned bloodshed amongst the Indians as well as their own destruction.

Friday 5th Completed the Discovery's Water.

Sunday 7th This forenoon were visited by Tawmehanno. The Mother of Kaavie being then on board, he could not be prevailed on to go into the great Cabin whilst she was there. Kaavie's party we are told, is likely to prove too hard for him.

In the Afternoon, Kaavie himself made a visit to the Ships. He is a very handsome boy, but appears to be of a sickly constitution.

All this time continued trading for provisions, Salting pork etc. Considering the shortness of our stay at Atoui, the Ships were supplied with a greater number of Hogs than at any Island in the South Seas, and to judge by the great concourse of people that constantly flocked round us at the watering place, I believe no Island we know of is more populous in proportion to its size. Whilst we lay here, none of us ventured to walk about or Straggle on Shore amongst the Indians as formerly.

Monday 8th This Morning Weighd our Anchors and sailed out of Atoui Road. In the Afternoon Anchord near the SW part of Neehow in 24 fathoms fine white Sand, and Moored with the Small Bower to the Westward. Latitude 21°48′ North, Longitude 199°46′ East . . . Distance from shore half a League. A small Island (Outoura) S52°W 5 or 6 Leagues. Sounded and found good bottom about the Ship.

9th and 10th The Launches on shore trading for Yams and Canoes alongside with provisions and Salt.

Thursday 11th The launches were sent in the morning as usual to trade for yams, but found a Tabu (prohibition) had been laid on them. This was done by some Chiefs just arrived from Atoui in consequence of a present which they said was coming for the Ships. The people of Neehow hesitated whether or no they should submit to this order and appeared disposed to be refractory [stubbornly disobedient]. Our making a small present to the Atoui Chiefs got the Tabu taken off and trade went on again as before.

There are at Neehow many priests and, what we have not seen at any other of these Islands, priestesses, who all act as if they were inspired by some supernatural power, performing numberless mad and strange pranks.

Saturday 13th The Resolutions Boats were sent to examine the West Side of Neehow. In the Evening they returned having found Anchorage in a Sandy bay and water ¼ of a Mile from the Sea Side, in small wells. This Bay is open to the North winds.

Sunday 14th This forenoon our launch was sent to a Small Cove on the West Side of the Southernmost point of the Island to look for Water, the Resolution having got some there last year, found none now. Parties on Shore all day trading for Yams and cutting broom Stuff.

Monday 15th At 7 in the Morning Weighed and Sailed from Neehow. Steered to the Westward in search of a low flat Island which the Indians told us lay to the west of the little Island Outoura. They call it Tomogoopapappa. It is uninhabited and abounds in Turtle . . .

One Canoe belonging to some Atoui Chief staid with us till Sunset, and then went towards the Island Outoura which was 4 miles distant to the SE. Their business, they told us, was to catch red birds, and that next day they intended going to Tomogoopapappa for Turtle . . .

Tuesday 16th At Daylight found we had fell greatly to leeward, the Island of Outoura being above 6 Leagues to the Windward of us. Bore away. At 7 the Resolution made our Signal to keep 6 miles distant from her and on her Starboard Beam. At 8 the Island Outoura (which was the last we Saw of the Sandwich Islands) bore ENE, distant 8 or 9 Leagues. Imagine we drifted past Tomogoopapappa in the Night.

Steered a little to the Southward of West to keep the trade wind, which was but light and variable from NE to ESE. Every day for the first week saw numbers of Tropic birds, Boobies, and Men of War birds.

Journal of Henry Roberts

Wednesday, February 24, 1779 At Daylight standing in for an Island lying to the SW of Mow-wee (called by the Natives Ka-ow-ra-nia) [Kahoʻolawe] with a stiff Gale. This island appeared to be destitute of every necessary. Its of a middling height and its shores rocky and broken, not the least show of trees [and] not any signs of Inhabitants nor even a house to be seen.

Thursday 25th Standing on between Mow-whe and an Island lying to the west of it that the Natives called Morrotoy [Moloka'i]. At this time we had several Canoes about us, mostly laden with roots & fruit, but a small number of pigs. These people were no doubt acquainted with our unfortunate accident of Karacacooah, by their questioning us after the principle Chiefs that had been killed. They took no further notice, but appeared peaceable and friendly.

A light breeze springing up from the SW, we stood on for the west point of Mow-whe when the Canoes returned to the Shore. Before Dark we were within 2 leagues of the point & could perceive a Shoal extending off it to a considerable distance, the small advantage we should reap in getting through this passage was thought not worth a risk. We therefore tack'd & stood to the Southward. This point is very remarkable by a small hillock being on it, to the South of which appeared to be a fine sandy Bay with several dwellings of the Inhabitants & Cocoa Nutt Trees. The Country appears pleasant & fruitful, the hills fall in Deep Chasams, which in all probability afford runs of fresh water.

In the Night a fresh breeze from the Eastward. Brought too, till Morning, when we bore away for the South end of Oanai [Lana'i]. Many Canoes came off to us with small supplys of refreshments.

Friday 26th Several Canoes trading with us. The Southern & Western shores of this Island is steep & rocky & carries a barren aspect. The eastern parts is low & apparently fruitful. We continued our course on all night for the west part of Morrotoy with a moderate breeze, but baffling. Three Canoes came off. Sold the effects of William Watman, deceased.

Saturday 27th The western part of this Island is low and the Shores in general rocky. It has a barren appearance & seemingly but thinly inhabited. We saw no houses or people on the shore, but some large fires were burning inland. The Eastern part is very high land which gradually descends in sloping hills.

At 11 saw low land stretching off the Northern point sett before & breakers extending out for near a mile and half at the distance of 4 miles. This island from its situation we find to be the same that was first discovered to the Westward by us on January 7, 1778 in our Route to the Northward, called by the Natives Wou-ah-oo [O'ahu]. Its very low and flat with a fine sandy beach round it. The surge beats very violent on the reef. On the point are many houses of the Natives, well shaded, with Cocoa Nutt and other trees.

Sunday 28th Standing in for a bay on the NW side of Wou-ah-oo. At 1 we struck soundings at 20 fms about 3 miles from the Shore. A low point, which was rocky & steep, projected out that appeared to give shelter for anchorage. We hauled in for it, the shores crowded with people. Hoisted out the boats & Captain Clerke went on shore accompanied with Mr. King. They landed upon a fine sandy beach under a point of rocks which sheltered it from surf opposite to the

Gully of fresh water. Many of the Natives were assembled at the landing place who, upon our people exiting the boats, prostrated themselves on the Ground and continued this submissiveness with the greatest affability & good nature during the whole of our stay. Their behaviour appeared friendly & not a Man arm'd with any kind of weapon. At this time some few Canoes were alongside with a small number of pigs, Taro & plantains.

Soon after Captain Clerke returned on board, the other boat sent to leeward to examine the Land of the bay, having received intelligence from the Inhabitants that there was a good harbour. Our principle object at this time being to get a supply of Yams, which this fertile Country did not appear to afford and compleating the water would be attended with almost & endless trouble, having to roll the casks through a muddy swamp, which lay within the beach, of brackish water, to a considerable distance before we could reach the run [water source]. On this account, therefore, it was resolved on leaving this place. Immediately the boat came on board and made the best of our way to Atoui [Kaua'i] in order to fill our water casks. At 6 the boats returned, having been misinformed by the Natives, finding no harbour. The reef of coral rocks extending some distance from the Shore and with a heavy surge boiling on, at ½ past 6 we got underway.

The Northern part offers the most fruitful country. The hills, being covered with different kinds of Trees with a rich verdure interspersed with the Dwellings of the Inhabitants, render the most pleasing prospect. The hills were high & form deep Valleys, but the Shore is low and fertile. The NW side of the Island is equally fruitful, but a greater extent of low land on which are several large Towns, shaded with groves of fine tall Trees. At the back of this the land takes a gentle ascent to the summits of the Mountains. The most parts cultivated and the plantations lain out with a degree of taste among the houses near the sea, are several high pyramidical buildings built and thatched. A fine sandy beach encircles this low land and a reef of coral rocks receives the heavy surge that rumbles in with great Violence. These beds of rocks extend themselves upwards of a mile into the sea. On this part of the Island the bay is situated sheltered from the Eastern and Southerly winds, the anchorage is good, being a firm sandy bottom of regular soundings from 12 to 20 fms at 2 miles from the shore, but oppen entirely to the Northerly winds, which most send in a great Sea.

We continued our Course all night upon a wind to the Northward and at Day break bore away for the Island [of Kaua'i]. At Noon Latitude 22°08′ North, Longitude 201°08′ East. A fresh trade wind & pleasant weather.

Monday, March 1st, 1779 A fresh Gale and pleasant weather. At 4 when the eastern point, being the Northernmost land in sight [was] 6 or 7 miles, a very remarkable sugar loaf hill which is low and rocky when we took a reef on each topsail and hauled off to the Southward. At this time a few Canoes came off to us with a small number of Roots etc. Stood off & on during the Night and at Daybreak bore away for the Anchoring place on the SW part of the Island [Kaua'i]. We got soundings at 26 fms 2 or 3 miles from the Shore. Its necessary to observe when you stand into the Roadstead not to keep within 2 miles of the previous point to avoid a shoal which runs from it to the Eastward of this point. [This place] which is about 3 miles from the Anchoring place, appeared a good bay in which is several Houses of the Natives & by the form of the hills over, it should conclude there was fresh water. This place although small seemed to afford shelter & good landing for boats, the bluff head to the West of the Valley or watering place [is] 2 miles. Hoisted the launch out.

Tuesday 2nd Sent the launch for a Turn of Water, and the pinnace with Men under Arms. Several Canoes [were] alongside trading with hogs, Tarro, sweet potatoes & sugar cane etc. In the evening the launch returned with a load of Water. They had not been any considerable time on Shore before the Natives committed several thefts and, at our embarking, they stole the officers hanger from his side and very insolent in every respect. A stone being thrown at our people in the boats, two or three Musketts were fired. When one of the Indians was killed, the others immediately fled. It did not appear at this time that any Chief were among them to keep any kind of order.

The proceeding morning the Launches of boats from each Ship were well Man'd and Arm'd and went on Shore to Water under the Command of our first Lieut, Mr. King. The Natives did not offer any molestation but kept at a respectable distance from the party upon the side of a steep hill to the Eastward of the Watering place and the opposite side to our people. The river is deep and in many places not fordable. By Noon got on board one turn of Water, a number of Canoes round us trading & very friendly & gracious. Our Carpenters with the assistance of the Discovery's caulking the Ships sides round, which were found very open.

Wednesday 3rd In the evening received on board another launch load of Water. The Natives quiet, but most of them Arm'd. The party came off. At Daylight the boats & people, armed as before, sent again to Water & by Noon got off two Turns. Many Canoes along side, trading with very large hogs, Tarro roots, potatoes, plantains & sugar cane, with a few small Yams. The Natives peaceable. This Morning we were visited by the Mothers & Sisters of the Young Kings, whose name is Tee-aa-ve. They brought on board a present consisting of a few Hogs etc, with several Matts, some of which were curiously worked. Latitude 21°56′45″ North.

Thursday & Friday 4th & 5th Compleated our Water and the party came on board without any interruption from the Natives. The Chiefs [were] on Shore, keeping them in great order. The carpenters caulking the sides. The young Chief, Tee-aa-ve, visited us with a few attendants & a small Ceremony, bringing a You-vah Cup. (You-vah is a root, well known, and used by the Natives of most of the South Sea Islands, the juice of which they drink, that stupefies the brain & brings on a sleepy intoxication.) This cup was presented to the Captain with a few Matts.

The Queen Dowager, during the time we were on shore, brought down a great present which was made up of vast quantities of roots, sugar Cane, fruit etc, with a large bundle of Matts, wrought extremely curious, besides bracelets made of Boar's Tusks, very neat, & Implements made of Feathers, the handles of which were human bones. This was given with much Ceremony. The Matts being spread out and every particular thing carried by a particular person and presented by the Queen whose name is Tumuttanah. The Natives alongside and trading as usual.

Saturday 6th PM the Boats returned from the Shore without receiving any insult from the Indians. At the time of our leaving the Shore they came from all quarters opposite the boats upon the beach but a few of them arm'd. But the multitude was immense, not being less than 7 or 8,000, which Concourse had been collecting since the morning, by fires made upon the hills, that we judged to be a signal for that purpose. Many alongside as before, the old Queen paid us another visit.

Monday 8th Unmoored and at 9 Weighed & made sail for O'neehow [Ni'ihau]. Many of the Natives came off loaded with provisions.

Imayak Bay is on the SW side of the Island of Atoui. Its Latitude 20°56′45″ North & Longitude 200°20′ East of the Meridian of Greenwich, the result of many observations. [It] may be known by a Steep Cliff to the Westward of a deep Valley lying over a fine sandy beach within which is a large Village and a fine fresh water river to the East of it. Both the opposite side[s] of the River is many detached Towns alongshore and even extend out to the East point of the Bay or the Southern point of the Island, which is low and covered with a kind of long coarse Grass. From this point as I have before observed, lies a shoal at the distance of 2 or 3 miles. The West point of this Road is very low, almost even to the waters edge, with shoals lying off every part of it. This low part is covered with small shrubs or trees, behind which the land rises in high hills, as it does on each side of the aforesaid Valley. In most parts [it is] well clothed with Wood. The best anchorage is in 25 fms when the steep Cliff [is] about 2 Miles from the beach.

The Country exhibits a most pleasing prospect. Its to a degree fertile & well Cultivated in every part that's capable of receiving it. While we lay at this place we purchased a great number of the largest & finest Hogs, by far superior to those of the other Islands, which supply enabled us to Cure eight more puncheons of pork. We were likewise Daily brought a sufficient quantity of Roots to serve to the people. The Natives at our first arrival was extremely insolent and troublesome, merely from there being no person of any distinction on the spot, but latterly, when the principle chiefs of people made their appearance, they were altogether as quiet and friendly. They gave us to understand that they had been very lately at War with O'neehow, in which action several of their Chiefs fell. The dispute and difference between these people seems to have arisen in consequence of the Goats and other things given by us the last season to the inhabitants of O'neehow, which most probably created a jealousy in those of the other Island.

Tuesday 9th PM we passed the high bluff head [Ni'ihau], which is the Southernmost promontory of the Island, joined to the Northern Range of Hills by a neck of low land, which appeared to produce long shaggy grass only, not a Tree or Shrub to be seen. Upon the higher part of the bluff were two Men waving white flags, possibly signals to the other parts of the Island, or possibly meant as a welcome to us upon peaceable terms. At Noon a continuance of the Gale, but few Canoes ventured off. Carpenters employed caulking the Main Deck.

Wednesday 10th Strong Gales & Squally. Employed drawing yarns. Carpenters caulking the Main Deck & painting the quick work. The Launch [was] sent on shore to trade for Yams. The landing place is in a small sandy bay edged round with Rocks, in which Cove is a Village, the only one on this side of the Island. To the Eastward of it is a few straggling houses. This place affords very good shelter for the boats with the trade wind. In the Evening the launch came on board with a few Yams.

Saturday 13th The Master was sent with the pinnace and cutter to look round the high point for a more convenient anchoring place. Some Canoes [were] along side trading, bringing large quantities of root, which is very sweet. The Natives call this root "Tea," which we afterward learn't was the root of a Fern that this Island produces in abundance. The Launch bringing off but few Yams, being but a small Number of the Inhabitants at the located place. Yesterday several of the Chiefs came from Atoui and visited us.

Sunday 14th In the evening the boats returned. [They] found a good anchorage round the West point in a small sandy bay, sheltered from the trade winds and in every respect much superior to this roadstead. We also found good water in three or four wells about ¼ of a mile inland. This appeared to be spring water from its clearness. The rolling way [of water casks] to the beach [is] extremely level and good. AM unmoored and loosed the sails today to dry. Carpenters finished caulking the Main Deck. Many of the Natives alongside bartering with a few Roots.

Its with sorrow that, I apart, that these poor innocent people universally accuse and condemn us in leaving the Venereal Disease among them. It appears to have made great ravages from the most part of our Crew, who has at this time contracted it from the Women.

Monday 15th The Launch as usual on Shore trading for Yams. Hoisted the boats in and at 7 Weighd & came to sail, standing to the SWBW for a small low sandy Island that the Natives gave us information of. [It is] in that direction from where they get Turtle. Its a passage of two days for them, generally sleeping, at the Island Tasora.

Since our first anchoring at these Islands, our Cables [have] suffered to a great degree, although the best precaution [h]as always been taken, the bottom will appear clear & good, with the lead at times, but theres no doubt a bedd of broken coral intermitted with the sand, which at all times will not appear in the lead.

Its therefore very requisite at these places not to Veer any great scope of Cable without a fresh of wind, for in little Winds the Cable will certainly hang under foot, and by that means drag & Chafe against the bottom.

Read the Articles of War to the Ships Company at Noon.

The anchoring place is situated on the SW part of the Island. Within this the bottom is foul and not more than 10 fms, which renders it an oppen roadstead, & a fresh of wind to the South of east causes a great Swell, & the bottom being loose sand & broken Coral, theres great Danger to be apprehended in drawing off the Bank. We generally found a Current setting to Windward, more or less.

During our continuance at this place, we purchased but a small quantity of Yams, not more than will supply the people a month, having had but an indifferent season & the Natives foreseeing our want of this article, they immediately assumed a prodigious price, which we were necessitated to comply with. Hogs was but scarce & those commonly ran small. Potatoes was also far from being plenteous. The Fern root, which was exceedingly sweet & luscious, was bought in great quantities.

The Natives, during the whole of our stay, were affable, friendly & courteous. This Island [Ni'ihau] has by far the most barren appearance of any of the Windward Isles. The Southern parts are covered with very long grass. Otherwise, [this Island is] destitute of Tree or Shrub. The Northern parts, which is hilly, we have but little knowledge of its produce, but with our glasses could distinguish wood on the sides of the steep hills. Nor are the Inhabitants Numerous or wealthy.

We have now salted & cured at the whole of these Island 40 puncheons of pork and a stock of salt consisting of 16 puncheons, besides the quantity expended in Curing the Meat.

Sandwich Islands are a group consisting of 12 in Number situated between the Latitude of 18°50′ & 22°15′ North and Longitude 199°30′ & 205°15′ East from the Meridian of Greenwich and lying in the Direction of ESE and NWN per Compass. The most Eastern one, called by the Natives Haw'yhe'e or O'why'he, is the largest and is to be seen at least 30 or 35 leagues in a clear day. The high snowy peak is a Mountain of immense height on the NE part of the Island, nor does the Land on the SW part fall much short of this, whose summit is also Covered with snow. We frequently try'd soundings on the Northern Coasts, but could get no bottom with our greatest scope of line. The Southern parts were almost equally fathomless, except a small bight we stood into to the Eastward of the Southern point, where we had regular soundings of 50 & 55 fathoms over a bottom of fine sand. This Island is divided into six provinces or Districts, the names of which are, agreeable to the Natives, distinguished by A'poo'na, A'Kon'a, Ka'oo, Ka'har'ra, A'Macooa and A'Tee'doo. The Bay of Karica'coo'a lies in the third of these provinces, & the great bay of the Tee-yah-yah in the fourth.

The Isle of Mow-wee is situated to the NNW of this extensive Island, whose hills are also of great height. We saw it at the distance of two or three and thirty leagues. Its divided by an isthmus into two distinct provinces, the names of which we were not able to procure. The northern shores of this Island, like the other, is steep and affords no soundings, but to the SE, between it and the adjacent Isles, we got regular depths with 150 fms, a bottom of sand. From off the West point, which is low, runs a shore extending across towards the other Islands at some considerable distance. To the Southward of this is a fine spacious sandy beach, shaded with Cocoa Nutt Trees and many habitations of the Indians. It appeared to afford good shelter for landing and doubtless a good anchorage. The high land over this is extremely steep, falling in deep Chasams, & conveys the most romantic appearance. The Natives gave us information of a good harbour lying to the Southward of the Easternmost point, which they affirm'd was superior to that of Karicacooa.

The other Islands, Morrotoi, Ranai, & Ka-hoo-nowee, fall short of the two latter in point of fruitfulness. The hills are quite barren and, as is the low land, destitute of Shrub or house. Morrotoi in appearance in respect to its produce is very similar to the Island O'neehow. We had occasion therefore to conjecture this to be a Yam Country. The Western parts of Ranai is some little wood with a few dwellings of the Indians.

Wou'ahoo is the next. This Island is inferior to none in fertility. Those parts that fell under our observations are to a degree fruitful, well clothed with wood, as well Cocoa Nutts & other fruit trees, which afford the most pleasing prospects. Most parts of this Country was Cultivated & the Villages equally numerous with many plantations. We have therefore reason to believe as well from these circumstances, as the number of Natives we saw along its Shores, that the Island is well peopled. The Shores are very low but the hills rise to a great height.

Atoui [is] the next westernmost Island which abounds with every refreshment and necessarys of the other Islands. It lies 23 leagues to the WNW of Wou'ahoo. We could get no bottom on the West coast, being steep and rocky. The inland parts are mountainous and woody.

O'neehow is the last of any note, and that but a barren spot yielding scarcely any other refreshment than Yams & Salt. Its distance from Atoui is 6 leagues in the direction of SW. The other small Islands are Onnehou'a, Ta'oora, and Tamatta-papapa. This latter lies to the SW of O'neehow, Ta'oora to the SW also & Onnehou'a lying to the NW. Tamatta-papapa is situated to the SW of O'neehow, its just place we were not able to find, steering too much to the westward.

March 16th The Island of Ta'oora distance about a league. A Canoe came along side with a quantity of sweet root, which we purchased. They afterwards left us & directed their course towards Ta'oora. At ½ past 5 bore away in search of the Island Tamatta-papapa.

March 17th [We] made the Signal for the Discovery to come under our stern, a swell continuing from the Northward. Brought too for our Consort. At ½ past 5 bore away again. In the evening the horizon was extremely clear, not the least appearance of any land, we therefore hauled our wind, having given over our search of Tamatta-papapa, which island I am firmly persuaded lies in a more Southerly direction than that which we steered, our true Course from Ta'oora being SEBW, distance 50 miles.

PART FOUR
HOMEWARD

INTRODUCTION

With Cook dead, Clerke and the remaining officers could have easily abandoned the voyage and returned to England. But Clerke was implacable. In happier times, he and Cook decided to return to the Arctic the following summer to learn if the ice pack could be penetrated at an earlier time of year. Despite failing health that often confined the captain to his cabin, the expedition sailed north again.

Leaving Hawai'i in mid-March, the ships sailed to the northwest for six weeks. As they entered northern latitudes the weather became cold and foggy until they reached Avacha Bay and the port of Petropavlovsk on the Kamchatka Peninsula, which was then called the Village of St. Peter and St. Paul. From this remote Russian outpost on the Pacific, Vitus Bering embarked on his two voyages fifty years earlier. It was still ice-bound in late April. Based on the reports of Ismailov in Unalaska, they anticipated a significant and prosperous colony of Russians, but it was only a small village with a handful of soldiers. Ledyard said the Russian guard amounted to "just 15 or 20 miserable looking men commanded by a serjeant and about 60 Indians." Although friendly, the Russians were overcome by a difficult winter themselves, with most of them disabled by scurvy, so they were alarmed when two armed ships entered the bay. They refused all assistance, perhaps because they had little to give.

The English needed supplies before they tested the ice again, so King, Gore, and Webber bravely embarked on a four-day river and dogsled journey overland for supplies. When they reached Bolsheretsk on the other side of the peninsula, over one hundred miles away, they found it no more impressive than Petropavlovsk, with just a few more buildings and a handful of cattle to distinguish it. But they also found Major Magnus von Behm, the fort's commander, who was eager to support the voyagers. He quickly undertook a substantial return expedition from his meager colony, plodding back over the spine of the peninsula to stock the vessels for their northward journey.

The English were in Avacha Bay for six weeks and in that time Behm fully resupplied the expedition without charge. But soon it was time to test the Arctic Sea. As they readied to sail, a nearby volcano exploded, the ash and cinders falling as they left the bay. "We had again the small shock of an earthquake and heard a hollow rumbling noise in the air," Ledyard wrote. "It became almost as dark as night. The mountain exploded with a tremendous shock that convulsed everything around us . . . the atmosphere was one continuous sheet of flame. Soon after it began to thunder there fell showers of small fragments of lava about the size of a walnut." The travelers were just twenty miles from the volcano, so the two ships and nearby shore were soon covered with mud and ash, which Burney later wrote "lay several inches thick on our decks."[1]

Leaving the eruption behind, for nearly three weeks the explorers followed the Kamchatka coast, usually enshrouded in a thick fog, passing Bering Strait on July 6.

They soon came to the ice pack, a continuous, impassable wall that prevented further progress. Cook had hoped that entering the Arctic Sea in July would allow further penetration in the ice, but the ice held fast to shore and impeded forward progress. On July 19 they reached 70°31′ in a deep bay formed by this solid ice, a few miles short of Cook's northernmost point from the prior summer.

Clerke's health deteriorated quickly. On July 21, still anticipating another opening north, he considered his plans to move along the ice to the Siberian coast, writing,

> I therefore think it the best step I can take for the good of the service to trace the Ice over to the Asiatic Coast, try if I can find a Hole that will admit me any farther North, if not see whats to be done upon that Coast where I hope but cannot much flatter myself with meeting better success, for this Sea is now so Choak'd with Ice that a passage I fear is totally out of the question.[2]

This was his final journal entry. Burney then took up Clerke's pen to continue the log of the expedition. After again challenging the ice along the barrier from Alaska to Siberia, on July 27 Clerke abandoned the search and ordered the ships to return to Avacha Bay. On August 10 he wrote his final letter to Joseph Banks, offering his personal commentary of the voyage outcome. He also wrote Gore and King, who he knew would soon take command of the two ships, on the prospects for returning to England. On August 22, 1779, he died at age thirty-eight in sight of the Kamchatka coast, a year after Anderson and six months after Cook.[3]

Two days later the ships reached the harbor and Clerke was laid to rest. Unlike Cook, whose few remains were committed to Kealakekua Bay, Clerke was buried ashore on the grounds of a church in a nearby village. Gore insisted the burial be given the most solemn ceremony, so the crew and local Russian soldiers marched in procession offering "great respect and solemnity." King wrote,

> in the afternoon we paid our last offices to Captain Clerke, with all the decency and ceremony we could, the officers and men of both ships walking in procession to the Grave whilst the ships fyred minute guns, and the service being over, the marines fyred three vollies. Captain Gore was prevailed upon, by our good friend the priest, to bury Captain Clerke here, rather than at Paratoonca, as that church is so soon to be removed. This Reverend Gentleman walked in the procession with the gentleman who read the service, and all the Russians attended with a great deal of respect.

After the burial the crews planted willows around the grave, and Gore inscribed a wooden plaque or escutcheon that was posted in the nearby Russian Orthodox Church.[4]

The expedition stayed in Kamchatka another seven weeks, the longest stop on the voyage. The first day the temperature was 70°, a marked improvement from their time in the same bay several months earlier, let alone after nearly two months in the fog and ice. The Virginian, John Gore, took command, returning to Cook's flagship, and King was appointed as captain of the *Discovery*. Burney also moved to the *Resolution*, now second in command of the flagship, and stopped writing in his journal.

The English found the Native people of the village of Petropavlosk peaceable and reserved, but they kept their distance from the British. Like their time in Unalaska, it seemed the Native people were restrained by the Russians and were allowed little contact with visitors. At the same time the Russian soldiers were roundly criticized in British journals, as they seemed lazy and ineffectual, simply collecting tribute in furs and otherwise relying on Native servants to do the work. "The settlements at this Bay appear to be more in a state of decay than improvement," Gilbert wrote, "for the Russians don't seem to make any effort either to extend their Navigation, or increase the number of their vessels. And so great is their indolence that they rather choose to live in the most wretched state of any people we ever saw, than to be at the least labour to cultivate the Country."

King wrote of the dismal record of Russian conquest of the Aleutians and Kodiak Island, particularly how they had recently suffered a setback in Kodiak. He speculated that the only way the Russians would come to dominate Kamchatka, the Aleutian Islands, and Alaska would be through the ravages of time. He was told that smallpox and other diseases had killed a large part of the Native population in the region near Okhotsk, where as many as 20,000 had recently died. Whole villages were depopulated, and the people who survived intermarried with the Cossacks to form a new population. He expected the same for the Aleutians. "Such has been the effects of this terrible visitation which having so diminished them," he concluded, "and at the same time fresh supplies of soldiers, Cossacks and banished men being sent here who intermix by marriage with the natives, that I should suppose in a short time there will be very few of the original natives remaining, which I think will be of little service to the country, for the Kamskadales are a laborious quiet set of people as I ever saw, whereas the Soldiers and Cossacks are the Idlest drones one can conceive, glad enough to connect themselves with the Kamskadales and to be kept by them."

In early October the spruce beer ran out, about the same time the carpenters, coopers, and sail makers completed refitting the ships. The Siberian terrain also began to turn to winter again. "The Summer here is of a very short duration," Gilbert wrote, "being little more than four months; for by October the Country began to have quite a wintry appearance; the trees and Bushes having entirely lost their verdure, and the weather grown cold."[5]

In a week the ships were underway, finally bound for England, returning down the coast of Russia, past the little-known Kurile Islands and Japan, then to Canton for supplies. While they sold many of the sea otter furs they collected along the Northwest Coast in Kamchatka, several sailors were wise enough to save their furs for the merchants of China, where they realized astounding profits. "One of our Gentlemen purchased eleven prime Skins for double the number of large green beads," King wrote, "which here would have sold for 80 or 100 Dollars each." Midshipman George Gilbert reported "We sold the remainder of our furs to much greater advantage than at Kamchatka, the Chinese being eager to purchase them and gave us 50 to 70 Dollars a skin . . . for what we bought with only a hatchet or a saw."

When the sailors learned the value of the sea otter furs, they wanted to return to Alaska and the Northwest Coast to trade for more furs. King complained, "the rage with which our Seamen were possessed to return to Cook's River and buy another cargo of skins to make their fortunes was at one time not far short of mutiny." He feared the sailors would insist on an immediate return north, despite the condition of the ships, but England was at war and the sailors were already "too much chagrined at having been so long out of the road of honourable achievements" that they continued home. Nonetheless, rumors of the fantastic profits made by the sailors in Canton soon fueled a new fur industry on the Northwest Coast and, after returning to England, many of the sailors led the effort.

After nearly four years away, in China they finally had some news from home. The greatest surprise was that the American colonies were at war with England and that the French had joined the colonists in the fight. Gore and Ledyard were both Americans, so reports of the rebellion must have prompted a few anxious moments between them and the other crewmen. "What a conflict of passions did this mighty flood of new matter occasion," King remarked, "America declaring herself independent so soon after our departure, supporting for a length of time her declaration at last aided by France. England our dear long absent and distant country, so often wished for, to be so situated with Spain also preparing to annoy her was intelligence sufficient to rouse the dullest and most slavish mind amongst us."

Leaving Macao in mid-January, the ships made good progress sailing to Africa, but a gale in the Indian Ocean damaged the *Resolution,* requiring them to put into port at the Cape of Good Hope to again repair and refit the beleaguered flagship, the ship's last renovation. Here Williamson and Phillips fought a duel, as they bitterly blamed each other for the death of Cook in Hawai'i.

In mid-July, four years after leaving England, the weary travelers entered the English Channel. They expected a triumphant return, but an easterly storm drove them northwest into the Irish Sea. The winds did not abate for several days until they anchored in Stromness harbor in the Orkney Islands, north of Scotland. King and Webber disembarked and went overland to deliver the journals, sketches, and charts to the Admiralty. With King gone, Gore promoted Burney to command the *Discovery.* After a month favorable winds finally took them down the east coast of England. On October 7, 1780, the ships anchored at the Royal Dockyards at Deptford, on the southern bank of the Thames River near Greenwich.[6]

Thanks to Major Behm, the death of Captain Cook in Hawai'i was already well-known throughout England and the rest of Europe. Clerke gave Cook's journal and other expedition papers to Behm when the expedition met him in May 1779, and they were safely delivered to the Admiralty the following January. The earlier letter Cook gave to Ismailov in Unalaska arrived in March. On January 11, 1780, ten months before the ships returned, the *London Gazette* offered the following solemn report:

> Captain Clerke of His Majesty's Sloop *Resolution*, in a letter to Mr. Stephens, dated the 8th of June 1779, in the Harbour of St. Peter and St. Paul, Kampschatka, which was received yesterday, gives the melancholy account of the celebrated Captain Cook, late commander of that Sloop, with four of his private Marines having been killed on the 14th of February last at the island of O'Why'he, one of a group of new discovered

> Islands in the 22nd Degree of North Latitude, in an affray with a numerous and tumultuous Body of the Natives.

An obituary for Cook appeared the same day:

> This untimely and ever to be lamented Fate of so intrepid, so able, and so intelligent a Sea-Officer, may justly be considered as an irreparable Loss to the Public, as well as to his Family, for in him were united every successful and amiable quality that could adorn his Profession; not was his singular Modesty less conspicuous than his other Virtues. His successful Experiments to preserve the Healths of his Crews are well known, and his Discoveries will be an everlasting Honour to his Country.[7]

There was little excitement when the vessels arrived nearly a year after the announcement of Cook's death, except for the pleasure of families seeing the safe return of the weary sailors. Promotions and appointments were awarded, wages were paid, and the artifacts and collections of flora and fauna were sent to the Royal Society for safekeeping. But for Britons still at war with their rebellious colonies there was no reason to celebrate. The Northwest Passage had not been found and both Captains Cook and Clerke were dead.

"Thus ended a long, tedious and disagreeable voyage," Gilbert concluded, "of four years, and three months, during which we lost only seven persons by sickness, who all belonged to the Resolution, and three by accident belonging to Discovery, exclusive of those who were killed with our great and unfortunate Commander." At that time the third voyage was the longest single exploring voyage in history. Remarkably, no one died from scurvy, a true testament to Cook's determination and commitment to the health of his crews. A century earlier it would not have been uncommon for such lengthy voyages to lose one-third of their crews to scurvy.[8]

The news of Cook's death overshadowed the results of the voyage, as he had come to represent the best of the Age of the Enlightenment in Europe, a humane explorer and great gentlemen. He singularly enjoyed the great variety of people, cultures, and civilizations he met while introducing the western world to the near boundless limits of the globe. It was said that King George III openly wept when told of Cook's death. Just as important, he revolutionized shipboard hygiene. When news of his death reached London, the *London Evening Post* praised Cook for losing just one sailor to sickness on the entire second voyage.[9]

The published accounts of the first and second voyages had already gone into several editions so the anticipated demand for the published account of the third voyage was high. The Admiralty hired John Douglas, who had helped Cook with the second voyage account, and he merged Cook's manuscript with the entries from King's journal after Hawai'i. King received credit as co-author. John Webber oversaw production of the engravings and Henry Roberts prepared the charts. It took several London engravers four years to complete the task. Despite a discouraging delay, the official account of the third voyage finally appeared in June 1784.[10]

Later that year Roberts prepared the comprehensive general chart of the three voyages, which for the first time offered a reasonably accurate map of the Pacific

Ocean. Roberts wrote a long memoir about how he worked with Cook to construct the map, then embellished the chart with other source material after Cook's death:

> Soon after our departure from England I was instructed by Captain Cook to complete a map of the world as a general chart from the best materials he was in possession of for that purpose and before his death this business was in great measure accomplished. That is, the grand outline of the whole was arranged, leaving only those parts vacant or unfinished which he expected to fall in with and explore. But on our return home, when the fruits of our voyage were ordered by the Lords Commissioners of the Admiralty to be published, the care of the general chart being consigned to me, I was directed to prepare it from the latest and best authorities, and also to introduce Captain Cook's three successive tracks, all his discoveries, that the different routes he had taken might appear together, by this means to give a general idea of the whole.
>
> This task having been performed by me, it is necessary for the information of the Reader to state the heads of the several authorities which I have followed in such parts of the chart as differ from what was drawn up immediately under the inspection of Captain Cook. And when the Public are made acquainted that many materials necessary to complete and elucidate the work were not at the time on board the *Resolution*, or in his possession, the reason will appear very obvious why these alterations and additions were introduced contrary to the original drawing.

After listing the materials he used that supplemented Cook's personal work, Roberts concluded by explaining "Every other part of the chart not mentioned in this account is as originally placed by Captain Cook."[11]

1

Reaching Avacha Bay
March–June 1779

Sailing north from Hawai'i, shipboard routine was interrupted by a sudden flood below decks in the *Resolution*. Roberts offered an animated description of the catastrophe, where strong winds drove waves over the deck in a terrible gale in the middle of the Pacific. Soon the coal hold was awash with seawater and supplies and equipment were floating in the holds. The men bailed and pumped for their lives, finally gaining on the flood when the storm abated. As a reward, Clerke ordered an extra allowance of grog and provisions to the crew. In the same storm, Burney reported that the *Discovery* fell behind, lumbering north on shortened sails.

In late April the *Resolution* was the first to observe the coast of Kamchatka, which was still covered in deep snow. The weather was so frigid, the coldest temperature since leaving England, fires were lighted to warm the sailors below. Even so, one day the temperature in the cabin fell to 38°F. Struggling north in fog, sleet, and snowy weather, the rigging froze, slowing progress. The land was only seen occasionally through the mists. When they finally reached Avacha Bay, it was still frozen in the grip of winter, filled with ice. So the shore boats were used to pick their way through broken ice to reach shore. There the British found the fortification, or "ostrog," was small and poorly made, nothing like what they were told by Ismailov in Unalaska the previous fall.

Today this is the thriving port of Petropavlovsk-Kamchatsky, a town of over 250,000 people, but in the early spring of 1779 it was a bleak and foreboding place, covered in snow, with just two buildings and a handful of smaller log dwellings. "We saw a few log houses, and Conic shaped huts upon Poles," King wrote, "but their miserable appearance, and Smallness in Number, would not allow us to take it for St. Peter and St. Pauls Village . . . with our glasses we could discern two men Walking about the huts; we look'd round the bay but saw no more huts, no boats, no living Soul. Some few flocks of duck was all that enlightened this very silent solemn, waste prospect."[12]

The fort was in a desperate condition after a difficult winter so it could not offer provisions when the ships arrived. So King, Gore, and Webber, along with two Cossacks, went overland on foot and by dogsled to Bolsheretsk on the Sea of Okhotsk. There the sailors found Major Magnus von Behm, the governor of Kamchatka, who offered considerable aid, sending twenty head of cattle and nine hundred pounds of rye meal, as well as tobacco, tea, fresh butter, and rice overland to the ships. When Behm later arrived at the village, the ships saluted him as if he were royalty.

Burney was quite frank in reporting his impressions of the region and its inhabitants, especially the ravages of disease on the Native population and the tribute system imposed to collect furs, particularly the "sea beaver" or sea otter found in the islands to the west. Roberts was focused on repairs to the *Resolution* after the near disaster at sea. Even after reaching the relative safety of the bay, he observed "The Ship at this time making 7 or 8 inches [water] in the course of 24 hours." The carpenters found most of the protective planks under the water line so decayed that they disintegrated when touched. He wrote, "the sheathing entirely eaten by the worms to a perfect honeycomb." Fortunately, Roberts was more lucid after the ships returned from the Arctic to Avacha Bay, as he had considerable free time as the crew repaired the damaged ships. Meanwhile, Burney was burdened with new duties after Clerke's death, so he discontinued writing in his journal.

After suffering from the privations of Siberia on their arrival, soon the ice melted and the ships were able to reposition closer to shore. After several weeks provisioning the ships, taking advantage of advancing spring weather, they sailed for the Arctic again. Although Avacha Bay was free of ice, the ships' departure from Petropavlosk was as difficult as its entry. There were baffling winds, opposing seas and fog and, as they sailed out of the bay, a nearby volcano exploded, raining ash on the ships. Burney reported the volcano had been smoking for several days and "broke out in a violent eruption throwing out such a quantity of Ashes as darkened the Air and several times covered our decks." Roberts said the blasts generated lightning and thunderstorms throughout the region, as pumice stones fell on the ships, "some of which were ½ an inch in Diameter."

Journal of James Burney

Friday, March 26th, 1779 In the forenoon the Resolution made the Signal for Seeing Land, which however proved to be only a haze bank.

Saturday 27th At Noon Latitude in 19°49′ North, Longitude in 182°40′ East. From this Day Noon steered to the Northward of West [in the following days the crew observed turtles and sea birds from the deck . . . bearings omitted].

Tuesday, 30th At Noon Latitude 20°20′ North, Longitude 180°15′ East. The Trade wind being light and unsteady, Shaped our Course more towards the North.

Tuesday, April 6th This last week have steered nearly on one Course (between NW and NWBN). The Winds continuing Easterly till this forenoon. Latitude at Noon 30°06′ North, Longitude in 170°21′ East. Wind Northerly. Steering to the Westward.

Thursday, 8th Variable Winds and Squally Weather with much rain. Latitude at Noon 30°41′ North, Longitude in 167°32′ East. Course to the NNW.

Monday 12th Both the Ships Companies were put to whole allowance of Spirits. Many Sea birds about us. Passed a Log of Wood . . . From the 12th to the 17th Saw many Sea birds and passed a good deal of drift wood. 17th at Noon Latitude in 43°19′ North, Longitude 160°16′ East.

21st and 22nd Saw Geese, Ducks and other birds.

Friday 23rd Wind NE. A fresh breeze with Snow and Sleet. At 6 in the morning Saw the Coast of Kamtschatka bearing from NBE to WBS [and] made the Signal [to the *Resolution*]. At ½ past 6 had Soundings at 70 fathoms, Sand, 3 or 4 Leagues from the Shore. Our Latitude then 52°18′ North, Longitude 158°54′ East, the Land Broken, mountainous and covered with Snow.

From this to the 28th trying to get to the Northward towards the Bay of Awatscha. A fresh Gale from the NE with constant Snow, Sleet and foggy Weather.

23rd and 24th Frequently lost sight of the Resolution, but were lucky enough to join her again.

Sunday 25th In the Afternoon, again lost sight of the Resolution. Our Ship has some time past gone considerably worse than the Resolution. Shortening Sail for us these 3 last days has considerably detained her. As we did not see or hear any thing of her in the night or next day, we continued turning to the Northward for the Bay of Awatscha.

Wednesday 28th The Wind became moderate. At Noon Saw the Awachinskoy Mountain . . .

Thursday 29th Light Winds and fair. At Noon Saw the Entrance of the Bay of Awatscha, our Latitude Observed 52°39′ North. At 6 in the Evening were within 4 miles of the Eastern point of the Entrance into the Bay, on which is a lookout house. Saw the Entrance blocked up with Ice. Night coming on and the wind right in, hauld off till next morning. Fired guns in the Night as a Signal to the Resolution in case she should be within hearing.

Friday 30th At Daylight were 4 Leagues South of the lookout house point, light Northerly winds till 9, when it came round to the Southward. Stood towards the Bay again [with] the Ice Drifting out in large, broken fields . . . All the bays alongshore full of low Ice. Served Biscuit again, the yams being expended . . . caught plenty of Cod.

At 3 a breeze [came] from the Southward [so we] Weighd and Stood towards the Bay, the Entrance appearing quite clear of Ice. At 5 the Resolution's Cutter came out to us, the Resolution having Anchord in Awatscha Bay 2 days before. At 6 were in the entrance of the bay. At ½ past 10 Anchord in 7 fathoms about 4 miles distant from the Town of St. Peter and Paul . . .

Saturday, May 1st In the Morning got under Sail and ran father in, where we Anchord and Moored near the Resolution and about half a League from the Ostrog of St. Peter and Paul, not being able to get nearer for the Ice. The harbour of St. Peter and Paul is froze up. No part of the Shore is yet clear of Ice, nor the land clear of Snow. The Country all round the Bay, woody.

The Resolution Anchord in the Bay of Awatscha April 28th in the Afternoon. The Next Morning an Officer was Sent to the Ostrog of St. Peter and Paul with 2 Letters which Ismiloff, the Chief of the Russian factory at Oonalaska had given to Captain Cook: one directed to Major Behm, Governor of Kamtschatka, and the other to the Commanding Officer at this place. The Russians were much alarmed at the first appearance of Strangers; however, they sent sledges drawn by Dogs to the edge of the Ice for our people, boats not being able to get within a mile of the Ostrog. The Commanding Officer here, who is only a Serjeant, immediately sent an express to Bolcheretzkoi with the letter for Major Behm.

John Webber, "A View of the Town and Harbour of St. Peter & St. Paul, [Petropavlovsk]," circa 1781-83. Pen, wash, and water color panorama of the expedition's two lengthy 1779 visits to the Kamchatka community. The view looks east toward the entrance of Avacha Bay, with the tiny village shown on a sandy peninsula with raised native summer huts ("balagans") and Russian log homes. Dixson Library, State Library of New South Wales, PXX 2, f. 41.

The Inhabitants of St. Peter and Paul are about 40 Soldiers, some of whom have families, and scarcely so many Kamtschadales. These with the Men belonging to a Sloop in the Harbour (50) were all the people we found here. The evening after the Resolution arrived, we were within 4 miles of the lookout house. The Bay then appeared to be full of Ice, occasioned by part fast to the Shores within the Bay breaking off, which in Drifting out had choaked up the entrance. Night coming on, prevented our examining closer. This last winter, the Russians tell us has been the severest felt at Kamtschatka for many years past.

Our communication with the Ostrog would have been difficult and dangerous but for the civility of the Russians, who sent Sledges whenever a boat went to the edge of the Ice. The Sledges carrying safely over Ice and Snow that will not bear walking upon.

The Carpenters of both Ships were employed in Caulking the Resolutions Side and under her bends. All the latter part of our passage to Kamtschatka she had been very leaky.

Monday 3rd This morning our Jolly boat landing some Gentlemen, got closed in by the Ice. Sent the Launch to assist in getting her clear. The loose Ice setting in Shore hemmed in the Launch and one of the Resolutions Boats. The people belonging to the three boats went to the Ostrog and were entertained by the Russians till the next morning, when the Ice broke loose and we got the boats off again.

Tuesday 4th A Russian Merchant and a German, who was sent as an interpreter, arrived from Bolcheretzkoi and went on board the Resolution to wait on Captain Clerke. They made an excuse for the Major's not having sent an Officer down, it being understood from Ismiloffs letter that we were trading Ships. The

Major had sent directions to the Serjeant to give what assistance to the Ships he was able, without receiving any thing in return. Indeed, the Russians of St. Peter and Paul were as much in need of Assistance as able to Supply our wants, many of them being very bad with the Scurvy, on which account our Surgeons visited them every day. They complain that in the whole province of Kamtschatka there is not one Surgeon. They supplied us with fish and as much Game as they could Spare. They had Scarce any thing else we Stood in need of except 3 or 4 head of Cattle that belonged to private persons. Bullocks are the only live Stock [that] can be kept in Kamtschatka, Hogs, poultry, etc. being always destroyed by the Dogs, who are too necessary an Animal to part with.

Friday 7th Captain Gore, Lieut King and Mr. Webber, who Speaks German, set out with some Russians for Bolcheretzkoi. They went to the head of the bay in the Ships Boats and from thence in Sledges.

Tuesday 11th The Astronomers Observatory was erected on Shore at the Ostrog. The Ice having cleared away as far as the entrance of St. Peter and Paul Harbour, we unmoored and warped within ¾ of a mile of the Ostrog, where we Moored again, the point of the Peninsula on which the Ostrog Stands bearing NNW.

Thursday 13th The ground beginning to be clear of Snow, Sent a party on shore to cut Wood. Found nettle tops and Onions in every clear Spot. We likewise tapped the birch trees, which gave a good quantity of a clear sweet juice; with this the Ships companies allowance of Brandy was mixed every day. The Ice having in some places broke off from the Shore, caught with our Seane [seine] plenty of Salmon, Cod and flatfish.

Sunday 16th Got a Small Bullock from the Ostrog, which was killed for the use of the Ships Companies.

Monday 17th Alexander Macintosh, Carpenters Mate on board the Resolution, departed this life of a flux [dysentery or other infection].

Wednesday 19th This Afternoon, the Ice broke up and drifted out of the harbour of St. Peter and Paul.

Friday 21st At 8 in the Evening, the Governor (Major Behm) with Captain Gore, etc. arrived at the Ostrog from Bolcheretzkoi.

Saturday 22nd The Governor was Saluted with 13 Guns at going on board of the Resolution.

Tuesday 25th This Evening both Ships Saluted him with 13 Guns at his taking leave. The next morning early, he set off for Bolcheretzkoi. He made a present to the Officers of both Ships of Tea and Sugar, and to the Ships Companies of Tobacco, which was shared out 3 lbs. to every man that used Tobacco and one pound to each of those that did not. 20 head of Cattle are now on the Road from Bolcheretzkoi for the use of the Ships. As the melting of the Snow is likely to detain them, Captain Clerke is at liberty to use the Cattle belonging to private people at St. Peter and Paul, which the Major will see replaced. We are to be supplied with flower [flour]. Cordage or Ship Stores they have none. The Major has promised to Send for those Articles from Ochotzk [Okhotsk] and have them ready for us in case we should call here again in returning from the North.

An Order dated 1775 has been sent from the Empress to Kamtschatka, directing the Governor to assist any European Ships belonging to her Allies, that might stop here, on which account, nothing except a receipt was taken for these things the Ships were supplied with.

The Major had intelligence from the Tschuktschi [Chukchi] of two Ships being in these Seas. By their description it could only be known we were Strangers, the Russians having no larger Vessels hereabouts that Galliots. We likewise found the Meaning of the Russian Note given us on the Coast of America, which was a receipt for Skins given as tribute. The discovery of this Note was unlucky for Ismiloff at Oonalaska, who is suspected of underhand dealing, as it was not known before at Kamtschatka that any tribute was collected so far to the Eastward as where we got the note.

Friday 28th The Ships Companies were put to full allowance of bread, having been at 2/3rd since the 30th of November 1776. Biscuit and Flower now served alternately 1 lb. per Day. A much larger proportion of provisions remaining in our Ship than in the Resolution. She was supplied from us with 2 Hogsheads of Brandy and 7 Puncheons of Biscuit.

Thursday, June 3rd Received from the Shore for the use of the Ships 250 poods [about 36 pounds, Russian measure] of Flower equal to 8354 lbs . . . , of which we took only 428 lbs and the Resolution the remainder, to make the proportion of provisions equal in both Ships.

Friday 4th Fired 21 Guns, being the Anniversary of his Majesty's birth day.

Saturday 5th Twenty head of Cattle arrived from Bolcheretzkoi for the Ships, part of which was killed for present expense, and the remainder corned for Sea Service.

Mr. Baily's Observations make St. Peter and Paul in 53°00½' North Latitude and 158°37′ East Longitude from Greenwich, which differs very little from what it is laid down by the Russians . . .

The Ostrog of St. Peter and Paul stands on a low, narrow Slip of land behind which is the harbour. It consists of about 20 Balagans [beehive-like summer dwelling on stilts] and 8 or 9 log houses. The Sides of these houses are Stout timber piled horizontally, and the ends where they Cross at the corners so cut as not to hinder them from laying close to each other. The houses have in general a Small outer room, which serves for an entry and to keep lumber in, and a large inner room which occupies all the remaining Space. Within this is an Oven for Cooking and for heating their Apartment, which they do to an unwholesome degree, almost to suffocation. This and their eating scarce any vegetables may be the reason why they are so much afflicted with the Scurvy.

John Webber, "Summer and Winter Habitations in Kamschatka," circa 1781-83. Pen, wash, and water color view of local habitations on a peninsula of Petropavlovsk showing four summer huts or "balagans" with conical roofs resting on poles, with a partially buried winter house in the foreground. Three Natives in traditional dress are seating on a platform and walking into view. There is an upturned boat on the right. Dixson Library, State Library of New South Wales, PXX 2, f. 42.

In Behrings time there was a Church at the upper part of the harbour, and there is yet a Store house which he built and another house, which serves occasionally for Barracks or Hospital. The Church is removed to the West Side of Awatscha Bay at a small Kamtschadale Village called Paratunka, where except the pastor and his family, none but Kamtschadales reside. The pastor is himself half Kamtschadale, and a very friendly sensible old man.

There is in every Town a Chief of the Kamtschadales, called a Toyon, who is chosen by themselves and confirmed by the council at Bolcheretzkoi. His power is limited to the punishment of Small crimes only, such as neglect of business, etc. He is accountable for the tribute which is a fox skin and in some parts a Sable annually from every Male about the age of 18.

The Country is now very thinly inhabited. Great numbers were destroyed by the Small pox which was communicated to them by a Vessel from Okhotsk in the year 1768. This distemper spread like a plague through the Country, depopulating whole towns. The year after, the Natives made an insurrection in which Captain Nieloff the then Governor, was killed. The leader of this was a Polander sent hither as an exile, who seized upon a Vessel belonging to some Merchants and escaped to China and from thence to Europe. By the small pox and these commotions, upwards of 20,000 Kamtschadales perished, 8,000 of them males who paid tribute.

To quiet these disorders Major Behm was sent here, and is now on the point of returning to Petersburg, having already solicited and obtained leave. He is much beloved and respected here, particularly by the Kamtschadales, who speak of his departure as a misfortune and as such dread the approaching time. Captain Smealoff, who is next in command, is to succeed him. The present tribute to the Crown from Kamtschatka is valued at not much more than 10,000 Rubles yearly (about £2000). In almost every little cove round the Bay of Awatscha we saw the remains of Old Towns and Houses now desolate but which bespeak the Country to have been formerly well peopled. At this time there are no Towns or Villages near Awatscha Bay except St. Peter and Paul, and Paratunka, in both of which cannot be reckoned two hundred Kamtschadales including those married to the Russians.

The Fur Trade in Kamtschatka is mostly carried on by a company of merchants instituted by the Empress. They are distinguished by wearing a gold medal and their number limited to 14. This company have not an exclusive right, but only some peculiar privileges, which are not granted to other Merchants. This Trade employs but few vessels and those small ones. The furs are mostly collected among the Islands between Kamtschatka and America, where are Russian Settlements. They have one Settlement to the East of the Island Oonalaska near the high Mountains. They likewise trade and receive tribute from the Northern Kuriliki [Kurile] Islands. With the Southernmost they have scarce any communication. They are said to be inhabited by hairy people. Two children not long ago were brought to Kamtschatka, who had hair growing on all parts of their bodies. This fact was attested by Major Behm. Spangberg likewise mentions these people as inhabiting Urupe, one of the Jep Islands.

The Merchants at Kamtschatka will give 15 Rubles for a good Sea Beaver Skin. Considering the Taxes, expence of Carriage, Risks, etc. etc. besides profits to different Merchants, one may very well venture to credit the accounts told of their value being above 90 Rubles in China. Their trade to China is not direct; all goods are landed at a Russian Settlement called Ookoi, which lies North of the River Amur, from where they are sent partly by Rivers and partly by land Carriage.

The forces at this time in the province of Kamtschatka, which includes all the Country East of the Penghinska Sea (the whole being under one command) are about 700, part Russians, part Cossacks.

The Anadirskoi Ostrog is abandoned as being too remote. The Strongest garrison the Russians have to the Northward is Indjiga, which lays West of the Penghinska Gulf and is within the district subject to the Commanding Officer at Okhotsk.

We get no intelligence or information concerning the Seas beyond Behrings Straits, none of the Russian Charts extended so far North but what were copied from Behrings.

Saturday 12th This Afternoon got under Sail and Stood towards the mouth of the Bay. At 7 Anchord again 4 miles below the Ostrog.

Sunday 13th Kept in all day by baffling winds.

Monday 14th In the Morning Weighd, but at 9 the Wind came right in from the Sea with a thick fog. Anchord about 2 miles within the lookout house point, in 8 fathoms mud. Boats on Shore all the Afternoon gathering greens.

Tuesday 15th This morning, the Awachinskoi [Avachinsky] Mountain, after burning very fiercely these 3 days past, broke out in a violent eruption throwing out such a quantity of Ashes as darkened the Air and several times covered our decks. This Mountain is the Easternmost of the two on the North Side of Awatscha Bay. The other is likewise now smoking.

Wednesday 16th At daylight Weighed with a light breeze Northerly, and Sailed out of the Bay. The remainder of this and the next day, Standing alongshore to the Eastward with light variable winds.

Journal of Henry Roberts

[After leaving Hawai'i, the journal records four weeks of bearings, coordinates, soundings, wind, weather, and ship duties with the *Discovery* in company. At first Roberts observes moderate trade winds and pleasant weather. This changed to frequent gales and cold weather as they sailed north entering the latitude of Siberia.

In the first days at sea Roberts reported sighting several porpoises, turtles, albatross, boobies, and men of war birds about the ship. The crew even caught several sharks. It was "disagreeably hot and sultry." There was an "appearance of land" on March 26, which proved false, and instead, was just a "cloud or haze bank." In the dreary time at sea, Roberts reported the crew kept busy on menial tasks. The carpenters painted and caulked the quarterdeck while the marines exercised in the hot sun until an unexpected flood occurred in the cargo deck in mid-April.

But after sailing north for two weeks, the weather changed. The first hostile weather featured lightening and rain, which soon increased to a gale with rain squalls. Later Roberts observed snow showers and sleet as they approached Kamchatka. He complained of "cold raw weather" and reported that the thermometer reached its lowest point on the voyage in the three years since leaving England. Despite the weather, the crew regularly observed puffins, sea gulls, ducks, and drifting rafts of sea weed.]

Wednesday, April 14th On examining the Cole [coal] hole found a great quantity of water had lodged there, the place being full up to the middle deck, which with the violent pressure of that body of water, was blown up on the larboard side. Our situation was somewhat alarming. The assistance of a pump through the Decks would be rendered useless by immediately being choked with the Coals, and to back it at this time was impossible, being a number of weighty things afloat, which would endanger a mans limbs or life by the velocity of the surge occasiond by the violence of the Ships motion. We were therefore reduced to skuttle the bulk head in the Fore hold, which task was not executed without great trouble and fatigue to the people, until two O'Clock in the Morning, when it answered the desired affect. The water finding a course to the pumps, we were then employed bailing out the Cole hole & pumping the remainder of the Night, and whole of the Day. The Carpenters sustained some little life, by most with pain.

Hard gales and squally. The leak we now find to have increased very much. The water flowing tolerable freely to the pumps keeps the hands constantly at them. A continuance of the Gale with thick hazy weather and a high sea. Employed bailing and pumping.

Thursday, April 15th Strong Gales and Squally weather. The Ships Company at two Watches, one watch continually bailing and pumping. Burnt a false fire to the Discovery, not Answered. Repeated the Signal which was answered. Served the people an extra allowance of Grog. PM The Gale decreasing. Served the people an extra allowance of provisions.

Friday 16th The Water appearing discoulor'd, sounded with 160 fms but had no bottom. We have now the satisfaction to find the water drain aft to the pumps, which delivered us from the disagreeable fatigue of bailing. Put the people to 3 watches as usual. Kept our pump in motion.

Monday 19th Fresh Gales with showers of snow and Sleet. The Weather intense, cold and raw. Showers of thick snow with a great Western Sea. This morning ¾ of a Degree lower than any time since our leaving England. 48°28′ North Latitude and 161°43′ East Longitude.

Friday 23rd Thick misty weather. Saw many wild fowl. The Discovery fired a Gun which was answered. Tack'd Ship, imagining ourselves near the Eastern coast of Kamtschatka.

At 6 Saw Land appearing through the haze bearing NW. At ½ past we Tacked about 5 leagues from the nearest shore, which was a bluff head bearing WBS. The extremes to the Southward of this point, which is remarkable for its spiral rocks, appeared something like a bay, the Country affording a most dreary aspect, the hills being totally buried in snow & the shores steep and rocky. The summits of the Mountains hid in the haze.

Saturday 24th A moderate breeze and close cloudy weather. Saw the land again [and] At this time large flocks of wild fowl about. Tacked about 4 leagues from the Shore. We had now a tolerable sight of the Coast, which in general is straight, although there are appearances of bays, which most probably is a deception of the snowy land that lies within the skirts of the shore, which are so steep & broken that snow cannot possibly lie on these parts. They therefore make like so many different points and head lands to people who are unacquainted with these Snowy Coasts. One point seem to form an Inlet that is before Mentioned, being the spiral point, and another bluff head due North [is] a rocky head. It was some people's opinion that they saw wood upon particular parts of the shore.

Sunday 25th Wore Ship and stood in for the land [which was] under our lee when two openings appeared. At Noon we Tack'd 3 or 4 leagues from the Northernmost, which we judge to be the Bay of Awatscha, from the situation of the ship, the latter being by Dead Reckoning. Peterpawlowska harbour lies agreeable to their [Russian map] account 9 or 10 miles from the mouth of the bay. This distance accordingly applied to our distance from the entrance gives the latitude of 53°07′ North. This was the Northern point of the Entrance, which shows itself with several high detached rocks lying near it.

Monday 26th Saw nothing of the Discovery. Tack'd and stood in for the land again, the Northern point of the Entrance about 3 leagues, which we still judge to be the bay of Awatscha. Standing off all the Night with the thick weather and a severe frost being piercing cold. Wore Ship, it blowing very hard at times, with a heavy fall of snow, which rendered it so exceedingly thick that it was absolutely impossible to distinguish any object a quarter of a Mile. Our rigging being Froze to a Degree very solid cake of Ice, found the Time had stopped, probably occasioned by the intense cold weather, as the Thermometer was 38° in the Cabin where it hung.

Tuesday 27th The weather very thick occasioned by the heavy fall of snow. Tackd & made the most of our sails endeavouring to turn into the bay before night. The weather cold & raw and our rigging still covered with ice.

Wednesday 28th Turning to windward, endeavouring to reach the bay. At 6 in the evening we were close in with the Shore, not more than 2 miles distant. We sailed past an Island with two remarkable spiral rocks lying to the Northward of it with a spit of rocky Ground. The point which we take for Awatscha is cliffy with a rock lying at a small distance off it. The Country near the water side is of a middling height, much covered with snow & most parts well clothed with a small kind of brush wood.

We stretched off during the night under single reefed topsails and at 12 Tackd & stood in for the bay of Awatscha when at 3 the wind, shifting to our disadvantage, we were obliged to stand off again until 7, when the wind somewhat favouring us, we tackd & made all sail for the harbour with a light breeze.

At 8 the wind lessening with fine weather being much clearer than at any time we have had it since our falling in with the Coast. The haze clearing away from over the land shew us several Mountains of immense height intirely covered with snow with many ranges of hills not equally high but equally buried in snow. The highest of the Mountains is situated to the Northward of the bay of Awatscha, which we conjecture to be the same the Russians make mention of as being a Volcano. Yet we could perceive no appearance of smoke issuing from its top, which makes in a peak & descends gradually on all sides to a base of a great extent.

At Noon the weather exceedingly clear & pleasant, which gave us a gentle thaw that rid us of our burden of Ice that had froze to the rigging.

Thursday 29th At 5 we were in the entrance, having brought soundings from 22 fms. From the Northern head there's a reef of sunken rocks extending 3 or 4 miles from the Main. The outer land to the Northward, which we apprehend to be near the Kronotsckoi [Kronotsky] Cape, stands a watch tower belonging to the Russians, with a staff to hoist a flag when necessary (as a signal most probably) to their settlement in the Bay. The entrance of the Bay is about 4 miles in extent.

At 6 we were in the narrowest part of the bay, that is about 3 miles wide and depth of water 52 fms. Sent the Cutter ahead to sound and followed under an easy sail. Having sailed about 4 miles from the mouth of the Bay, we were obliged to anchor in 6½ fms away to the upper part of the Bay, being froze entirely across, with thick field ice. We perceived a few houses in a Cove on the NE Shore, which we concluded to be the settlement of St. Peter and Paul.

The following morning at daylight sent the boats away in quest of a more commodious harbour, when Mr. King and some other of the officers went to the Village. In a short time the boats returned from sounding, having found convenient anchoring abreast of the Town at the Distance of a Mile or a Mile & half from it, a Shoal bank also a little to the Southward of it, with not more than 1½ or 2 fms water on it. To the SE of this the water deepens and seems to afford a good channel into the harbour, which is at present choak'd with Ice, as the Shores in general are at the distance of ½ a mile or more fairly blockaded by it. The land round the bay is of a moderate height, much covered with snow and tolerably cloathed with wood of the birch specie.

Friday 30th Towing in towards the harbour, Mr. King and party came on board, having been received on shore with the greatest politeness by the Russians, consisting of a Serjeant, his guard & several others, with a number of Kamtschadales likewise in their service. The Town is situated on a low point of land stretching off from the East shore towards a high bluff head, & somewhat within it, forming a narrow passage, which afterwards oppens into a small but good harbour, in which place they have a Sloop or more properly a dogger of about 60 Tons. To the Northward of the harbour are two large buildings, one of which is the Magazine for stores & provisions, the other an hospital for the sick & hurt. The Harbour [is] entirely frozen over & the shores before the Town much encumbered with Ice for a considerable distance off.

In the evening we anchored close to this Ice about a mile and a half from the settlement. The nearest part of the East shore about ¾ of a mile. Carried out a warp and moored ship NE & SW, the hardest gales generally blowing from that quarter (which is also most oppen to the Sea) when moored. Carpenters preparing a floating stage to repair and stop the leak. [We] could have no connection with the shore but by the Sledges drawn with dogs upon the Ice, which we were furnished with from the Russians. Thermometer Noon 38°. Saw the Discovery in the offing, standing in for the Harbour. Sent the cutter out to assist her in getting in.

Saturday, May 1st Great quantities of drift Ice floating about with the tides. The Carpenters employed caulking the bends, the Ship concealing very much in those parts, which we were not able to get seamed at our last port. We filled a number of water casks along side and got them aft in the quarter deck in order to bring the ship by the stern to enable the Carpenters to get at the leak, which we find to be under water. The Ship at this time making 7 or 8 Inches [water] in the course of 24 hours. We endeavoured to cutt through the Ice but we found it so very thick and impenetrable that we failed in the attempt. The Discovery anchored near us.

Sunday 2nd Thick snowy weather with a SE gale [so we were] not able to employ the people or get any communication with the shore.

Monday 3rd Great quantities of Ice drifting over from the opposite shore occasioned by the wind blowing from that direction. Punished Robert Davies, quarter master, with 12 lashes for neglect of duty & for mutinous expressions. Thermometer Midnight 28°.

Tuesday 4th Came on board a Russian merchant and Linguist from Bolchaiscka [Bolsheretsk] sent by the Governor. Much ice floating in the bay. Thermometer Midnight 30°.

Wednesday 5th Vast quantities of Ice drifting about. Heald the Ship, being already as much by the stern as we could get her, having everything out of the Fore hold. The Carpenters, on stripping the sheathing off round & under the bends upon the bow, found the seams quite oppen & many parts in the plank, as well that of the Trunnel, entirely decayed. But it was not owing altogether to these defects that the leak had been occasioned for on examining the butt ends at the stern we found them oppen and in a bad condition.

Thursday 6th A fresh Gale from the NE with a thick fall of snow. Carpenters caulking under the fore castle, the weather not permitting them to work on the leak. Thermometer Midnight 32° Noon 39½°.

Friday 7th Less wind and Cloudy with some snow showers. Part of the Ice broke up from the shore when a large piece drifting all night with the tide. The Carpenters, repairing the defects under the bow, found many of the Trunnels so rotten as to take them out with their fingers. Captain Gore and Lieut King set out for Bolchaiscka to wait on the Governor, accompanied by those Russians who visited us on the 4th.

Saturday 8th Sent to see if there was a possibility of cutting wood, when we found impracticable the snow lying so very deep. Thermometer Midnight 32° Noon 36°.

Sunday 9th The Ice breaking up from the shore very fast. The Ship still on a heel & the Carpenters hard employed.

Monday 10th Blowing a strong Gale with cold but dry weather. Our Carpenters were not able to work on the leak, the water working over the stage, as was the case many days when a moderate Gale only blew. The Cooper on shore repairing, having cleared the snow away from a spot abreast of the Ship, where there was a run of water in which place we fixed a tent. Thermometer Midnight 32° Noon 39½°.

Tuesday 11th Weigh'd the anchors and warped the Ship nearer the Shore, as it would be more convenient to wood & water when the season should permit. Carpenters employed on the leak were obliged to strip more sheathing off, finding the Bends very much decayed and the seams, as before, intirely oppen.

Wednesday 12th Came too again in 9½ fms and moor'd as before, the Russian Ostrog bearing NW ¾ mile, the mouth of the bay being shut in with this part that where we now lay [was] landlocked. Sent a party of hands on shore to fall Trees for wood, which was yet impossible to cut up, for the snow that now thaws fast. Thermometer Midnight 37° Noon 45°.

Thursday 13th The Ship yet on the heel & the Carpenters at work found great part of the sheathing entirely eaten by the worms to a perfect honeycomb, which they were obliged to shift with new plank. Cooper repairing the Casks & Sailmakers on the sails. Hands wooding. Boild a quantity of wild parsley & other Greens in portable soup every morning for the peoples breakfast. Thermometer Midnight 32°.

Sunday 16th Sent the people to haul the seine abreast of the Ship. Caught a large quantity of fine flat fish & trout sufficient to serve the Ships Company. Boiled greens in the broth as usual. Sent the Butchers on shore to kill a small Bullock sent on board for the use of the people weighing 272 lbs. AM Served the Crews of both sloops 1½ lbs. per man.

Monday 17th Employed giving the Ship a heel to port, the Carpenters having finished the larboard side. People on shore wooding. Hauled the Seine and met with equal success as before. At midnight departed this life Alexander MacIntosh, one of the carpenters mates, who had been long ill of a flux. At 11 AM committed his body to the Deep.

Tuesday 18th Carpenters employed stripping the starboard bow, which they find in as bad a state as the starboard one. Hauled the seine with the usual success. Thermometer Midnight 35¼°.

Saturday 22nd Having intelligence of Captain Gore's return from Bolchaiscka accompanied by the Governor, sent boats to the mouth of the River Awatscha to wait on them. [When] the Governor came on board & was saluted with a guard and 13 Guns. There were with him a priest, who resides at an Ostrog to the west of this named Paratounka, with some merchants of consequence in the Empresses service. Thermometer Midnight 38° Noon 52°.

Monday 24th The Governor (Major Behm) made a present of a considerable quantity of tobacco to the companies of both ships. The Bay quite clear of Ice. Latitude Observed 53°00′ North.

Wednesday 26th The Governor took his leave of the Ships and was saluted with 13 Guns & cheers from the People for his extraordinary civilities & unbounded generosity. A fog in the night, as was most frequently the case. The Cooper preparing a Cask to take in a quantity of Flour, a considerable supply, out of the Russian store house granted by the Major. Received on board 415 lbs of beef. Sent the Discovery her proportional part. Thermometer Midnight 40° Noon 56°.

Tuesday, June 1st Punished Job Clay with a dozen lashes for Insolence & contempt. Employed getting on board wood & water. Sent hands to gather greens. Received from the Discovery 2912 lbs of bread & 125½ gallons of brandy. Got the powder on Shore to dry & sift.

Wednesday 2nd AM received on board 250 pood of Flour or Rye Meal, which is equal to [over 8,000] lbs. This supply with the quantity of bread we have taken from our Consort makes an equal division between the two of bread and flour. Served the people whole allowances of Flour in lieu of bread.

Friday 4th A strong Gale from NE to SE with rain & sleet. The weather was so bad as to prevent our forwarding the work. Sent the Discovery some of her meal as her proportional part. This morning came down from Bolchaiscka 23 head of Cattle for the use of both Ships Companies with a quantity of leathern caps & stockings etc, which was equally distributed to the people at the common standard price of the Country. The merchants purchased most of the Beaver skins in the two ships, the best selling for about 30 Rubles & the coarser kind for 15 & 10 (a Ruble we reckon to be about 4 shillings Sterling). The Captain & officers were also presented with a good stock of tea & sugar from the Major & Captain Ishmyloff of Bolchaiscka.

Saturday, 5th Fired 21 Guns, being the anniversary of his Majesty's birth day.

Monday 7th Employed stowing away wood whilst others on shore were hard employed cutting more & the Carpenters sawing plank. Served fresh beef to the people, 1 pound per man. Thermometer Midnight 47° Noon 53°.

Thursday 10th Employed getting ready for sea. Corned 4 puncheons of beef. This morning intended to unmoor but the wind being in the SE quarter & blowing fresh, could not venture it.

Friday 11th The wind increased to a hard Gale & shifted to the NE. Sent the pinnace to observe the wind in the entrance of the Bay & see if there was a possibility of getting to sea. Soon after she returned & found the wind blowing from the ESE and a great sea setting in. Finding from this report an attempt impracticable without danger, we hove in & secured the Ship. Served fresh meat to the people every day.

Sunday 13th With the assistance of the Tide weighed the small bower, hove up the Best Bower and came to sail. Stood across the Bay with the wind at SE, [but] at 8 it falling little wind and the tide making against us, we came too in 10 fms off the mouth of the harbour. At 4 in the morning hoisted the launch in & got under way with the Ebb tide in favor, the Boats ahead towing.

Monday 14th At 6 weighd with the Ebb & plyed to windward, when it fell little wind & came on a thick fog, which obliged us to anchor again. It continued little wind all night and the fog was equally thick. The Boats ahead towing with not a Breath of Wind. At ½ past 9 the flood made with a foul wind setting in for we came too again. Until noon it continued to blow strong from the SE. Sent the Boats on Shore to pick Greens.

Tuesday 15th This afternoon it continued to blow from SE until Night when it veered more round to the east, which brought in a fog. Towards morning it backed round to the Southward again, so as to prevent our getting out. The weather cloudy & unsettled, occasiond by an eruption from the Volcano to the North of Peterpawloska. It emitted vast quantities of mineral Ashes, rising in immense Collumns, with the smoke that darkened the whole element. Our Decks & rigging were covered with this filth. Clean'd the Ship between Decks. Sent the two boats with partys to pick up Greens, of which we now get great plenty, such as Wild parsley, Nettle, a kind of Wild Celery, & abundance of Onions or Leeks. Thermometer Midnight 40° Noon 41½°.

Wednesday 16th A Moderate Gale and cloudy, with Thunder & much lightening, which we apprehend to arise from the heavy Clouds & the great bodys of smoke from the Volcano counteracting with each other. Several violent eruptions we heard from the Mount. The smoke and ashes overspread the Element to that degree which almost occasioned a total darkness. With this we had rain that mist itself, with the latter, which created a fall of mud with heavy showers of cinders or pumey [pumice] stone, some of which were ½ an inch in Diameter. These severe blasts continue till 10 O'Clock in the evening, when it cleared away & a light breeze sprung up from the NW.

At Day light we got under way & stood out of the Bay not without some trouble, for the tide setting immediately over on the Eastern Shore & the wind rather faltering. It was with difficulty we clear'd the Monkey rocks [harbor entrance]. By Noon, with the Assistance of the Boats, & making the most of what wind we had, got an offing of 2 leagues. In this situation we had 43 fms over a bottom of small stones, which its probable, fell from the Volcano.

2

Confronting Arctic Ice
June–July 1779

The ships took nearly a week to get out of Avacha Bay because of adverse winds and tides, as well as the sooty darkness from the eruption of Avachinsky Volcano. Once the ships cleared the land they turned north, sailing in and out of fog and hazy weather along the Siberian coastline until they reached Bering Strait. Passing the Diomede Islands, they viewed both the American and Asian coastlines simultaneously. In early July they came to the solid ice pack, which they found further south than the previous year. Cook had speculated the pack would be easier to penetrate in July, but that was not the case. Clerke lingered several days to give the pack time to disperse, but by mid-July he turned east, sailing along the ice front to the coast of Alaska. Roberts found the ice rough and jagged, in many places twenty feet high. As Cook had reported the previous year, Roberts found it was "as compact as a wall."

Clerke was more aggressive than Cook had been, often challenging the ice despite the constant fog, wind, and tides. They were frequently embayed, forced to punch through field ice to avoid entrapment. Both journals reflect the growing anxiety of the crews, who must have been astounded by the risks taken, particularly the constant shocks to the vessel hulls as they attempted to force their way through the pack. Roberts said the *Resolution*'s Cutwater, the framework of a ship's bow, was cracked and broken. After two weeks in the ice, Burney reported the *Discovery* was taking on a foot of water a day, which later increased to three inches every hour. When the ships finally returned to Kamchatka, the carpenters found the jolts had come with such violence that many of the bulkheads had shattered and much of the sheathing was missing below the waterline.

The final weeks of July were spent in constant contact with the ice. Roberts offers a frightful report of the daily interaction with the pack. On July 19 the ships reached the farthest north for the year at 70°33′ North Latitude. The previous year, on August 18, 1778, Cook reached 70°44′ North Latitude. That same evening the crew briefly saw two polar bears. When the bears returned the next day, the shore boats were hoisted out and the sailors gave chase, killing them both. The largest weighed nearly 500 pounds. The crews found polar bear meat to be a worthy dietary enhancement. Roberts wrote, "These were looked upon by us to be wholesome food, which afforded hearty meals and in every respect well tasted."

After reaching the Alaska coast, it was clear the pack was fast and impenetrable, so the ships turned east again for Asia. By late July, after sailing along the pack from Alaska, they reached the coast of Asia. Like the previous year, they could not find a northerly route through the ice and abandoned the search for any passageway. Roberts wrote, "We have now beyond all doubt traced the Ice evidently from the one Continent to the other and in the many attempts we made to get to the westward, [it] does appear that we had the ill fortune not to succeed once, although no pains or labour was spared in our researches with the assistance of great perseverance and good conduct."

Clerke then altered course, returning south for Bering Strait and Avacha Bay. Overcome by his own escalating illness, the captain died three weeks later when the ships first viewed the Kamchatka coastline.

Journal of James Burney

Friday, June 18th At 11 in the forenoon the Easternmost of the Land in Sight, which we supose to be the Shupinskoi Noss, bore . . . 7 or 8 Leagues distant. Our Latitude then 52°47′ North, Longitude in 159°45′ East. After 11 the weather became foggy and wind freshened from the SW. Lost sight of the Land. Steered towards the NE.

Saturday 19th Kept more to the Northward. Foggy. No Land in Sight nor Soundings.

Sunday 20th At 2 in the Morning, being clearer weather, saw the Coast of Kamtschatka to the NW but the foggy weather coming on again soon hid the Land. This must be somewhere near the Cronotskoi Noss. At Noon, Latitude in 54°57′ North, Longitude in 163°08′ East.

Monday 21st Clear Weather. At 2 in the morning Saw Land to the NW. At Noon the Kamtschatka Noss bore NW about 7 Leagues distant. We make this Noss in 56°01′ North Latitude and 163°18′ East Longitude, which is more to the Eastward than laid down in the Russian Charts. The Land in sight all the Afternoon at 5 or 6 Leagues distance, high and uneven. Our Course between the North and NNE.

Tuesday 22nd At Noon the Land still in Sight to the WSW at 12 or 14 Leagues distance. Our Latitude in 57°02′ North, Longitude in 164°33′ East. In the afternoon Cloudy with variable winds. Lost Sight of the Land.

23rd to the 27th Winds between the South and SW with foggy Weather. Running to the NE without land, Soundings or any remarkable occurrence. The 27th at Noon, Latitude observed 59°52′ North, Longitude in 175°20′ East. Wind WSW with fair Weather. Hauled up to the NNW per Compass to make the Land.

Monday 28th At ¼ past 5 in the Morning, Saw the Land to the NW. At 9 were within 3 Leagues. Stood to the ENE along shore. From 9 to Noon had Soundings of 26 to 30 fathoms . . . this is the Coast of Koreki. At Noon the Land bore from SW to NE distance off shore 4 or 5 Leagues. An Opening which I take to be the River Kalinka [Velikaya River in Chukotka] NWBW Latitude 61°58′ North, Longitude 175°35′ East. In the Afternoon and Night running along the Coast to the Eastward about 6 Leagues distant from the Shore . . .

Tuesday 29th Hazy weather. Running to the Eastward along the Coast which from the thickness of the Weather was only seen at times. Had Soundings at 56 fathoms 6 Leagues from the Land, at Noon, Latitude 62°02′ North, Longitude 178°25′ East. St. Thadeus Noss bore (per Compass) . . . 6 or 7 Leagues distant. [Bearings omitted.] All this part of the Coast is high and Mountainous.

Wednesday 30th Light winds. Steering all day to the ENE without losing sight of St. Thadeus Noss. In the Afternoon caught Cod, . . . 16 Leagues from the Shore.

Thursday, July 1st At 4 this morning St. Thadeus Noss bore W¼S per Compass 20 Leagues distant . . . As we ran towards the ENE found the depth decreasing though at the same time we distanced the land. At Noon no land in sight. Foggy weather. [Bearings omitted.]

Friday 2nd A Moderate breeze from the Southward with a thick fog. Running towards the ENE.

Saturday 3rd At Noon Latitude is 63°37′ North, Longitude is 186°38′ East. At 4 in the Afternoon, Saw the Tschuktichi Coast to the NW and at 6 saw land to the Eastward, which we take to be the Island of St. Lawrence. At 11 ran by the NW part of the Island at 3 or 4 miles distance. After Midnight Steered more Northerly for Behrings Straits. Had Soundings all night from 20 to 23 fathoms.

Sunday 4th Steering North per Compass. Thick foggy weather. No land in Sight. Soundings 23 to 26 fathoms.

Monday 5th Wind SSE. At Noon Latitude 65°50′ North, Longitude 190°16′ East. The Weather clear and hazy alternately. At Noon saw the Islands in Behrings Straits [Diomede Islands]. Ran between them and the Asia Coast . . .

Tuesday 6th At Noon Latitude 67°07′ North, Longitude 190°58′ East . . . no land in Sight. Have been set to the Northward by a current these 3 last days. Afternoon at ½ past 1 fell in with loose Ice. The Resolution sent her boats after Seahorses but caught none. Stood on to the NNE, a continuation of loose fields of Ice in sight to the Eastward till midnight . . .

Wednesday 7th At 6 in the morning saw Ice to the Eastward and beyond it the Coast of America about 10 Leagues distant, bearing from NEBN to ENE. The weather becoming hazy, soon lost sight of the Land. From 6 to Noon ran 9 Leagues to the Northward along the edge of the Ice, which appears to be fixed to the Shore, or one continued field. Latitude at Noon 68°24′ North, Longitude 192°52′ East.

All the Afternoon running towards the North and NNE. At 8 came on a thick fog, lost Sight of the Ice. Sea Gulls and Sea Parrots about us in great Numbers. Passed some drift wood. At Midnight saw the Ice again to the Eastward. Depth 19 fathoms, which according to the Sounding we had last year, is not above 6 or 7 Leagues from the Land.

Thursday 8th Continuing our Course to the NNE. Ice in sight to the Eastward of us. In the morning . . . stood to the NW and lost sight of the Ice. At Noon Latitude 69°29′ North, Longitude 192°55′ East. In the Afternoon. At 2 Saw

Ice to the Northward. This does not appear fixed like the Ice we left this morning, but is a continuation of loose fields too close to attempt forcing a passage through and extending to the Northward beyond Sight of our horizon. Steered to the Westward along the edge of the Ice, a great many Sea horses on it.

Friday 9th In the Afternoon . . . having ran near 40 Leagues along the edge of the Ice, without seeing an Opening or a clear Sea to the Northward beyond it, Bore away to the SSE and lost sight of the Ice, depth 24 to 29 fathoms these 2 last days . . . Saw Whales, drift wood and Sea birds.

Steered all Night to the SSE, Captain Clerke intending to run as far as the Serge Kamen and return to the Northward again towards the end of the month when we might expect to find the Sea clearer of Ice.

Saturday 10th In the forenoon fell in with large bodies of loose Ice. At Noon Calm. The Resolutions boats after Sea horses. Latitude 68°02′ North, Longitude 188°35′ East. In the Afternoon, a breeze from the Eastward. All Night turning to the SE to clear the Ice, which extended from the Westward to the SE.

Sunday 11th Not being able to weather the Ice and it appearing tolerably clear and open, attempted to run through under an easy sail that the Ships might not suffer by Striking too hard against the large pieces. After running 8 miles to the Southward amongst broken Ice, Saw the Ice to the SW, SE and NE, one compact body. Tackd and Stood back again . . . [keeping] to the Northward.

Monday, 12th In the forenoon little wind. Much loose Ice about. Caught 4 Sea horses. Tried for fish without success. At Noon, Latitude 68°38′ North, Longitude in 187°53′ East . . .

Running to the Northward.

Tuesday 13th Wind Easterly. At 5 saw a large body of Ice to the Westward extending towards the North. Continued our Course in that direction along the edge of the Ice, which is one continued field. At 8 seeing the Ice extend towards the East, hauled close on a Wind . . . Passed some large pieces of driftwood.

Wednesday 14th Little wind and foggy. Turning to the Eastward near the Main body of the Ice which was to the North of us. At Noon, Latitude 69°35′ North, Longitude in 189°02′ East.

Thursday 15th The Wind came round to the westward. Ran to the East by the edge of the Ice, which we kept on our Larboard hand. [Bearings omitted.] All the afternoon and Night, coasting the Ice along one continued body.

Friday 16th Wind SW. In the morning running to the NE close to the edge of the Ice. Foggy weather till 8, when the wind freshening, cleared away the fog and we found ourselves embayed, the Ice taking a sudden turn to the SE, one close body. Hauled on a wind to the SSE, a fresh Gale with Snow. At Noon, were out of sight of the Ice [bearings omitted].

Saturday 17th Wind Westerly. The weather becoming Moderate. Bore away to the NE again. [Bearings omitted.] In the Afternoon, past a good deal of small drift wood . . .

Sunday 18th In the Morning, wind NE. Stood to the NNW. Saw Whales, Sea parrots and other Sea birds. At ½ past 8 Saw the Ice again. At Noon, Latitude 70°28′ North, Longitude in 195°50′ East. At ½ past 1 were close to the Main Body of the Ice to the North of us, extending towards the East and West beyond our Sight. The wind veering to the westward of North, ran to the Eastward along the edge of the Ice, Steering more Northerly or Southerly according as it trended. Large herds of Sea horses. At 9 in the evening a White Bear swam close to our Ship, and afterwards made for the Ice on which we Saw 2 others. At 11 a thick fog on, wind WSW. Hauled to the Southward from the Ice. Half an hour after Midnight, being Clear, tackd and Stood for the Ice again.

Monday 19th Wind variable. At 2 in the morning found the Ice. Turned Short to the South, and after running 3 miles in that direction along the edge which we kept constantly on our larboard hand, it turned towards the SW, in which line we coasted it all this day. At Noon, Latitude 70°16′ North, Longitude 196°41′ East. Our distance from the Coast of America we judge to be about 7 Leagues. The Weather fair, but hazy in the horizon, prevents our seeing it.

Afternoon at 1 two White Bears swam from the Ice towards the Ships. Hoisted our boats out and sent in pursuit of them. Killed and took both. At 6 got a glimpse of the land beyond the Ice to the SE . . . hazy towards the Land.

Tuesday 20th The Ice turned more to the Westward. In following it, deepened our Water. At 6 in the morning, foggy. Lost sight of the main body of the Ice. Much loose Ice and small drift wood about us. At 8 Clear. Saw the Main body of the Ice to the SE, and at 11 the Land beyond the Ice bearing SEBS 5 or 6 Leagues. [Bearings omitted.] In the Afternoon running to the Westward through loose Ice. Lost sight of the continued body of the Ice, which seems to be as yet fixed to the American Shore. At 8 in the evening, little wind. Tried and found a current setting to the ENE . . . , ripling in the night and much small drift wood, which are signs of our being near the entrance of a River.

The large drift wood we have seen at different times in the Sea, most probably has drifted hither from Norton Sound or from the Coast to the Southward of it. Between Norton Sound and Sledge Island we found a constant current setting to the Westward and NW towards Behrings Straits, and in Behrings Straits, the current near both Shores set to the Northward.

Wednesday 21st Running to the Westward. At 9 Saw the Coast of America to the SE 7 or 8 Leagues distant. At Noon neither Land or Ice in Sight. Latitude 69°48′ North, Longitude 193°40′ East. In the Afternoon passed much loose Ice.

Tuesday 22nd Wind Easterly, running to the Westward. All the morning a clear Sea. [Bearings omitted.] Saw Ice to the Westward . . . Hauled on a wind on the Southward to clear it . . . At 8 found ourselves amongst loose fields of Ice. Most part of the Night Standing to the SSE expecting to get clear of the Ice. The Weather foggy.

Friday 23rd A fresh breeze ESE. Turning towards the SE to regain an open Sea. At 4 in the morning were obliged to shorten sail on account of the Ice being so thick about us that we could not avoid running against many large Clumps, which tore off much of our Sheathing. Continued turning towards the SE [but] when almost clear out, got entangled amongst some large pieces which stopped the Ships way so much that she fell bodily to leeward. After having with poles pushed these pieces clear of us, we made 2 or 3 short trips, but our run was so shortened on each tack by the Ice closing that instead of gaining ground, we fell broadside foremost on the edge of a Small field. Having almost an open Sea to Windward, the Surf made the Ship strike violently. The field at length breaking, we set all our Sails for another trial, but before the Ship gathered way enough to be under command, we again fell to leeward on some more.

As the Swell made it very dangerous and unsafe to lay to windward of all, and as there was no chance of getting clear, we pushed for a small opening into the Ice. As soon as we got within the first large piece, furled all our Sails and made fast with Ice hooks. Having smooth water. At Noon, Latitude 69°20′ North, Longitude 187°17′ East. The Resolution bore SEBE 3 miles distant 3 miles under Sail and seemingly clear of the Ice. Half an hour after Noon lost sight of her. Found the Ship drift with the body of the Ice towards the NW at above half a Knot.

At 4 in the Afternoon the Ice was close all round and as far as could be seen except between the South and ESE, where at the distance of ¾ of a mile from us it was still loose and open. At 5 the wind veered round to the NE and at 6 to the North, which made the Ice begin to Separate. Took up our Ice hooks, and made Sail towards the SE, the Ice slowly giving way as the Ship pressed against it. Heard a Gun from the Resolution which we answered. At ½ past 7 were without the edge of the close Ice. Heard the Resolutions Guns to the SE, by the sound of which we joined her half an hour before Midnight being then in a clear Sea. The Weather foggy.

Saturday 24th Wind SSW. Running towards the SE. At 11 in the forenoon were stopped by a large body of loose Ice to the Eastward from SSE to NNE. At noon, Latitude 68°54′ North, Longitude in 188°17′ East. In the Afternoon falling Calm sent our Boats after Sea horses. Caught Eleven, which served for lamp oil.

Sunday 25th Wind SW. Seeing a clear Sea beyond the loose Ice to the SE, made Sail that way to force through. At 6 were clear past all. The remainder of this day running to the SE without seeing any more Ice. [Bearings omitted.]

26th and 27th Standing backwards and forwards to clear bodies of loose Ice. Condemned our Worst Foresail to repair other Sails. Have found a leak in our larboard Bow about 2 feet below the water line. Since getting amongst the Ice (the 23rd) have made a foot water every 4 hours. Before then only made 9 inches in two days. 27th at Noon, Latitude 67°55′ North, Longitude 188°26′ East.

27th In the afternoon were surrounded by loose Ice. Wind SE. Standing to the SW. At ¼ past 4 saw the Coast of Asia, a Bluff point . . . distant about 15 Leagues. Between us and the land a body of close Ice. Stood towards the East.

After this finding our run to the Northward, as well as our approaches to either Continent, obstructed by the Sea being so full of Ice, it was judged fruitless to make any more attempts.

Journal of Henry Roberts

Thursday, June 17th Light baffling winds round the Compass with Rain at times, endeavouring to get a good offing. In the evening hoisted in the boats, the North head of the entrance about 4 leagues. At day light the North head of the Bay about 5 leagues, the land at the back of this appears level & has a gradual ascent to the foot of the Volcano & the other ridge of Mountains lying to the NE of it.

Friday 18th From 6 in the morning to Noon found the Ship had gone 8 miles to the Southward, which I attribute to the Ebb tide making strong out of the Bay. At 6 this morning Latitude 52°44′ North, Longitude 159°29′ East.

Saturday 19th From Noon we continued to stand out to get an offing until 2, when we hauld more to the Northward with an intention to range the Coast. At 7 we imagined we saw the land NW, but the weather being very thick & hazy, it remained a doubtful point. The Gale increasing, took in the single reefs of each Top Sail, the weather continuing Dark & gloomy. Near the horizon was a brightness which we took to be the reflection from the high snowy land, the glare lying in that quarter. The Course we shaped for the Night was agreeable to the direction of the Coast according to the Russian Charts. The weather still very thick, which toward morning changed to a perfect fog, which confined our sight to less than ¼ of a Mile. Many divers about and at times drift weed.

Sunday 20th The fog continuing so thick that rendered it impossible to stand in for the land. At 10 the fog cleared away when early in the morning [we] shaped our Course towards the land, willing to Coast it if possible. In less than ½ an hour we made it, extending from NBE to NWBW. This we take to be the Kronolskoi Noss, the Russians placing it nearly within our track in Latitude, which is 54°42′ N.

We stood on till 4 when the Gale increased, which forced in our double reefs & soon after accompanied with a very thick fog, which obliged us to haul off the land, when we made the signal to our Consort with 4 Guns to alter the Course. The Land near this Cape appeared very high & the inland Mountains much covered with Snow. The Shores to appearance steep & the coast straight, without the least sign of Inlets.

The weather continued exceedingly thick, which made it necessary to fire Guns hourly to prevent a sepperation with the other Ship. A brisk Gale running under single reefed Main Top & fore sails, with a proper spread of canvas to haul on the Wind in case of an emergency. Towards Noon the weather made several attempts to clear away, which enabled us to get a Meridian Observation.

Monday 21st At Noon hauld in to make the land, being favoured with clear weather. At this time many sea parrots & other sea fowl about, with a number of Whales blowing. We expected to have seen the land in the evening, but the haze still continuing on the horizon destroyed our sight. We remained on the same course during the night, when at Day break, which was 2 O'Clock, we saw the Continent extending from NWBN to WNW at the distance of 11 leagues. This part from its situation we judge to be near the Kamtschatkoi Cape, the wind being light and changeable. Having lost the Southerly Gale obliged us to stand to the Eastward until it appeared more settled, when at 5½ hours Tackd & made sail, standing in again.

The observed Latitude was 55°51′30″ N. The land appeared either to have a separation by a river towards the Northern part or else connected by the low land, which we could not see. The Southernmost extreme of this land falls in a low sloping point, nor are the other parts of any great height or even so much covered with snow, as with the land near the Chupoonskoi Cape. It was several peoples oppinion that they saw land in the direction of WBS. A fog bank was also observed to lie there most of the morning, which might easily be mistaken for land. Therefore, makes it a matter of doubt.

Tuesday 22nd We continued our course following the direction of the Coast agreeable to the Russians. We find the Northernmost part to be the Kamtschatkoi Cape, its surface is flat and of a moderate height forming a bluff head. About 3 leagues to the Southward of it was a small oppening, which had the appearance of a river. The land on each side very low. In the Russian accounts this Noss is described as a peninsula, which most probably is the Case, as it never appeared as an Island to us, nor could we perceive the least rising about the low land. Therefore its certain the hills must lie at a considerable distance within it & these single range of Mountains connected by a neck of flat land. The Great River of Kamschatka we judge to lie further South to the westward of the Southern extremity of this peninsula.

In the Night we passed a dead whale with a number of sea Birds about it that created an abominable stench. Towards the Morning the breeze lessened. [Gulls, shags, divers and puffins observed. So much fog it is difficult to see the coast, so they move away from land, with regular signals to Discovery.]

Tuesday 29th [Their Latitude was 59°49′ N on June 27 and because of rapid, following seas they reached 62°02′ N on June 28. A small river caused rippling of the water off shore that was feared to be a shoal.] Continuing the Course along shore carrying a regular depth of water from 20 to 32 fms, the nearest part [of the land] 5 leagues. This part of the Continent appeared quite barren, not the least wood to be perceived even with the assistance of our Glasses. The Tops & sides of the hills free from snow, lying only in some of the Valleys. The land in general is hilly, but far from being Mountainous. The sea Shores [are] low. In the evening, imagining we saw land extend to the NEBE we steered more to the East, but this afterwards proved to be a fog bank, for at 12 we had 38 fms, which before morning deepened to 46 & 50 fms. To the Southward of this point of land to the NE (which from its situation we judge to be the Noss of St. Thadeus) the land forms in a deep bight to the west, conformable to the Russian discoveries in which part they place the river Kalinka.

The winds but light & changeable with thick rainy weather in which interval we caught a few Cod. A little before Noon a breeze sprung up from the NW but the rain still continuing, prevented our getting a meridian at observation. Latitude 62°02′ North, Longitude 176°51′ East. [Walrus, which the crew called "sea horses," as well as seals, gulls, and divers observed. The fog came in and out from the shore, making navigation difficult. The crew caught cod from the decks and they had soundings of 65 fathoms.]

Friday, July 2nd At ½ past 3 the weather cleared for the space of a few minutes, which gave us an imperfect View of the land. Our great distance from this part of the Coast & the ill opportunities that offered, most consequently render the determination of its boundaries but inaccurate. We however traced the Land so far as to settle the direction of its Coast from the Northern point of the River Opuka to the Noss of St. Thadeus. The land near the last mentiond Cape is of a considerable height, whose hills are much covered with snow. The coast to the Northward seemd to take a more westerly direction, agreeable to Captain Behring's account, this point being the SW promontory of the Gulph of Anidar.

Sunday 4th At 4 [we came to the] southern part [of the coast] that we explored last season, the western point being the same that Behring calls the Tuchotskoi and is the SE promontory of the Gulph of Anidar. Its Latitude 64°13′ N, longitude 186°33′ East. Soon after we saw the Island St. Lawrence & more land to the southward of it. We hauld close upon a Wind with an intention to get a nearer View of it, but in this attempt we failed, not being able to clear the weather side of the Island St. Lawrence. We therefore were obliged to bear up & leave the extent of this new land undetermined.

By midnight we were abreast of the Island St. Lawrence at the distance of 4 or 5 miles. This Island is at a distance of 18 leagues and 14 from the nearest part of the Main. Its of a moderate height and the snow appeared to lay very thick, nor is the Island to the Southward less free from it. We now shaped a Course more Northerly, making the best of our way up to Behring's Straits, deepening the water to 20 fms, which by Noon had increased its depth to 27.

Monday 5th Many whales blowing. The haze lying very thick on the horizon, hauld more to the westward to make the land Tchutskoi, imagining ourselves about 6 leagues off.

Tuesday 6th Soon after noon we saw the land to the NE and the NW, supposing the first to be the islands lying in the passage between the two Continents

[Diomede Islands]. In the Latitude 65°48′ N we steered for it. When at 3 we were abreast of them at the distance of 4 or 5 miles, the snow appeared to lie very deep upon them, considerably more than on the beginning of August last season. At the time we discovered them.

Bore away & resumed the Course to the Northward, the weather continuing very thick, we however could just perceive the Asia Coast to the westward. We haule up in that direction to make it more distinct. In a short time we saw the East Cape bearing WBS distance 3 leagues. Altered the Course & steered to the Northward. By 10 the weather cleared and shew us the peaked hill on the American Shore and the East Cape of Asia at the same time. The shores near this promontory were greatly encumbered with ice and the hills burdened with Snow. In the course of the Night passed several small pieces of Ice & from the dirt that was on it, should naturally conclude it had broken from the Shores.

Many sea horses about & flights of small birds (a kind of diver). The number of these Animals rather indicate a near approach to the Main Ice.

Wednesday 7th Several Sea horses seen. At 3 we saw Ice ahead & by 5 we were among it. This was a quantity of loose Ice in drift and appeared very rotten. Some of the pieces were large uppon which there lie a number of the aforementioned animals. In the evening we could perceive more Ice to the Northward and for the greatest part of the Night were sailing through large quantities that drifted.

In the morning we could perceive the horizon much covered with Ice to the Northward [and] the Coast of America distant about 15 leagues. At this time we found the Ice in a firm body, apparently connected to the Continent, which was seen over it. We therefore were obliged to bear up to the Westward along the edge of this immense body, whose surface was exceedingly rough & jagged & in many places 20 feet in height. Our situation was in Latitude 68°02′ N & Longitude 192°33′ E. This part of the Main now discovered was not seen in our Route last season.

Thursday 8th Standing along the edge of the firm field Ice & passing many large pieces and great quantities of small loose ice. Passed a trunk of a stout Tree & some pieces of wood. The field Ice extended from NE to SE. Made fires below to Air the Ship & put Canvas round each hatchway to screen the people from the weather.

Friday 9th At 3 we meet with the Ice again. This part appeared to be quite a solid body and much higher than any we had before seen. The surface, like the other, very rough & uneven. The edge of it seemingly as compact as a wall with immense quantities of Drift Ice lying before it. We stood along the skirts of the Main Ice, forging our way through large drifts of loose ice, when at 8 we were again brought up by the main body, which obliged us to bear away to the South. The Southernmost part bearing SW, at this time we had a fresh Gale. Took the single reefs in each Topsail and stood on under an easy sail all Night, running amidst abundance of loose Ice, some of which were composed of weighty pieces floating very deep under the surface of the sea. We continued this way till Noon, keeping sight of the firm Ice, Latitude 69°12′ N, Longitude 189°30′15′ East. Fires below as Yesterday to Air the Ship.

Saturday 10th Sailing through the midst of drift Ice. At 4 the firm body of Ice extended from SE to WSW. The drift Ice still forcing us to the Southward, we endeavoured to bore our way through it, but we found it so very thick & the flakes large that we were necessitated to give the point up and steerd to the Southward. The ship receiving considerable shocks from the large pieces. Found that the Cutwater [framework of ship's bow] was in some places hurt & the sheathing rubbed.

Sunday 11th Passing quantities of loose Ice. At 4, seeing a number of Sea Horses on it, hoisted the boats out & set them to kill some of these Animals. By 6 we were brought in by a close drift of packed Ice extending from Easterly to SW. After getting on board the boats, who brought a few Horses, Tackd & stood to the Northward with an intention of plying to windward round the eastern part of the Ice. At 12 we were again within ½ a Cables length of the edge of the packed Ice.

Sailing past immense quantities of drift Ice, some of which were in large & heavy pieces, were stopped with a great tract of close packed Ice, finding it impossible to force the Ship through it. Tackd & stood to the Northward, forging our way amidst the drift and large broken pieces upon which we saw great numbers of sea horses & many whales in the Sea blowing.

Monday 12th Continued forcing the Ship through the large flakes of partial Ice. By 1 we were intirely free from it when we stretched to the Northward with a clear Sea, having little or no ice in sight.

Tuesday 13th A clear and smooth sea, with a depth of water. At 7 in Latitude 69°22′ N, seeing no appearance of Ice to the Northward, bore away. Passed some driftwood. At 8 Saw the Ice ahead extended from NE to SW and by 9 we were close to its edge, which was in a small degree broken, but the inner parts appeared firm & closely connected.

Wednesday 14th At 5 we were again close in with the solid body of Ice [with] much loose & many large pieces floating near its edge, upon which the surge of the Sea washd with some force. The extremes bore from NE to WBS. Tackd & stood to the Southward. Our latitude at this time was 69°41′ N.

Thursday 15th Stretched on towards the Ice until ½ past 4 O'Clock, at which time we saw it appearing through the fog close under our lee. Made the signal with 2 Guns & Tackd, continuing to fire a swivel every half hour till 6, when our Consort came in sight. A thick fog & frost all Night. Flights of Divers flying round us. Made fires between Decks to Air the Ship. Standing to the Eastward following the direction of the Ice, it being a firm field. At Noon it bore from the West to NNE when we hauld more to the Northward to get a nearer view of it.

Friday 16th We again reached the brink of the Ice, which was in some measure broken, but the inner parts were quite firm. We bore away & continued to range its course at the distance of a mile or two from the edge until 8 in the morning, when the weather clearing up, we found ourselves embayed by the Main body, which extended from East to SW. At this time the Gale increasing, forced in the double reefs of each topsail, and hauld the wind to the Southward. What drew us into this snare was our mistaking the solid body of Ice for that of a floating field, having sailed round its point to the North a considerable distance before we discovered the firm ice & perceived our error. Our latitude was 70°07′ N.

Saturday 17th At 2 the wind increasing to a strong Gale, close reefd the Fore & handed the Mizzen Top Sail. Got down Top Gallant Yards. Bore down to the Discovery. Cleaned below & made fires to air the Ship.

Sunday 18th Standing to the Northward with no Ice in sight in Latitude 70°15′N, Longitude 196°31′15′ East. At 10 saw the ice ahead and at Noon it extended from NE ½ E to WBN about 2 miles from the Ships.

Monday 19th At 1 we were close to the Ice, which we found to be a solid body extending from West to ENE. Tackd & saild along its edge to the Eastward. At ½ past 10 the weather coming on awful foggy & the firm body of ice close to the northward of us, we were obliged to haul the wind to the south, our Latitude at this time proving to be the greatest that we were able to penetrate this season, which was 70°31′ North & Longitude 196°52′ East.

All the Night ranging the boundaries of the Ice, passing amidst great quantities that drifted near. The firm body with numbers of Sea horses about. The weather being rather thick & unfavourable, obliged us at times to lye bye. At ½ past 12 found ourselves nearly encircled by the Main Ice, bearing from SSE to SW. Bore away & resumed the course to the East when at ½ after 2, finding the Ice take still a more southern direction, forced us to slant the wind to weather it.

Tuesday 20th Ranging as before the boundaries of the solid body of Ice and sailing through much loose & many large pieces among which we saw two white bears that we pursued in one of the boats and killed them. These were looked upon by us to be wholesome food, which afforded hearty meals and in every respect well tasted. The largest, weighing 463 lbs. without the entrails, its length 7 ft. 2″ and circumference in the broadest part 4 ft. 10″. This was the female. The Male not so large weighing only 253 lbs.

At ½ past 12 we were brought up by the Main body of ice, which was at first thought to be land from its height and firm appearance. We again had got ourselves embayed, bearing from NBW round Eastward to SWBW. Bore away in this last direction. Having the limits of the Ice, the weather very unfavourable, a thick fog every few minutes, at ½ past 10 we saw the land bearing SSE being that part of the Coast of America we discovered last year. Lying to the Northward of 69 [North Latitude], we stood in for it as far as the Ice would possibly admit of that. By Noon [it] prevented our nearer approach, extending in a westerly direction, being a compleat barrier. The edges [were] a little loose & broken with large pieces drifting. The fog at this time dissipating, we had a tolerable sight of the land, which was in the cavities of the hills much burdened with Snow. A thick fog bank which had the appearance of land lying to the south of it.

Wednesday 21st Sailing amidst much loose ice which lies near the edges of the solid body. Saw the land again having a strong rippling in the water. Tryd the Current & found it setting from the westward at the rate of a knot an hour.

Great quantities of drift ice in large pieces. At 8 the weather clearing [to] shew the land to the SE, hauld in for it, when at ½ past 9 we were brought up by the Ice, the edges of which was broken, but the inner parts appeared to unite in a compact body as firm & solid as the land itself and apparently joined to the Coast, distance 12 leagues. [We have] now determined that there is neither a passage to the North or eastward but that this immense Mass of Ice makes an intire barrier in those quarters, and does also evidently connect with the great American Continent. It was therefore judged proper to make a second attempt on the Asiatic coast in hopes of meeting with better success. We accordingly bore away to the westward, making all sail.

Thursday 22nd At 5 saw the Main ice bearing WNW. Passed many large and loose pieces. Steerd more Southerly. ½ after 9 we perceived the ice through the fog, hauld our wind to the Northward, when the weather clearing we could trace the firm body of ice nearly round us, only oppen to the SE. Tackd and stood on in that direction to get clear of it. At 7 PM in Latitude 69°32′ N and longitude 189°46′ East. At Noon no ice in sight. Shaped the Course more to the Northward to make it.

Friday 23rd Some drift Ice seen to the SE. Bore away to the westward when at ½ past 8 we fell in with a great quantity that we were fearful was near the edges of the Main body, which obliged us to haul the wind to the Southward. Immediately after the fog clearing, found that our fears were not groundless. The solid Ice, being close under the lee, extended to the SE & Northward. Got the jacks on board and beat to windward, endeavouring to weather the East part. [This] was not accomplished until 4 in the morning when we found the loose Ice very thick and great abundance drifting upon us occasioned by the fresh wind. We however persevered in forcing a passage to the South, which fortunately was compleated by 7, not without great trouble and difficulty, and the ship on her part receiving some heavy shocks. Our Consort was not so successful for at ½ past 10 we had the mortification to see her caught up in the ice, which appeared to be quite fast. At this time a thick fog came on and more ice driving down from the windward. We kept standing off and on waiting for her.

Saturday 24th Standing off and on for the Discovery, having shore packed ice on each side of us, both to the North & South. At 6 fired a Gun as a signal but heard no return. When at 9 we had the satisfaction to hear a gun from the westward, which was answered, we repeated the signal 2 times hourly (having returns from her) until ½ past 11, at which time she came in sight & joined Company. When we bore away to the Eastward to clear the ice, they informed us of having received some damage in her bottom, making 3 inches of water an hour.

Continued to stand on to the SE with the appearance of much ice to the southward, having the blink of it on the horizon in that direction, which by the morning shew itself. By ½ past 10 we were brought up, being a large track of close packed Ice, which extended to the NNE & SE as far as the Eye could trace it from the Masthead, with much broken Ice lying about it in large & heavy lumps. We tackd ship and the Gale freshening, took the single reefs in each topsail. In the course of the night's run we had an extreme smooth sea that evidently indicates an extensive body of Ice to the South, the wind blowing from that quarter.

Sunday 25th At 1 Tackd Ship & stood on for the Ice, extending from NBW round southerly to NE, leaving only 5 points of the compass oppen & that to the Northward. At 4, being in with the Ice, we perceived many hundreds of sea horses lying in herds upon it. Hoisted the boats out to kill some of them. At 12 made sail and steered along the Ice to the NE, having killed 10 Sea horses and the boats hoisted in.

Following the course of the Ice, which appeared very thick & close, and impenetrable for the Ships, until ½ after 4, when it became more oppen & loose and so narrow that we could distinguish a clear sea over it to the South. Bore away & attempted to force our way through with success after receiving many severe strokes upon the bows, which occasioned by a swell tumbling in from the southward, that acted powerfully on the Ice and Ships. The facing of the cutwater received some damage. At 6 we were entirely clear of it. Stood away to the SE with a stiff breeze from the SSW which before Noon forced in the single reefs of the Topsails. Bore down to the Discovery.

Monday 26th Many Whales blowing. At 10 saw the Ice ahead. Hauled the wind and at Noon it extended from the west to SE and appeared to be loose and drifting fast with the force of the wind to the NW. Latitude 68°08′ N and longitude 189°40′ East.

Tuesday 27th At 1 Tackd close in with the ice, part of it very loose and broken, but most of it packd and appeared to increase its substance to the South & westward. Saw the firm ice to the NE, the weather being thick and unfavourable. Hauld the wind to the SW when at ½ after 3 we were again brought up with another field (or probably connected with the last). Tackd Ship and stood on to the Northward, sailing amidst much large and loose pieces.

Wednesday 28th At 1 the fog clearing away we saw the Ice extending from SE to NE. Soon after we also saw the Land, being the Coast of Asia, the haze lying heavy on it. At 4 we perceived more ice ahead which took a SE and NW direction as far as the eye could carry it from the mast head. Tackd close to the edge of the field ice with great quantities of loose [ice] lying before it and not the least signs or appearance of a clear sea to the westward. The most part of the Night we passed continually large sheets of drift and loose pieces and seemd apparently to join with the land, being that part of the Coast to the NW of the Serdze Kamen [prominent Siberian coastal feature named by Bering].

We have now beyond all doubt traced the Ice evidently from the one Continent to the other and in the many attempts we made to get to the westward, [it] does appear that we had the ill fortune not to succeed once, although no pains or labour was spared in our researches with the assistance of great perseverance and good conduct. The Ships on their part has received in the course of this business many heavy shocks with the Cutwaters in a great measure bruised, and their bows much subdued. The Discovery started and lost part of the sheathing, being in a leaking condition, and in danger of more sheathing hourly washing from her bows. At 4 in the Morning the Coast bore from S35°E to S65°W and Cape Serdze Kamen being the nearest point distant 5 leagues. Towards Noon the weather grew very hazy, which deprived us of a sight of the Coast.

3

RETURN TO KAMCHATKA AND ENGLAND
JULY–NOVEMBER 1779

After finding the pack impenetrable between Alaska and Asia the expedition abandoned the search for the imagined passageway, returning through Bering Strait to Avacha Bay and Petropavlosk. Overcome by the ravages of tuberculosis that effectively kept him in his cabin since leaving Hawai'i, Clerke died in late August when the ships first viewed the Siberian coastline. When a boat was sent to the *Discovery* to advise Captain Gore, Roberts reported, "Capt. Gore succeeded to the Command, the Discovery therefore the leading Ship."

The Burney journal concludes with the return of the expedition to Kamchatka, two days after Clerke's death, almost a year before the expedition returned to England. Burney was promoted and transferred from the *Discovery* to the *Resolution* after the captain's death, which presumably explains the premature end to his work. Likewise, Lieutenant John Gore transferred to the *Resolution*, where he assumed command of the expedition until it returned to England. King took command of the *Discovery*.

Settling in for a long stay in the Siberian village, Gore had tents erected for all the crew on shore, not just for the carpenters and sail makers. For a time, the captains considered scuttling the *Discovery* because of the damage it had received in the Arctic. The most essential repairs were to the ruined sheathing and the broken hull, which is where the ice had punctured the vessel below the water line. In addition, there were open, uncaulked timbers throughout. When the officers found similar problems with the *Resolution*, the thoughts of abandoning the consort ship were dismissed, so the crews settled in for a long stay until both ships could be made seaworthy. Crew not engaged in retrofitting the ships were free to explore the countryside, usually occupying their time collecting berries, hunting bears, and brewing spruce beer.[13]

As Master's Mate, Roberts was responsible for preparing charts and overseeing supplies, as well as the maintenance of the *Resolution*, yet his journal expanded with the passage of time ashore, particularly after the deaths of Cook and Clerke. Given the premature end to Burney's writing, it is fortunate that Roberts' text flourishes after the expedition returned to Avacha Bay in August, particularly as he described the repair of the vessels.

Roberts also made extensive remarks about the burial of Clerke. Before his death the captain said he wanted to be buried ashore at the church he had seen near the harbor in the village of Paratoonca. Gore and King both insisted that the burial be undertaken with a solemn ceremony, with all the pomp and dignity they could muster in such a remote place. When the time came, all the crew, even the local Russian soldiers, marched in procession with the local priest. Roberts was moved by the occasion, writing the funeral was "with all the honours suitable to his Rank."

In early October the carpenters, coopers, and sail makers finished refitting the ships just as the spruce beer ran out, so the vessels were soon underway for the long journey back to England.

Although Burney was now silent, Roberts' journal followed the voyage south past the Kurile Islands and Japan. While the wind and tides kept the vessels offshore, he observed local vessels, sea life, and the Japanese coastline—even the lofty summit of Mt. Fuji. There must have been considerable volcanic activity in the region at the time, as floating pumice was observed for weeks in the water as they approached the China Sea. Driven east by repeated gales, Roberts' last observation is of an island he described as "a perfect lump of Lava," which the British called "Sulphur Island." This is the solitary volcanic island six hundred miles south of Tokyo, now called Iwo Jima. It is an unusually flat and featureless volcanic island, with a small summit at one end, made famous by the horrific World War II battle in 1945.

Gore and King collected the personal journals of the officers and crew as they approached Macao. British tradition demanded that all the personal accounts would be combined into a single voyage journal, so Roberts concluded his journal on November 30, 1779. He explained, when they reached the Coast of China, he could not write any more, as "the Journals, Charts and papers, etc. were demanded by the Captain through order of the Lords of the Admiralty from the officers and people." It is unclear when the Admiralty returned the journals to Burney and Roberts, but it would have been many years later, after the official account was published.

Journal of James Burney

July 28th and 29th, 1779 Turning towards the SE in sight of the Coast of Asia.

Friday 30th Wind NW. In the Night ran through Behrings Straits, keeping to the west of Midchannel Islands.

Saturday 31st Steering to the Southward, the Coast of Asia in sight all day. Latitude at Noon 65°08′ North, Longitude in 189°08′ East.

Sunday, August 1st Wind SW. At Noon saw land to the SSE which we supposed to be an Island to the Eastward of St. Lawrence. Latitude 64°22′ North, Longitude 189°12′ East. All the Afternoon and Night, endeavouring to weather the Island. Thick foggy Weather.

Monday 2nd In the Morning, the fog cleared away. Found we had fell to leeward. At Noon being very clear, Saw the land . . . making in a number of high Clumps which appear like separate Islands. Our distance from the nearest 4 or 5 Leagues.

This Land we did not approach near enough to determine whether it is all one, or a cluster of Islands close together. The Westernmost part is what we passed July 3rd in the Night. The Easternmost part we ran close by in September last year and found to be a number of high Cliffs joined together by very low land, which makes it most probably that the whole is but one Island. Its extent is from 62°54′ North Latitude to 63°49′ [North Latitude] and from 188° to 191½° East Longitude. Most part of the Afternoon Calm. In the evening a light breeze ENE. Steered to the Westward.

James Burney, "St. Lawrence Island to Icy Cape," August 1779. Burney was the only cartographer to chart the expedition's second attempt to breach Arctic Ice during the summer of 1779—Captain Clerke's search for the Northwest Passage. Burney carefully traced the tracks of the ships during their month-long attack on the ice pack, which nearly wrecked both ships. Burney Journal p. 181, Mitchell Library, State Library of New South Wales, Safe 1/64 and 1/79.

Tuesday 3rd Light winds, running round to the NW point of the Island Saint Lawrence.

Wednesday 4th In the Afternoon a fresh Gale at East. Lost Sight of the Land. Steered towards the SSW.

5th and 6th Winds between the North and West with rainy weather.

Saturday 7th At Noon Latitude 59°38′ North, Longitude in 183°07′ East. In the Afternoon, little wind . . . Caught Cod.

To the 17th making the best of our way towards the SW, without any occurrence worth remarking.

Tuesday 17th At ½ past 4 in the Morning Saw Land to the NW which we could not approach, the wind being from that quarter. At noon, Latitude 53°50′ North, Longitude 168°06′ East, the Land in Sight, NBW distance 10 or 12 Leagues. This we take to be the Island Meadnoi [Medny in the Komandorski Islands], laid down to the SE of Behrings Island in the Charts of the Russians at Kamtschatka.

Saturday 21st At Daylight saw the Coast of Kamtschatka, the Shupanovcokaya Mountain [Klyuchevskaya Sopka, the highest active volcano in Eurasia] bearing NW½N per Compass, 25 or 30 Leagues distant.

Sunday 22nd This morning, the Resolutions boat came on board to Inform us of the death of Captain Clerke. At Noon were off the Shupinikoi Noss [Avacha Bay], its Latitude 53°08′ North Longitude 159°56′ East.

Monday 23rd In the evening Saw the lookout house of Awatscha Bay, on which a good light was shewn us after dark. At Midnight Anchord in the entrance of Awatscha Bay in 11 fathoms.

Tuesday 24th In the morning weighd and Stood towards the Ostrog. In the Afternoon Anchord and Moord in the harbour of St. Peter and Paul. The Country has now a most beautifull appearance. Kamtschatka in Summer and Kamtschatka in winter, one would Scarcely call the same place.

Major Behm, we hear, set off for Petersburgh soon after our departure (in June). Captain Smealoff is Commander in Chief of Kamtschatka. The Ostrog of St. Peter and Paul is under the same Serjeant who commanded when we were here before.

Journal of Henry Roberts

Thursday, July 29th Standing in shore until 8 when Cape Serdze Kamen was 7 leagues [from the ships]. This point is situated in the Latitude of 67°03′ N and Longitude of 188°11′ East. Its shores are steep & cliffy. The inland country to the west of it rises to hills of a moderate height, the summits of which are irregular, owing to small rocky parts which at some distance have the appearance of buildings. The Coast to the North of the Cape takes a more western direction. We could perceive no wood on the shores, which is tolerably clear from Snow. Continued standing to the eastward all night under single reef'd Topsails with flurries of wind & Calms occasioned by the hills and a great head sea, so that we made but little way through the water. At 4 we saw the East Cape of Asia, distance from the Cape 15 leagues.

Saturday 31st At ½ past 5 the haze somewhat cleared away, which enabled us to get a sight of the land, the American Coast shewing itself. Hauled the wind when seeing the Islands that lie between the two Continents (or the islands of St. Demetrius) [Diomede Islands], we altered course & steerd in for the Asiatic shore to make the East Cape. At this time we saw Cape Prince of Wales on the American side.

Monday, August 2nd In the afternoon the weather turning foggy and shoaling our water to 17 fms we made the signal to our Consort and tackd and fired a Gun every hour until 7 in order to keep Company, which was answered, at which time we Tackd. Having clear weather, soon after it became thick as before when we were obliged to stand to the West again, which course we continued all night. At 2 in the morning tackd & stood to the SE, some part of the Coast bearing WBS.

At 5 the fog having dissipated we saw the Land to the Southward and appeared as three different Islands. That which we ever took to be St. Lawrence being the westernmost, with a flat surface. The other two however was afterwards found to be joined by low land. [We were] offshore 5 leagues and could perceive low land to unite them with the same also stretching from the westernmost towards the Island St. Lawrence, but whether this connected like the other we were not able to determine at this time. We saw the land situated to the westward of Andersons Island and may likewise join, yet we could observe no risings between them, but off the eastern extremity of this nearest land is some rocks, so that if there should prove to be a sepparation it will be found very inconsiderable & most likely not a fit channel for ships to pass through. We had a tolerable good view of this Country with the assistance of our Glasses and appeared to be the same as the former.

Tuesday 3rd We now saw the land we discovered to the SE of St. Lawrence in our route up to the North and by every appearance should conclude that it made the SW extremity of this Isle. The highest parts of the Island in general are hills of a moderate imminence with a broken surface where cavities are filled with snow and not the least prospect of Tree or shrub. The low places are quite level and from a light green verdue that lay on it, it may possibly produce good Grass and heath berries, the only production of Islands in these advanced Northern Climates.

Wednesday 4th Saw the Island St. Lawrence distant 7 leagues. The weather at this time was so obscured with haze banks that we could not determine whether this joined to the other land, but from its situation & size layd down by Capt. Behring, should apprehend it to be a distinct Island. Otherwise, he never had an opportunity of determining its extent. At this time caught a good number of Cod. Latitude 58°48′ N.

Wednesday 11th The fore Top Gallant sail, being much torn and bad in many places, it was cut up to repair other sails. Latitude 57°33′ N and Longitude of 173°24′ East.

Friday 13th Many whales blowing, with large flights of Sea Gulls, divers and parrots about.

Tuesday 17th At ½ past 4 we saw land supposed to be the Southernmost of Behrings Islands, corresponding nearly with its latitude agreeable to the Russians. At Noon the haze lying over it we had but an indistinct sight but that part which shew itself distance 15 leagues. This is high land and appeared quite clear of snow. It lies in the latitude of 54°28′ N & longitude of 167°52′ East. Try'd soundings but had no Ground at 150 fms.

Sunday 22nd At 8 the Chupoonskoi Cape distance 10 leagues. We now had sight of three very high mountains, whose summits were peaked, the southernmost bearing due west, the last being the same as first seen Yesterday. Very little snow on the land.

At ½ past 8 this morning departed this life Captain Charles Clerke, our Commander, after a lingering Consumption of many months. Sent a boat on board the Discovery.

Monday 23rd Capt. Gore succeeded to the Command, the Discovery therefore the leading Ship. At 5 latitude of 53°01′ N and longitude of 161°34′ East. Passed a number of riplings during the course of the night, which was occasioned by the currents or tides, as we could reach no bottom with 160 fathoms. At ½ past 9 AM a breeze sprung up and made all sail shaping a course for the bay of Awatscha. Saw the land through the haze bearing NW.

Tuesday 24th The gale increasing that shew us the Entrance of Awatscha Bay we continued standing on when at 10 we were in the mouth of the Bay and having little wind hoisted the boats out to tow, the Russians keeping a good fire on the North head. At 1 the tide making against us, anchored in 7 fms. In the morning we were agreeably surprised to find so great an alteration in the aspect of the Country, as at that time we quitted it in June, [now] every hill were most elegantly diversified with Trees of different bloom, each having the greatest verdue conceivable. In short the whole face of the Country [was] carrying a most butiful prospect.

Wednesday 25th At 9 AM the flood making, we got under weigh with the boats ahead towing. At Noon we were about 4 miles from the Ostrog of Peterpawloska [and] by 2 O'Clock [a light breeze] carried us into the harbour of St. Peter & Paul, the Discovery close to us.

In the Morning fixed the Tents and observatorys on shore and sent partys to cut wood, others to boil pine Tops for beer, and sailmakers to repair the sails.

Capt. Gore took Command of this Ship, appointed Lieut. James King to that of the Discovery and Mr. Burney and Rickman first and second Lieutenants of the Resolution. Sold the effects of Captain Clerke.

Thursday 26th Our carpenters at work on the Discovery's bows. Hauld the Seine and caught plenty of fine Salmon, sufficient for the Ships Company. Hands sent daily to gather Greens, which were boiled in the soup. Thermometer Noon 65°.

Friday 27th The Carpenters find the Discovery wants much repair. Sent the Launch for a Load of Wood, the people being obliged to cutt it about 2 miles from this up the Bay, being scarce near this place. AM sent hands to clear a place for the Burial of Captain Clerke at the head of the harbour.

Sunday 29th Interred the body of Captain Charles Clerke (at the foot of a Tree to the Northward of the harbour) with all the honours suitable to his Rank. His Escutcheon [an emblem bearing his coat of arms] was afterwards put up in the Church at Paratounka with an Inscription relating his succession to the Command of the two Ships after the fall of his great predecessor, Captain Cook. Another inscription was also fixed on the Tree over his grave, which was staked round and made conspicuous.

Tuesday 31st Employed cleaning the Fore hold and lighting the Ship forward to enable us to repair the Cutwater, which is much hurt. Sent hands to haul the Seine. Punished Matthew Beach, Seaman, with 12 lashes for Insolence. Thermometer Midnight 50° Noon 53°.

Saturday, September 4th PM an officer arrived from Bolchaisetokoi, being a praporschuck, in the Russian services. Thermometer at Noon 82°. Gave the people liberty on shore to refresh themselves after their Northern campaign. Carpenters finished repairing the Discovery. Received 472 lbs of fresh beef, which was serv'd to the Companys of both Sloops.

Tuesday 7th Employed making ready for hauling aground to repair the Cutwater. Dropped the Sheet and other Anchors from the Bows and carried out the stream on the Town point and hauld near the Shore. Punished John McDonald, Marine, with a dozen lashes for drunkenness and Insolence. Thermometer at daylight 48° at Noon 51°.

Wednesday 8th Hauld the Ships bow on the ground, being sheathed with quarter fasts. We were obliged to wait the morning tide for the Carpenters to work [who] found the defects further under the water than was expected, when we were forced to lighten the Ship more by getting the Fore top mast & Fore yards with all the booms etc on Shore and hove her bow further on. Thermometer at daylight 49° at Noon 55½°.

Friday 10th Carpenters repairing the Cutwater. Sent hands to cut brooms. A Russian Sloop appearing off the Bay. Sent a boat out to her. Found her at Anchor, having come from Ochotsk, loaded with meal, cordage & other stores, some part of which was for us. AM sent the Boats to give them assistance in getting in. At Noon she anchored in the Harbour. Thermometer 49° at Noon 55½°.

Saturday 11th The Carpenters being finished, hauld the Ship afloat. AM heeld the Ship and secured by the hands on both sides. Received from the Sloop [listing of stores received from the Russian storeship, particularly cables, coils, tubs of tar and pitch, and twine necessary to renovate the vessels after their near destruction in the Arctic]. Thermometer 48° at Noon 55°.

Tuesday 14th Employed storing the last side of the main hold. AM got wood on board & the small Bower in the hold. Punished John Fisher with 12 lashes for drunkenness and insolence. The praporschuck this morning set out for Bol-

Henry Roberts, "Awatcha [Avacha] Bay [Kamchatka]," April-October 1779. Many of the expedition chartmakers prepared maps of this bay, as they spent more time here than any other anchorage on the expedition. Roberts' chart shows his usual precision and careful penmanship. Roberts Journal p. 119, Vol. II, Dixson Library, State Library of New South Wales, DLMSQ 151-52 and DLMSF 2.

chaisetokoi. Another officer came in the Sloop who took precedence of this, an elderly Man called a praporschuck. Thermometer 48° at Noon 54°. [Journal records a further two weeks at port, especially repairing the sails and rigging.]

Monday 20th Received from the Russian Sloop 81 Skin bags of Rye Meal weighing 241½ poods gross weight (or) 8059 lbs. Thermometer Noon 57°.

Wednesday 22nd Arrived at the Town Captain Ishmyloff from Bolchaisetokoi, Commander in Chief of all Kamtschatka.

Thursday 23rd At 1 this being the anniversary of His Majesty's Coronation, saluted with 21 Guns. Came on board Captain Ishmyloff, when we saluted him with 11 Guns.

Saturday 25th Captain Ishmyloff went off for Bolchaisetokoi. Saluted him with 11 Guns.

Saturday, October 2nd Warped out of the Harbour and anchored in 7 fms between the low point which runs off the west head of the harbour and the ostrog point, distance ½ mile, steadied with the stream [anchor]. Served fresh meat to the people.

Sunday 3rd At Noon fired 21 Guns in honour to the Empress of Russia. Thermometer from 47° to 60°. [Wood, water, and ballast brought aboard, getting ready for sea with killing of remaining cattle and corning the meat. Lengthy and delayed departure due to winds, weather, and tides.]

Awatscha Bay is situated on the West Coast of Kamtschatka, the mouth of which lies in the Latitude of 52°50′ N and Longitude East of Greenwich 158°45′. The Bay itself is nearly Circular of 3 or 4 leagues in Extent on every part. The depth of Water is regular. The greatest depth is 15 fms over a Bottom of muddy Clay. It affords three extremely good Harbours (viz. Terieira, Rackowina & Peterpawloska). The latter is the place Resident by the Russians, having their Settlement on a low sandy point, which forms the Harbour.

Terieira was at the Time I surveyed the Bay Blocked up with Ice in the Month of May but before we sailed the shores were totally clear, yet had no opportunity to compleat the survey. Major Behm however gave it the Character of a very convenient good Harbour. The soundings in the Mouth of it is regular and clear of Rocks.

The Bay is well diversified with hills of a Moderate Elevation bearing in general the Birch Tree and a small specie of the pine. The low land which lies at the head of the Bay is also well clothed with wood of immense thickness, so as to render it impassable. This Bay may be known by the North head of the Entrance on which stands a look out belonging to the Russians. Its a steep cliffy projecting head land and might be seen at least 8 leagues. The Harbour of Peter & Paul lies from this in about 9 Miles in the direction of N ½ W.

The Refreshments we procured at this place was very considerable, exclusive of the Beef and Flour supplied us by the great hospitality of the Russian Commander. Our nets brought us Cod, Salmon, Herrings, Plaice [halibut], and other different fish in great abundance and our Guns plenty of Game and wild fowl. The sides of the hills afforded nettle tops, wild Celery & Garlick, etc all of which was most commonly boiled in the peoples Broth, and pease, which makes it savory and nourishing.

Sunday 10th At 3 the weather became clear with a gentle gale from the NW. Weighd and came to sail. In heaving up the Messenger being but indifferent gave way several times, which obliged us to seize a purchase to break the Anchor from the ground. Stood out for the harbours mouth and by 6 we were abreast of the watch tower head, upon which the Russians kept a good fire. Standing to sea all Night to get an offing against a swell rolling in from the SE.

Light winds accompanied with Calms in which intervals caught a number of very fine Cod. Began to serve spruce beer to the people and continued every other day, with their allowance of Grog alternately.

Monday 11th Standing along the Coast with changeable winds. At 3 another head land oppend with the Southernmost sett at noon (which is called by the Russians Cape Gavarra) about 7 leagues from the last mentioned point. Between them were two small inlets which probably might unite and form a small Island. The shores here are steep and cliffy and the hills fall suddenly into Valleys that are mostly well wooded. The Northward of Cape Gavarra are appearances of several Inlets, but the information we received from the Russians assures us that its nothing more than deep Valleys closed up with low land.

Wednesday 13th To the Northwest of the Cape is a remarkable high mount whose elevated peak out topped the Clouds. We at this time also saw the first of the Kurile Islands to the southward of the Cape called Shoom [Shumshu] by the Russians. The passage between this Isle and the Cape is described by them dangerous from the rapidity of the Tides motion and sunken rocks lying off the Cape. Its breadth is 3 leagues.

When at day break we saw the next Island to the Southward of Shoom, named Pourimtchin [Paramushir], the land high and much covered with snow. A peaked mountain [on it] was thought issued out smoke. This most probably was the case as [there were] many Volcanoes on these Islands. [The expedition observed beds of sea weed and flights of gulls and other birds as it sailed south past the Kurile Islands during the next two weeks. On the 14th they passed Paramushir, which Roberts noted as one of the largest of the Kurile Islands in Latitude 49°47′ North and Longitude 156°43′ East. A gale and haze prevented them from getting a good view.]

Tuesday 26th [In a week the ships passed the southernmost of the Kurile Islands, but repeated gales and rain squalls forced them away from land. Later the Isles of Jeso, north of Japan, were expected, but the weather remained hazy and no land was observed.]

At daybreak in the Morning saw high land to the westward that we know to be part of the great Isle of Nippon or Japan Latitude 39°59′ North and Longitude 142°05′ East. At this time the land [had] a point with a sugar loaf hill upon it to the Northward of which appeared to be a deep Inlet the surface of which was level. We stood on until ½ past 9 when we were within 2 leagues of the nearest part. The shores here were steep and cliffy, the hills of a Moderate height agreeably diversified with fine tall wood. The back land out top'd this considerably but these hills carried a gentle account to the very summits, the sides of them well clothed with trees. We tackd to stand off in a depth of water of 50 fms, put over our fishing lines, but had no success. At Noon having light baffling winds, we found the Ship drifted considerably to the NNW by a strong Current or Tide. Saw several smokes upon the hills.

Wednesday 27th Soon after noon the southern Gale again renewed its force when we took in our single reefs & stretched off to the ESE. The weather exceeding hazy that we shortly lost sight of the land. The Northernmost part we saw by an estimated distance is in Latitude 40°30′ N and should suppose it to be the Nabo Noss [Nemuro Peninsula, Hokkaido], agreeing nearly with the situation. It made in a low shelving point with high land some distance at the back of it, which probably is an Island. To the Southward of this point as I before observed appears to be a Bay, the same I judge thats distinguish'd in the Charts by the name of Port Nambu [Nanbu]. We find the longitude of this Northeastern Coast very justly described by G. Muller. The most eastern in 142°30′ East of Greenwich.

Thursday 28th The Coast here is not so high as the land we first saw. Several points seem to form but whether they afforded shelter or not remains a great doubt as our situation was too distant to determine.

Friday 29th [Coasting south] this part appeared to be quite a straight shore, which was low and woody. The land behind moderately high and the tops of the hills level. We had at this time 20 fms water over a bottom of coarse sand and gravel. Saw a Country Vessel in shore standing to the Northward soon after we saw another to windward, when we tackd and brought too with an intention of getting a nearer View of them on coming to some parley. They passed within 2 miles of us. We then wore and stood after them for a few minutes without following them. Afterwards hauld our wind to the Eastward. She appeared to be net 40 Tons, built high at each end and low in the middle, with only one mast which supported one large square sail. There appeared to be but few people on board. Towards Noon the Gale increased with thick weather. [The ships kept a distance from the Japanese coastline, but a shark, Mt. Fuji, and a series of Japanese vessels were observed nearer shore. The current was ever changing, with a "confused sea," and the *Resolution* struggled in the hot, humid weather.]

[Leaving Japanese waters for China, Roberts frequently observed large quantities of pumice stone suspended in the water, suggesting a recent volcanic explosion nearby. He also noted grass and logs floating as debris, as well as porpoises, flying fish, a large shark, and land and sea birds from the deck. They also suffered severe squalls and gales with a heavy sea that caused the ship to roll violently.

When the gales subsided, they experienced thick weather so they could not see one quarter mile.]

Sunday, November 13th A hard gale with heavy squalls and rain. The sea running very high, we shipped one [a wave], which struck us with great violence, carrying away the weather gunwale sail, with some of the stanchions overboard, and filled between decks knee deep with water our forehatch way, at this time not being closed. Many dolphins about. Saw a Tropic bird & albatrosses, with quantities of pummice stone passing.

Monday 15th We had now a tolerable sight [of a peaked volcanic mountain, known today as Iwo Jima]. The shores appeared very steep and the mountain rise with a quick ascent on all sides. The other land (to the south) made in a hummock with low land stretching off it to the Northeastward. At 9 we were abreast of the hummock when we perceived sulphur lying on its top and also smelt it to be very strong. The whole Mass of it appeared to be a perfect lump of Lava, being quite steep & barren. The other part to the Northward was level, covered with grass and small shrubs in many places, with small rocky and broken precipices. The west side is well guarded by a reef, within which was a good sandy beach. Besides this reef there are many detached rocks to the west of it and a ledge flying off the Eastern part.

This island obtained the name of Sulphur Island and had no doubt every appearance of being very recently a Volcano. Latitude 24°51′ North and Longitude 140°42′ East.

Tuesday 16th We intended landing on this Island but found no place that we could do it with safety. Many flying fish. [They continued to observe rafts of floating pumice, as well as bonitos, albatross, sheerwater birds, and porpoises. Later they experienced another gale with high seas, which kept them well off the coast. Thick, foggy weather followed. In the fog they fired a gun to the Discovery as a signal. While fishing from the decks, the Resolution caught a dolphin and a shark. They soon looked for the Bashee Islands, seven islands in the China Sea. Although breakers and reefs were detected through the rain, gales, and cloudy weather, they did not see any land.]

Monday 29th The water appearing very white, being on the China fishing ground. Saw several of the China fishing Boats and other country Vessels.

Tuesday 30th Many fishing Vessels about. At 4 hours afternoon we made the Coast of China when the Journals, Charts and papers, etc, were demanded by the Captain through order of the Lords of the Admiralty from the officers and people.

Henry Roberts, Mate.

NOTES

PROLOGUE

1. J. C. Beaglehole, *The Life of Captain James Cook* (Stanford: Stanford University Press, 1974). There have been many biographies of Cook. The first was published less than a decade after his death by Andrew Kippis, *The Life of Captain James Cook* (London, 1788). The Kippis biography is as collectable as the published accounts of the voyage. See also Nicholas Thomas, *Cook: The Extraordinary Voyages of Captain James Cook* (New York, Walker & Company, 2003) and John Gascoigne, *Captain Cook: Voyager Between Worlds* (London: Humbledon Continuum, 2007). Cook had already established himself as Europe's pre-eminent explorer after completing his first two voyages. While struggling to find land in the ice during his second voyage in Antarctica, on Sunday, January 30, 1774, Cook wrote of his personal ambition and the limitations of the sailing ships of the era, "I who had Ambition not only to go farther than any one had done before, but as far as it was possible for man to go, but was not sorry at meeting with this interruption as it in some measure relieved us, at least shortened the dangers and hardships inseparable with the Navigation of the Southern Polar Regions." Fifty years ago the quotation evolved into "to explore strange new worlds, to seek out new life forms and new civilizations, to boldly go where no man has gone before," in the title sequence of the television series, *Star Trek*, reflecting Cook's lasting impact in the exploration of new frontiers. The Cook quote is found in J. C. Beaglehole, *The Voyage of the Resolution and Adventure, 1772-1775* (Cambridge: Cambridge University Press, 1961), 323. In this vein, a more lighthearted look at the story of Captain Cook's three voyages of exploration can be found in Tony Horowitz, *Blue Latitudes: Boldly Going Where Captain Cook Has Gone Before* (New York: Henry Holt and Company, 2002). See generally, James K. Barnett, *Captain Cook in Alaska and the North Pacific* (Anchorage: Todd Communications, 2008) and James K. Barnett and David S. Nicandri, eds., *Arctic Ambitions: Captain Cook and the Northwest Passage* (Seattle: University of Washington Press, 2015).
2. Glyndwr Williams, *Voyages of Delusion: The Search for the Northwest Passage in the Age of Reason* (London: Harper Collins, 2002), 287–306. Beaglehole, *Life of Cook*, 478, 483. See also, Glyn Williams, *Arctic Labyrinth: The Quest for the Northwest Passage* (Berkeley: University of California Press, 2009), 135–36. An excellent summary of the purposes and preparations for the third voyage is found in Glyndwr Williams, "James Cook and the Northwest Passage: Approaching the Third Voyage," in Barnett and Nicandri, *Arctic Ambitions*, 21–44.
3. J. C. Beaglehole, *The Voyage of the Resolution and Discovery, 1776-1780* (Cambridge: Cambridge University Press, 1967), Part Two, Appendix IV, 1478–79. This is the edited version of the voyage journal, written by Captain Cook until just before his death in early 1779. After his death the official journal continues with contributions from Lieutenant James King, as well as Charles Clerke until Clerke's death six months later in Kamchatka. Beaglehole, *Life of Cook*, 610.
4. Beaglehole, *Life of Cook*, 498. Andrew David, ed., *The Charts and Coastal Views of Captain Cook's Voyages: The Voyage of the Resolution and Discovery 1776-1780* (London: Hakluyt Society, 1997), xx. An excellent summary of the consequences of the first two voyages is found in John Gascoigne, "James Cook: Navigator and Explorer, The Pacific Experience, 1768-1776," in Barnett and Nicandri, *Arctic Ambitions*, 3–20.
5. Beaglehole, *Life of Cook*, 448. See also Anne Salmond, *The Trial of the Cannibal Dog: The Remarkable Story of Captain Cook's Encounters in the South Seas* (New Haven: Yale University Press, 2003). Mai's extraordinary time in England during 1773–76 is described at 293–317.
6. Anne Salmond, *Between Worlds: Early Exchanges Between Maori and Europeans, 1773-1815* (Honolulu: University of Hawai'i Press, 1997), 140.
7. Beaglehole, *Voyage of the Resolution and Discovery*, Part Two, Appendix V, 1535. The death of Cook has been described by many onlookers, and repeated by biographers, all carefully examining the facts and implications, looking for a rationale for the loss. Beaglehole is the accepted authority on Cook and accounts of his three voyages to the Pacific. See J. C. Beaglehole, ed., *The Journals of Captain James*

Cook on His Voyages of Discovery (Cambridge: Cambridge University Press for the Hakluyt Society, 1967). His accounts of Cook's death in Hawai'i are found in *The Voyage of the Resolution and Discovery, 1776–1780,* which he summarizes in Part One, cxlvii-clvii. Clerke's account carefully reconstructed events from the English perspective, almost as a court of inquiry, and can be found at Beaglehole, *Voyage of the Resolution and Discovery*, Part One, 531–39. King was with Cook on the *Resolution* when events unraveled that morning. His version is at Beaglehole, *Voyage of the Resolution and Discovery*, Part One, 549–61. The most concise examination is found at Glyn Williams, *The Death of Captain Cook: A Hero Made and Unmade* (Cambridge, MA: Harvard University Press, 2008).

8. Williams, *Arctic Labyrinth*, 141–48.
9. An insightful interpretation of the consequences and accomplishments of the third voyage and Cook's temperament on the voyage is found in David Nicandri, *A New Look at Cook: Reflections on Sand, Ice and His Diligent Voyage to the Arctic Ocean*, in Barnett and Nicandri, *Arctic Ambitions*, 109–29.
10. Beverly Hooper, ed., *With Captain James Cook in the Antarctic and Pacific: The Private Journal of James Burney, Second Lieutenant of the "Adventure" on Cook's Second Voyage, 1772-1773* (Canberra, ACT: National Library of Australia, 1975), 1–8. Beaglehole, *Life of Cook*, 498. David, *Charts and Coastal Views of the Resolution and Discovery*, lxxiv.
11. Hooper, *Private Journal of James Burney*, 23–93. Suzanne Rickard, *Sailing with Cook: Inside the Private Journal of James Burney RN* (Canberra, ACT: National Library of Australia, 2015). Beaglehole, *Voyage of the Resolution and Discovery*, Part One, 534.
12. David, *Charts and Coastal Views of the Resolution and Discovery*, lxxix. David discusses Roberts' personal relationship with William Bligh at lxxi.
13. See, for example, Beaglehole, *Voyage of the Resolution and Discovery*, Part Two, 1560–65. This is a letter from Bligh to Roberts telling him of errors in the published charts. Bligh also declares all the surveys were of his making and that Roberts had just copied them. There is no record of Roberts' response. See also Beaglehole, *Voyage of the Resolution and Discovery*, Part One, ccxv-ccxvi. Bligh's complaints were usually addressed to Burney, but Beaglehole confirms Roberts was a careful draftsman.
14. Beaglehole, *Life of Cook*, 691. David, *Charts and Coastal Views of the Resolution and Discovery*, xciv. For example, Burney wrote of Ledyard's "ardent disposition" and his "passion for lofty sentiment and description" in his reminisces in *A Chronological History of North-Eastern Voyages of Discovery and of the Early Eastern Navigations of the Russians* (London: Payne and Foss, 1819), 280–81. According to Burney, Ledyard's "ideas were thought too sentimental, and his language too florid." Beaglehole, *Voyage of the Resolution and Discovery*, Part One, lxxxix-lxxxx. Samwell's version of the events of February 14, 1779, is found in Part Two, 1194–1207.
15. Beaglehole, *Life of Cook*, 684–85. Burney's explanatory note for this version is found in Beaglehole, *Voyage of the Resolution and Discovery*, Part One, clxxxiii, "On the arrival of the Resolution and Discovery to Macao Roads, we learnt that Great Britain was at War with France and with the North American States, which gave us some apprehension of being captured on our passage homeward, and in such event that we should lose our journals. Under this apprehension, I made a copy of my journal on China paper in so small a compass as to be easily concealable, that if bereft of our other journals there might be one saved for the Admiralty." This version is now mounted on four slides between sheets of glass and maintained as a curiosity in the British Museum.
16. David, *Charts and Coastal Views of the Resolution and Discovery*, cxxxi. Beaglehole, *Voyage of the Resolution and Discovery*, Part One, 697–701 (Ships in the ice above Bering Strait, July 22–August 24, 1779) and 1340–42 (Description of Tongan music, June 12, 1777).
17. Beaglehole, *Voyage of the Resolution and Discovery*, Part One, 697–701.
18. Burney, *North-Eastern Voyages*, 266. Chapter XXI, entitled "Sequel," is 252–70.
19. Beaglehole, *Voyage of the Resolution and Discovery*, Part One, clxxxv; David, *Charts and Coastal Views of the Resolution and Discovery*, cxx.
20. David, *Charts and Coastal Views of the Resolution and Discovery*, lxxxv-lxxxvii.
21. Beaglehole, *Life of Cook*, 501. The comprehensive catalog of the original drawings and engravings from Captain Cook's three voyages is Rüdiger Joppien and Bernard Smith, *The Art of Captain Cook's Voyages* (Melbourne: Oxford University Press in association with the Australian Academy of the

Humanities, 1987). Two of the four volumes are dedicated to the third voyage drawings, principally those of John Webber and William Ellis. Webber's appointment is discussed in Volume Three Text, 1–2. See also John Frazier Henry, *Early Maritime Artists of the Pacific Northwest Coast, 1741-1841* (Seattle: University of Washington Press, 1984), and David, *Charts and Coastal Views of the Resolution and Discovery*, lxxix-lxxx.

22. Joppien and Smith, *Volume Three Text and Catalog*, 171–215. A careful review of the work of the many artists on Cook's three voyages, which features the contributions of Webber and Ellis, can be found in Rüdiger Joppien, "The Artists on James Cook's Expeditions," in Adrienne L. Kaeppler, Curator, *James Cook and the Exploration of the Pacific* (London: Thames & Hudson, 2011), 112–18.

PART 1: THE SOUTH SEAS

1. Thomas, *Extraordinary Voyages of Captain James Cook*, 285–86, 289.
2. Beaglehole, *Voyage of the Resolution and Discovery*, Part Two, 784–85. Salmond, *Trial of the Cannibal Dog*, 310–11.
3. A careful examination of the *Adventure*'s second visit to the Sound, including the struggle that led to bloodshed and claims of cannibalism at Grass Cove, is offered in Salmond, *Between Worlds*, 100–105. Once recovered by Burney and his crew, the remains of the ten murdered men were returned to the *Adventure*, tied in a hammock with ballast and shot and, in the naval tradition, buried at sea.
4. Hooper, *Private Journal of James Burney*, 95–99. Salmond, *Trial of the Cannibal Dog*, 228–31. Burney did not think the attack on the Europeans was premeditated, but Furneaux and his men should have anticipated the volatile outburst. John Rowe, the leader of the party, was indifferent toward the Maori and assured of the superiority of British firepower. Nonetheless, cannibalism by the local people, a greatly disputed theme during the European Enlightenment, was apparently confirmed by this incident. A careful analysis of Cook's many visits to *Tōtara-Nui* or *Tōtaranui* (Queen Charlotte's Sound) can be found in Salmond, *Between Worlds*, 65–160. Scholars have attributed the massacre to growing hostilities with Europeans after earlier attacks and because it was a part of their culture for the absolute destruction of their enemies. "Cannibalism among Maori was not arbitrary," Salmond writes at 144, "but a devastating act of retribution."
5. The details of Cook's final visit are found in Salmond, *Between Worlds*, 119–30. Salmond titles her iconic book, *Trial of the Cannibal Dog*, to substantiate the sailors' reaction to the slaughter when they returned to Queen Charlotte Sound at the beginning of the third voyage. They held a mock court martial of a Maori "cannibal dog" on board the *Discovery* after learning the captain was not planning to take revenge for the massacre. See 6–10, 312–17. See also Beaglehole, *Life of Cook*, 446–47 and Thomas, *Extraordinary Voyages*, 300–306.
6. Thomas, *Extraordinary Voyages of Captain James Cook*, 310–12. Salmond, *Trial of the Cannibal Dog*, 320–21.
7. Mai's presence as an interpreter was frequently applauded in the journals, particularly given the closeness of the visitors to the people, including relations with the women. "Omai is of great use to us, not only as an interpreter," King wrote, "but in keeping up a good understanding between us and the Natives, for they pay him great attention and listen to the stories he tells them about Brittannee, which doubtless tends to keep up our consequence, too apt to be lessened by the familiarity of our intercourse; and from which we find out that the Venereal disorder has been left among them. So it is wherever we go we spread an incurable distemper which nothing we can do can ever recompense." Beaglehole, *Voyage of the Resolution and Discovery*, Part One, 99 note. In 1789, after leading a failed watering party two days earlier on Nomuka, which was interrupted by hostile Natives, Fletcher Christian and his mutineers seized the *Bounty* from Captain Bligh on April 28, in open ocean thirty miles south of the nearby Tongan island of Tofua, setting in motion a notorious episode of British South Seas maritime history. Caroline Alexander, *Bounty* (London: Harper Collins, 2003).
8. Beaglehole, *Voyage of the Resolution and Discovery*, Part One, cii–civ. Beaglehole, *Life of Cook*, 531–46. Salmond, *Between Worlds*, 134. Thomas, *Extraordinary Voyages of Captain James Cook*, 316–21.

9. Beaglehole, *Life of Cook*, 549–50. Salmond, *Trial of the Cannibal Dog*, 351–54.
10. The first European to reach Tahiti was Samuel Wallis of Great Britain, who arrived in 1767 in the *Dolphin*. His crew included John Gore, who sailed on both Cook's first and third voyages. Louis Antoine de Bougainville arrived less than a year after Wallis, commanding a large French voyage with two ships and over 300 men, including the first woman known to have circumnavigated the world. Unaware of Wallis's earlier visit, he claimed Tahiti for the King of France and named it *New Cythera*. But Cook left the most indelible mark. See generally Anne Salmond, *Aphrodite's Island: The European Discovery of Tahiti* (Berkeley: University of California Press, 2009), which examines Cook's legendary interplay with the island nation, particularly at Matavai Bay, where he anchored on four occasions between 1769 and 1777. The final time to Tahiti on the third voyage is discussed at 417–52. See also Salmond, *Trial of the Cannibal Dog*, 354–78, and Thomas, *Extraordinary Voyages of Captain James Cook*, 334–40.
11. Beaglehole, *Voyage of the Resolution and Discovery*, Part One, cxii–cxiii. Beaglehole, *Life of Cook*, 552–70. Burney wrote of Clerke's request to stay in Huahine in his chronicles, *North-Eastern Voyages*, 233–34, writing "Mr. Anderson and Captain Clerke had been in a declining state the last twelve months. When the ships were at Otaheite in August 1777, Anderson represented to Captain Clerke their inability to encounter the severities of a frozen climate and they mutually agreed to ask leave of Captain Cook to resign their appointments to the voyage, that they might remain where they were and trust themselves to the care of the Natives, as the only hope left them of being restored to health." Burney explained that Anderson and Clerke deferred leaving the vessels in Huahine and again Ra'iātea, because Clerke said his papers were not yet in order. By the time they reached the final island stop at Bora Bora, where they did not land, Cook had apparently convinced them to continue with the expedition.
12. Gavan Daws, *Shoal of Time: A History of the Hawaiian Islands* (Honolulu: University Press of Hawai'i, 1968), 1–8. Beaglehole, *Voyage of the Resolution and Discovery*, Part One, cxv–cxx.
13. Beaglehole, *Voyage of the Resolution and Discovery*, Part One, 279. Beaglehole, *Life of Cook*, 574–80. Thomas, *Extraordinary Voyages of Captain James Cook*, 354–56. Salmond, *Trial of the Cannibal Dog*, 380–85.
14. Beaglehole, *Voyage of the Resolution and Discovery*, Part One, xxxi and Part Two, 1459, 1486–87.
15. The bottle inscription probably meant "In the reign of Louis XV, King of France, the lord de Boynes being Secretary of the Marine, in the years 1772 and 1773." Beaglehole, *Voyage of the Resolution and Discovery*, Part One, 31–32.
16. Beaglehole, *Voyage of the Resolution and Discovery*, Part One, 60.
17. The confusion with the winds is discussed in Beaglehole, *Voyage of the Resolution and Discovery*, Part One, xcix–c. Cook expected westerly winds and he had easterlies. Such changes are common to the seasons and months of the year, but unknown to Cook, who had only passed this region in June-August 1773.
18. Beaglehole, *Voyage of the Resolution and Discovery*, Part One, 80, 87.
19. Beaglehole, *Voyage of the Resolution and Discovery*, Part One, ci, 94–95.
20. Mai told Cook that the local people built a large fire in late afternoon, and he was quite alarmed that "he and his companions were going to be roasted and eat[en]," but soon hogs were killed and roasted on the spit over the fires, feeding the multitude. These apprehensions and the press of the crowd convinced the four to abandon the island at sunset and not return for the provisions they originally sought. Beaglehole, *Voyage of the Resolution and Discovery*, Part One, 84–86.
21. Cook wrote that when he approached his people on shore, "the natives were ordered out to meet him and paid their obeisance by bowing their heads to their feet, so there was no room to suspect him being anything less than a King." Beaglehole, *Voyage of the Resolution and Discovery*, Part One, 100.
22. Cook was less sanguine about the Tongan attitude at their departure. "Thus we took leave of the *Friendly Islands* and their Inhabitants after a stay of between two and three Months," Cook wrote, "during which time we lived together in a most cordial friendship, some accidental differences its true now and then happened owing to their great propensity to thieving, but too often incouraged by the negligence of our own people." Beaglehole, *Voyage of the Resolution and Discovery*, Part One, 160.

23. According to Captain William Bligh, who returned to the island in 1789 on the *Bounty*, Mai's European possessions were soon stolen by his fellow islanders after Cook left for America and he died a natural death three years later. Salmond, *Between Worlds*, 140.
24. "Fished" refers to dropping a line into the bottom to fish out the broken wood from the spar.
25. Cook explained the Tahitians were frightened by the display. "The 7th in the evening played of some fire works before a great concourse of people, some were highly entertained but by far the greatest part were terribly frightened, in so much that we had enough to do to keep them together to see the end; a table rocket was the last, it flew of[f] the table and despersed the whole crowd in a Moment, even the most resolute fled." Beaglehole, *Voyage of the Resolution and Discovery*, Part One, 207.
26. Cook was irresolute in recovering the goat. He explained, "The loss of this Goat would have been nothing if it had not interfered with my views of Stocking other Islands with these Animals but as it did it was necessary to get again if possible." In securing its return Cook laid waste to much of the island, burning canoes and homes, then finally cutting off the ear of the perpetrator. Cook contemplated shooting him. On Huahine ten days later, a thief stole a sextant and was given the same punishment. "He appearing to be a hardened Scoundrel, I punished him with greater severity than I had ever done any one before and then dismissed him." Beaglehole, *Voyage of the Resolution and Discovery*, Part One, 228, 230, 236.
27. Cook wrote, "[When] Omai went ashore, after taking a very affectionate farewell of all the Officers; he sustained himself with manly resolution till he came to me, then his utmost efforts to conceal his tears failed, and Mr. King, who went in the boat, told me he wept all the time in going ashore. . . . His gratifull heart always retained the highest sense of the favours he received in England nor will he ever forget those who honoured him with their protection and friendship during his stay there." Beaglehole, *Voyage of the Resolution and Discovery*, Part One, 240–41.
28. Although there has been speculation that Spanish galleons saw the Hawaiian Islands as early as the sixteenth century, this is the first recorded western contact with the islands. The following day, Cook wrote of his first contact with Hawai'i and its inhabitants, "On the 19th at Sun rise the island first seen [O'ahu] bore East. This being directly to windward there was no getting nearer to it so that I stood for the other [Kaua'i], and not long after discovered a third island [Ni'ihau] in the direction of WNW and as far distant as an island could be seen. . . . At this time we were in some doubt whether or not this land before [us] was inhabited, this doubt was soon cleared up by seeing some Canoes coming off from the Shore towards the Ships. I immediately brought to give them time to come up, there were three or four men in each and we were agreeably surprised to find them of the same Nation as the people of Otaheite and the other islands we had lately visited." Beaglehole, *Voyage of the Resolution and Discovery*, Part One, 263–64.
29. Williamson was in command and failed to tell Cook of the death until after the expedition left Hawai'i, presumably fearful of a denunciation or punishment from the captain. Williamson is the same man who would be criticized a year later when he failed to rescue Cook in the moments before the commander's death at Kealakekua Bay. Beaglehole, *Voyage of the Resolution and Discovery*, Part One, 267.
30. Gore and twenty men were stranded on Ni'ihau for three days, with the captain explaining, "the sea run so high we had no manner of communication with the people on shore." Beaglehole, *Voyage of the Resolution and Discovery*, Part One, 276.

Part 2: The Northwest Passage

1. Beaglehole, *Life of Cook*, 477–78. See also Christian Feest, *James Cook in America*, in Adrienne L. Kaeppler, Curator, *James Cook and the Exploration of the Pacific* (London: Thames & Hudson, 2011), 108–11, which offers a general discussion of the voyages' accomplishments on the Northwest Coast, Alaska, and Siberia. A general review of the third voyage accomplishments along the Northwest Coast in Alaska can be found in Barnett, *Captain Cook in Alaska and the North Pacific*. The discussion of the voyage purposes and instructions are at 12–14.

2. Cook and King introduce the von Stählin map in the voyage journal at Beaglehole, *Voyage of the Resolution and Discovery*, Part One, 338n5, 342n9. They soon came to lament the maps for their inaccuracy, especially the von Stählin version, beginning on 414. See also Beaglehole, *The Voyage of the Resolution and Discovery*, Part One, cxxiv–cxxvi and Beaglehole, *Life of Cook*, 593. An analysis of the map and why it was so inaccurate can be found in Glyndwr Williams, "Alaska Revealed, Cook's Explorations in 1778," in Antoinette Shalkop, ed., *Exploration in Alaska, Captain Cook Commemorative Lectures* (Cook Inlet Historical Society, 1980), 69–87. Glyndwr Williams, "Myth and Reality: James Cook and the Theoretical Geography of Northwest America," in Robin Fisher and Hugh Johnson, ed., *Captain James Cook and His Times* (Seattle: University of Washington Press, 1979), 58–80, and Carol Urness, "Russian Mapping of the North Pacific to 1792," in Haycox, *Enlightenment and Exploration*, 132–46.
3. Cook knew he was in the area of the "pretended" Strait of Juan de Fuca, it having been placed on the maps by theoretical geographers after the apocryphal voyage of the Greek pilot of that name in the late 1500s. Cook wrote, incorrectly as it turned out, ". . .we saw nothing like it, nor is there the least probability that iver any such thing existed." Beaglehole, *Voyage of the Resolution and Discovery*, Part One, cxxi.
4. Beaglehole, *Voyage of the Resolution and Discovery*, Part One, 295–96. Robin Fisher, "Cook and the Nootka," in Robin Fisher & Hugh Johnson, eds., *Captain James Cook and His Times* (University of Washington Press, 1979), 81–98. The contact between the Cook expedition and the local Mowachaht people has been well documented in J. C. H. King, *First People, First Contact: Native Peoples of North America* (Cambridge, MA: Harvard University Press, 1999), 122–45. John Ledyard, *A Journal of Captain Cook's Last Voyage . . . in the Years 1776, 1777, 1778, and 1779* (Hartford, CT: Nathaniel Patten Publisher, 1783), 71–77.
5. Beaglehole, *Voyage of the Resolution and Discovery*, Part One, 298–99, 333. Thomas, *Extraordinary Voyages*, 361–65. Barnett, *Captain Cook in Alaska and the North Pacific*, 79–80.
6. Beaglehole, *Voyage of the Resolution and Discovery*, Part One, 346–47, 352–54, n. 1 and n. 4. Beaglehole, *Life of Cook*, 596–97. Samwell's report on the encounter with the people of Prince William Sound is in Beaglehole, *Voyage of the Resolution and Discovery*, Part Two, 1106–14. Barnett, *Captain Cook in Alaska and the North Pacific*, 93–104.
7. Beaglehole, *The Voyage of the Resolution and Discovery*, Part One, 352–60. Beaglehole, *Life of Cook*, 598–99. Williams, *Voyages of Delusion*, 287–334. Williams, *Arctic Labyrinth*, 132–48. Barnett, *Captain Cook in Alaska and the North Pacific*, 107–28.
8. Christine Holmes, ed., *Captain Cook's Final Voyage, the Journal of Midshipman George Gilbert* (Honolulu: University Press of Hawai'i, 1982), 81. See also Aron L. Crowell, "The Cook Expedition and Russian Colonialism in Southern Alaska," in Barnett and Nicandri, *Arctic Ambitions*, 149-69.
9. Beaglehole, *Life of Cook*, 599. Beaglehole, *Voyage of the Resolution and Discovery*, Part One, 368; the irrepressible optimist, Gore had already named a feature in Prince William Sound as "Cape Hold with Hope," Beaglehole, *Voyage of the Resolution and Discovery*, Part One, 343. After his death the Admiralty named two important geographical features in the Pacific to honor the dead captain. The waters between the two islands of New Zealand were called "Cook Strait" and the great Alaska inland waterway was called "Cook's River." Today New Zealand's Maori call Cook Strait *Raukawa* or *Raukawa Moana*. The Dena'ina call Cook Inlet *Tikahtnu*. Williams, *Voyages of Delusion*, 318–19. Williams, *Arctic Labyrinth*, 141–48. Barnett, *Captain Cook in Alaska and the North Pacific*, 127. An examination of the significance of such European acts of possession is found in Robert J. Miller, "The International Law of Discovery: Acts of Possession on the Northwest Coast of America," in Barnett and Nicandri, *Arctic Ambitions*, 191–210.
10. Ledyard, *Journal*, 83–84. Beaglehole, *Voyage of the Resolution and Discovery*, Part One, 388–89, 416. Williams, *Voyages of Delusion*, 322–24.
11. Holmes, *Gilbert Journal*, 90–92. Beaglehole, *Voyage of the Resolution and Discovery*, Part One, 418–20. Williams, *Voyages of Delusion*, 323–24. Williams, *Arctic Labyrinth*, 141–48. Beaglehole, *Life of Cook*, 623. Barnett, *Captain Cook in Alaska and the North Pacific*, 146–47.
12. Burney, *North-Eastern Voyages*, 251.

13. Cook's thorough description of the Aleuts of Unalaska is found at Beaglehole, *Voyage of the Resolution and Discovery*, Part One, 459–68. See also Aron L. Crowell, "The Cook Expedition and Russian Colonialism in Southern Alaska," in Barnett and Nicandri, *Arctic Ambitions*, 149-69. Williams, *Voyages of Delusion*, 325–32.
14. Beaglehole, *Voyage of the Resolution and Discovery*, Part One, cxxxix. Williams, *Arctic Labyrinth*, 146. David, *Charts and Coastal Views of the Resolution and Discovery*, cii–cix.
15. In the first twelve years perhaps two-dozen Russian expeditions harvested millions of rubles in furs and the local sea otter populations were decimated. As each island's treasure of furs was wiped out, the Russian conquerors sailed further east along the Aleutian chain and, after several decades, to Kodiak Island and mainland Alaska. The tale of conquest was often repeated, given the superiority of Russian firepower. After a brief fight and almost certain destruction, local families were overpowered and held hostage, while the Russians coerced male hunters into the sea to kill as many sea otters as possible. Lydia T. Black and R. G. Liapunova, "Aleut: Islanders of the North Pacific," Lydia Black, "The Story of Russian America" and Aron Crowell, "Prehistory of Alaska's Pacific Coast," in Fitzhugh and Crowell, eds., *Crossroads of Continents, Cultures of Siberia and Alaska* (Washington: Smithsonian Institution Press, 1988), 52–57, 70–82, 130–41. See also Michael Krauss, *Alaska Native Languages in Russian America*, in Barbara S. Smith and Redmond J. Barnett, ed., *Russian America: The Forgotten Frontier* (Washington State Historical Society, 1990), 205-13
16. Holmes, *Gilbert Journal*, 97. Beaglehole, *Life of Cook*, 635–36. David, *Charts and Coastal Views of the Resolution and Discovery*, cii–cix. Beaglehole, *Voyage of the Resolution and Discovery*, Part One, cxxxix–cxl, 458, 470. Beaglehole, *Life of Cook*, 630–35.

PART 3: REVISITING HAWAI'I AND THE DEATH OF COOK

1. Holmes, *Gilbert Journal*, 99.
2. Beaglehole wrote, *Voyage of the Resolution and Discovery*, Part One, cxli, "no place in the eighteenth century Pacific has been more fully described for us than this bay, the northern half of which stands for so much in the history of exploration." Beaglehole, *Life of Cook*, 648–51. Cook's description of the reception on the Big Island is located at Beaglehole, *Voyage of the Resolution and Discovery*, Part One, 490–91. King's description of the lavish greeting is found at Beaglehole, *Voyage of the Resolution and Discovery*, Part One, 502–504. Salmond, *Trial of the Cannibal Dog*, 389–94. Thomas, *Extraordinary Voyages*, 380. Both Hawaiian historians and 19th century American missionaries believe Cook's sailors introduced venereal disease to the islands. See generally Beaglehole, *Voyage of the Resolution and Discovery*, Part One, 266, clix–clxi.
3. The Gilbert quote is found at Holmes, *Gilbert Journal*, 101. See also Glyn Williams, *The Death of Captain Cook: A Hero Made and Unmade* (Cambridge, MA: Harvard University Press, 2008), 24–25.
4. Beaglehole, *Voyage of the Resolution and Discovery*, Part One, cxl–cxlviii. Daws, *Shoal of Time*, 8–15. Williams, *Death of Cook*, 25–30, 117–22. Salmond, *Trial of the Cannibal Dog*, 390–406. Thomas, *Extraordinary Voyages*, 381–84.
5. Williams, *Death of Cook*, 31–34. Salmond, *Trial of the Cannibal Dog*, 408–11. King was in the Observatories, on the south side of the bay, so his view of the theft was from shore. Beaglehole, *Voyage of the Resolution and Discovery*, Part One, 528–31. Samwell was aboard the *Discovery*, so observed the incident close at hand. It turns out that Edgar and Vancouver gave chase to the thief to avoid bloodshed, as the culprit could have easily been killed as he jumped into his small craft alongside. Samwell's description of the events of February 13, 1779, is found at Beaglehole, *Voyage of the Resolution and Discovery*, Part Two, 1191–94.
6. Roberts' whereabouts during the fracas is well documented by King. He commanded the pinnace, taking Cook and Lieutenant Molesworth Phillips to shore, and then positioned it a few yards offshore to keep away from the bottom, which is underlain with lava rock. Only Phillips, who happened to be Burney's closest, lifelong friend, was with Cook; the others just watched the drama unfold. Phillips did not write his own account, though his first-hand account was the basis of Clerke's report and was

certainly recounted to Burney. Since he was only yards from shore, presumably Roberts' account was the closest first hand report. It was later said that Roberts and Phillips "behaved with great courage and resolution" during the affair. See Beaglehole, *Life of Cook*, 669, and Beaglehole, *Voyage of the Resolution and Discovery*, Part One, 537–38, 550, 555.

7. The death of Cook has been described by many onlookers, and repeated by biographers, all carefully examining the facts and implications. Beaglehole's careful accounting is found at Beaglehole, *Voyage of the Resolution and Discovery*, Part One, cxlvii–clvii and Beaglehole, *Life of Cook*, 662–72. Clerke and King each carefully reconstructed events at the time, summarizing them at Beaglehole, *Voyage of the Resolution and Discovery*, Part One, 531–61. Salmond, *The Trial of the Cannibal Dog*, 386–416. See generally, Williams, *Death of Cook*, 34–37; Salmond, *Trial of the Cannibal Dog*, 411–16; Thomas, *Extraordinary Voyages*, 391–96. There was considerable debate amongst the sailors on the voyage, as well as scholars since that time, whether Cook was intemperate or simply outmanned when he fired the gun and whether the marines provided him adequate support. Most of the sailors blamed Lieutenant Williamson, who was in command of a boatload of marines. He apparently retreated when Cook motioned him to pick him up on shore, leaving Cook, Lieutenant Phillips, and a few marines alone at the mercy of the unruly crowd. Burney wrote in *North-Eastern Voyages*, 263, that Cook was a man of "cool discernment" for his own safety and did not act in an irritated, exasperated, or unseemly manner. Beaglehole suspects Burney was simply trying to protect Cook's reputation in the aftermath of the various published journals, which offer an unfavorable view, writing from recollection 40 years later. See Beaglehole, *Voyage of the Resolution and Discovery*, Part One, clvi–clvii.

8. Holmes, *Gilbert Journal*, 107–108. Daws, *Shoal of Time*, 16–28. "Natives at Kealakekua Bay and elsewhere looked back on Cook's death with a mixture of genuine sorrow and mournful relish," Daws writes at 24, "the kind of feeling shared by people who have shared a great catastrophe and cannot stop talking about it." See also Beaglehole, *Voyage of the Resolution and Discovery*, Part One, 548, Salmond, *Trial of the Cannibal Dog*, 418–25 and Anne Salmond, "The Death of Cook," in Kaeppler, *James Cook and the Exploration of the Pacific*, 37–38.

9. Williams, *Death of Cook*, 158–64. The myths and reality of the death of Cook and whether the Hawaiians really looked upon him as a reincarnated god or other deity, as well as British and Hawaiian versions of the death, have been discussed in a lively debate found in Marshall Sahlins, *How "Natives" Think, About Captain Cook, For Example* (Chicago: University of Chicago Press, 1995), and Gananath Obeyesekere, *The Apotheosis of Captain Cook: European Mythmaking in the Pacific* (Princeton, NJ: Princeton University Press, 1992). See also Pauline Nawahineokala'i King, "Some Thoughts on Native Hawaiian attitudes towards Captain Cook," in Glyndwr Williams, ed., *Captain Cook: Explorations and Reassessments* (Rochester, NY: Boydell Press, 2004), 94–109, esp. 103, discussing the Sahlins-Obeyesekere controversy on whether the Hawaiians accepted Cook as *Lono*, a deity Hawaiians associated with fertility, agriculture, rainfall, music, and peace, and whether Western scholars can understand non-Western cultures.

10. Beaglehole, *Voyage of the Resolution and Discovery*, Part One, 619–20.

11. Cook's final journal entry describes the ceremony at the Hawaiian temple. Beaglehole, *Voyage of the Resolution and Discovery*, Part One, 491.

12. Beaglehole, *Voyage of the Resolution and Discovery*, Part One, 527. Ledyard, *Journal*, 143.

13. After the crowd assembled on shore and began shouting, Cook told Phillips they should abandon plans to take the king onboard, observing "We can never think of compelling him to go onboard without killing a number of these people." Cook then planned to embark, when interrupted by a man brandishing a spear and stone. When the man threatened to throw the stone, Phillips explained that Cook "discharged a load of small shot at him but having his Mat on, the small shot did not penetrate it, and had no other effect than farther to provoke and encourage them. . . . just at this time they began to throw stones and one of the Marines was knocked down, the Captain fired a ball and killed a Man. They now made a general attack and the Captain gave orders to the Marines to fire and afterwards called out 'Take to the Boats.' . . . the Shouts and Yells of the Indians far exceeded all the noise I ever came in the way of." Instead of retreating in the hail of fire, the warriors charged, overwhelming the English on shore. Phillips did not see Cook again. Badly injured, he struggled to climb aboard the

pinnace, where Roberts waited, fearlessly withstanding the hail of rocks hurled by the crowd. They saved two Marines before retreating. Beaglehole, *Voyage of the Resolution and Discovery*, Part One, 535–36.

14. Clerke wrote, "Hoisted out the Pinnace and Cutter in which I went ashore. On landing I was received with every token of respect and friendship by a great number of the Natives who were collected upon the occasion; they every one of them prostrated themselves around me which is the first mark of respect at these Isles, indeed I don't know how any People can devise a more expressive one; however I immediately made motions for them to rise." After a brief ceremony, Clerke asked for the nearest source of water for the ships. When told it was a mile, Clerke decided to leave for Kaua'i. Beaglehole, *Voyage of the Resolution and Discovery*, Part One, 572–73.
15. Samwell wrote that the day after the shooting Clerke sent his shore party with eighty armed men, the largest force he could muster. Clerke and Burney said it was more like fifty men, reflecting Samwell's flirtation with facts that probably permeate his journal. The chiefs and Queen Dowager of the island soon arrived to restore order and on the following days the shore parties did not require any armed support. The troublesome Williamson wrote an apologetic account absolving himself of blame for the killing in January 1778, even though he did not report it to the captain for a month. Beaglehole, *Voyage of the Resolution and Discovery*, Part One, 575–86, Part Two, 1223–25, 1347–50.
16. King explains the sudden change in temperament, "On going on board we were told that many great Chiefs had visited Captain Clerke and advised him by all means to kill whoever was insolent to us on shore, but that in future they would take care that no molestation should be given." The next day he reports "The Watering Party went on shore under the Command of Lieutenant Burney to compleat the Discovery; as they had with them the old Queen and other Chiefs, the Mob were kept in perfect good Order, the Discoverys water was completed today." Beaglehole, *Voyage of the Resolution and Discovery*, Part One, 589–90.

PART 4: HOMEWARD

1. Burney, *North-Eastern Voyages*, 266–67. Beaglehole, *Voyage of the Resolution and Discovery*, Part Two, 1240. Ledyard, *Journal*, 165–69. Anichtchenko, "From Russia with Charts," in Barnett and Nicandri, *Arctic Ambitions*, 80–84.
2. Beaglehole, *Voyage of the Resolution and Discovery*, Part One, 696–97.
3. Burney, *North-Eastern Voyages*, 268–69. Beaglehole, *Voyage of the Resolution and Discovery,* Part One, 695, clxiv–clxv. See also Beaglehole, *Life of Cook*, 681–82 and Barnett, *Cook in Alaska*, 207–209. Compare the accomplishments of the two captains during their time in the Arctic ice pack in Nicandri, "A New Look at Cook," in Barnett and Nicandri, *Arctic Ambitions*, 109–29.
4. David, *Charts and Coastal Views of the Resolution and Discovery*, 274–76.
5. Holmes, *Gilbert Journal*, 140–49. See King's general remarks on the return to Avacha Bay in David, *Charts and Coastal Views of the Resolution and Discovery*, 282–87. Anichtchenko, "From Russia with Charts," in Barnett and Nicandri, *Arctic Ambitions*, 69–80. Barnett, *Cook in Alaska*, 202–203.
6. David, *Charts and Coastal Views of the Resolution and Discovery*, 297–310. Holmes, *Gilbert Journal*, 154–58. Barnett, *Cook in Alaska*, 218–21. On the duel and arrival in England, see Beaglehole, *Life of Cook*, 685–86.
7. Thomas, *Extraordinary Voyages*, 402–404. Williams, *Death of Cook*, 11–15. Williams, *Voyages of Delusion*, 336–38.
8. Holmes, *Gilbert Journal*, 158. Beaglehole, *Life of Cook*, 364. Barnett, *Cook in Alaska*, 217–30.
9. See Bernard Smith, "Cook's Posthumous Reputation," in Robin Fisher & Hugh Johnson, eds., *Captain James Cook and His Times* (Seattle: University of Washington Press, 1979), 159–85. A fascinating look at Cook's contribution to the Pacific, particularly in light of recent changes in historiography, can be found in Glyndwr Williams, "As befits out age, there are no more heroes, reassessing Captain Cook," in Williams, *Explorations and Reassessments*, 230–45.

10. See generally, I. S. MacLaren, "Narrating an Alaskan Cruise: Cook's Journal (1778) and Douglas's Edition of *A Voyage to the Pacific Ocean* (1784)," in Barnett and Nicandri, *Arctic Ambitions*, 231–59. See also Anthony Payne, "The Publication and Readership of Voyage Journals in the Age of Vancouver, 1730-1830," in Haycox, *Enlightenment and Exploration*, 176–86.
11. David, *Charts and Coastal Views of the Resolution and Discovery*, 248, which was reprinted from the *Political Magazine* for December 1784, 403–404. Beaglehole, *Voyage of the Resolution and Discovery*, Part One, clxxxiii. See generally, John Robson, "Cook on the Coasts of the North Pacific and Arctic America: The Cartographic Achievement," in Barnett and Nicandri, *Arctic Ambitions*, 211–29 and Andrew David, "From Cook to Vancouver: The British Contribution to the Cartography of Alaska," in Haycox, *Enlightenment and Exploration*, 116–31.
12. Beaglehole, *Voyage of the Resolution and Discovery*, Part One, 650. Beaglehole, *Life of Cook*, 679.
13. David, *Charts and Coastal Views of the Resolution and Discovery*, 276, 280.

BIBLIOGRAPHY

The main source document for Cook's third voyage is the original three volume account published four years after the expedition returned to England, John Douglas, ed., *A Voyage to the Pacific Ocean in the years 1776, 1777, 1778, 1779 and 1780... Vol. I and II written by James Cook, Vol. III by Captain James King,* 3 vols., London, 1784. It is difficult to find, particularly in the prized first edition, and any edition is very expensive.

The more reasonably priced version is the comprehensive and annotated two-volume work edited by J. C. Beaglehole, *The Voyage of the Resolution and Discovery,* Cambridge University Press, 1967, which is part of a larger series published by the Hakluyt Society for the three voyages. Beaglehole (1901-1971) was professor of British Commonwealth History at the Victoria University of Wellington, New Zealand. His unparalleled work contains Cook's journal, extracts from several other journals kept by members of the expedition, the list of seamen on the voyage, the voyage instructions, and letters and other documents from members of the expedition. It is supplemented by the author's biography of the explorer, J. C. Beaglehole, *The Life of Captain James Cook* (Stanford, CA: Stanford University Press, 1974).

In addition to the journals reprinted by Beaglehole, the following first-hand voyage journals are available:

Ellis, William. *An Authentic Narrative of a Voyage ... in Search of the Northwest Passage.* 1782.

Holmes, Christine, ed. *Captain Cook's Final Voyage, the Journal of Midshipman George Gilbert.* Honolulu: University Press of Hawaii, 1982.

Ledyard, John. *A Journal of Captain Cook's Last Voyage ... in the Years 1776, 1777, 1778, and 1779.* Hartford, 1783.

Rickman, John. *Journal of Captain Cook's Last Voyage to the Pacific Ocean.* E. Newberry 1781.

A comprehensive catalog of the original drawings and engravings from the third voyage is Rüdiger Joppien and Bernard Smith, *The Art of Captain Cook's Voyages* (Oxford: Oxford University Press, 1987). Two of the four volumes are dedicated to the third voyage drawings, principally those of John Webber and William Ellis. See also John Frazier Henry, *Early Maritime Artists of the Pacific Northwest Coast, 1741-1841* (Seattle: University of Washington Press, 1984).

The charts and coastal views drawn by Cook and his officers can be found in the three-volume work edited by Andrew David, *The Charts and Coastal Views of Captain Cook's Voyages* (London: Hakluyt Society, 1997). Volume III is dedicated to the third voyage and includes original maps, coastal views drawn on the voyage, and the "lost" journal of Captain King beginning at the time of Captain Clerke's death in August 1779 until the end of the voyage.

Numerous biographies exist on Cook, probably more than any other explorer in history, but only a few concentrate on the third voyage. The reader should consider the following ten selected titles:

Barnett, James K. *Captain Cook in Alaska and the North Pacific.* Anchorage: Todd Communications, 2008.

Barnett, James K., and David S. Nicandri, ed. *Arctic Ambitions: Captain Cook and the Northwest Passage.* Seattle: University of Washington Press, 2015.

Fisher, Robin, and Hugh Johnson, ed. *Captain James Cook and His Times.* Seattle: University of Washington Press, 1979.

Gascoigne, John. *Captain Cook: Voyager Between Worlds.* London: Humbledon Continuum, 2007.

Horowitz, Tony. *Blue Latitudes: Boldly Going Where Captain Cook Has Gone Before.* New York: Henry Holt and Company, 2002.

Hough, Richard. *Captain James Cook: A Biography.* London: Hodder & Stoughton, 1994.

Rigby, Nigel, and Pieter van der Merwe. *Captain Cook in the Pacific.* London: National Maritime Museum, 2002.

Salmond, Anne. *Trial of the Cannibal Dog: The Remarkable Story of Captain Cook's Encounters in the South Seas.* New Haven: Yale University Press, 2003.

Thomas, Nicholas. *The Extraordinary Voyages of Captain Cook.* London: Walker & Co., 2003.

Williams, Glyndwr, ed. *Captain Cook: Explorations and Reassessments.* London: Boydell Press, 2004.

Hundreds of books consider topics presented in this book as they impact the North Pacific. The reader might examine the range of topics in the following thirty selected titles:

Anderson, Bern. *Surveyor of the Sea: The Life and Voyages of Captain George Vancouver.* Toronto: University of Toronto Press, 1960.

Barnett, James K. *Captain George Vancouver in Alaska and the North Pacific*. Anchorage: Todd Communications, 2017.

Barratt, Glynn. *Russia in Pacific Waters, 1715-1825.* Vancouver, BC: University of British Columbia Press, 1981.

Bown, Stephen R. *Madness, Betrayal and the Lash: The Epic Voyage of Captain George Vancouver.* Vancouver, BC: Douglas & McIntyre, 2008.

Brown, Steven C., ed. *Spirits of the Water: Native Art Collected on Expeditions to Alaska and British Columbia, 1774-1910.* Seattle: University of Washington Press, 2000.

Cook, Warren L. *Flood Tide of Empire, Spain and the Pacific Northwest 1543-1819.* New Haven, CT: Yale University Press, 1973.

Cordy, Ross. *Exalted Sits the Chief: The Ancient History of Hawai'i Island*. Honolulu: Mutual Publishing Co., 2000.

David, Andrew, Felipe Fernandez-Armesto, Carlos Novi, and Glyndwr Williams, eds. *The Malaspina Expedition.* Volume II. London: Hakluyt Society, 2003.

Daws, Gavin. *Shoal of Time: A History of the Hawaiian Islands*. Honolulu: University of Hawaii Press, 1974.

Engstrand, Iris H. W. *Spanish Scientists in the New World: The Eighteenth Century Expeditions.* Seattle: University of Washington Press, 1981.

Fisher, Robin. *Contact and Conflict: Indian-European Relations in British Columbia, 1774-1890.* Vancouver, BC: University of British Columbia Press, 1977.

Fisher, Robin, and Hugh Johnston, ed. *From Maps to Metaphors: The Pacific World of George Vancouver.* Vancouver, BC: University of British Columbia Press, 1993.

Fitzhugh, William W., and Aron Crowell, *Crossroads of Continents: Cultures of Siberia and Alaska.* Washington, DC: Smithsonian Institution Press, 1988.

Ford, Corey. *Where the Sea Breaks Its Back.* New York: Little, Brown and Company, 1966.

Gough, Barry M. *Distant Dominion: Britain and the Northwest Coast of North America, 1579-1809.* Vancouver, BC: University of British Columbia Press, 1980.

———. *Fortune's a River: The Collision of Empires in Northwest America.* Maderia Park, BC: Harbour Publishing, 2007.

———. *The Northwest Coast: British Navigation, Trade and Discoveries to 1812.* Vancouver, BC: University of British Columbia Press, 1992.

Haycox, Stephen, James Barnett, and Caedmon Liburd, ed. *Enlightenment and Exploration in the North Pacific 1741-1805.* Seattle: University of Washington Press, 1997.

King, J. C. H. *First People First Contacts: Native Peoples of North America.* Cambridge, MA: Harvard University Press, 1999.

Lamb, W. Kaye, ed. *The Journals and Letters of Sir Alexander Mackenzie.* London: Hakluyt Society, 1970.

———, ed. *The Voyage of George Vancouver, 1791-1795.* 4 volumes. London: The Hakluyt Society, 1984.

Pethick, Derek. *First Approaches to the Northwest Coast.* Vancouver, BC: J.J. Douglas, 1976.

Rigby, Nigel, Pieter van der Merwe, and Glyn Williams. *Pioneers of the Pacific: Voyages of Exploration, 1787-1810.* Fairbanks, University of Alaska Press, 2005.

Steller, Georg W. *Journal of a Voyage with Bering, 1741-42.* O. W. Frost, ed., Margritt A. Engel and O. W. Frost, translators. Stanford, CA: Stanford University Press, 1988.

Vaughan, Thomas, and Bill Holm. *Soft Gold, the Fur Trade and Cultural Exchange on the Northwest Coast of America.* Portland: Oregon Historical Society, 1990.

Wagner, Henry R. *Cartography of the Northwest Coast of America to the Year 1800.* Berkeley: University of California Press, 1937.

———. *Spanish Voyages to the Northwest.* San Francisco: California Historical Society, 1929.

Waxell, Sven. *The American Expedition.* New York: William Hodge and Company, 1952).

Williams, Glyndwr. *Arctic Labyrinth: The Quest for the Northwest Passage.* Berkeley: University of California Press, 2009.

———. *Voyages of Delusion: The Search for the Northwest Passage in the Age of Reason.* London: Harper Collins, 2002.

INDEX

About the Author

James K. Barnett has been an Alaska attorney in private practice in Anchorage since 1974. A fourth-generation Californian, his principal leisure pursuit is the early history of the west coast of North America, from California to Alaska.

He was the long-time president of the Cook Inlet Historical Society in Anchorage and helped organize the 1994 exhibition and international symposium commemorating the bicentennial of Captain George Vancouver's voyage to Alaska, the 2004 exhibition featuring Ernest Shackleton's Imperial Trans-Antarctic Expedition, and the 2015 centennial commemoration of the founding of Anchorage.

He was co-editor and contributor to the Vancouver Symposium papers, *Enlightenment and Exploration in the North Pacific 1741–1805* (Seattle: University of Washington Press, 1997) and instrumental in a more recent exhibition of Captain Cook's third voyage in the North Pacific, presented at both the Anchorage Museum at Rasmuson Center and the Washington State History Museum in Tacoma. He was co-editor and contributor to the companion publication, *Arctic Ambitions: Captain Cook and the Northwest Passage* (Seattle: University of Washington Press, 2015).

He has written two complementary volumes about the voyages of Captain James Cook and Captain George Vancouver for Alaska and the Northwest Coast audiences. The author's study of Cook's expedition, and particularly that part of his third voyage to reach Alaska, is titled *Captain Cook in Alaska and the North Pacific*. It was published by Todd Communications in 2008. His later study of Vancouver's expedition is called *Captain Vancouver in Alaska and the North Pacific*, and was published by Todd Communications in 2017. The author also wrote a pocket-sized history of Alaska in 2011, also published by Todd Communications, *Alaskan History - In Brief*. He is co-editor of *Imagining Anchorage: The Making of America's Northernmost Metropolis*, due in 2018 from the University of Alaska Press.